The Policy Process

A reader

edited by
Michael Hill
University of Newcastle upon Tyne

HARVESTER
WHEATSHEAF

New York   London   Toronto   Sydney   Tokyo   Singapore

First published 1993 by
Harvester Wheatsheaf
Campus 400, Maylands Avenue
Hemel Hempstead
Hertfordshire, HP2 7EZ
A division of
Simon & Schuster International Group

Typeset in 10/12pt Times by
Keyset Composition, Colchester

Printed and bound in Great Britain by
Redwood Books, Trowbridge, Wiltshire.

British Library Cataloguing in Publication Data

A catalogue record for this book is available from the
British Library

ISBN 0-7450-1272-8 (hbk)
ISBN 0-7450-1273-6 (pbk)

5 97 96 95

Contents

Preface

This reader has been written to complement the textbook on the policy process by the editor and Chris Ham, *The Policy Process in the Modern Capitalist State*. It has been produced as a result of a suggestion that Clare Grist of Harvester Wheatsheaf made to the editor when he was discussing with her the production of a second edition of the textbook. A special acknowledgement is due to her for all the work she has done to guide the process of compiling it and to negotiate the contributions.

The eight parts do not exactly parallel the chapters of *The Policy Process in the Modern Capitalist State*. Whilst the shape of that book has influenced its design, this reader has been organised to stand alone in its own right. The first part inevitably picks up some of the key issues from the introductory chapter of the textbook; the second one is concerned to look at the debate about power which so crucially underpins any study of the policy process, and in so doing it takes in issues covered in Chapters 2 and 4 of Ham and Hill. The third part parallels the textbook's consideration of bureaucracy and the state, but the fourth uses two articles which take an overview of all the issues in what may be described as the policy-making part of Ham and Hill. The next three parts all follow the lines of three chapters in *The Policy Process in the Modern Capitalist State* on the rationality/incrementalism debate, on implementation and on the contribution of organisational studies. The final part picks up themes related to the study of implementation, like street-level bureaucracy and discretion, discussed in Chapters 8 and 9 of Ham and Hill. There is no reading selection to parallel the concluding section of the textbook, but the extracts in Part IV and the extracts from Elmore and from Degeling and Colebatch in Part VII share the concern of that chapter to integrate approaches to the subject.

Each part is preceded by a brief introduction by the editor. These highlight key issues to look out for, and sometimes it may be appropriate to re-read them afterwards. They also indicate links between the various parts, and stress the way in which normative issues about what constitutes a desirable policy-making or implementation process continually arise.

Acknowledgements

Grateful acknowledgement is made to the following sources for permission to reproduce in this book material previously published elsewhere. Every effort has been made to trace copyright holders, but, if any have been inadvertently overlooked, the publisher will be pleased to make the necessary arrangement at the first opportunity.

Michael Adler and Stewart Asquith for 'Discretion and power', in M. Adler and S. Asquith (eds), *Discretion and Welfare*, Heinemann, 1981.

The Australian Journal of Public Administration, Pieter Degeling and Hal Colebatch for 'Structure and action as constructs in the practice of public administration', *Australian Journal of Public Administration*, **XLIII**, 1984.

Basil Blackwell Ltd for extracts from the following: G. McLennan, *Marxism, Pluralism and Beyond*, Polity Press, 1989; C. Pollitt, *Managerialism and the Public Services*, Blackwell, 1990; P. Dunleavy, 'Explaining the privatization boom: public choice versus radical approaches, *Public Administration*, **64**, 1986, pp. 13–34; M. J. Hill, 'The exercise of discretion in the National Assistance Board', *Public Administration*, **47**, pp. 75–90.

Andrew Blowers for 'Masters of fate or victim of circumstance – the exercise of corporate power in environmental policy-making,' *Policy and Politics*, **11**, 1983, pp. 393–415.

Cambridge University Press and Theda Skocpol for material from P. B. Evans, D. Rueschemeyer and T. Skocpol, *Bringing the State back in*, 1985.

Cambridge University Press and Paul A. Sabatier for P. A. Sabatier, 'Top-down and bottom-up approaches to implementation research: a critical analysis and suggested synthesis', *Journal of Public Policy*, **6**, 1986, pp. 21–48.

Falmer Press Ltd for B. Hudson, 'Michael Lipsky and street level bureaucracy: a neglected perspective', in L. Barton (ed.), *Disability and Dependency*, 1989.

The Free Press, a Division of Macmillan, Inc., for material from *The Theory of Social and Economic Organization* by Max Weber, translated by A. M. Henderson and Talcott Parsons. Edited by Talcott Parsons. Copyright © 1947, copyright renewed 1975 by Talcott Parsons. Reprinted with the permission of The Free Press.

Ian Gordon, Janet Lewis and Ken Young for an extract from 'Perspectives on policy analysis', *Public Administration Bulletin*, **25**, 1977, pp. 26–30.

Robert J. Gregory for 'Political rationality or "incrementalism"? Charles E. Lindblom's enduring contribution to public policy making theory', *Policy and Politics*, **17**, 1989, pp. 139–53.

The President and Fellows of Harvard University for R. Elmore, 'Organizational models of social program implementation', *Public Policy*, **26**, 1978, pp. 185–228.

Bob Hudson for 'Collaboration in social welfare: a framework for analysis', *Policy and Politics*, **15**, 1987, pp. 175–82.

The Institute of Economic Affairs for an extract from G. Tullock, *The Vote Motive*, 1976.

W. I. Jenkins for material from *Policy Analysis*, Martin Robertson, 1978.

Macmillan Education Ltd and Humanities Press International, Inc., Atlantic Highlands, NJ, for material from S. Lukes, *Power: A radical view*, 1974.

Macmillan Education Ltd and New Amsterdam Books for material from P. Dunleavy and B. O'Leary, *Theories of the State*, 1987.

Macmillan Education Ltd for material from C. Ham, *Health Policy in Britain*, 2nd edition, 1985.

Martin Minogue for 'Theory and practice in public policy and administration', *Policy and Politics*, **11**, 1983, pp. 63–85.

Oxford University Press for material from B. W. Hogwood and L. A. Gunn, *Policy Analysis for the Real World*, 1985. © Brian W. Hogwood and Lewis A. Gunn 1985. Reprinted by permission of Oxford University Press.

Policy and Politics for G. Smith and D. May, 'The artificial debate between rationalist and incrementalist models of decision making', *Policy and Politics*, **8**, 1980, pp. 147–61.

David O. Porter and Benny Hjern for 'Implementation structures: a new unit of administrative analysis', *Organization Studies*, **2**, 1981, pp. 211–27.

The Russell Sage Foundation for an extract from M. Lipsky, *Street-level Bureaucracy: Dilemmas of the individual in public service*, © 1980, The Russell Sage Foundation. Used with permission of The Russell Sage Foundation.

Sage Publications Ltd for an extract from S. R. Clegg, *Modern Organizations*, © 1990, Sage Publications Ltd.

Part I

Policy and policy analysis

Introduction

In the first of the extracts in this reader Gordon, Lewis and Young highlight a crucial distinction – between 'analysis for' and 'analysis of' policy. This book of readings is concerned with 'analysis of' policy, and even more specifically with 'analysis of policy determination' rather than 'analysis of policy content'. The extract from Gordon, Lewis and Young shows clearly the relation between this aspect of the study of public policy and other aspects.

Readers will continually find that those who write about the policy process, from almost any perspective, are very concerned to answer ultimate prescriptive questions about how policy *should* be made and implemented. In trying to do this they have been very preoccupied with the extent to which the policy process can be evaluated in terms of how far it measures up to what Gordon, Lewis and Young describe in their useful discussion of 'assumptions' as 'the "rational system model" [having a] status as a normative model and as a "dignified" myth which is often shared by the policy-makers themselves'.

Whilst it is possible to conceive of the study of policy as a detached academic study, and it is at times important to try to achieve detachment to have a clear view of what is going on, nevertheless the ultimate rationale for our subject is bound to be a concern about improving the policy process. That, of course, need not at the same time imply an identification with the goals of those who control the process; we may want to understand it better in order to subvert it in its present form. The complex relationship between policy analysis as a form of 'management science', in which the goals of management are very much at the forefront, and as an academic development out of political science is explored in the article by Minogue, who makes his overall point pithily in a section heading 'Management versus politics: united they stand, divided they fall'. Within Minogue's exploration lies an important argument on why those who are principally interested in analysis 'for' policy should give some attention to analysis 'of' policy. If they fail to understand policy making and implementation as a *political* process they will prepare recommendations which are ill adapted to the real world.

A leading textbook on policy analysis (Hogwood and Gunn, 1984) proclaims in its title that it offers 'policy analysis for the real world', yet its very adherence to the rational model detracts in places from that goal. Yet to discard entirely the rational model is to collude cynically with those who care neither about good policy nor about good policy processes. We must not forget, moreover, that the concept of the rational model is here particularly applied to solving policy problems in a systematic way. It may also be applied to solving them in a democratic way. But, perhaps most importantly, we may want to reserve the use of the concept of rationality for the policies adopted. There is an important conflict of notions of 'rationality' here, explored further in Part V in this book (in the introduction and in the article by Gregory).

The extract from Jenkins' book takes us rather more directly into the issues about studying the policy process in a systematic way. He offers us a conceptual scheme, and comments upon some of the pitfalls in approaching this in too mechanical a way. Later in the book, some of the readings may suggest that even Jenkins' careful approach is too systematic to make sense of some aspects of the policy process, where clear policies are hard to ascertain and policy output emerges out of grass-roots interactions.

All of these introductory readings have been chosen to introduce readers to some of the terminology, to sensitise them to some of the distinctions (which may or may not be made in practice) and to highlight some of the key characteristics of the study of the policy process.

Reference

Hogwood, B. W. and L. A. Gunn, *Policy Analysis for the Real World* (Oxford, Oxford University Press, 1984).

Perspectives on policy analysis

Ian Gordon, Janet Lewis and Ken Young

A typology of policy analysis

The most obvious distinction in varieties of policy analysis is in terms of explicit purpose and/or client, separating analysis *for* policy from analysis *of* policy. In terms of established lines of research this is probably the most important distinction, and it also reflects a division of disciplinary concerns. Yet within this dichotomy lies a continuum of activities from policy advocacy at one end to the analysis of policy content at the other.

Analysis for policy		Analysis of policy		
Policy advocacy	Information for policy	Policy monitoring and evaluation	Analysis of policy determination	Analysis of policy content

Policy advocacy
We use this term to denote any research that terminates in the direct advocacy of a single policy, or of a group of related policies, identified as serving some end taken as valued by the researchers. The connection of such research with the decision network may be rather less direct. It may be aimed at policy-makers, in which case it assumes a degree of value correspondence (which may or may not be a tenable assumption), or it may serve to challenge existing policies and appeal to rival groups or public opinion at large. In some cases policy advocates argue from their findings toward a particular conclusion, which is offered as a *recommendation*. In other cases, where a very strong commitment to a particular course of action predates the research, whatever analysis was conducted may have been designed, consciously or unconsciously, to

From I. Gordon, J. Lewis and K. Young, 'Perspectives on policy analysis', *Public Administration Bulletin*, **25**, 1977, pp. 26–30.

support the case to be argued. Information is gathered and organised in order to sustain a point. This style of policy analysis [. . .] is often carried out by reformist pressure groups, although it is by no means entirely absent from some types of university research.

Information for policy
In this mode, the researcher's task is to provide policy-makers with information and perhaps advice. It assumes a case for action, in terms of either the introduction of a new policy, or the revision of an existing one. It may be carried out within the research branch of a government department; by outside researchers funded by that department; by independently funded researchers; or by unfunded individuals or associates who have simply chosen to address their scholarly activities to policy issues. The activity itself may be confined to the provision of useful data (e.g. on demographic change) for consideration in policy-making. It may, however, go beyond this to elucidate causal relationships, and thereby to suggest definite policy options. [. . .]

Policy monitoring and evaluation
Policy monitoring and evaluation frequently take the form of *post hoc* analysis of policies and programmes. In an obvious sense, all public agencies perform monitoring and evaluation functions in respect of their own activities, although some may be facile, uncritical or self-legitimising. Evaluation for policy *review* is, on the other hand a more self-conscious business, particularly where the policy or programme in question has an experimental aspect. [. . .]

Monitoring and evaluation can be aimed at providing direct results to policy-makers about the impact and effectiveness of specific policies. But it can do more than this. *Post hoc* review of policy impact may be used for feasibility analysis in future policy design, via the specification of a feasible *set* of actions. In this mode, the object of policy analysis is to inform policy-makers of the limits of possibility. 'Better' policies might then be those which are more closely tailored to the constraints of feasibility imposed by the intractable external world of the policy-makers.

Analysis of policy determination
The emphasis here is upon the inputs and transformational processes operating upon the *construction* of public policy. Attempts to analyse the policy process are inescapably based upon explicit or implicit models of the policy system. In some cases the model is seen as being 'driven' by environmental forces, in others by internal objectives and goals, in yet others by the internal perceptions of the external environment. In contrast with 'advocacy' or 'information' this mode can tend to

over-emphasise the constraints upon action to the point where patterns of activity are portrayed as the necessary outcomes of a confluence of forces.

Analysis of policy content
This category of activity includes many studies which have been carried out, within the social administration and social policy field, of the origin, intentions and operation of *specific* policies. Typical of this category are the numerous descriptive accounts which have been given by academics on such policy areas as housing, education, health and social services. While their results may help to inform policy-makers, this is not usually an explicit aim of such studies, for they are conducted for academic advancement rather than public impact. In their more sophisticated variants, content studies engage in 'value analysis' and show social policies as institutionalising social theories.

Assumptions about 'policy' and 'policy-making'

Before discussing the varieties of policy analysis further it is necessary to clarify certain assumptions about the nature of policy and policy-making, since a misunderstanding of these can lead to an unduly narrow view of appropriate research strategies.

Assumptions about the process
The common threads in 'policy' studies can be seen to include some interest in the *content* (as well as the institutions, ideology and procedures) of government activity, some concern for its *outcomes* and an assumption that this activity is in some degree instrumental or *purposive*. The basic orientation is compatible, however, with very different implicit models of the policy process, leading to different strategies for analysis and its application.

   To take ideal cases, researchers may on the one hand adopt the assumption that policy-making is essentially a rational process based on the classic steps from problem formulation and evaluation of alternatives through to implementation. Conflicts over goals or perceptions of the situation may be admitted, but these are assumed to result in stable and determinate outcomes which do not interfere with the consistency of the system's operations. Typically the problem is seen as technical, the climate as consensual and the process as controlled. On the other hand, policy-making may be seen as an inescapably *political* activity into which the perceptions and interests of individual actors enter at all stages. In this case implementation becomes a problematic activity rather than something that can be taken for granted, as in the rational process model; policy is seen as a bargained outcome, the environment as conflictful and the process itself is characterised by diversity and constraint.

The power and survival ability of the 'rational system' model is surprising, given that its assumptions have been undermined by empirical studies of the policy process, and that its predictive record is uneven. The main explanation for its continuing existence must lie in its status as a normative model and as a 'dignified' myth which is often shared by the policy-makers themselves. Acceptance of the rational model helps the researcher towards a comfortable life; it enables him or her to appear to engage in direct debate with the policy-makers on the basis that information provided by the researchers will be an aid to better policy-making. If, however, as we believe, policy-making systems approximate more closely to the 'political' model, these prospects can only be superficially attractive.

Assumptions about policy
The concept of 'policy' has a particular status in the 'rational' model as the relatively durable element against which other premises and actions are supposed to be tested for consistency. It is in this sense that we may speak of 'foreign policy' or 'social policy' or 'marketing policy' as if the terms denoted local variants of a universal theme. Yet each of these examples represents very different ways of manipulating, via purposive action, the external environment of particular organisations. Moreover, the term 'policy' is used even within ostensibly similar governmental agencies to describe a range of different activities including (i) defining objectives (ii) setting priorities (iii) describing a plan and (iv) specifying decision rules. These characterisations of 'policy' differ not only in their generality and the level at which it is supposed to occur but also in whether 'policy' is assumed to be entirely prior to action or (as we believe is often the case) at least partly a *post hoc* generalisation or rationalisation. We suggest here that there is a *recursive* relation between policy and action, with 'policy' itself representing an essentially dynamic set of constructions of the situation. In this case, we argue that it is a mistake to conceive of policy analysis as the study of identifiable things called policies which are produced, or crystallise, at a particular stage in the decision process.

Assumptions about 'boundaries'
A feature of the rational model of policy-making is that it conceives the policy system as tightly bounded, and its operations upon the external world as unproblematic. To depart from the assumptions of classical rationality is inevitably to widen the boundaries of the 'relevant' in the analysis of policy-making. 'Policy-makers' are seen as negotiating both

within their own organisations and externally, with a host of other organisations and actors whose concurrence may be necessary to policy implementation. The focus shifts from 'decision analysis' to encompass the range of activities from formulation to implementation and impact. Inter-organisational politics and the manipulation of networks (*réseaux*) enter the picture, and it becomes less plausible to speak of locating the 'real' policy-makers. Policy-making, like 'power', appears as a dynamic yet diffused element in the relations between public actors and the world on which they act. This, *the analysis of policy systems*, is perhaps the most neglected aspect of the field.

Assumptions about problem definition
In addition to the assumptions made about the policy-making process, assumptions about problem definition also affect almost all policy analysis. It has been suggested that in every government department there are 'deep structures' of policy – the implicit collection of beliefs about the aims and intentions of the departments and about the relevant actors who influence or benefit from the policy. These constitute what Laski called the 'inarticulate major premises' of the policy-makers. Policy analysts are in the position either of having to accept the 'deep structures' and the consequent assumptions made about problem definition and the range of possible solutions, or of trying to stand outside the organisational consensus and bring new perceptions to old problems. The former role may be more congenial to the policy-makers themselves, but the major potential contribution of the social scientist lies in challenging the deep structures of policy-making. In order that this potential be realised, policy studies must engage in the analysis *of* policy processes, systems and content – a narrowly utilitarian approach to funding policy research will in the long term be self-defeating.

Theory and practice in public policy and administration

Martin Minogue

Introduction

Both the interest and the complexity of the study of public policy lie in its propensity to disrupt disciplinary boundaries, and to call for examination of the social, economic and political environment in which the state operates. The search for a general explanatory theory of public policy necessarily implies a synthesis of social, political and economic theories, for 'what governments do' embraces the whole of economic, social and political life.

Public policies do things to economies and societies, so that ultimately any satisfactory explanatory theory of public policy must also explain the interrelations between the state, politics, economy and society. This is also why people from so many 'disciplines'—economics, politics, sociology, anthropology, geography, planning, management and even applied sciences—share an interest in and make contributions to the study of public policy. But synthesis here becomes a matter of considerable controversy: the scale of interest and intellectual develop- ment allows speculation, hypothesis, theorising, argument, much of it brilliant and suggestive; but our state of social knowledge is such that no one theory is capable of proof. Theories themselves may become both heuristic tools and practical ideologies: a good example is provided by Marxist and neo-Marxist political economy. This complexity breeds competition between theories, conflicts over methods, and disagreement over what constitutes the proper mode of analysis.[1]

From M. Minogue, 'Theory and practice in public policy and administration', *Policy and Politics*, **11**, 1983, pp. 63–85.

The interests of policy students are inexhaustible. They may seek to examine:

- a particular public policy system, for example, the policy processes of British or Nigerian or Indian government; or
- a particular area of policy within or across these systems, e.g. foreign policy, health policy, industrial policy, rural development policy.
- a particular decision, e.g. to mount a military attack on another country, to establish free health services for all, to devalue the pound, to increase income tax, to build a motorway, to abolish corporal punishment.

Whatever the particular interest of the student of policy, what cannot be avoided is the need to incorporate the other dimensions. The 'system' cannot be understood without reference to particular areas of policy; areas of policy cannot be understood without reference to specific decisions and actions; specific decisions and actions may be interesting in themselves but have no meaning beyond themselves except to the extent that they contribute to understanding of the policy area within which they are located, and to the general policy system which provides the context for both decision and policy. In brief, the policy analyst, who seeks to provide description of and prescription for specific decisions on particular policies, cannot ignore the overall policy process which is created by the interaction of decisions, policy networks, organisations, actors and events. Nor can he avoid the broader environment within which the public policy process is located; that is, he must pay due regard to the interaction of society and economy, in the effort to understand the political consequences of this interaction. Wildavsky, indeed, identifies 'interaction' as the crucial focus for policy studies, whether at the level of individuals or organisations or within society as a whole. A central concern with interaction will tend to produce an obsession with inter-relationships, which might be dealt with as discrete behavioural patterns, or simplified into systematic models, or elevated into 'grand theory'.

The danger, then, to which policy analysis is notably prone is to downgrade the significance of cause and effect: this frequently shows itself in the ahistorical approach of the bulk of policy studies. It is useful, sometimes, to establish systemic patterns, in which the parts contribute through clearly established relationships to a recognisable whole; but to think that this is enough, or that such analysis can be a reliable guide to present or future practice, is to be very shortsighted about what constitutes an adequate form of explanation. How did the parts come to look as they do? Were they always like that or have they changed? That is, what relationships of cause and effect underlie the relationships of action and interaction? Some analysts who embrace the comfortable rationality of systems theory are, of course, aware of this: but awareness leads them invariably into the position: 'if only we didn't have to start from here, we could much more easily reach our destination'. This can even lead to what Wildavsky terms 'retrodiction', or the prediction of the past.

Policy theorists, on the other hand, concerned to avoid such pitfalls and to establish a working set of theoretical propositions, exhibit a rather different fault, though one to which 'comprehensive rationality' adherents are vulnerable: that is, in their concern with policy process and social interaction they are liable to treat particular events and cases with something akin to contempt. In their understandable concern to build up explanatory models at a level which transcends the messy complexity of activities on the ground, they must needs extract some bits of actuality and leave out (suppress?) others. In doing so, they may establish a useful set of regularities, which recur often enough to manipulate into matrices, models, even general theories, but they then, inevitably, falsify any particular piece of actuality;[2] and their 'theory' will quite fail to predict any future piece of actuality, even if it manages to predict a general pattern within which actualities will be likely to occur. This falsification of reality, and so of prediction, is the greatest weakness of theory in the policy sciences. It is scarcely surprising that we therefore find the field full of alternative, competing constructions of reality. Nor is it surprising that the practitioner shuns theory because the gap between theory and practice is more self-evident to the practitioner than it is to the theorist.

This problem lies at the heart of the theoretical catholicity of policy studies, and resides partly in the lack of experience of policy in practice among those who predominate in the theoretical field. The greatest problem for most policy analysts is their inability to cope with politics. I turn, therefore, to a consideration of the place of politics in policy studies, and will proceed by counter-posing political science and management science as competing disciplinary approaches.

Management versus politics: united they stand, divided they fall

The study of politics and the state has a long tradition; the study of administration and management is a much more recent phenomenon. A conventional and dominant tradition in the study of the state has always been the study of constitutions and laws, and the treatment of the state as a neutral instrument of law. In such an approach the principal activity of the state was administration of law and regulation of society within

established law. As the scope of the state expanded, so did the scale of its operation and its administrative activities. The academic outgrowth which responded to these developments came to be known as 'public administration'. Public administration is still in use as a terminology, but is now essentially devoid of conceptual meaning. The idea that there is something called public administration which can be defined and recognised as distinctive from other 'disciplines'—like politics, or economics or management science—would be regarded as absurd by any social scientist. [. . .]

We can see at once, if we think about the great variety of disciplines which contribute to the study of activities carried out by 'the public administrator', that the term 'public administration' only has any meaning if it is given an extremely narrow connotation, that is of the administrative rules, procedures and routines which characterise the public service in action. If we shift our gaze beyond this narrow frame, say, to administrative practices, we are at once in a much bigger arena, where there are few certainties and fewer concepts with which to label the phenomena we observe. If we broaden our view to policies, increasing complexity increases our uncertainty: and we must employ some sort of conceptual apparatus if we are to make any sense of it all. 'Public administration' offers no such conceptual framework: it is rather an empty receptacle ready to receive whatever people prefer to put in it.[3] We can then discern a battle of preferences, or competing forms of explanation of what happens in public administration (which naturally become alternative prescriptions as to what *should* happen). Peter Self has said that 'the study of administration could be viewed as a battleground between the contending perspectives of the political scientist and the organisation or management theorists; but the potential contestants are on such different wavelengths that the battle is rarely joined'.[4]

Management science is a house with many rooms: but it is distinguished principally by the claim to offer a superior application of rationality both in making decisions (policy) and in implementing decisions (administration); it would also lay claim to more rigorous methods of investigation, and more effective regard for efficient means of operation. In short, management science holds out to us the promise of better policies which are better administered. We can see how attractive this promise must be to practical men of affairs, particularly so in a period of public concern about the effective use of scarce public resources. The political scientist interested in policymaking is, by contrast, disinclined to give hostages to fortune. His claim rather would be to provide a superior mode of explanation, which would strip away the outer disguises of government and lay bare the structures, processes and relationships of power which constitute the flesh and bones of 'real' government. The argument here would be that there exists a political rationality which may be defined as 'the capacity to make decisions in the future, to mobilise support for substance' which is 'at least as important as generating economic growth so that there will be resources to allocate'.[5] But how are we to choose between these opponents: managerial rationality and political rationality?

In the public sector, it is difficult to draw distinctions between 'management' and 'policymaking'. If we examine the three conventionally defined stages of government activity (decision making, implementation, and evaluation) it can be argued that at each stage the 'policy' perspective provides a more plausible account of events than the 'managerial' perspective. It follows that the policy perspective gives us a more plausible account of the whole governmental system; and that the contribution to public affairs of the managerialist, and of managerial ideologies, is always in the long run likely to be inferior to the contribution of the policy analyst and of policy studies. This is a debate of considerable appositeness at a time when the ideology of management has made strong progress in numerous state bureaucracies, and where "better management" is all too frequently and simplistically offered as a solution to what is said to be the central problem of bureaucratic inadequacy; whereas the real issue is that of policy failure.

Decision making

It is, of course, arbitrary to reduce complex processes to distinct categories, but orthodox accounts do this as a matter of course, and regard such neat formulations as virtuous. The primary theoretical characteristic of managerialism is the emphasis it places upon rationality. Processes must be orderly. Structures must be logical, and relate clearly to functions. Activity must be systematic: that is, it must flow in a predictable way through the established structures, with predetermined consequences. Decisions must also be rationally ordered, in discernible stages: a stage of formulation, in which clear objectives will be established; a stage of implementation, by which these objectives will be translated into actions; and a stage of evaluation, where practice will be monitored and information fed back systematically into a new cycle, starting with the reformulation of objectives. This type of rationality implies that there can be a perfect system of decision making and that decisions can be perfectly administered.

But managerialism goes beyond the provision of a decision making system; it also tells us that there are rational means for making the choices which the system will translate into action.[6] Numerous devices are offered for our inspection, the principal devices being cost-benefit analysis, systems analysis and programme budgeting. All are rather different, both in theory and practice (and for some governments they are very much in practice), but share at least two characteristics. First, they are all essentially drawn from the work of economists interested in efficiency, here defined as meeting specified objectives at the least possible cost. Secondly, all such techniques rely on hard information, and lots of it, which should be quantifiable.

In *cost-benefit analysis* (CBA) allowances are made for variations in available information by postulating separable categories of decision making:

- decision making under certainty: where a specific action will lead to a predictable specific outcome;
- decision making under risk: where action is broken down into a set of possible specific outcomes, to each of which a quantified level of 'probability' can be attached:
- decision making under uncertainty: where range of possible outcomes may be predicted, but where it is not possible to attach levels of probability to specific outcomes.

In theory, the information and the arithmetic combine to produce the most profitable, or 'best', choice or decision, and therefore the best outcome.

In *systems analysis*, there is less reliance than in the CBA on quantitative methods, more reliance on judgement. Essentially, systems analysis builds models which abstract from 'reality', but represent what are held to be the crucial relationships in reality. Objectives are taken as specified, but as likely to be imprecise and in need of clearer definition. The claim made for systems analysis is that it can clarify objectives, cut the costs of meeting these objectives, and identify bottlenecks which are causing problems: in short, the aim of systems analysis is to eliminate inefficiency, and to create a more effective 'system'.

Programming budgeting cannot be so easily defined as the foregoing devices, except by reference to its application in practice (for example in the USA and in the UK). The general idea is to relate expenditure budgeting to defined goals and outputs, again with the intention of controlling the costs of achieving set objectives.

Most managerialists and many self-described policy analysts would embrace these devices with enthusiasm, stoutly defend their merits, and seek to apply them in the real world of government. But what of the student of public policy who is primarily concerned to locate decision making in the 'real world of government' within an explanatory framework related to political analysis? His reaction will be almost to ridicule such procedures, on the ground that they are so far removed from what a literary critic recently called 'the odd unsymmetry of actual life'.[7] These managerialist approaches incorporate assumptions which in the context of *public* policy processes and *public* organisations are simply not tenable. The assumptions most open to objection relate to *objectives* and *information*.

Objectives
The assumption is either that objectives are given, and the question is only what are the best means to achieve these ends; or that objectives, if not already properly established, can be given clear definition and closely related to specific means; and in both instances, an assumption that public organisations are predominantly concerned with a rational relationship between means and ends.

The policy scientist knows that the 'actual life' of government does not offer much support for these assumptions. First, governmental organisations rarely have clear and precisely defined goals; indeed, such stark definition is deliberately avoided. This is because, characteristic- ally, any specific policy arena is marked by conflict over objectives. The conflict may take a partisan form: i.e. conflict between political ideologies, or between political groups competing for office. Or conflict may take an organisational form: i.e. conflict within public organisa- tions, e.g. ministers vs. officials, higher officials vs. lower officials, departments vs. departments, ministers vs. ministers, and so on; yet again partisan conflicts and organisational conflicts will frequently be inter-related, through interaction between the executive and the legisla- ture, or between the executive and interest groups. In this sort of political-organisational setting, to specify objectives is to pre-empt, or try to pre-empt, someone's interest in an alternative objective. Typical- ly, decisions emerge from a complex process of bargaining[8] and, in a bargaining process, to specify objectives too clearly or too quickly is to invite difficulty. To make clear your objectives is to make a concession to opponents or competitors, and gives them information upon which they can base more effective resistance.

A second assumption to be challenged even where objectives are specified is that these are the real objectives, and that there is unity over objectives. Organisational analysis tells us[9] that organisations are made up of interests, which are engaged in a competition for resources and power (or influence). The competition may be far more significant than the policies upon which competition turns; means are likely to be of much greater concern than ends. Indeed, characteristically, the means— the construction of powerful organisation—often becomes the principal end for those who inhabit the organisation. In relation to British government, you only have to read the Crossman Diaries[10] to see the force of this statement: or note, for example, a quotation from

Crossman's famous *éminence grise*, Lady Evelyn Sharpe, who said of the British machinery of government that the distribution of functions did not proceed on the basis of analysis and judgement, but on a basis of guesswork and personalities. In British central government the definition of the whole range of organisational objectives would be (and is) impossible for the outsider, and undesirable (if possible) for the insider. Yet managerial philosophies insist that objectives can be rationally defined and efficiently achieved. In truth, objectives are the products of interaction between key participants, not the prime mover of such interaction.[11]

Information

A further managerial assumption is that necessary and sufficient information is available to the decision maker. There are two comments to be made here. First, in public policymaking, information is frequently inadequate or simply not available, yet these are constraints supplied by time and events; the decision maker cannot wait until he has all the information he needs. Second, information is a resource, to be used and manipulated. It may even be denied to key participants (like one policy adviser to the British Secretary of State for Health and Society Security; he was the Minister's personal representative and informant on a departmental working party on social security benefit, but at the point where crucial decisions had to be made, the officials changed the venue of the meeting at the last minute and 'forgot' to tell the policy adviser).

Moreover, too much information may be an embarrassment. Maynard Keynes once wrote: 'there is nothing a Government hates more than to be well-informed; for it makes the process of arriving at decisions much more complicated and difficult.'[12] This emphasises again the highly political nature of decision making in public life: rational methods may be in principle more desirable than 'the hurried judgements of bargainers' but a political system needs ambiguity if bargains are to be negotiated.

An assumption related to the question of information is that choices between competing objectives can be rationally determined on the basis of accurate formulations of knowledge. But practice has appeared to offer other lessons. For example, in relation to 'big' issues, CBA cannot deal with the problem of choosing between programmes which serve different objectives and constituencies: in what 'rational' way could you choose between the allocation of resources to education as opposed to health, or health as opposed to industrial subsidy? Such choices must, can be and are made: but they are made through political processes in which groups representing different policy areas bargain, and construct trade-offs; or alternatively, where some groups, or one group, succeed in imposing their political power (however based) to the extent of winning a larger share of resources than other groups. Moreover, similar competitive struggles take place not only between policy arenas but within specific policy areas. The outcomes of such struggles are not determined by rational techniques of decision making.

A major problem for rational methods is the reliance upon knowledge which is quantifiable. As Henderson put it in his analysis of Concorde, 'only that which can be counted is permitted to count';[13] and he suggests sardonically that on this score CBA represents 'a greatly superior design of fig-leaf'.[14] It is almost trite to make the point that in the complex social and economic world to which public policies are addressed, and from which in part they spring, a considerable range of factors simply cannot be quantified, except in the most arbitrary manner: how do you put numbers to the quality of a lively sixth form, or the worries of an old, sick person, or the desperation of an unemployed youth? Yet it is factors such as these which generate political enthusiasms and hatreds, and it is just such passions which will, in part at least, influence the political process through which real decisions will emerge. Within such processes, numbers can sometimes be seen to be useful, but only where their projections accord with some strong interest in the decision making arena. As Lord Beveridge once put it: 'Reason and special knowledge have their chance only if there is a channel of access to those who have power.'

Henderson comments that CBA analysts always have excellent statistics of the future, but not of the present or the past. E. S. Quade, the Rand Corporation expert who is said to have 'invented' systems analysis, admitted that 'systems analysis is still largely a form of art'.[15] The major result of the application of programme budgeting in Britain appears at first glance to be public expenditure deficits of breathtaking proportions. We may, I think, conclude this part of the discussion with the view that the claims for rational techniques to make an actual and potential contribution to better public decision making need to be treated with considerable scepticism.

Implementation

Let us turn, then, to an alternative claim for managerialism: that it offers both a method and a philosophy for achieving efficient and effective administration. Here the focus must be on implementation, the crucial business of translating decisions into events: of 'getting things done'. It is, perhaps, the claim to be able to 'get things done' which distinguishes the management system and the management man. It is an appealing philosophy and a seductive promise, and it is this promise (explicit or implicit) which has made management so fashionable in the last decade or so. When governments fail, the problem is frequently identified as 'poor management', and the remedy, of course, is better management: frequently, 'better' management is construed as the practices and attitudes of private sector business management.[16]

The policy scientist can at least agree that getting things done, or implementation, is a crucial aspect of the real world of public policy-making, and one which has been neglected in theoretical literature.[17] He would seek to make a significant distinction, though, between implementation and outcome. Implementation relates to 'specified objectives', the translation into practice of the policies that emerge from the complex process of decision making. Outcome, by contrast, refers to the results of decision-plus-implementation, or what actually happens. My *motif* here would be a quotation from B. J. Loasby: 'It is dangerous to assume either that what has been decided will be achieved, or what happens is what was intended.'[18] This can be explained partly by reference to the problem of objectives: that organisations do not quite know what they are, or cannot agree on them, or pursue conflicting objectives, or even set objectives (either deliberately or unintentionally) which cannot be implemented. But it is also a matter of administration, which means 'good management', and may also mean planning. I do not take the view that administration is in practice redundant, or in theory so dependent a variable as to lack explanatory significance. An extreme view of the first notion was expressed in early Marxist-Leninist ideology, with the belief that planned administration would be rendered unnecessary by the pervasiveness of socialist ideals throughout Soviet society: in *The ABC of Communism* (1920) Bukharin and Preobrazhensky wrote: 'The main direction will be entrusted to various kinds of book-keeping offices or statistical bureaux . . . and since all will understand that this work is necessary and that life goes easier when everything is done according to a pre-arranged plan . . . all will work in accordance with the indications of these statistical bureaux. There will be no need for special Ministers of State, for police and prisons, for laws and decrees—nothing of the sort. Just as in an orchestra all the performers watch the conductor's baton, so here all will consult the statistical reports and will direct their work accordingly.'[19]

But we see that in practice, the Soviet state has notably failed to 'wither away', and indeed represents a strong example of the pervasiveness of state bureaucracy, and arguably of the 'bureaucratisation of politics'. Soviet ideology places the strongest possible emphasis on directive planning of policies, and upon the efficient management of those policies. So do most new states. Similar views have everywhere been gaining ground in the industrialised capitalist states. Management of state policies might be said, then, to be of universal interest, which makes more essential a proper scrutiny of the claims of managerialism.

The policy scientist is likely, in a word, to be sceptical of those claims; sceptical of planning, but not opposed to commonsense attempts to forecast future problems; sceptical of how much effect 'management' can have on the success or failure of public policies, but not opposed to attempts to dispose resources and activities in an orderly way. In particular, he would question two propositions which are implicit and explicit in managerialist literature and practice:

(i) that the expression of efficient management fathers the deed: all managers claim that they are good managers, though many are not; and many public organisations claim that they have introduced 'good management' despite the evidence that they have not (an excellent example of the latter is the British civil service response to the Fulton reforms).[20]

(ii) that a virtue of management is the exclusion of politics: management is 'good' and 'rational'; politics is 'bad' and 'irrational'. Management can deliver desirable results; politics frustrates desirable results. Management represents an instrumental rationality which is functionally necessary; politics represents a dysfunctional irrationality, which is both objectionable and unnecessary; management is 'clean', politics is 'dirty'.

Two questions arise here. First, what is 'good' administration/management; second, is politics necessary? The first point may be dealt with by borrowing the formulation (by Christopher Hood) of a model of perfect administration. Hood proposes the model and then 'relaxes' it to accord with real administration. It take fives pages to propose the perfect model; and 195 pages to give an account of real organisational life which leaves the model in shattered pieces.[21] The model may be summarised as follows:

(a) An administrative system should be unitary like a large army with a single line of authority: there must be no conflicts of authority, for this would weaken administrative control;

(b) Objectives must be given, uniform, explicit, and known throughout the system;

(c) Clear and authoritative objectives must still be implemented: to achieve this the system must ensure either perfect obedience, or perfect control (to eliminate resistance): the assumption must be that every action of every individual can be recorded and scrutinised;

(d) There must be perfect information and communication, with all tasks unambiguously specified and precisely coordinated;

(e) All these conditions require an adequate time-scale for fulfilment.

Simply to state this model is to highlight the absurdity of the managerialist position: such systems do not, and could not, exist. The 'limits of administration' are clear enough: limited resources, ambiguity of objectives, internal organisational competition. Above all stands the political limit, which might be described thus:

(i) nothing gets done which is unacceptable to dominant or influential political groups, which may be defined to include the 'bureaucratic leadership' group;
(ii) activities which 'get done' externally may generate a hostile and uncooperative response, referred to by Hood as 'recalcitrance'.

There are two insurmountable problems for the analysis which wants to exclude politics. First, the internal world of the organisation cannot be isolated from the world external to the organisation. This is overwhelmingly the case with the public administrative system, which in myriad ways is inter-related with the wider political system; at the centre of affairs the two systems are almost inextricably intertwined. External politics cannot simply be left out.

Secondly, the approach contains the assumption that internal organisation does not involve politics. This assumption could only be sustained by defining politics so narrowly as to render it meaningless. All organisations have politics, in the sense that they contain groups of people, and individuals, who will compete with each other to control and manipulate resources, policies, practices, each other, and the organisation itself. In public organisations, no meaningful distinction between policy and administration is possible; and policies proposed and authorised by formal political institutions and participants are in a wide variety of ways influenced, mediated, even altered by formal administrative institutions and participants at both the higher and the lower levels. (Hood calls this, in the implementation stage, knocking off the corners to get the policy through the front door.)[22]

The problem of making clear definitions of what is involved in good management can be further illustrated by reference to the question of information. Hood's model says that information must be accurate and must be communicated. So does textbook management. There are endless examples to show that the assumption is over-optimistic, mainly because it treats information as neutral. We have already noted that information is a resource which in practice is manipulated by competitors within organisations; and in the case of the state information is an instrument which can be manipulated to maintain domination over policies, to deny influence to external competition for influence over policies and to reduce 'recalcitrance' in the external political environment. Perhaps the most telling examples may be drawn from Soviet and

Chinese economic planning, where we might assume the highest possible combination of specified objectives and administrative control. For example, Stalin used to be shown films of tables groaning with fruit, poultry and agricultural produce to illustrate the successful implementation of the rural collectivisation programme; in actuality, the collectives were famine-stricken and impoverished.[23] A different sort of example is provided by World War II fighter pilots, who consistently exaggerated the number of enemy planes they had shot down: they gave to each other, and their superiors (and thence to the wider public), not the truth, but the false information that everyone wanted to hear.[24] We know from studies of real organisations that not only may real information be screened out if it doesn't accord with established beliefs and preferences;[25] but that competent critical people may also be 'screened out' in favour of incompetent uncritical people: we need to look no further than the Nixon Administration in the USA for an example.

Evaluation

A closely related question is that of ignorance, the lack of information or knowledge. This may be an organisational matter too; for as Michel Crozier says, 'People who make the decisions cannot have direct first-hand knowledge of the problems they are called upon to solve. On the other hand, the field officers who know these problems can never have the power necessary to adjust, to experiment, and to innovate.'[26] Even if policymakers had the best of intentions, they would still come up hard against the real limits imposed by ignorance. Public policies are addressed to a world of social and economic interaction of such complexity and scale that our ignorance of it is probably more substantial than our knowledge. In this context, public policies might more usefully be described as social experiments; experiments, moreover, distinguished by guesswork rather than scientific method. It is this facet with explains the need to conceptualise the outcome or impact of public policy. We often do not know what the results and consequences of policies will be until we see them in action.

Clearly it is essential for governments to estimate results, to measure these results, and learn from them. The literature, too, places considerable emphasis upon evaluation: systems analysis calls it feedback, and technically such feedback operates as a self-adjusting mechanism; alternatively, evaluation might generate more data on which to base improved calculations of 'best' future policies. A rather different approach is Lindblom's concept of disjointed incrementalism, which through processes of 'partisan mutual adjustment' ensures that experience is learned from and policy adjusted within the limits imposed by internal organisational politics and external social and political configurations.[27]

Both approaches considerably over-emphasise and contain values of stability and continuity. They make few allowances for conditions of marked economic and social change: conditions which prevail in most countries in the latter part of the twentieth century. Not only is our knowledge of how societies work so limited that policies addressed to societies frequently turn out to be misjudged, or ineffective; but the time scale required for the construction and operation of a major policy is so great that it is highly likely, when operated, to be addressed to a problem which has already changed its nature. In this sense, policy always lags behind events, except to the extent that policies themselves provide part of the social framework within which changes take place. Therefore, the argument is not that policies cannot have effective consequences; but that policies at the very least are always likely to have unintended consequences. If we seek to improve policymaking, we must improve our stock of social knowledge; and as part of this activity, analysis of the results of policies is of profound importance.

Major problems arise here with the nature of political leadership and organisational behaviour. Political leaders will not be anxious to have too critical an examination of their failures; this will be particularly so if, as with many national economic plans in new states, political leaders have never intended implementation (with all its real difficulties and resource-hungry characteristics) but sought only the easy fruits of political rhetoric.[28] For similar reasons, bureaucratic leaders do not frequently show an interest in serious evaluation of policies: this may be because of the fear that the information which results may provide a resource to the enemy/competitor of the organisation. It is, of course, possible that top policymakers well understand the gaps which exist between their policies and the real external world, and so avoid evaluation because they do not wish these frailties to be exposed.

We need to understand yet again that evaluation is not merely a technical matter, nor even a question of good practice: it is, or may be, a highly political issue. We are always, therefore, likely to find that an absence of evaluation contributes further to the uncertainties and unsystematic nature of public policy, and in its analysis, the uncertainty principle must be given great regard. It is worth quoting again that wise man of public affairs, J. M. Keynes: 'The sense in which I am using the term uncertainty is that in which the prospect of European war is uncertain, or the price of copper and the rate of interest twenty years on, or the obsolescence of a new invention . . . About these matters there is no basis on which to form any calculable probability whatever. We simply do not know . . .'.[29]

The limits of managerialism

I propose now to set out some judgements based on these prior
arguments, about the limitations of managerialism as an approach to the
study, teaching and practice of public policy.

(1) Managerialism constructs a false and naive view of the policy
    process; in leaving out politics, it puts out the baby with the
    bathwater. Decisional 'systems' which leave out politics will produce
    unreal, unworkable or unacceptable decisions.
(2) Efficiency is not enough, if it leaves out problems of choice, and the
    analysis of choice is inept if it leaves out values. In short,
    managerialism leaves out morality. Can we say that a state, like the
    German Third Reich, which cheaply and with great efficiency
    achieves a specified objective, that is, the extinction of a significant
    group of its citizens, is a 'good', a well-managed state? Insofar as
    managerialism leaves aside consideration of the desirability of
    objectives it may actually be dangerous. Indeed, Rein suggests that
    the dilemmas posed by competing objectives are 'desirable, because
    they pose moral choices and hence permit a debate about moral
    purposes'.[30]
(3) Managerialism addresses itself too much to the future, too little to
    the past or the present. The answer to 'bad management now' is
    'better management in the future'; in the end, managerialism is an
    'if only' conception. It is not rooted in present realities. Far from
    addressing itself in a practical way to practical men, it is principally
    in the business of mythmaking.
(4) Managerialism conceals the inner politics of bureaucracies, by
    bureaucratising political exchanges which are articulated as organi-
    sational exchanges.[31] This is a deception convenient both to
    managers and to managerial analysts. The danger here is that
    managerialism may lead to enormous policy errors if it succeeds in
    neutralising political exchanges or reducing political intervention in
    policy discussion: Henderson's account of the AGR reactor pro-
    gramme gives a good example.[32] British local government also
    provides an interesting example of the bureaucratisation of
    politics.[33]
(5) Managerialism can be successfully turned against itself merely by
    assertion, e.g. by using managerial concepts and language to
    describe 'reality' but avoiding real analysis by constructing a false
    reality; examples are provided by:
    (i) the practice of economic ministries in new states of reporting the
        achievement of planned objectives when these objectives have
        not really been met, or even implemented;

(ii) the assertion that there exists, say, a system of management by objectives, or financial programme management, where these are not in practice effective, nor intended to be, but aim to provide the semblance of a response to calls for 'better management'. One example here is the history of British government's fairly brief flirtation with 'management by objectives', now in effect discarded, and 'programme analysis review', now defunct (a recent internal report suggested that one way to achieve more efficiency would be to reduce the number of efficiency experts!).

Finally, this counterposition of 'managerialism' and 'politics' in public policy analysis depends upon a counterposition of types of rationality. Let Wildavsky sum up the view consistently argued in this section: 'the method called the "rational paradigm" (order objectives, compose alternatives, compare the highest ranking) is mistaken as describing either how decisions are or ought to be made. This paradigm conveys the wrong-headed impression that all one has to do to answer a question is to ask it.'[34] By contrast, political rationality consists of identifying what are the problems to be answered; then, in constructing support for the solutions proposed: here, 'rationality resides in results'.[35]

The limits of policy science

This section might be subtitled: if managerialism fails, can policy science do better? The answer is yes, in that the policy scientist insists on including the political context of public service management in his explanations and analysis, and would incorporate the political dimension into his prescriptions; and yes, in that the policy scientist penetrates real organisational life, seeking to lay bare the political and behavioural processes which generate actual policies, and govern the form, style and pervasiveness of state bureaucracies. But policy science too has serious limitations, and must not, any more than managerialism, state its claim too confidently.

A principal limitation resides in the problem of theory alluded to briefly in the first part of this paper. Policy 'science' has no real claim to be a science; it has no agreed theoretical foundation on which to build models and test hypotheses, but encounters several theoretical possibilities. As always in situations of theoretical fragmentation, policy scientists spend an excessive amount of energy in addressing each other, and in struggling to incorporate a variety of disciplinary approaches. To say this is not to attack the search for a workable and distinctive theory; but to point up the limitations which this continued search produces, at a time when the main contributing disciplines (economics, sociology and politics) are themselves, arguably, in a state of crisis.

One significant effect is to widen the gap which exists between theory and practice. The gap is created in a variety of ways. The most obvious problem is the absence of real political or administrative experience in those who teach and theorise about public policy. This partly explains the 'remoteness' of theory from the real world of policy, but also tends to promote a greater respect for theory than for practice, since academics move in a world where the highest value is placed upon the construction and refinement of theory; even the application of theory may be pursued in an intellectual rather than a practical context. Indeed, some policy studies specialists would quite deliberately avoid any involvement in the real world of policy on the ground that this might impose upon them unwanted intellectual constrictions, as well as quite practical constraints. It is not difficult to understand this tension between academic and practitioner: each threatens to interfere with the activities and preferences of the other. The theorist wishes to distance himself intellectually from the real policy world to avoid the ideological contamination which inevitably comes from actual participation in an area of policy. The practitioner tends to avoid over-exposure to a wide range of ideas, and is rarely anxious to cultivate external critical analysis. C. H. Sisson, himself a former British civil servant, put this rather well: 'the official is a man who has been trained to a practical operation, not to an exposition of theory or a search for truth. There is no need for the administrator to be a man of ideas. His distinguishing quality should rather be a certain freedom from ideas.'[36]

An unfortunate consequence of the gap between the theoretician and the practitioner is that each manifests something uncomfortably close to contempt for the other, a contempt strengthened rather than weakened by being based in a defensive insecurity (the academic insecure about the crisis of theory, the practitioner insecure about the failures of practice). It might be held that decisional and other techniques at least offer to bridge the divide; but the antagonistic feelings of the practitioner are strengthened when he perceives the weaknesses and limited use of such techniques; in any case, the able official will manipulate these techniques and their findings in the political arena, and is able therefore to manipulate the policy analyst. The policy adviser, who is concerned less with techniques than content, and perceives the real policy process more accurately than the 'technician', will be a stronger opponent. But the danger then is the tendency for the policy adviser to think that he is the sole repository of truth, and that his perceived truth must prevail of its own force. Martin Rein makes the point that the policy adviser who seeks to influence practice enters an arena in which several holders of 'truth', as they see it, fight their corner.[37] It is not a question so much of 'speaking Truth to Power':[38] Power decides what Truth is. To the extent that the policy adviser wishes his version to be chosen, he must enter the power struggle: and once he does so, to the extent that he has to participate in bargains and accommodations, so will the value of his real insights or knowledge be reduced. Rein makes some other interesting suggestions:

(i) that action is significant to the policy analyst because it generates inquiry, not (as the purist would like to think), the other way about;
(ii) knowledge is not always cumulative: decision makers do not always learn from experience even when it is analysed for them, or rather, the factors which condition policymaking may screen out unwanted learning or knowledge (a point recently emphasised in *New Society*: 'not only does social science cost money, but it persists in finding out things the government does not want to know.')[39]

On the basis of these arguments, Rein suggests that it is not so much social science which is important for public policymaking, as the social scientist; the values, personality, ambitions and preferences of the individual policy adviser may combine to make a distinctive contribution to real policy. Wildavsky's idea is rather similar: that policy analysis is synonymous with creativity, and with defining problems rather than offering handy solutions: 'in policy analysis the most creative calculations concern finding problems for which solutions might be attempted.'[40]

Rein and Wildavsky are optimistic about the possibility of a genuine role for the external policy analyst, and so for the improvement of public policies. Wildavsky places what can only be described as faith in the possibility of producing better policies and better government through a process by which bright graduates are trained in the 'art and craft', as well as the techniques, of policy analysis. This approach envisages that Graduate Schools of Public Policy will provide a stream of well-trained, knowledgeable policy analysts who will move into governmental agencies and actively participate in policy activities. Yehezkel Dror, ostensibly more attached to 'rationality', shows a similar enthusiasm for the 'preparation of policy sciences professionals'.[41] Other writers, geared to narrower formulations of policy analysis in terms of decision making skills, also take a highly optimistic view of the utility of professional analysts. For example, one recent work of this type promotes the concept of 'performance administration' as an antidote to ineffective policymaking: 'performance administration combines the traditional approaches of public administration with contemporary concepts of systems analysis and comprehensive planning in an attempt to achieve a coordinative process capable of yielding more rational public policies and decisions': this 'must be more than a handful of strategies and techniques . . . it is a set of attitudes . . . a management style.'[42]

But neither the stylish perceptiveness of Wildavsky, the earnest idealism of Dror, nor the careful reasonableness of Steiss and Daneke really gives us much help in relating their varieties of analysis to the sheer messiness of real-world political and organisational life. These political realities are acknowledged, but not dealt with in any convincing way when it comes to prescription. There is no sense of the conflicts and problems which these brave new policy sciences professionals will encounter, no attempt to discuss the limitations by which they will be hamstrung. For example, Dror makes out a case for a code of ethics as part of the 'professionalisation' of the policy scientist, which includes:

b. When the goals and values of a particular client contradict basic beliefs of the policy scientist, the policy scientist should resign . . .

c. . . . a policy scientist should not hide an alternative because it contradicts his own personal values and preferences . . .

e. . . . a policy scientist should refuse to prepare studies, the sole purpose of which is to provide a supporting brief to an alternative already finally decided upon for other reasons . . .

f. . . . policy scientists should not work for clients who do not provide necessary access to information . . .[43]

Dror clearly believes that such 'policy science professionals' do not exist; but the equally implicit assumption that they should, and can, exist is based on a fundamental lack of understanding of what real life in real public bureaucracies is like. If Dror's graduates were to follow his recommendations, there would soon be none of them left in public service jobs, and this can scarcely be Dror's intention. Dror has left a gap between the ideal and the actual, and gives no guidance on how this gap is to be bridged. There is, in formulations like this, a sort of implied wish that awkward political realities would somehow wither away: but of course they will not, and the failure here is to understand the functional rationality of what might appear otherwise to be irrational political behaviour. Too many policy scientists share the management scientists' tendency to 'leave out the politics', or assume it away. But there will be no adequate theory of public policymaking which does not convincingly account for political phenomena as well as organisational reality. And it is unlikely that an adequate theory can be produced, when it is primarily in the hands of those who do not inhabit the actual world of public political organisations and only get occasional glimpses of that world. These glimpses mean that much theoretical work is shot through with flashes of illumination, but the flashes seem so bright because of the prevailing darkness.

The problem does not rest only with the theorists: they are, at least, trying to make sense of a puzzling, half-hidden world, illuminated less by a flaming torch than a spluttering candle. Practitioners themselves constitute part of the problem. Self-interest pushes them towards concealment rather than open dealing, towards disguises rather than revelations. It becomes an organisational virtue to keep apart policy information and policy analysts, especially if these analysts are outside the organisation; even 'insider' analysts may often find themselves treated with reserve and suspicion. The greatest weakness of the practitioner is the inability to perceive himself, and to understand that all his own actions and activities are just as ideologically framed as the theories of the non-practitioner. The 'pragmatic' bureaucrat is just as beset by values, beliefs and preferences as the 'objective' academic. Both produce work which rests on assumptions, even on world views. Neither can really sustain a claim to objectivity. Just as there is no such thing as value free social science, so there is no such thing as value free administration or value free public policy-making. At least some policy scientists acknowledge the impossibility of detachment: most bureaucrats would not, and the failure of the official to comprehend the ideological nature of his own activities brings a myopic vision which is thoroughly damaging to public policy itself.

The distaste often shown by practitioners for the work of academics is less subtle and more visible. But it is equally damaging to public policy when it involves a deliberate evasion of knowledge; and since knowledge is subject to manipulation by power, the practitioner is invariably well placed to ensure that his version of knowledge prevails. The policy analyst who wishes to influence 'real policy' may follow one of two paths. He may choose to work inside the decision making bureaucracy, using whatever influence he can muster to support his authoritative knowledge. Or he may work through the political process, by way of specific pressure groups or political parties; or in some types of political system, through specific political authority figures, or patronage networks.

What the policy analyst can never assume is that authoritative knowledge will do the trick by itself;[44] though the dissemination of such knowledge may well, in the long run, have important effects upon those who control policy decisions. There is, of course, a view that knowledge will inevitably assert itself in the long run, that it will cause changes in general social values and that these social values must eventually find expression in the public policies which form the framework for social action. But this gradualist view runs into serious opposition, notably from the contrary view that social values reflect economic and social configurations which are deterministic in nature: so that, as Marx said:

'The ruling ideas are everywhere the ideas of the ruling classes', and all knowledge, too, is subject to this formulation, having no political authority except that bestowed by attachment to power.[45]

Whichever underlying view one adopts, political practice seems to indicate that expert knowledge may be necessary to the achievement of desired public policy, but is not sufficient for such achievement. This is probably as it should be: for there is no reason to suppose that the public policies 'desired' by the expert will conform to the policies generally desired by the public, or even that what the expert analyst believes to be the public interest is in actuality in the public interest. We could only rely on a firm connection between the policy analyst and the general public interest if the recent past were more comprehensible and the near future more predictable than they are. If we cannot rely on the state of knowledge of the academic theorist, we can rely even less on the state of knowledge of the professional bureaucrat or politician: as the rate of social and economic change seems constantly to increase, and as political, social and economic systems come more and more to be characterised by 'turbulence', then we might agree with the comment that 'public officials often do not know where they are, let alone where they are going.'[46] In short, social systems are simply not predictable enough to be described as manageable; rational management and control in such circumstances are impossible.

Conclusion

The foregoing analysis might seem to lead to pessimistic conclusions: if the prospects for the efficient management of effective public policies are so constricted and uncertain, is there any point in teaching policy studies, and pursuing policy research and analysis?

The study of public policy is fashionable, of practical importance, and theoretically incoherent: it follows that, though it increasingly attracts students, it is not an easy subject either to teach or to learn: indeed Wildavsky once wrote that policy analysis may be learned but not taught! A subject which holds immense fascination can be turned into a tedious rehearsal of tired concepts, especially where too much emphasis is laid on theory, too little on the investigation of real issues and problems. In the last resort, teachers will follow their own noses, but should be careful to remember that students have noses too, and may not relish the same smells. It is tempting, given the current disarray of the social sciences, to suggest that we should avoid the worship of what usually turn out to be false gods, and seek to develop new ways of tackling the subject, and new ways of involving students in it. Yet the thrust of this paper suggests that the pursuit of the timehonoured method of discrete analysis of issues and problems, on the basis of sound historical groundwork, and informed by a strongly developed consciousness of the primary influence of politics remains the most interesting and illuminating method; for it combines a decent analytical method with the theoretically sound perception that issues of public policy do not lend themselves to neutral, value free, scientific analysis. As Charles Darwin once wrote: 'How odd it is that anyone should not see that all observation must be for or against some view if it is to be of any service.'[47]

Notes

1. Marxist political economy has been strangely neglected in public policy studies: yet the burgeoning interest in the state and its relations with society owes at least as much to this radical strand as it does to the work of more conventionally located policy theorists; for example, Ian Gough, *The Political Economy of the Welfare State* (London: Macmillan, 1979); R. K. Mishra, *Society and Social Policy* (London: Macmillan, 1977); R. Miliband, *The State in Capitalist Society* (London: Weidenfeld & Nicolson, 1970); N. Poulantzas, *State, Power, Socialism* (London: New Left Books, 1978). For a stimulating discussion of the possibilities for radical theory in the field of public administration, see Patrick Dunleavy, 'Is there a radical approach to Public Administration?', *Public Administration*, Vol. 60, No. 2 (1982), 215–24.
2. This is a crude summary of a detailed and convincing argument in Q. R. D. Skinner, 'The limits of historical explanations', *Philosophy*, Vol. 41, No. 157 (1966) 199–215.
3. The same comment holds good for 'Social Administration': see Michael Hill, *Understanding Social Policy* (Oxford: Blackwell and Martin Robertson, 1980), Chap. I.
4. P. Self, *Administrative Theories and Politics* (London: Allen & Unwin, 1972 edn.), 14–15.
5. A. Wildavsky, *The Art and Craft of Policy Analysis* (London: Macmillan, 1980), 3.
6. The following analysis draws on Wildavsky's articles, 'The political economy of efficiency: cost benefit analysis, systems analysis, and program budgeting', *Public Administration Review*, Vol. 26 (1966), 292–310; and 'Rescuing policy analysis from PPBS', *Public Administration Review*, Vol. 29 (1969), 189–202.
7. Graham Hough, *The London Review of Books*, 1980.
8. Note C. E. Lindblom's concepts of 'disjointed incrementalism' and 'partisan mutual adjustment', elaborated as a critique of the 'comprehensive rationality' approach; see *The Intelligence of Democracy* (New York. Free Press, 1965) and *The Policymaking Process* (New York: Prentice Hall, 1968). Lindblom's incrementalist approach has attracted much criticism, most notably from Y. Dror, *Public Policymaking Re-examined* (Chandler, 1968).

9. The literature is well surveyed in A. Dunsire, *The Execution Process*, Vol. 1 (Oxford: Martin Robertson, 1978), 16–90.

10. R. H. S. Crossman, *The Diaries of a Cabinet Minister* (3 vols, London: Jonathan Cape and Hamish Hamilton, 1975–7).

11. For a discussion of the ways in which problem definition is manipulated and can be linked to policy failure, see Joan K. Stringer and J. J. Richardson, 'Managing the political agenda: problem definition and policymaking in Britain', *Parliamentary Affairs*, Vol. 33 (1980), 23–39.

12. Quoted in Michael Ellman, *Socialist Planning* (Cambridge University Press, 1979).

13. P. D. Henderson, 'Two British errors; their probable size and some possible lessons', *Oxford Economic Papers*, July 1977.

14. *Ibid.*

15. E. S. Quade, quoted in Wildavsky (1966).

16. Notable examples in the British system are provided by the Fulton Committee's Report on the Civil Service (1968); and more recently by the initiatives endorsed by the Thatcher administration: see especially Michael Heseltine, 'Ministers and management in Whitehall', *Management Services in Government* (May 1980), and J. M. Lee, 'The machinery of government under Mrs Thatcher's administration', *Parliamentary Affairs* (Autumn 1980). For a full account of the 'management movement' in British central administration, see John Garrett, *Managing the Civil Service* (London: Heinemann, 1980).

17. A useful survey of this literature is provided by Michael Hill and Susan Barrett in 'Implementation theory and research: a new branch of policy studies, or a new name for old interests?', unpublished paper based on their report to the SSRC Central–Local Government Relations Panel.

18. B. J. Loasby, *Choice, Complexity and Ignorance* (Cambridge University Press, 1976), 89.

19. N. I. Bukharin and E. Preobrazhensky, *The ABC of Communism* (1920, trans. Penguin, 1969).

20. Garrett, *op. cit.*

21. C. Hood, *The Limits of Administration* (John Wiley, 1976).

22. *Ibid.*, 10.

23. Ellman, *op. cit.*, 70.

24. Len Deighton, *Fighter* (Panther, 1979), 186.

25. See J. D. Steinbruner, *The Cybernetic Theory of Decisions* (Princeton, 1974): 'information which is threatening to established belief systems is not processed in a fashion wholly dominated by the reality principle.'

26. M. Crozier, *The Bureaucratic Phenomenon* (Tavistock, 1964), 190.

27. Lindblom, *op. cit.*

28. See C. Leys, 'The analysis of planning' in C. Leys, ed., *Politics and Change in Developing Countries* (Cambridge University Press, 1969); and A. Killick, 'The possibilities of development planning', *Oxford Economic Papers* (July 1976).

29. J. M. Keynes, in 1937, quoted in Ellman, *op. cit.*

30. M. Rein, *Social Science and Public Policy* (London: Penguin, 1976), 259.

31. For an elaboration of this argument, see B. Schaffer, 'Insiders and outsiders: insidedness, incorporation, and bureaucratic politics', *Development and Change*, Vol. II (1980), 187–210.

32. Henderson, *op. cit.*

33. For a detailed account see John Dearlove, *The Reorganisation of British Local Government: Old orthodoxies and a political perspective* (Cambridge University Press, 1979).

34. Wildavsky (1980), 8.

35. *Ibid.*, 10.

36. C. H. Sisson, *The Spirit of British Administration* (London: Faber, 1959), 23.

37. See especially the chapter 'Social science for social policy'; Rein, *op. cit.*, 247–68.

38. Wildavsky (1980), 401–5.

39. *New Society* (28 May 1981), 341.

40. Wildavsky (1980), 3.

41. Y. Dror, *Design for Policy Sciences* (Elsevier, 1971), especially 'Teaching of policy sciences', Chap. 14, 100–16.

42. A. W. Steiss and G. A. Daneke, *Performance Administration* (Lexington, 1980), Chap. 1.

43. Dror (1971), 119.

44. See, for example, the extent to which expert evidence commissioned by governments is disregarded. There are many examples in development planning in the third world; for British examples, see Martin Bulmer, ed., *Social Research and Royal Commissions* (London: Allen & Unwin, 1980).

45. For a surprisingly similar, since non-Marxist, view, see David E. Apter, ed., *Ideology and Discontent* (New York: Free Press, 1964), 18.

46. R. Rose and E. Page, 'Incrementalism or instability?: managing local government financial systems in a turbulent time', paper to SSRC/CSPP Conference, Strathclyde University (June 1981).

47. Quoted in Ralph Ruddock, *Ideologies*, Manchester Monographs 15 (Department of Adult and Higher Education, University of Manchester, 1981).

Policy analysis
Models and approaches

Bill Jenkins

Models and approaches: some attempts to cope

What *is* public policy and why the current concern to focus on it, analyse it and reform it? Pursuit of the first question leads one down the tangled path towards a definition where many have been before and from which few have emerged unscathed. There is, as Lineberry and Masotti point out, little in the way of a consistent conceptualisation of the term 'policy' itself and pages could be, and have been, filled with competing definitions.[1] The problem may be to provide an account that captures the detail and density of the activities embraced by the policy arena. With this in mind, it is worth considering the following definition of public policy:

Definition of Public Policy.

A set of interrelated decisions taken by a political actor or group of actors concerning the selection of goals and the means of achieving them within a specified situation where these decisions should, in principle, be within the power of these actors to achieve.[2]

Such a definition should not be seen as all-encompassing. For example, it points to the adoption of a course of action and the means of implementing it, but it does not build implementation into the policy itself. However, the definition has strengths, in that it incorporates the possibility of inaction (the decision not to move), and separates policy from ambition by linking policy decisions to available resources. Further, it stresses the point that policy is more than a single decision. As Anderson has argued, 'policy making typically involves a pattern of action extending *over time* and involving *many decisions*' (author's italics).[3] Public policy, therefore, must be considered to be much more

From W. I. Jenkins, *Policy Analysis* (1978), Oxford: Martin Robertson, Ch. 1.

than simply governmental outputs. Moreover, there may be *types of policy* corresponding to distinctive sets of decisions taken within the political system. Thus to focus on outputs alone may result in a partial and incomplete view of the dynamics and totality of public policy.[4] Further, policies have identifiable characteristics, according to which they may occupy different parts of the political spectrum and may need to be dealt with in different ways. For example, policies concerning national defence involve different actors and different structures and are likely to be processed in a different fashion from those concerning welfare matters. To pursue this line of argument indicates another conceptual issue with which the analyst must deal: the separation of *policy content*, the substance of policy, from *policy process*, the given set of methods, strategies and techniques by which a policy is made. To make such a distinction is not to deny that content and process can be, and often are, interdependent. In fact, some would go as far as proclaiming that content may determine process [. . .]. However, for many process is a central, if not the central, focus, to the extent that they argue that a conceptual understanding of the policy process is fundamental to an analysis of public policy.

Issues enter the political system; information feeds into decision; policies emerge and are implemented. How can such fragmentary events be linked? Is there an inherent and consistent logic connected with the way that policy is made in political systems? To address oneself to this problem is to conceptualise the policy process, and here one of the simplest and most frequently used models is that of the functional set of categories first offered by Harold Lasswell and adopted and developed by others since. An indication of this model is given in Figure 1. Basically, it assumes that policy emerges via a logical path; an issue moves through the political system in a processual way from point of entry, through decision and implementation, until a final choice is made to proceed with or terminate a course of action. Such a scheme, it is argued, is useful in drawing attention to the ordering of policy activities—certain bodies at certain times are more likely to be connected with one stage of the process rather than another. Few who offer this model would consider it as anything but an ideal representation of reality and fewer still would claim that political behaviour ever takes place in such an ordered fashion. Given such reservations, the utility of such an approach, particularly as a vehicle for hypothesis generation, becomes problematic and, in the face of such criticism, some have argued that it may be more productive to consider the policy process in terms of an adapted input–output model of the political system derived from the work of David Easton. Such a perspective is favoured by Sharkansky, Dye and others.[5][. . .] Its major dimensions are indicated in Figure 2, from which it will be clear that the focus of

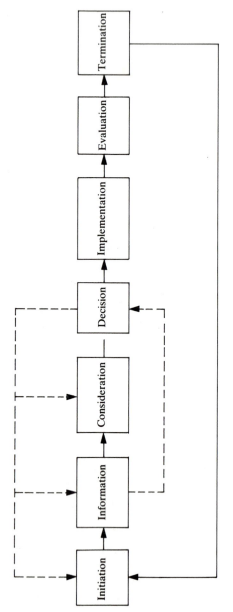

Figure 1 Schematic presentation of process perspective on policy (Source: Suggested by G. K. Roberts in a private communication)

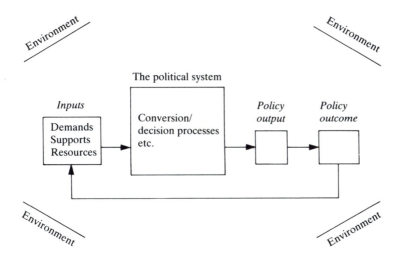

Environment: includes social, economic and political influences
on inputs, systems variables, policy outputs and
policy outcomes.

Figure 2 Systems model of the policy process

this approach is the dynamics and processes of a political system
operating in its environment. Thus its advocates would wish to
differentiate between:

(i) *policy demands*: demands for action arising from both inside and
outside the political system;

(ii) *policy decisions*: authoritative rather than routine decisions by the
political authorities;

(iii) *policy outputs*: what the system does—thus, while goods and
services are the most tangible outputs, the concept is not restricted
to this;

(iv) *policy outcomes* (or *impacts*): consequences intended or unintended
resulting from political action or inaction.

In this way, it becomes possible to define and explore the process of
policy while becoming aware of the various interconnections existing
within this process. Once more, the model may be too neat and too
simplistic. Still, granted such caveats, a systems model indicates
possibilities of coping with some of the conceptual problems of policy
analysis already mentioned: the questions of linking variable patterns of
political action with varying political demands [. . .], of explaining

outputs, and of distinguishing outputs from outcomes. [. . .] Thus, via systems approaches, policy analysis can clearly be seen as an activity involved in disaggregating and understanding the specific policy-related aspects of the political process.

At this juncture, however, it may be as well to indicate some wider points concerning the development of policy theory, in particular the preferred directions in which some observers would like analysis to go. Hence for many, undoubtedly, the ultimate goal is the 'scientific' study of policy, in which central concepts would be open to scientific verification and ideas such as 'responsibility' or 'rational policy forma- tion' would be eliminated. According to this view, what policy analysis should aim for is a conceptual framework which yields variables capable of systematic and rigorous testing. Such an approach has much to commend it, although it also introduces problems by downgrading certain variables, in particular behavioural ones. Rigour of this nature may be no bad thing. It also has its disadvantages.[6] [. . .]

The move towards a scientific attack on policy has also been accompanied by moves towards comparative research and a suspicion of, if not a positive disregard for, case studies. Case studies are considered static, with a tendency to isolate decisions unreasonably and to confine an investigation too closely to central actors. The limitations of case studies, it is argued, can be overcome by careful comparative analysis. But comparison over what time period and taking into account what variables? Many case studies may well misuse historical explana- tion, but the problem with much comparative policy research is that it is blatantly and erroneously ahistorical. Perhaps a major task facing policy studies is to synthesise comparative theory and case study. [. . .] In the long run, indeed, this may offer possibilities; in the short run it would seem too early to jettison case-study material and the concepts that arise from it simply in exchange for quantitative sophistication.[7]

Moves towards scientific hardness, comparative research and a more careful conceptualisation of variables mark recent trends in academic interest in the policy field, many of which can be linked with the increasing popularity of systems models of analysis. Associated with these trends, although often separate from them, is the use of a variety of other conceptual approaches to explore problems such as policy formation and implementation. The majority of such approaches have emerged from within the area of political science although, more recently, others have been drawn in from outside. The political science contribution has, in the major part, been met before in, for example, rational and incremental theories of policy making and élite and group models of political behaviour. Again, since full details of these are available elsewhere, they will only be noted in passing here.[8] Broadly, however, their development and use in the policy field indicates a problem of choice, i.e. how does the analyst choose between theoretical approaches to attack the issues of policy? In confronting this problem the first point to remember is [. . .] simply that there is no one best way. The nature of the policy problem is such that a variety of approaches are required to deal with the complexity of the process. As Anderson argues:

> Each [of the models] focuses attention on different aspects of politics and policy making and seems more useful for some purposes or some situations than others. Generally, one should not permit oneself to be bound too rigidly or too dogmatically to a particular model . . . It is my belief that the explanation of political behaviour, rather than the validation of a given theoretical approach, should be the main purpose of political inquiry and analysis.[9]

This quotation is significant. Indeed, we would extend Anderson's argument by stressing that any analysis of policy and the policy process can only be achieved through the linking of a number of differing perspectives. [. . .]

The need for an extended perspective?

The focus on policy here is primarily a systemic one. We would argue that public policy is best understood by considering the operation of a political system in its environment and by examining how such a system maintains itself and changes over time. This is basically, very basically, a starting point.[10] The more detailed perspective we adopt is somewhat broader (see Figure 3). But even this is offered primarily as a guide to thought, since it is grossly oversimplified as it stands, such simplifications being particularly apparent with regard to the model's representation of (a) *the policy environment* and (b) *the political system* itself.

In traditional systems models inputs arise out of the environment, are aggregated in some fashion, and impact on the political system. In all this the environment is defined broadly in socio-economic, physical and political terms. For the general purpose of understanding political life, and for the specific purpose of analysing policy, such a conceptualisation is too crude. The environment is not structureless. It may be made up of individuals, groups and organisations with values and interests, operating alone or together *over time*. Further, the strength of environmental influences may vary with their proximity to the political system, although this is not to argue for a linear relationship between proximity and demand pressure. Interestingly enough, arguments concerning environmental change and environmental structure have been a feature

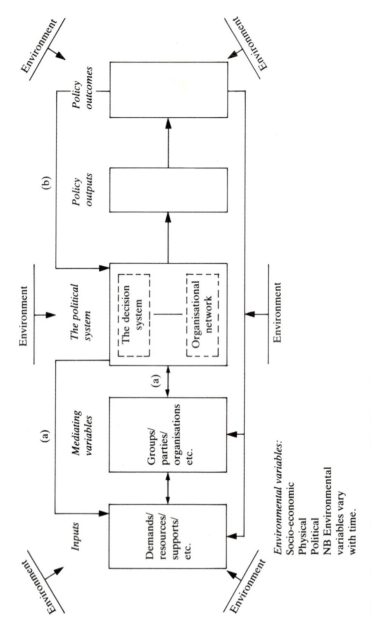

Figure 3 Amended systems model of the policy process

of organisational sociology for some years, the thesis being that, to account for organisational behaviour, one requires a better conceptualisation of environmental influences.[11] The same point would seem to hold in the study of public policy. In particular, one needs to explore the relationship between demand patterns and what have been termed here 'mediating variables' (see Figure 3). Further, it seems crucial to investigate whether there is any relationship between political action and the presence or absence, over time, of such variables. [. . .] What passes for the 'environment', therefore, requires thought and attention. Indeed, because of the way systems models are usually presented, the all-embracing nature of environmental influences is rarely realised. As usually defined, the environment surrounds the whole process, influencing anything and everything (see Figure 3). While useful as a first approximation, this is too gross a representation of environmental influences. A more detailed focus on environmental variables may be crucial for policy studies.

Much of the comment and criticism in the discussion above could be applied with equal force to the usual conceptualisation of the 'political system'. Too often this has been taken as a black box from which policies emerge or, at best, in which the solution to patterns of political action can be found in the size and variation of political majorities or modes of élite control. In terms of understanding policy such a position is simply not adequate. [. . .] Often the *process of choice* may be as important as the *actual choice* itself. Moreover, decision systems may be constrained by the networks within which they operate. [. . .] The latter question touches on an issue already referred to above: the possible role of administrative systems in the *formation* rather than in the *execution* of public policy, a feature often missed by an analysis that concentrates on political decision-making élites. In brief, the argument here is that policy analysis needs to disaggregate and explore the political system. This point is illustrated by Figure 3, in which a distinction is made between decision systems and organisational networks, and to this should be added another often-ignored factor, the capacity of political systems to influence their environment directly (indicated by (a) in Figure 3). Too often policy is seen simply as the response to pressure, but why is there sometimes no pressure? Why [. . .] may demands fail to emerge? Such problems, again, are the concern of the policy analyst, especially if he purports to explain the non-action as well as the action of political systems.

It is, therefore, doubtful whether the policy process can be captured in any great detail by the simple linear feedback model which political systems theory initially offers. Interactions both across and within systems must be considered, while it may also be important to account for stances and positions adopted by political actors which have no immediate and tangible policy output. A separate point concerns the relationship between decisions and outcomes. The tendency to see the latter relationship as a discrete sequence, initiated by changes in demand or support inputs, is problematic in that it may lead to the neglect of the possibility of a direct relationship between outcome and decision (see (b) in Figure 3). [. . .]

Thus the policy analyst needs to explore in more detail the nature of the political system and the relationship between such variables as decision processes and outcomes. To explain outcomes, however, involves another vital but often downgraded aspect of the whole problem: the need to establish some conceptual grasp of motivation and behaviour. Without such a grasp, responses to policy can be neither understood nor anticipated. To assume individuals or organisational élites behave rationally (perhaps the most elementary behavioural model) is often an oversimplification. An understanding of behaviour and motivation is central to an understanding of policy outcome and impact. More than this, however, such an understanding also appears crucial to an investigation of other aspects of the policy process, in particular the internal operation of the political system itself: for example, why are attempts to rationalise policy or change decision systems so often resisted? [. . .]

To explore the policy world, therefore, demands a more detailed conceptual schema than has previously been offered. To this end, an extended systems model acts as a useful heuristic map; useful in alerting one to areas that need more attention (e.g. the environment, the political system); useful in emphasising links on which theory could be usefully brought to bear (e.g. the extent to which the political system itself controls inputs rather than inputs determine political action). Moreover, to articulate the problem in such a way has value in demonstrating the view, already expressed by Anderson above, that different conceptual models may be required to explore different aspects of the overall process. Figure 3, therefore, presents in the first instance a guide for thought and analysis. As it stands, however, it is open to much of the usual abuse directed at models of this type. Indeed, it cannot be denied that the very act of starting from a systems perspective may pose problems from which it is difficult to escape: the problems of accepting uncritically a goal model of organisations, of adopting the broad assumptions of welfare economics, of slipping towards a pluralistic model of politics. Nevertheless, it must be disputed that one necessarily falls into an ontological trap;[12] rather, in using an extended systems model as an initial focus it becomes possible to explore some of the diverse directions in which policy theory has developed.

Notes

1. On definitional problems, see J. Anderson, *Public Policy Making* (Nelson, 1975), Ch. 1; also R. L. Lineberry and L. Masotti (eds.), *Urban Problems and Public Policy* (Lexington Books, 1975), xi.
2. This definition is adapted from G. K. Roberts, *A Dictionary of Political Analysis* (Longman, 1971), 152–3, and private communications with the same author.
3. Anderson, *op. cit.*, p. 10. For a similar point, see also J. Stewart, 'Public administration and the study of public policy making', *Public Administration Committee Bulletin*, 11 (1971), 42–56.
4. For a perspective on this, see T. Lowi, 'Decision making vs. public policy', *Public Administration Review*, 30 (1970), 314–25, and 'Four systems of policy, politics and choice', *Public Administration Review*, 32 (1972), 298–310. Also note R. Salisbury and J. Heinz, 'A Theory of Policy Analysis', in I. Sharkansky (ed.), *Policy Analysis in Political Science* (Markham, 1970).
5. Lasswell's original process model appears in 'The decision process', in N. Polsby *et al.*, *Politics and Social Life* (Houghton Mifflin, 1963), while for a more contemporary perspective using a similar process schema, see R. Rose, 'Comparing public policy', *European Journal of Political Research*, 1 (1973), 67–94. An Easton-type model is used by a number of writers, who each give it a different emphasis; for example, see T. Dye, *Understanding Public Policy* (Prentice Hall, 1972); I. Sharkansky, *Public Administration: Policy making in government agencies* (Markham, 1970); and, in the context of urban politics, R. Lineberry and I. Sharkansky, *Urban Politics and Public Policy* (Harper & Row, 1971).
6. For a typical argument on the advantages of a scientific and comparative approach to policy-making studies, see R. L. Hofferbert, *The Study of Public Policy* (Bobbs Merrill, 1974), in particular Chs. 1–3.
7. Against case studies, see also Hofferbert, *op cit.*, but for a differing perspective, note P. Hall *et al.*, *Change, Choice and Conflict in Social Policy* (Heinemann, 1975), in particular Pts. I and II.
8. A full discussion of these and other approaches used in policy studies appears in Dye, *op. cit.*, and Anderson, *op. cit.*
9. Anderson, *op. cit.*, p. 25.
10. The 'black box' models appearing in policy studies are frequently only crude simplifications of the more elaborate systems framework developed by David Easton. For more comprehensive details of the latter, see D. Easton, *A Framework for Political Analysis* (Prentice Hall, 1965), or his earlier *The Political System* (A. Knopf, 1953).
11. For a discussion of organisational environments, see, for example, S. Terberry, 'The evolution of organisational environments', in J. Thomas and W. Bennis (eds.), *The Management of Change and Conflict* (Penguin, 1972); also, R. Osborn and J. Hunt, 'Environment and organisational effectiveness', *Administrative Science Quarterly*, 19 (1974), 231–46. More generally, note the discussion in J. Child, 'Organisational structure, environment and performance', *Sociology*, 6 (1972), 1–22.

12. These points are raised by G. M. Dillon, 'Policy, and dramaturgy: a critique of current conceptions of policy making', *Policy and Politics*, 5, No. 1 (1976), 47–62.

Part II

The role of the state

Introduction

In order to understand the policy process it is necessary to relate it to the power structure of a society as a whole. Policy is the product of the exercise of political influence, determining and setting limits to what the state does. Any detailed attention to the policy process, including policy implementation, needs to be set in this wider context.

Controversy about power in society has been centred upon a debate between pluralism, a theory which sees access to influence upon the state as comparatively open to citizens, and theories which emphasise structured power inequalities. Many of the latter derive from Karl Marx's analysis of power under the domination of capitalism. The first three extracts in this section all deal with aspects of this controversy. Lukes sets out the basic dimensions of the debate, linking it to the conceptual and methodological problems that were encountered by the simpler forms of pluralist theory. Pluralism was in the first place an adaptation of nineteenth-century individualist thinking, which had to be modified to recognise that in a complex society citizens relate to the state through intermediary groups. That adaptation, sometimes described as 'democratic elitism', had then to face the problem that the relationship between groups and the state is often complex and obscure, with the 'elitism' sometimes more evident than the 'democracy'.

Lukes' critique of pluralism is followed in this reader by McLennan's analysis of the way in which political scientists in the pluralist tradition have gradually modified their stance, conceding the importance of structured inequalities. McLennan's discussion of pluralism comes from a book in which he shows how the two traditions of pluralism and Marxism have converged as they have had to confront difficulties with their own models of the power structure.

The corresponding way in which the Marxist approach has been modified is explored in the extract from Dunleavy and O'Leary. It has had to come to terms with the way in which the complexity of economic and social relations in modern societies cannot simply be analysed in terms of a confrontation between two elements of capital and labour. Structural analysis has to recognise the importance of a number of

different structured conflicts in society, and a wide range of differences
within groups postulated, in simplistic Marxist theory, as having
opposing interests. In doing this, neo-Marxist theory, whilst holding on
to the importance of structured interests which may be obscured in the
ways discussed in Lukes' second and third dimensions of power, has
conceded that actual conflicts in society may have some of the more
open characteristics set out in the pluralist model.

Both pluralist and Marxist have long had to contend with a criticism
that they disregard the extent to which the state is itself a source of
power. They tend to treat it as something neutral to be captured. Early
in the twentieth century the main challenge to this view came from
writers like Pareto and Mosca, who opposed the Marxist view of the
state as 'the executive of the ruling class', seeing it instead as dominated
by elites. This approach always faced a difficulty in dealing with
questions about the original power source of these elites. More recent
writing tends to disregard this problem and simply emphasise the extent
to which, once complex state institutions were set up, the elevation of
individuals or groups to control these created a power elite, who were
then likely to take steps to develop and perpetuate that power. In doing
so they would not necessarily remain committed to the interests of the
classes or groups which initially enabled them to acquire these positions.
Rather they were likely to develop interests of their own, and start to
recruit to their own ranks and influence access to state institutions.
Further down the line, as we are in societies which have had massive
state institutions for a long period of time, this 'autonomy' has become
an important feature of power structures. Dunleavy and O'Leary discuss
the way some Marxist theory has tried to come to terms with this issue.
Then the last of the extracts in this section, part of Skocpol's
introductory essay in a collection which explores the importance of
'state-centred' theory, sets out some of the key concerns of the
'autonomous state' approach.

In the introduction to Part I it was pointed out that normative
concerns, that is concerns about how policy should be made, are never
far away in policy studies. It is interesting to note that even in this part,
where attention is being given to theories of power, such issues are
around. Pluralism emerged as an attempt to argue that even with power
concentrations individuals could have access to influence over the state.
Pluralist theorists have offered a defence of democracy, particularly
American democracy, in these terms. The pluralist ideal is offered as
one to which states should aspire. In contradistinction Marxism argues
that so long as class divisions exist such an ideal cannot be achieved.
The Marxist model has obviously been damaged by the evidence that
those governments which proclaimed that they were influenced by
Marxist principles clearly failed to rid their societies of concentrations of

power. That should not, however, lead us to disregard the sociological significance of Marxist theory in drawing our attention to the importance of economic power for political power. The shortcomings of both the pluralist and the Marxist ideal shift our attention to the issues about state autonomy, with the state seen by the New Right as an obstacle to the realisation of the pluralist ideal, and by the 'liberal' centre and left as a necessary counterweight to economic power. This is a theme to which we will return in the next part of this reader.

Three distinctive views of power compared

Steven Lukes

The distinctive features of the three views of power presented are summarised below.

One-dimensional view of power
Focus on (a) behaviour
         (b) decision-making
         (c) (key) issues
         (d) observable (overt) conflict
         (e) (subjective) interests, seen as policy preferences revealed by political participation

Two-dimensional view of power
(Qualified) critique of behavioural focus
Focus on (a) decision-making and non-decision-making
         (b) issues and potential issues
         (c) observable (overt or covert) conflict
         (d) (subjective) interests, seen as policy preferences or grievances

Three-dimensional view of power
Critique of behavioural focus
Focus on (a) decision-making and control over political agenda (not necessarily through decisions)
         (b) issues and potential issues
         (c) observable (overt or covert) and latent conflict
         (d) subjective and real interests [. . .]

From S. Lukes, *Power: A radical view* (1974), London: Macmillan, Chapter 7.

The three views compared

I now turn to consider the relative strengths and weaknesses of the three views of power I have outlined.

The virtues of the decision-making or one-dimensional view are obvious and have often been stressed: by means of it, to cite Merelman, the pluralists 'studied actual behavior, stressed operational definitions, and turned up evidence' (Merelman, 1968, p. 451). However, the trouble is that, by doing this, by studying the making of of important decisions within the community, they were simply taking over and reproducing the bias of the system they were studying. By analysing the decisions on urban redevelopment, public education and political nominations, Dahl tells us a good deal about the *diversity* of decision-making power in New Haven. He shows that these issue areas are independent of one another, and that, by and large, different individuals exercise power in different areas and therefore no set of individuals and thus no single elite has decision-making power ranging across different issue areas. He further argues that the decision-making process is responsive to the preferences of citizens because the elected politicians and officials engaged in it anticipate the results of future elections. It would, he writes, 'be unwise to underestimate the extent to which voters may exert *indirect* influence on the decisions of leaders by means of elections' (Dahl, 1961, p. 101): no issue of importance to the former is likely to be ignored for long by the latter. Thus Dahl pictures pluralist politics as both diverse and open: he writes, '[T]he independence, penetrability, and heterogeneity of the various segments of the political stratum all but guarantee that any dissatisfied group will find spokesmen in the political stratum' (p. 93). But the diversity and openness Dahl sees may be highly misleading if power is being exercised within the system to limit decision-making to acceptable issues. Individuals and elites may act separately in making acceptable decisions, but they may act in concert – or even fail to act at all – in such a way as to keep unacceptable issues out of politics, thereby preventing the system from becoming any more diverse than it is. 'A polity', it has been suggested, 'that is pluralistic in its decision-making can be unified in its non-decisionmaking' (Crenson, 1971, p. 179). The decision-making method prevents this possibility from being considered. Dahl concludes that the system is penetrable by any dissatisfied group, but he does so only by studying cases of successful penetration, and never examines failed attempts at such penetration. Moreover, the thesis that indirect influence gives the electorate control over leaders can be turned on its head. Indirect influence can equally operate to prevent politicians, officials or others from raising issues or proposals known to be unacceptable to some group or institution in the community. It can serve the interests of an elite, not only that of the electorate. In brief, the one-dimensional view of power cannot reveal the less visible ways in which a pluralist system may be biased in favour of certain groups and against others.

The two-dimensional view goes some way to revealing this – which is a considerable advance in itself – but it confines itself to studying situations where the mobilisation of bias can be attributed to individuals' decisions that have the effect of preventing current observable grievances (overt or covert) from becoming issues within the political process. This, I think, largely accounts for the very thin and inadequate character of Bachrach and Baratz's study of poverty, race and politics in Baltimore (Bachrach and Baratz, 1970). All that study really amounts to is an account of various decisions by the mayor and various business leaders to deflect the inchoate demands of Baltimore's blacks from becoming politically threatening issues – by such devices as making certain appointments, establishing task forces to defuse the poverty issue, supporting certain kinds of welfare measures, etc. – together with an account of how the blacks gained political access through overt struggle involving riots. The analysis remains superficial precisely because it confines itself to studying individual decisions made to avert potentially threatening demands from becoming politically dangerous. A deeper analysis would also concern itself with all the complex and subtle ways in which the *inactivity* of leaders and the sheer weight of institutions – political, industrial and educational – served for so long to keep the blacks out of Baltimore politics; and indeed for a long period kept them from even trying to get into it.

The three-dimensional view offers the possibility of such an analysis. It offers, in other words, the prospect of a serious sociological and not merely personalised explanation of how political systems prevent demands from becoming political issues or even from being made. Now the classical objection to doing this has often been stated by pluralists: how can one study, let alone explain, what does not happen? Polsby writes:

> . . . it has been suggested that non-events make more significant policy than do policy-making events. This is the kind of statement that has a certain plausibility and attractiveness but that presents truly insuperable obstacles to research. We can sound the depths of the abyss very quickly by agreeing that non-events are much more important than events, and inquiring precisely *which* non-events are to be regarded as most significant in the community. Surely not *all* of them. For every event (no matter how defined) that occurs there must be an infinity of alternatives. Then which non-events are to be regarded as significant? One satisfactory answer might be: those outcomes desired by a significant number of actors in the community but not achieved. Insofar as these goals are in some way explicitly pursued by people in the

community, the method of study used in New Haven has a reasonable chance of capturing them. A wholly unsatisfactory answer would be: certain non-events stipulated by outside observers without reference to the desires or activities of community residents. The answer is unsatisfactory because it is obviously inappropriate for outsiders to pick among all the possible outcomes that did not take place a set which they regard as important but which community citizens do not. This approach is likely to prejudice the outcomes of research. . . . (Polsby, 1963, pp. 96–7.)

Similarly, Wolfinger argues that the 'infinite variety of possible nondecisions . . . reveals the idea's adaptability to various ideological perspectives' (Wolfinger, 1971, p. 1078). Moreover, suppose we advance 'a theory of political interests and rational behavior' specifying how people would behave in certain situations if left to themselves, and use it to support the claim that their failure so to behave is due to the exercise of power. In this case, Wolfinger argues, we have no means of deciding between two possibilities: either that there was an exercise of power, or that the theory was wrong (p. 1078).

The first point to be made against these apparently powerful arguments is that they move from a methodological difficulty to a substantive assertion. It does not follow that, just because it is difficult or even impossible to show that power has been exercised in a given situation, we can conclude that it has not. But, more importantly, I do not believe that it is impossible to identify an exercise of power of this type.

What is an exercise of power? What is it to exercise power? On close inspection it turns out that the locution 'exercise of power' and 'exercising power' is problematic in at least two ways.

In the first place, it carries, in everyday usage, a doubly unfortunate connotation: it is sometimes assumed to be both individualistic and intentional, that is, it seems to carry the suggestion that the exercise of power is a matter of individuals consciously acting to affect others. Some appear to feel discomfort in speaking either of groups, institutions or collectivities 'exercising' power, or of individuals or collectivities doing so unconsciously. This is an interesting case of individualistic and intentional assumptions being built into our language – but that in itself provides no reason for adopting such assumptions. In what follows I propose to abandon these assumptions and to speak of the exercise of power whether by individuals or by groups, institutions, etc., and whether consciously or not. A negative justification for this revisionary usage is that there is no other available word that meets the bill (thus 'exerting' power is little different from 'exercising' it); I shall offer a positive justification below.

The second way in which the phrase 'exercising power' is problematic is that it conceals an interesting and important ambiguity. I referred above to Dahl's definition of the exercise of power in terms of A getting B to do something he would not otherwise do. However, this is, as it stands, too simple.

Suppose that A can *normally* affect B. This is to suppose that, against the background of (what is assumed to be) a normally ongoing situation, if A does x, he gets B to do what he would not otherwise do. Here A's action, x, is *sufficient* to get B to do what he would not otherwise do. Suppose, however, that exactly the same is true of A_1. He can also normally affect B: his action, y, is also sufficient to get B to do what he would not otherwise do, in just the same way. Now, suppose that A and A_1 both act in relation to B simultaneously and B changes his action accordingly. Here, it is clear, B's action or change of course is overdetermined: both A and A_1 have affected B by 'exercising power', but the result is the same as that which would have occurred had either affected him singly. In this case it is a pointless question to ask which of them produced the change of course, that is, which of them made a difference to the result: they both did. They both 'exercised power', in a sense – that is, a power *sufficient* to produce the result – yet one cannot say that *either* of them made a difference to the result. Let us call this sense of 'exercising power' the *operative* sense.

Contrast this case with the case where A *does* make a difference to the result: that is, against the background of a normally ongoing situation, A, by doing x, actually gets B to do what B would not otherwise do. Here x is an intervening cause which distorts the normal course of events – by contrast with the first, overdetermined case, where there are, *ex hypothesi*, *two* intervening sufficient conditions, so that neither can be said to have 'made a difference', just because of the presence of the other: there the normal course of events is itself distorted by the presence of the other intervening sufficient condition. In this case, by contrast, A's intervention can be said to make a difference to the result. Let us call this sense of 'exercising power' the *effective* sense.

(It is worth adding a further distinction, which turns on *what* difference A makes to the result. A wishes B to do some particular thing, but, in exercising effective power over him, he may succeed in changing B's course in a wide variety of ways. Only in the case where B's change of course corresponds to A's wishes, that is, where A secures B's compliance, can we speak properly of a *successful* exercise of power: here 'affecting' becomes 'control'. It is, incidentally, this case of the successful exercise of power, or the securing of compliance, on which Bachrach and Baratz exclusively concentrate. The successful exercise of power can be seen as a sub-species of the effective exercise of power – though one could maintain that, where the operative exercise of power issues in compliance, this also is an [indeterminate] form of its successful exercise.)

We can now turn to the analysis of what exactly is involved in identifying an exercise of power. An attribution of the exercise of power involves, among other things, the double claim that A acts (or fails to act) in a certain way and that B does what he would not otherwise do (I use the term 'do' here in a very wide sense, to include 'think', 'want', 'feel', etc.). In the case of an effective exercise of power, A gets B to do what he would not otherwise do; in the case of an operative exercise of power, A, together with another or other sufficient conditions, gets B to do what he would not otherwise do. Hence, in general, any attribution of the exercise of power (including, of course, those by Dahl and his colleagues) always implies a relevant counterfactual, to the effect that (but for A, or but for A together with any other sufficient conditions) B would otherwise have done, let us say, b. This is one reason why so many thinkers (mistakenly) insist on actual, observable conflict as essential to power (though there are doubtless other theoretical and, indeed, ideological reasons). For such conflict provides the relevant counterfactual, so to speak, ready-made. If A and B are in conflict with one another, A wanting a and B wanting b, then if A prevails over B, we can assume that B would otherwise have done b. Where there is no observable conflict between A and B, then we must provide other grounds for asserting the relevant counterfactual. That is, we must provide other, indirect, grounds for asserting that if A had not acted (or failed to act) in a certain way – and, in the case of operative power, if other sufficient conditions had not been operative – then B would have thought and acted differently from the way he does actually think and act. In brief, we need to justify our expectation that B would have thought or acted differently; and we also need to specify the means or mechanism by which A has prevented, or else acted (or abstained from acting) in a manner sufficient to prevent, B from doing so.

I can see no reason to suppose that either of these claims cannot in principle be supported – though I do not claim it is easy. Doing so certainly requires one to go much deeper than most analyses of power in contemporary political science and sociology. Fortunately, Matthew Crenson's book, *The Un-Politics of Air Pollution: A study of non-decisionmaking in the cities* (Crenson, 1971), provides a good example of how the task can be approached. The theoretical framework of this book can be seen as lying on the borderline of the two-dimensional and the three-dimensional views of power: I see it as a serious attempt empirically to apply the former, together with certain elements of the latter. For that reason, it marks a real theoretical advance in the empirical study of power relations.

It explicitly attempts to find a way to explain 'things that do not happen', on the assumption that 'the proper object of investigation is not political activity but political inactivity' (pp. vii, 26). Why, he asks, was the issue of air pollution not raised as early or as effectively in some

American cities as it was in others? His object, in other words, is to
'discover . . . why many cities and towns in the United States failed to
make a political issue of their air pollution problems' (p. vii), thereby
illuminating the character of local political systems – particularly with
respect to their 'penetrability'. He first shows that differences in the
treatment of pollution cannot be attributed solely to differences in the
actual pollution level or to social characteristics of the populations in
question. He then provides a detailed study of two neighbouring cities in
Indiana, both equally polluted and with similar populations, one of
which, East Chicago, took action to clean its air in 1949, while the other,
Gary, held its breath until 1962. Briefly, his explanation of the
difference is that Gary is a one-company town dominated by U.S. Steel,
with a strong party organisation, whereas East Chicago had a number of
steel companies and no strong party organisation when it passed its air
pollution control ordinance.

His case (which he documents with convincing detail) is that U.S.
Steel, which had built Gary and was responsible for its prosperity, for a
long time effectively prevented the issue from even being raised,
through its power reputation operating on anticipated reactions, then
for a number of years thwarted attempts to raise the issue, and
decisively influenced the content of the anti-pollution ordinance finally
enacted. Moreover, it did all this without acting or entering into the
political arena. Its 'mere reputation for power, unsupported by acts of
power' was 'sufficient to inhibit the emergence of the dirty air issue' (p.
124); and, when it eventually did emerge (largely because of the threat
of Federal or State action), 'U.S. Steel . . . influenced the content of the
pollution ordinance without taking any action on it, and thus defied the
pluralist dictum that political power belongs to political actors' (pp.
69–70). U.S. Steel, Crenson argues, exercised influence 'from points
outside the range of observable political behaviour. . . . Though the
corporation seldom intervened directly in the deliberations of the town's
air pollution policymakers, it was nevertheless able to affect their scope
and direction' (p. 107). He writes:

> Gary's anti-pollution activists were long unable to get U.S. Steel to take a
> clear stand. One of them, looking back on the bleak days of the dirty air
> debate, cited the evasiveness of the town's largest industrial corporation as a
> decisive factor in frustrating early efforts to enact a pollution control
> ordinance. The company executives, he said, would just nod sympathetically
> 'and agree that air pollution was terrible, and pat you on the head. But they
> never *did* anything one way or the other. If only there had been a fight, then
> something might have been accomplished!' What U.S. Steel did not do was
> probably more important to the career of Gary's air pollution issue than what
> it did do. (pp. 76–7)

He then moves from these two detailed case studies to a comparative analysis of interview data with political leaders taken from fifty-one cities, aimed at testing the hypotheses arising out of the two case studies. Briefly, his conclusions are that 'the air pollution issue tends not to flourish in cities where industry enjoys a reputation for power' (p. 145) – and that 'where industry remains silent about dirty air, the life chances of the pollution issue are likely to be diminished' (p. 124). Again, a strong and influential party organisation will also inhibit the growth of the pollution issue, since demands for clean air are unlikely to yield the kind of specific benefits that American party machines seek – though where industry has a high power reputation, a strong party will increase the pollution issue's life chances, since it will seek to purchase industrial influence. In general Crenson plausibly argues that pollution control is a good example of a collective good, whose specific costs are concentrated on industry: thus the latter's opposition will be strong, while the support for it will be relatively weak, since its benefits are diffuse and likely to have little appeal to party leaders engaged in influence brokerage. Moreover, and very interestingly, Crenson argues, against the pluralists, that political issues tend to be interconnected; and thus collective issues tend to promote other collective issues, and vice versa. Thus by 'promoting one political agenda item, civic activists may succeed in driving other issues away' (p. 170):

> where business and industrial development is a topic of local concern, the dirty air problem tends to be ignored. The prominence of one issue appears to be connected with the subordination of the other, and the existence of this connection calls into question the pluralist view that different political issues tend to rise and subside independently. (p. 165)

Crenson's general case is that there are 'politically imposed limitations upon the scope of decision-making', such that 'decision-making activity is channelled and directed by the process of non-decision making' (p. 178). Pluralism, in other words, is 'no guarantee of political openness or popular sovereignty'; and neither the study of decision-making nor the existence of 'visible diversity' will tell us anything about 'those groups and issues which may have been shut out of a town's political life' (p. 181).

I suggested above that the theoretical framework of Crenson's analysis lies on the borderline of the two-dimensional and the three-dimensional views of power. It is, on the face of it, a two-dimensional study of non-decision-making à la Bachrach and Baratz. On the other hand, it begins to advance beyond their position (as presented in their book) in three ways. First, it does not interpret non-decision-making behaviourally, as exhibited only in decisions (hence the stress on inaction – 'What U.S. Steel did not do . . .'); second, it is non-individualistic and considers institutional power, and third, it considers ways in which demands are prevented, through the exercise of such power, from being raised: thus,

> Local political forms and practices may even inhibit citizens' ability to transform some diffuse discontent into an explicit demand. In short, there is something like an inarticulate ideology in political institutions, even in those that appear to be most open-minded, flexible and disjointed – an ideology in the sense that it promotes the selective perception and articulation of social problems and conflicts. . . . (p. 23)

In this way, 'local political institutions and political leaders may . . . exercise considerable control over what people choose to care about and how forcefully they articulate their cares' (p. 27): restrictions on the scope of decision-making may 'stunt the political consciousness of the local public' by confining minority opinions to minorities and denying 'minorities the opportunity to grow to majorities' (pp. 180–1).

Crenson's analysis is impressive because it fulfils the double requirement mentioned above: there is good reason to expect that, other things being equal, people would rather not be poisoned (assuming, in particular, that pollution control does not necessarily mean unemployment) – even where they may not even articulate this preference; and hard evidence is given of the ways in which institutions, specifically U.S. Steel, largely through inaction, prevented the citizens' interest in not being poisoned from being acted on (though other factors, institutional and ideological, would need to enter a fuller explanation). Thus both the relevant counterfactual and the identification of a power mechanism are justified.

References

Bachrach, P., and M. S. Baratz (1970), *Power and Poverty*, New York, Oxford University Press.

Crenson, M. A. (1971), *The Un-Politics of Air Pollution: A study of non-decisionmaking in the cities*, Baltimore, Johns Hopkins Press.

Dahl, R. A. (1961), *Who Governs?*, New Haven, Yale University Press.

Merelman, R. M. (1968), 'On the neo-elitist critique of community power', *American Political Science Review*, 62, pp. 451–60.

Polsby, N. W. (1963), *Community Power and Political Theory*, New Haven, Yale University Press.

Wolfinger, R. E. (1971), 'Nondecisions and the study of local politics', *American Political Science Review*, 65, pp. 1063–80.

The evolution of pluralist theory

Gregor McLennan

Critical pluralism

The force of at least two of the standard sets of criticisms of conventional pluralism needs to be deflected to some extent. First, there was the issue of the different sorts of interest group brought under the same heading for analytic purposes. The problem with conventional pluralist analysis is *not* that the need for distinctions was ignored, nor that inequalities between groups were considered insignificant. Bentley finally plumped for a kind of materialism in arriving at a manageable categorization of the basis of group life. His 'underlying' groups were, in effect, principles of potential social stratification and included those based on differences of environmental conditions, race, wealth and trade (Bentley 1967: 462). Writers such as Pendleton Herring and Peter Odegard in the 1930s developed an approach to group analysis which deliberately undercut any all-purpose usage of the notion of interests. Under later pressure from critical voices such as those of Schattschneider and Easton, the pluralist persistence with the notion of interest groups was not so much a naïve and uncritical levelling of differences as the retention of a convenient label within which more detailed distinctions and comparisons could be made. Dahl's argument against marxism, for example, was not that class was unimportant, but that when considered as somehow more 'real' than other bases of social differences, the importance of the latter (e.g. language, religion, race) was undermined (Dahl 1971: 106–7). His argument – at least as reviewed in retrospect – was that the undeniable persistence of class division in modern society did not entail that class was always and everywhere the major determinant of politics (Dahl 1982: 62). In this context, Dahl is

From G. McLennan, *Marxism, Pluralism and Beyond* (1989), Cambridge: Polity Press, Chapter 2.

probably right to dismiss as 'rather absurd' the charge that the conventional pluralists theorized groups as being equally open, equally well resourced, and equally heard at the political level (Dahl 1982: 208–9).

Some pluralists, certainly, were more aware of group inequalities than others. V. O. Key, for example, was an influential 'empirical democratic theorist' whose wry tone and clear mind were not conducive to mystification. Key (1964, 1st edn. 1942) looked at a range of pressure groups with a view to their potential for coherence and internal division. He pointed out that while sectional interests cut across the business community, the latter was able to achieve solidarity on political questions due to their special powers of class unity in the face of challenges to their control of wealth (Key 1964: 73f.). Business, however, is a minority interest, so in a democracy the problem for businessmen (which they generally overcome) is to generate the kind of public opinion that acquiesces to their high status in the economic order (1964: 91). For Key, an element of 'economic determinism' here is quite palatable – provided it does not obliterate other, non-economic sources of interest-conflict (1964: 103).

A second objection to pluralism – that it ignores the organized power of the state – also stands in need of modification. It is true that group theory does play down 'the state' as a concept and focuses instead on the representative and responsive political system. But this is not merely a 'bias' of pluralism since the tradition in the US from the early part of this century has been unimpressed by idealist concepts of the general will and common good which the state was held to 'represent'. The turn to group interests was a more empiricist and behavioural approach, but it was also a substantive sociological impulse which can be defended as such. Additionally, it does not follow from pluralists' relative neglect of the state that they were wholly unaware of interest-group activity *within* the level of the political system. On the contrary, Latham for one pointed out the perpetual 'group struggle' within officialdom itself (1952: 35). And Dahl's whole concern was to establish the political as well as the social prerequisites for polyarchy, since societal pluralism could not of itself guarantee that a range of interests would be taken up by parties and leaders. The frequency in pluralist writings of terms such as 'leaders' as marking a contrast between the groups represented and the political representatives in a polyarchy indicates the pluralist awareness of self-interest on the parts of officials and politicians. Dahl's major empirical study of the interest group influence on local decision-making, *Who Governs?* (1961), comes out with quite 'anti-pluralist' conclusions, if pluralism is taken in any pure sense. The city government of New Haven is clearly perceived and portrayed by Dahl as an independent agent and the various interest groups identified do not appear to have great impact on the outcome of the political process (1961: 5–6).

The condensation of pluralist thinking on the state into a convenient metaphor suggesting responsive representation can therefore be misleading. Truman, for example, described the 'weathervane' picture, in which government as a single entity is moved this way and that by the balance of forces amongst social interests, as 'much too simple' (Truman 1951: 106). Latham not only saw officials as constituting interest groups, he accepted that in some sense the state had to act independently as the 'custodian of the consensus' (1952: 14). Clearly, this conception, like Dahl's continual assertion of the imperfections of modern democracy, entails a powerful semi-autonomous governmental interest. The bargaining amongst the various powers, interests and organizations in pluralist theory is not, after all, an even-handed process. Some groups in society are in a stronger position to bargain than others, and those in the political system itself are often in a position to brush off the pressures created by social constituencies.

The main critical charges against pluralism are therefore relative ones. It is true that in comparison with other types of political theory 'the state' is *relatively* neglected. It is true that in *some* expressions of pluralism, democratic consensus is assumed to operate and the impression is given that all serious interests can be both balanced out and partially satisfied. *Occasionally* pluralists tend to take suggestive images and parallels for real: the state as broker or umpire, for example, or the social system as tending to equilibrium. Overall, though, it is the contradictoriness of pluralist discourse which is striking, and this does involve a culpable theoretical forgetfulness. For example, in spite of his acute analysis of class interests amongst the most powerful group in society, Key is able to generalize – in a characteristic pluralistic phrase – that power remains widely dispersed and that groups interact in a 'complex and kaleidoscopic manner' (1964: 8). In parallel, and in spite of the recognition of the autonomy of political elites, the pluralists do frequently return to the constraints on leadership imposed by a variety of social interests and indeed the norms of the democratic culture.

This lack of a stable set of conceptual hierarchies is one reason why pluralism is seldom expounded as a specific theory. It also explains why attempts definitively to pin down conventional pluralism tend to run into trouble. For example, two recent commentators have argued that pluralism presents an 'image of society as an aggregate of interacting individuals socialized into cultural values and engaging in diverse communications and exchanges, especially in markets' (Alford and Friedland 1985: 17). This interpretation rightly highlights the role pluralism allots to the civic culture in providing the subjective bonding in an atomistic and competitive market society. Yet the characteristic

element which marks pluralism off from straightforward liberal indi-
vidualism – the sociology and psychology of *group* formation – is
glaringly absent from the sketch.

Another critical reviewer assimilates pluralism into the tradition of
the theory of political elites (Graham 1986: 125ff.). The logic of this
move is that pluralism's 'realistic' side is emphasized at the expense of
its 'normative' elements. Thus, the pluralists' emphasis on competing
groups, parties and organizations, plus their 'realism' about the necessary limitations of popular rule in a modern society, produce a
somewhat cynical rationale for the long-favoured 'iron law of oligar-
chies'. This interpretation is also plausible, but it does tend to
underestimate the normative aspect of pluralist theory. Although
minority groups do compete for power under the banner of self-interest,
pluralists believe (perhaps mistakenly) that a wide range of groups are
able to exercise a democratic voice. From below, pluralist society emits
a strong (and ever-changing) flow of citizen concerns. From above, the
condition of democratic stability is that groups ensconced in the political
system must show themselves to be sensitive to societal demands and to
the expectations of the democratic culture generally.

This unstable amalgam of hard-headed realism about the imperfect
democracy and a certain idealism about the virtues of pluralist market
society came unstuck in the later 1960s. The notion that deep social
polarity was a thing of the past and that an end to ideological politics
was in the offing simply evaporated as serious strife re-entered the fabric
of modern democracies. The complacency of the pluralist suggestion
that minority voices can be heard without resort to conflict was rudely
shattered by the racial and social violence which erupted in a spread of
major US cities. The rediscovery of millions of free Americans living in
poverty bluntly dented the feeling that democracy and affluence went
hand in hand. The onset of economic recession spoiled the technocratic
vision of smooth growth. The systematic questioning of the social order
by students – the very sons and daughters of middle America – revealed
that a concerned voice for internal change and for the rest of the world
would not, it seemed, be listened to in the normal process of
institutional democratic politics.

The impact of the political and cultural alternatives on respectable
America was closely connected to the fact that, and the way in which,
the strongest country in the world was conducting a war on one of the
poorest peasant societies: Vietnam. Not the cosy picture of articulate
pressure groups securing a response from a friendly local senator, but
harrowing images of the bombing and napalming of peasant communities, became part of the underbelly and substance of domestic western
politics in the late 1960s. Nothing could more dramatically reveal,
radical critics felt, the coercion which lay behind consensus, the

brutalization behind homilies on freedom, and the imperial interests which sustained an advanced economy upon which, according to pluralism, democratic norms depended. In response to the emergent radicalism behind that disillusionment, middle America turned to the more openly disciplinary politics of the Nixon era. But the promise of trust and openness could no longer be maintained without question, and the Watergate bugging scandal of 1973–4 seemed the apotheosis of the transformation of democratic promise to a polyarchy which was imperfect indeed.

The impact of these events on pluralist thinking was profound. Some political theorists were moved by these and parallel European developments to separate further the question of democratic *stability* from that of societal pluralism. By the mid 1970s a strong anti-pluralist current was prominent in international political science: the 'crisis' of the democracies was asserted to lie in the expression of *too many* turbulent group voices, *too much* responsiveness on the part of increasingly 'overloaded' government (cf. Crozier *et al.*, 1975). For several of the key conventional pluralists, notably Dahl and Lindblom, a more apt response was to move in a self-critical direction. In their important 1976 Preface to *Politics, Economics and Welfare*, these authors argue that polyarchy has taken an adverse turn, due to the growth of an 'imperial presidency', the entrenched accumulations of private wealth in the face of public squalor, and a singular failure to combat social inequality. The remedy, if one is to be found, must involve a far greater degree of active popular participation.

One aspect of the development from conventional to critical pluralism is the questioning of the somewhat functionalist and 'technicist' account of social evolution it embodied. Pluralism did not, as is sometimes alleged, lack a sense of history, or even of historical *conflict* (cf. Beer 1969), but it did assume that economic growth was a steady, necessary foundation for democracy, and that such a process is relatively independent of the social conflict surrounding it. In the later phase of pluralism, an element of this equation of growth, pluralism and democracy remains (e.g. Dahl 1971: 78), but there is a newly perceived sense of ecological and democratic danger in any neutral and limitless conception of economic advance. The realization that global resources are finite and that the choice of sources is itself a matter for careful moral consideration is one part of the questioning of growth. Another is the sense that the waste and pollution spawned by the very industry which sustained modern society now threatens to engulf and poison it. Yet another is the awareness of chronic 'underdevelopment' in some lands as a *consequence*, and not just a contingent accompaniment, of advanced development in others. This seriously undermines the idea that the west's 'lead' in technology is ultimately the hope for the rest of the world. These issues are mentioned only in passing in the new introduction to *Politics, Economics and Welfare* (1976, xxii) but they are seen as involving a qualitatively new set of problems for classical pluralism. Above all, as Dahl and Lindblom recognize, political issues of this sort are essentially *collective* in nature: of necessity they posit the need for action towards a common good. The theoretical currency of competing interest-group bargaining is not well equipped to provide a positive appreciation of such increasingly important items on the socio-political agenda.

Another – by now obvious – source of pluralist revision is an enhanced awareness of distinctions amongst groups. There is a greater sense than before that the configuration of interests requires an emphasis on profound social *division* rather than overlapping commonalities. Cleavage and conflict are now as much at the centre of analysis as consensus and freely undertaken negotiations (Dahl 1980: 20). The very notion of social 'interests' appears to have been sharpened too. In the earlier texts, the political importance of those interests which could take the form of *organized* pressure groups already went against the idea of spontaneously achieved democratic balance. In the last work of his 'conventional' phase, Dahl indeed had moved away from any temptation to convene totally different entities under the label 'interest group'. Organized political lobbies constituted one group-type; but the sociologically rich notion of 'subcultures' (Dahl 1971: 203) indicates a rather different order of analytic concern. An interest in the distinction between local, societal and international dimensions of interest-formation is evident too. True, Dahl for one continues to keep a line open to small group psychology when he asserts that local solidarities might simply be *recalcitrant* in the face of the rather abstract identities produced by structural reflection. But it is taken for granted that the complexion of local campaigns and attachments is likely to stem from the way in which general societal patterns and interests are locally embodied (Dahl 1982: 62f.).

The privileged role of business interests, as we have seen, was recognized to an extent in conventional pluralism. In the critical variety business is uniquely charged with having an effective *veto* on the entire political system (Dahl and Lindblom 1976: xxxvi–xxxvii). As well as acknowledging the personal influence of entrepreneurs in decision-making circles, a more general structural imperative is sketched whereby the political system is driven by its concern for business interests.

> It becomes a major task of government to design and maintain an inducement system for businessmen, to be solicitous of business interests, and to grant them, for its value as an incentive, intimacy of participation in government

itself. In all these respects the relation between government and business is unlike the relation between government and any other interest group in society. (Dahl and Lindblom 1976: xxxvii)

A conventional pluralist thought was that in a polyarchy business privilege could be neutralized. Lindblom, however, has now broken with that proposition, disturbing the hitherto implicit link between democracy and free market society.

The mere possibility that business and property dominate polyarchy opens up the paradoxical possibility that polyarchy is tied to the market system not because it is democratic, but because it is not. (Lindblom 1977: 168–9)

In other words, Lindblom is asking whether democracy-as-we-know-it (polyarchy) works in favour of a capitalist system precisely by giving the *appearance* (but not the reality) of equal pluralist participation in decision-making. This suggestion bears surprising resemblance to Lenin's well-known phrase that (bourgeois) democracy provides capitalism with its 'best possible shell' by conceding to the working class a degree of political freedom while continuing to enslave them economically. In a similarly quasi-marxist vein, Lindblom reasons that labour cannot possibly have a tendentially equal influence in the polity since the state has no need to offer workers inducements in the same way as it has to placate employers. On the contrary, workers will continue to contribute to the system without inducements 'because they have no choice but to do so' (Lindblom 1977: 176).

One of the real-world features which has caused the pluralists to become less sanguine about their earlier propositions is the continued centralization of the economy in private hands, in spite of considerable state intervention in the free market. That process overturns the impression that economic development represents a public good and a vital public domain. The interests of the giant corporations, pluralists now think, are governed principally by the imperatives of global expansion and profit. Rather than, as before, trying to theorize the role of business *within* polyarchy, the very accountability of private assets to public criteria of utility is seen as a threat to democracy. Critical pluralists are persuaded that in effect a systematic *rivalry* between business and polyarchy has developed, a contest between 'the voters' and 'the rich capitalists' (Duverger 1974: 5).

In order to appraise this problem adequately, pluralists have had to reverse exactly the terms of their analytical discourse. Not only is the previous idea of parity between interest groups now strictly 'unthinkable' (Lindblom 1977: 193), the very concept of pluralist politics as a market-place wherein groups bargain for advantage must be rejected.

The pluralists perhaps did not embrace this free-enterprise terminology as openly as Joseph Schumpeter (1943) or the 'economics of politics' theorists who regarded political choice as a species of consumer preference (Tomlinson 1981). And in an effort to emphasize the purely political character of pluralist theory, Truman (1951: 48) and Dahl and Lindblom (1953: 516–17) tried to theorize a 'third way' between the 'grand alternatives' of individual enterprise and state centralism, capitalism and socialism. Even so, the earlier pluralist work is pervaded by images drawn from 'bourgeois' economics.

Lately, Dahl in particular has jettisoned this terminology and its dominant paradigm. In an important switch of priorities, he is now concerned to examine economic organization itself in *democratic* terms, rather than the other way around, and he has come up with some radical equations. If the assumption of democracy is that binding collective decisions ought to be made only by those persons subject to them, then why does the principle not apply to a central arena of decision-making, namely economic enterprises (Dahl 1985: 57)? Currently, limited ownership and control of enterprises secures political inequality through its adverse effect on equal access, resources and life-chances. This is partly because capitalist enterprises are themselves fundamentally undemocratic in structure and decision-making. The democratization of capitalist firms is therefore a major prerequisite if a genuine pluralist democracy is to emerge. Here, much greater recognition is given by pluralists to the substantive conditions of formal democracy and participation. For full political liberty to be secured, the argument goes, workers must become 'citizens of the enterprise' (Dahl 1985: 92). And, in turn, for that to happen, there must be a substantial equalization of ownership and control.

On political grounds, corporate capitalism is inimical to democracy ('I do not see how private ownership of corporate enterprise can be a fundamental moral right') (1985: 74). The implication that it is capitalist economic organization which supports the pluralism which in turn sustains democracy has, with these arguments, dramatically been turned around. Without economic democracy and a radical spread of effective collective control, the new view suggests, pluralist democracy will remain superficial at best.

Dahl lays down some fairly stringent conditions for democracy, and his list in *A Preface to Economic Democracy* looks considerably more substantive in character than the somewhat formal analogue in *A Preface to Democractic Theory* almost twenty years before. In addition to equal votes, Dahl specifies effective participation, enlightened understanding, inclusive membership of the polity, and final control of the political agenda by the *demos* (Dahl 1985: 59–60). These considerations are far from constituting a technical checklist; yet they reflect a renewed concern for the norms of classical democracy, however 'unrealistic' these might appear in our complex civilization.

Some of the specified items clearly derive from reflections on the state of the civic culture. If societal pluralism cannot of itself produce effective polyarchy, never mind democracy, then the criteria of citizen participation and subjective commitment to political norms are ever more important. We noted that some doubt was expressed in conventional pluralism about how freely formed any democratic consensus could be. But there seemed a degree of genuine optimism that the people were at least content with the workings of the political system and that the level of participation was acceptable. Such optimism – or perhaps it is sheer contradictoriness – now strikes the critical pluralists as problematic. They perceive a decisively causal relationship between the very restricted terms of the political consensus and general 'indoctrinated complacency' (Dahl and Lindblom 1976: xxxix). This is secured, it is asserted, through the uniquely powerful mass media and education system. The narrowness of the basis of political agreement reflects and sustains, according to Dahl, an 'irrational and deformed public consciousness' (Dahl 1980: 29). Consciousness is deformed, the argument now goes, because the very legitimacy of the system itself is never placed before intelligent democratic judgement. Thus the grand or primary issues about the social system itself are removed from the political agenda, and indoctrination in the myth of balance encourages passivity and homogeneity in the public mind. The tones of a conspiracy theory in these sentiments involve no extraneous imposition of vulgar marxism on these democratic pluralist reflections. Lindblom especially sees the agencies of ideology as actively promoting business interests, and in general regards the 'core' beliefs of the polyarchies as 'the product of a rigged, lopsided competition of ideas' where the appearance of open belief-formation is secured mainly by the closed, circular operation of propaganda (Lindblom 1977: 202–12). [. . .]

Let me summarize the current political contours of pluralist theory by reference to Steven Lukes's influential analysis of models of power (Lukes 1974).

[The account of Lukes has been omitted as a section from Lukes's own work forms the previous chapter.]

The elaboration of this model represented an attempt to show the poverty of conventional pluralist theory. What is interesting for our purposes is that 'critical pluralism' as I have outlined its development now conforms to a large degree with the three-dimensional view. Lukes rightly noted Dahl's concern, in *Who Governs?*, to show how *indirect* were the influences on political decisions, thus in a way breaching the confines of the one-dimensional view. Phase two pluralism goes much further, revealing the strength of structural as well as personal influence by businessmen and corporations. It has sketched in greater detail the logic of non-participation in polyarchies and that of 'agenda-setting', thus enriching its understanding of popular democracy in the process. And it has openly asserted that inequalities of resources and responses, which themselves render the grand edifice of open government a façade, are systematically sustained by a *rhetoric* of consensus which is generated through the socialization process and the ideological institutions. Pluralist theory has always had two faces, one of which looked somewhat cynically towards the reality of elite rule in formally democratic nations. The other face was turned optimistically to the future in the hope that imperfect democracy could be steadily enhanced. On waking up from their American dream, the pluralists have attractively revised their previous, limited conception of democracy.

References

Alford, R. R., and R. Friedland (1985), *Powers of Theory*, Cambridge, Cambridge University Press.
Beer, S. H. (1969), *Modern British Politics*, London, Faber and Faber.
Bentley, A. F. (1967), *The Process of Government*, Cambridge, Mass., Belknap Press.
Crozier, M. J., *et al.* (1975), *The Crisis of Democracy*, London, The Trilateral Commission.
Dahl, R. A. (1961), *Who Governs?*, New Haven, Yale University Press.
Dahl, R. A. (1971), *Polyarchy*, New Haven, Yale University Press.
Dahl, R. A. (1980), 'Pluralism revisited', in Erlich and Wooton (eds.).
Dahl, R. A. (1982), *Dilemmas of Pluralist Democracy*, New Haven, Yale University Press.
Dahl, R. A. (1985), *A Preface to Economic Democracy*, Cambridge, Polity Press.
Dahl, R. A., and C. E. Lindblom (1953), *Politics, Economics and Welfare*, 2nd edn., 1976. Chicago, University of Chicago Press.
Duverger, M. (1974), *Modern Democracies: Economic power versus political power*, Illinois, Dryden Press.
Graham, K. (1986), *The Battle of Democracy*, Brighton, Wheatsheaf Books.
Key, V. O. (1964), *Politics, Parties and Pressure Groups*, 5th edn., New York, Crowell.
Latham, E. (1952), *The Group Bases of Politics*, Ithaca, Cornell University Press.
Lindblom, C. E. (1977), *Politics and Markets*, New York, Basic Books.
Lukes, S. (1974), *Power: A radical view*, London, Macmillan.
Schumpeter, J. (1943), *Capitalism, Socialism and Democracy*, London, Unwin.
Tomlinson, J. (1981), 'The "economics of politics" and public expenditure: a critique', *Economy and Society*, 10.
Truman, D. (1951), *The Governmental Process*, New York, Alfred Knopf.

The evolution of Marxist approaches to state organization

Patrick Dunleavy and Brendan O'Leary

State organization

Relatively detailed Marxist accounts of how state institutions operate have emerged only in the post-war period, and are associated chiefly with the growth of Western neo-Marxisms – new forms of expressing Marx and Engels' ideas, distinguished chiefly by their willingness to engage 'bourgeois' social science directly in debate. While orthodox Marxist–Leninism of the Comintern period offered no serious accounts of liberal democratic practices and institutions, neo-Marxists have tried to come to terms with phenomena which classical Marxists did not anticipate, especially the advent of some form of mixed economy and the growth of an extended welfare state in every advanced capitalist society. Previous Marxist descriptions of the democratic state as a nakedly repressive apparatus attuned only to the behests of capitalists sat unsatisfactorily with the apparent emergence of government planning and 'caring capitalism', at least in the period from the early 1950s to the late 1970s. The emergence of new-right governments in the 1980s has called in question the previous welfare consensus, and apparently signalled a drive towards the 'recommodification' of areas of social life previously handled by public policy decision. But no attempt to dismantle radically the fabric of state regulation or public service provision has yet been pushed through in any liberal democracy, so that the public policy configuration now remains quite distinct from that prevailing before 1945.

If the problems requiring analysis are thus quite novel, the Marxist

From P. Dunleavy and B. O'Leary, *Theories of the State* (1987), Basingstoke: Macmillan, Chapter 5.

toolkit available for constructing a response has remained heavily
influenced by the three approaches to the state articulated in Marx and
Engels' own work, namely, the instrumental, arbiter and functionalist
models. [. . .] We cover neo-Marxists' modern instrumentalist, arbiter
and functionalist models in turn, summarizing the differences from Marx
and Engels' classical accounts, and describing how each approach
analyses the workings of state institutions and policy-making. We
conclude our accounts of each approach by looking at some of its
distinctive variants to demonstrate the range of options in the neo-
Marxist literature.

Modern instrumentalist models
We noted above that Marx and Engels most commonly relied on an
instrumentalist account of the liberal state as a machine directly
controlled from outside by capitalists and hence bound to act in
furthering their interests. They refined their account to acknowledge the
possibility of indirect control of the state by capitalists, taking account of
the persistence of aristocratic and monarchical governments in late
nineteenth-century Europe. Modern instrumentalism has adapted this
strategy to explain how it is that the election of social democratic parties
into government, or the advent of other coalitions orientated in part to
working-class voters (such as Franklin Roosevelt's 'new deal' administration in the USA), has not qualified the fundamentally capitalist
character of the liberal democratic state. Modern instrumentalists
elaborate Kautsky's proposition that the capitalist class rules but does
not itself govern, contenting itself with ruling successive governments, a
claim which is commonly elaborated through a point-by-point critique of
pluralism. [. . .]
    The next stage of the modern instrumentalist argument has close
affinities with elite theory, arguing that capitalists, state bureaucrats and
political leaders are unified into a single cohesive group by their
common social origin, similar lifestyles and values, and by the existence
of numerous networks and forums where co-ordinated strategies for
public policy are hammered out. While direct participation in government by personnel from big business has characteristically declined in
modern liberal democracies (except in the USA), the state apparatus
remains staffed overwhelmingly by strata of society who can be relied on
to adopt pro-capitalist stances on economic and industrial issues – for
example, members of professions, lawyers, accountants and farmers.
Where leftist governments do gain power, international financial markets and the loss of business confidence automatically create unfavourable climates for radical social reforms, normally shaping the 'economic
facts of life' to constrain any fundamental alteration of capitalism long
before the ultimate weapons available to domestic business (such as
investment strikes) have to be brought into play.

The consequences of capitalist domination can be traced in the consistent orientation of much state intervention to supporting domestic capital against foreign competition, underpinning advanced technology, and imposing restrictive state controls on industrial relations. Most mixed economy interventions involve the state in subsidizing or taking over the organization of necessary economic activities unprofitable for capital; and most welfare policies can be understood as attempts to socialize labour costs falling on businesses, which become financed out of general taxation instead of showing up directly in employers' wage bills and production costs. The absolutely preponderant orientation of the state in capitalist society is towards 'the containment of pressure' from below (Miliband, 1982, pp. 54–93).

Instrumentalists have never paid great attention to the detailed institutional organization of the liberal democratic state. Most instrumentalists agree with Marx that parliamentary processes are meaningless charades, significant only as a means of maintaining the key ideological illusion that there is effective popular control of state policy-making. Legislatures are ineffectual, and real power is concentrated in the executive branch of government. For example, in the web of agencies which surround the US presidency and make key foreign and defence policy decisions, Domhoff (1970, 1978) claims to detect clear evidence of capitalist control over both popular and elite opinion-making agencies, which set the agenda for policy-making. The American executive branch of the state is overwhelmingly staffed by the upper class; Congress serves at most as a place in which dissident members of the upper class can air grievances. Debate and apparent pluralism in the institutions of representative government mask internal and technical disagreements amongst the ruling class about how to manage the discontent of subordinate classes. Instrumentalists regard administrative elites as simply functionaries who make policy according to the rational interests of the capitalist class. Bureaucracies exist primarily to respond to the problems and contradictions of a capitalist economy: there is no necessary reason for their existence independent of their class-biased role. This simple view also extends to the legal system. Instrumentalists agree with radical elite theorists that the class origins of the judiciary are reflected in the use of judicial discretion in a consistently biased fashion against labour unions and radical social movements. Judges consistently use the law of contract against trade unions (labour monopolists) as opposed to capitalist monopolists.

In instrumentalist writings the state is seen in the last resort as a unified organization. Federal decentralization of domestic policy responsibilities to regional governments, local government organizations and/ or the separation of powers are alike dismissed as window dressing. Any apparent fragmentation is a ruling-class stratagem designed to divide exploited classes which develop revolutionary or reformist consciousness. Should apparent fragmentation get out of hand, control over policy will be overtly centralized, or a new but equally fraudulent decentralization of state organizations will be devised. Reorganizations which alter the legal powers and managerial patterns of local governments are interpreted as the implementation of the national capitalists' will. Local or regional governments originally served as the executive committees for managing the common affairs of the local or regional bourgeoisie. In the modern period capital is instead organized at a national or transnational scale so that the previous (capitalist) rationale for sub-national government has withered away, except for a few spatially constrained sectors of capital, such as development interests or companies engaged in extracting mineral resources. Current local state functions are a microcosm of the repressive and class-biased strategies which apply at central state level (Cockburn, 1977). If this situation threatens to change, as when radical left parties gain control of local authorities, then sub-national government is simply by-passed, or its powers are drastically reduced. Conflicts between central and local governments are the only serious ones which can arise within the liberal democratic state, and are invariably resolved in favour of the centre, where the executive committee of the national bourgeoisie is located. In the absence of such conflicts the local or regional state acts as the instrument of local or regional capitalists, except when their interests are too parochial. [. . .]

The arbiter model
Marx and Engels' arbiter model of the state suggested that if class forces in society were for a time evenly balanced, then the state bureaucracy and a strong political–military leader could intervene to impose stabilizing policies which were not controllable by capital, although they would be bound to maintain capitalist predominance in economic life. The modern arbiter model suggests that this distinct policy stance by state agencies and political leaders could be a much more common and long-lasting phenomenon than Marx or Engels ever acknowledged. Poulantzas (1978) suggests that the state in liberal democracies acts as a condensation of class struggle, mirroring in a distorted and class-biased way the balance of class forces in the broader society. Elections, strikes, riots, pressure group lobbying, and decisions by law courts continuously serve to adjust state policies to keep them in touch with movements and realignments of multiple class fractions and strata. Within modern capitalist societies the monopoly corporations constitute the dominant class fraction. If their influence over public policy is to be maintained, it is essential that the state ensures a broader degree of support for state policy from other fractions of capital, from intermediate class categories (such as the petit bourgeoisie and non-manual groups), and from

significant sections of the working class. Flexible and adaptive public policy configurations co-opt popular struggles and disorganize working-class militancy.

Maintaining this configuration requires that the state apparatus should operate with a considerable degree of autonomy from the dominant class fraction, and that the leaders who assemble and co-ordinate the ruling 'power bloc' should appear on the political stage as independent actors. But this autonomy for stage agencies is *relative*, since in the last instance the requirements of capitalism as an economic system will always prevail over any contradictory state policies, even supposing that these should reach the point of being explicitly formulated. Nonetheless, because the relatively autonomous state in advanced capitalism acts in a way which gauges and responds to the balance of class forces, there is the possibility of a partial socialization of capitalism as an economic system – i.e. the introduction of elements of a socialist mode of production, an argument which purely repressive or instrumental models of the state emphatically deny.

The arbiter model has been developed to analyse major institutional changes in post-war liberal democracies by Poulantzas' concept of *authoritarian statism*. This model particularly set out to explain the consolidation of the Gaullist regime in France after the Fifth French Republic was established with a strong president in 1958, a change which inaugurated an unbroken dominance of French national politics by right-wing parties for over two decades. Poulantzas identified the rise of authoritarian statism as the principal trend in contemporary liberal democratic politics, and defined it as 'intensified state control over every sphere of socio-economic life combined with a radical decline of the institutions of political democracy, and with draconian and multiform curtailment of so-called "formal" liberties' (Poulantzas, 1978, pp. 203–4).

Five features are important. First, the decline of parliaments and the strengthening of executive power corresponds to the decline of liberal bourgeois politics and presages the possible demise of liberal democracy altogether. Second, the whole separation of powers doctrine – which prescribes no institutional connections between the executive, the legislature and the judiciary – has begun to dissolve, and liberal democratic states systematically violate their own laws. Third, political parties have declined as serious inputs into policy-making, either because a single party grouping has emerged as dominant over all alternatives (as in Japan or Gaullist France), or because where two party groupings alternate in power, executive authority is always monopolized by a centrist bloc which spans both possible parties of government (as in Britain or West Germany). Fourth, the 'legitimating process is shifting towards plebiscitary and purely manipulatory circuits (the media) dominated by the administration and the executive' (Poulantzas, 1978, p. 229). The fifth feature is the development of so-called 'parallel networks', which cross-cut the formal or official organization of the state, and cause a concentration of powers to accumulate at the very top of the executive. Political leaders and presidents increasingly seem to run government in a directly personalized, discretionary way. At the same time quasi-governmental agencies have multiplied beyond the reach of any effective control by representative politics. Authoritarian statism carries the 'seeds or certain scattered elements of fascism' and Poulantzas asserts in conclusion that 'All contemporary power is functional to authoritarian statism' (1978, p. 239).

The arbiter approach dismisses instrumentalist arguments that the state apparatus operates to support capitalism because the social backgrounds, values and networks of contacts for senior bureaucrats and political leaders tie them into a directly pro-business orientation. In Poulantzas' view the co-ordination of the capitalist state is achieved by the political executive and higher administrative civil service, irrespective of the type of personnel who staff these posts. The institutional separation of the state from the capitalist class is not simply a charade. The constitutional and organizational arrangements filter the interests of state personnel towards the long-run interests of the capitalists. The mechanisms of legal and political accountability were initially developed to serve the interests of particular capitalists in removing the corrupt exploitation of state offices. In the modern period the institutional separation preserves harmony amongst different types of capital and makes the state appear open to the interests of all citizens, including the working class. The state must appear class-neutral, the better to preserve the long-run interests of the capitalist class.

Civil servants in an advanced industrial state are meritocratically selected (Therborn, 1978) even though their tasks are to plan in the long-run interests of capitalism. State officials are dependent upon capitalist economic development and growth if they are going to be able to pursue their interests and sustain themselves in office, so they are constrained to act in the interests of capital, although not necessarily in its optimal interests (Offe, 1984). Planning cannot be socially rational, as it would be under socialism, where planning for need would replace production for profit. But planning can be made rational *for a particular class* or for the 'power bloc' created to sustain monopoly capital's predominance. A range of policy technologies, including Keynesian demand management, incomes policies, regional policies, indicative planning and welfare management, can be used by state officials. These interventions will be implemented despite short-term business protests if state managers deem them class-rational. In the long run administrators try to make capitalism a positive-sum game from which all classes can gain. Such strategies prevent the breakdown of capitalism into class conflicts. They can only succeed by imposing long-run discipline upon capitalists. Conspiracies or strong personal relations between business and state elites, such as corruption, nepotism or clientelism, are syndromes of underdevelopment for arbiter theorists. Such lapses from the liberal democratic ethos are the legacy of feudalism, not intrinsic features of bourgeois democracy.

Arbiter theorists have a comparatively complex outlook on law, which is regarded as a partly autonomous sphere of social action, not controllable by capitalists. Legal procedures bind judges against straightforward manipulation, and subordinate classes can take advantage of these legal procedures despite the obstacles placed in their way. Jury systems, and the segmentation of the legal system into spheres which are in no obvious sense class-based, are given due significance in this view (Thompson, 1975). The successful struggle of labour movements in various liberal democracies to transform the practice of contract and labour law is not ignored, as in instrumentalist models. However, arbiter theorists have no faith in the long-run neutrality of the courts. Concessions which judges make to workers at one moment in the class struggle may be removed at another. The relative autonomy of law has to be constantly maintained by successful working-class mobilization into politics and the labour movement.

Arbiter theorists also recognize that liberal democratic states vary greatly in their internal organization between federal and unitary forms. Local governments also possess very different degrees of policy-making and financial autonomy; and a historically given separation of powers may still significantly affect the cohesion of the state. Since the state as a whole is relatively autonomous from the short-run interests of capitalists, each state sub-organization is also relatively autonomous from the relevant short-run interests of the capitalists, and other class interests must be accommodated in some degree. The changing institutional structure of the state is a historical artefact of class struggle which follows a simple pattern. The successes of subordinate classes in capturing state organizations are met by reorganizations which benefit the long-run interests of capital, as in Britain, where local government units have been completely modernized and increased in size to make them less vulnerable to electoral capture by the labour movement (Dearlove, 1979). American federalism was also explained by Charles Beard (1935) as a device which promoted national integration in the long-run interests of the merchant class. The fragmentation of the state apparatus also conveniently diverts the class struggle to multiple fronts. A thoroughly centralized state is avoided by an intelligent bourgeoisie because it is not in their long-run interest to build a state machine which could quickly be converted to serve socialist purposes. Decentralization fragments the scope of radical change and raises the thresholds required for it to be achieved, a maxim which constitutional and administrative designers take seriously in many liberal democracies. That decentralized state structures serve to reduce the scope of welfare state expansion and socialist incumbency is one of the few findings in the comparative public policy literature on which there is near unanimity (Castles, 1985, p. 120). Constitutions embodying decentralization bind the bourgeoisie against the short-run pursuit of their material interests, reflecting an abstentionist strategic rationality.

There are no developed variants of the arbiter model. Indeed, as we shall see below, many of its key protagonists (such as Poulantzas and Therborn) also switch back and forth between the arbiter model and functionalist arguments. However, there is an interesting and well-developed literature which is worth considering in its own right, namely the application of the arbiter model to explain the existence of *authoritarian regimes under capitalism*. Marxists have traditionally agreed that liberal democracy is the 'normal' form of political system for an advanced industrial state. Marx explained the regime of Napoleon III as an arbiter state temporarily gaining autonomy from the balance of class forces, a situation which he insisted could occur only when the transition from capitalism to socialism was already in train. Orthodox Marxists in the inter-war period accordingly hailed the widespread growth of fascist exceptional regimes as a sign that the death agonies of European capitalism were imminent. But the strength and resilience of those fascist societies, none of which fell because of internal collapse, and their replacement after 1945 by liberal democratic capitalism seemed to refute such interpretations. Equally the long-lived persistence of authoritarian regimes in post-war capitalist societies (as in Spain, Portugal, Greece, Brazil and Argentina) reawakened Marxist writers' interest in explaining 'exceptional' regimes. Trotsky (1971) suggested that fascist governments emerge not where class forces are 'balanced', but rather when the bourgeoisie has already lost its battle with the working class; only in these circumstances will capitalists concede a very high level of autonomy to a fascist political party or social movement which they cannot control. In trying to explain post-war authoritarian regimes Poulantzas radically extended the arbiter model to suggest that an autonomous state is the generalized form of political system for advanced capitalism, and that 'exceptional' and liberal democratic governments are both equally possible and common alternatives by which a necessary degree and appropriate form of state autonomy can be achieved.

Modern functionalist approaches

The functionalist model in Marx and Engels' work stressed the shaping of state organization and policy-making by the fundamental imperatives of maintaining capitalist development. Changes in the economic base of society determine shifts in the political and legal superstructure. Modern functionalist approaches continue to emphasize that state intervention is best explained by an impersonal logic of the development of advanced capitalism. Like the views of their predecessors in classical Marxist thought, modern functionalist views do not regard it as useful or necessary to demonstrate the precise mechanisms by which state policy responds to structural imperatives; instead they focus on macro-social issues and trends. Some important Marxist functional approaches have been defined as attempts to respond to grand sociological theories formulated in the USA and Western Europe. Conservative writers have developed complex theoretical systems to explain the maintenance of social stability and legitimacy [. . .]. Neo-Marxist functionalist schemas try to match their conceptual sophistication, and to adapt the concepts of system theory to demonstrate the necessary class biases and contradictions of state interventions. Although economic imperatives remain dominant in these schemas, all modern functionalist accounts acknowledge the existence of separate political–ideological structures or cultural processes with their own distinctive logic of development. For example, Althusser argues that revolutionary situations can only occur when the economic system is in crisis at the same time as the political and ideological structures are in crisis. Habermas argues that crises have been displaced from the economic realm into the state apparatus itself or into the cultural system.

There are few if any developed functionalist accounts of state institutions, although Therborn's (1978) analysis of the decline of parliaments is a mixture of functional and arbiter model arguments. He argues that the traditional forms of representative government, which effectively excluded the popular masses or isolated and controlled them through local notables, is 'no longer an adequate instrument'. In most liberal democracies it has gradually been supplemented by a new plebiscitary politics, based on the cult of charismatic leaders built up through the mass media. Plebiscitary politics enhances, indeed exalts, executive preponderance in policy-making and implementation, at the expense of legislatures. This change is functional for the stability of monopoly capitalism because the pseudo-democracy of direct voting by a mass electorate for leaders or policies increases the legitimacy of the political system, allows the mass of citizens to be co-opted into compliance, and poses no real risk of losing control over key state decisions to the masses. Similarly O'Connor (1973, p. 78) argues that the American executive branch remains independent of particular class interests, and serves the interests of monopoly capital as a whole. These interests are sifted, ranked and transmitted by the state administration to the president and his key aides, who initiate appropriate political action on them.

The characteristics of politicians or civil servants on which instrumentalist accounts focus barely matter in a functionalist analysis. State personnel simply fill given roles; their behaviour is largely predetermined by structural forces in line with the functional imperatives of the capitalist mode of production. Their policy-making styles vary according to what is optimal for the function concerned. Similarly the state's organization at any time is assumed to be *optimally* organized for the needs of capital at that time. Specify capitalism's need at any time and the structure of state organization is explained – except of course in periods of acute crisis. A strictly functionalist Marxist must accordingly believe that problems of state co-ordination cannot exist, except in a revolutionary crisis. In normal circumstances the capitalist state can successfully conceal its class character. The state's function is to co-ordinate and manage the economic crises generated by the mode of production through political and ideological interventions. Threatening co-ordination difficulties can arise if and only if the system's managers cannot resolve the displacement of crises because of serious dysfunctions in the economy or some sort of collapse in the cultural–ideological system.

But since Marxists believe that capitalism as a social system is doomed, it follows that capitalism cannot be rationally planned for ever. Ruling-class strategies and responses to functional imperatives from an internally contradictory mode of production are permanently unstable. Even in the functionalist version of Marxism the state's performance is contingent on class struggle (although the two explanatory mechanisms, classes in struggle and functional imperatives, are never combined convincingly). Functionalist Marxists continue to insist that rational comprehensive planning is only possible under socialism, despite a complete lack of evidence for this judgement in the operation of planning in the Soviet Union or its allied states (Nove, 1983). Many Western Marxists still deny that the experience of Eastern bloc countries has any direct relevance for the future planned performance of Western economies following their transformation into socialism. However, there is some evidence of a recent reappraisal of this entrenched attitude.

Yet there have been some areas where functionalist accounts have been elaborated to try to explain the persistence of both stability and internal tensions within the state apparatus. A quite developed model of the reasons for fragmentation of government into different tiers and sectors is provided by *the dual state thesis*, which presents a Marxist alternative to liberal corporatist theory [. . .].

The thesis has three main stages (O'Connor, 1973; Wolfe, 1977; Cawson and Saunders, 1983). First, three functions of the state in the capitalist mode of production are deduced from the functional requirements of the mode of production. They are the preservation of order, the promotion of capital accumulation and the manufacture of legitimation. Second, forms of state expenditure corresponding to each of these functions are identified. Order is maintained through 'social expenses' policy; accumulation is fostered directly by 'social investment' expenditures to reduce production costs; and social cohesion is boosted by 'social consumption' spending, which boosts workers' living standards (and hence only indirectly contributes to increased profitability). State organizations can be classified according to which function is furthered by their budgets. Thus police organizations which preserve order fall in the social expenses category, nuclear power plants supposedly providing cheap electricity constitute social investment, and welfare agencies which promote legitimation fall in the social consumption category. Third, the direction of state organizations is structured so that accumulation functions are ranked higher than legitimation functions. An appropriate ranking is achieved by creating two sets of institutions. The central government or politically uncontrolled quasi-governmental agencies monopolize social investment functions of critical significance for capital. Here decision-making is characteristically corporatist, future-orientated, and concerned to integrate external interests in achieving state policy goals. The central government also monopolizes social expenses functions of key significance for social stability, but these are administered in a rigidly bureaucratic way, without any attempt to co-opt external interests. At the same time local government structures, and perhaps some politically visible sections of the national state apparatus, are entrusted with responsibility for social consumption spending. Policy-making in this area is deliberately pluralist, mopping up political energies, providing a reassuring appearance of controversy and popular influence, and sustaining a needs-orientated ideology which seems to indicate the social neutrality of state policy. In practice local governments or elected regional governments are rigidly controlled by the centre to prevent them adopting policies hostile to capital interests, and their decisions are extensively determined by prior central state commitments of resources. Nonetheless, conflicts in central–local relations reveal the structural tensions between the accumulation and legitimation imperatives acting upon the capitalist state.

Critics of the dual state thesis argue that in practice public expenditures can be classified according to their function only through a *post hoc* evaluation of their consequences or by knowing which organizations implemented the programmes (which would make the whole schema tautologous). Thus only after the event can one evaluate whether

expenditure on public health services contributed to capital accumulation, legitimation, and/or social order (Dunleavy, 1984). Nor is the
comparative evidence of the allocation of functions between state
organizations in liberal democracies very favourable for the theory
(Sharpe, 1984). In some countries major social consumption functions
are controlled by the central government and social investment functions by local governments.

A second major area of functionalist thinking is in *accounts of the
legal system* which are based on Marx's base–superstructure metaphor
(Cohen, 1978). The legal system existing at any time is explained as
functional for the development of the productive forces at that time, or
(in another version) for the relations of production at that time. As
Cohen presents the functionalist model, law changes in accordance with
changes in the power relations between classes, a feature particularly
true of the law of the labour contract. There may be time lags and a
degree of sub-optimality in the correspondence between relations of
production and legal relations, but otherwise law is functional for the
economic base. Critics of the functionalist base–superstructure distinction argue that law is in fact part of the property relations governing
production, so it is not possible to separate the two (Lukes, 1983).
Nonetheless, the base–superstructure model is the dominant Marxist
approach to law. Renner (1949) argued with some plausible empirical
evidence that legal norms which appear to persist for lengthy historical
periods, spanning different modes of production, in fact change their
substantive functions in response to developments in economic structures. However, Renner's arguments did not imply that law is a passive
reflection of its class-divided environment. Judges and the legal system
play an active role in the maintenance and alteration of social relations.
Pashukanis (1979) stressed the formal resemblance between law and
capitalist rationality. Law mirrors the abstract individuality and formal
equality of contracting parties in the capitalist market. Law will
consequently disappear under socialism, where substantive collective
goals (embodied in the plan) will replace formal legal equality, which
would be dysfunctional to socialism. However, in some functionalist
versions of Marxism, the legal system does have the capacity to be
class-neutral, because it does not recognize classes, only abstract
individuals (Poulantzas, 1973). Nonetheless, this judicial fiction functions in a class-biased way, maintaining the capitalist mode of production through the 'juridical illusion' that social conflicts can be settled or
refereed outside the class struggle.

There has been a considerable fashion for functionalist accounts
among Western Marxists, since an apparently more elegant intellectual
apparatus than those of orthodox instrumentalists can be constructed.

Three distinctive variants of the functionalist approach have been noteworthy: structuralist Marxism, the capital logic school, and German neo-Marxism.

Structuralist Marxism originated in France in the 1960s, especially in the work of the communist philosopher Louis Althusser, although other key writers have included Poulantzas (who sometimes uses the arbiter model and sometimes a functional approach). In structuralist accounts the state is seen as essentially a factor of cohesion in society, which functions to organize the dominant class and to disorganize the subordinate classes through the use of either repressive or ideological apparatuses (Althusser, 1969). Repressive state apparatuses (RSAs) are new labels for armies and police forces. Ideological state apparatuses (ISAs) include a very wide range of institutions which are said to perform the 'state' function of ensuring social stability. Althusser's list includes religious, educational, trade union and mass media organizations, and the family. But remarkably no mention is made of welfare agencies, public enterprises or planning bodies, all of which are major additions in the extended welfare state. RSAs and ISAs continually create the 'conditions of existence' of the capitalist mode of production, producing docile, disciplined and fragmented 'individuals' whose viewpoints and behaviour are suitable for capitalist life. It is to capture this function that Althusser defined the state to include almost all non-economic organizations, except the revolutionary party of the working class, in the process definitionally obliterating the difference between input politics and state organization, or between the state and society (Polan, 1984, pp. 34–5).

Althusser denies that there is anything specific to explain about liberal democracy except its illusory existence. His ISA concept implies that the populations of the capitalist state are living under a dictatorship, a bourgeois dictatorship. What they think is private is in fact public. Liberal democracy, private life, civil rights and interest groups are all simply ideological constructs designed to pacify and mislead. [. . .] Althusser insists that political and ideological structures exist with their own rhythm and laws of development quite distinct from those in the economic sphere. One might have expected an examination of the non-economic bases of liberal democracy or of bureaucracy in understanding the distinction between 'class power' and 'state power', or 'the specificity of the political' (Laclau, 1977). However, structuralist Marxists fail to carry through their qualification of economic determinism. Social classes, political parties, ideologies and state organizations still seem to be 'explained' by the logic of the mode of production. Some critics also argue that any qualification of economic determinism threatens the distinctiveness of Marxism. For example, neo-Marxist analyses of bureaucracy and the division of labour have converged on the accounts given by elite theorists (Parkin, 1979); and post-Althusserian and post-Gramscian Marxism is indistinguishable from pluralism except in its vocabulary (Laclau and Mouffe, 1985).

A further problem for structuralist Marxists is the relation between class struggle and functionalist state theory. They later came to argue that class struggle goes on in state institutions (Althusser, 1976; Poulantzas, 1978). But such class struggle cannot originate in the political and ideological levels of the mode of production, because in their scheme the functions of these levels are to stabilize the mode of production. On the other hand, if the class struggle going on inside the state originates at the economic sphere, then surely there is no separation of the economic and the political–ideological levels at all?

The capital logic school of neo-Marxist theories (sometimes also called the 'state derivation' approach) set out to deduce the functional necessity of the state from analysis of the capitalist mode of production (Altvater, 1973; Holloway and Picciotto, 1978). For example, legal and monetary systems necessary for the production and exchange of commodities and the circulation of capital are 'deduced' from the functional needs of capitalism. The state as a whole functions as 'an ideal collective capitalist' (Altvater, 1973), a political institution which corresponds to the common needs of capital. Whereas public choice theorists explain state activities, such as the production of public goods, as a result of intentional rationality [. . .], the capital logic school deduces the functional necessity of the state from analysis of the imputed needs of capital. They similarly deduce the need for the contemporary state to intervene extensively to regulate the crisis-prone capitalist economy in four ways – providing the general, material conditions of production; establishing general, legal relations; regulating and suppressing conflicts between capital and wage-labour; and protecting national capital in the world market (Altvater, 1978, p. 42). However, there are limits to the functional capacities of the state – it cannot transcend the contradictions of capitalism.

German neo-Marxism is influenced by the Frankfurt School of critical theory and by systems thinking (Jay, 1973). A leading author in the genre, Claus Offe, defines the capitalist state as an institutionalized form of political power which 'seeks to implement and guarantee the *collective* interests of all members of a class society dominated by capital' (Offe, 1984, p. 120). This conception mixes an organizational and functional definition of the state. It presupposes that the functionally optimal capitalist state is in some senses class-neutral. Offe believes that the institutional operations of the state are guided by three conditions. First, the state is excluded from organizing production according to its own 'political' criteria. This 'exclusion principle' means that investment decisions in any liberal democracy lie with capitalists, outside direct state control. Second, state policy is constrained because government depends for taxation revenue upon maintaining successful capital accumulation. State officials must be interested, for the sake of their own power, in guaranteeing and safeguarding healthy capital accumulation, an argument which anticipates the neo-pluralist position of Charles Lindblom [. . .]. Third, the capitalist state is built upon this combination of exclusion from direct production and dependence on capital accumulation, but an ideal form of state also requires democratic legitimation. The state's function, *par excellence*, is to manage potential crises which may occur in the economy, in its own fiscal resources, or in the legitimacy of existing social arrangements.

Marxist critics argue that functionalist accounts of the state are vacuous because they consist of citing the consequences of particular actions as their causes (Elster, 1986 [. . .]). Because a particular action achieves a given result, the action is seen as made necessary in order to achieve that result, and a loose typology of the 'needs' of capital is constructed to demonstrate the functionality of any particular outcome. Thus we 'know' that the creation of an extended welfare state was functional for capital in the three decades after 1945 because that was what occurred. Equally we know that cutbacks and retrenchment of welfare services have become functional for capital since the mid-1970s because that too has occurred. In short, whatever the state does is functional for the capitalist class in the long run, so the theory is immunized against any conflicting evidence. Instrumentalists also claim that Poulantzas' conception of the state as the factor of cohesion in the social formation is equally unhelpful. To say that the reproduction of the capitalist mode of production requires a number of conditions to be met is not an explanation of how they are met, of what happens if they are not met, of whether they can be met in 'functionally equivalent ways', or of *why* these needs are met.

The relative autonomy of the state

All neo-Marxist word-processors have been programmed with the phrase 'the *relative autonomy* of the capitalist state', so it may be useful in rounding off this section to recap very briefly on how the three approaches actually use this concept. In fact there are two different meanings hidden away in this phrase: the state can be relatively autonomous of the capitalist class, which is appropriate for an organizational model of the state (Figure 1). Alternatively the state may be relatively autonomous of the capitalist mode of production, which is appropriate for a functionalist approach.

Figure 1 Marxist conceptions of the 'relative autonomy' of the state

References

Althusser, L. (1969) *For Marx* (Harmondsworth: Penguin), translated B. Brewster.

Althusser, L. (1976) *Essays in Self-Criticism* (London: New Left Books).

Altvater, E. (1973) 'Notes on some problems of state interventionism', *Kapitalstate*, 1 and 2.

Altvater, E. (1978) 'Some problems of state interventionism', in J. Holloway and S. Picciotto (eds.), *State and Capital* (London: Arnold).

Beard, C. (1935) *An Economic Interpretation of the Constitution of the United States* (New York: Macmillan).

Castles, F. G. (1985) *The Working Class and Welfare: Reflections on the political development of the welfare state in Australia and New Zealand, 1890–1980* (Wellington: Allen & Unwin).

Cawson, A. and Saunders, P. (1983) 'Corporatism, competitive politics and class struggle', in R. King (ed.), *Capital and Politics* (London: Routledge & Kegan Paul).

Cockburn, C. (1977) *The Local State* (London: Pluto Press).

Cohen, G. A. (1978) *Karl Marx's Theory of History: A defence* (Oxford: Oxford University Press).

Dearlove, J. (1979) *The Reorganization of British Local Government* (Cambridge: Cambridge University Press).

Domhoff, W. (1970) *The Higher Circles* (New York: Random House).

Domhoff, W. (1978) *The Powers that Be* (New York: Random House).

Dunleavy, P. (1984) 'The limits to local government', in M. Boddy and C. Fudge (eds.), *Local Socialism? Labour councils and new left alternatives* (London: Macmillan).

Elster, J. (1986) 'Further thoughts on Marxism, functionalism and game theory' in J. Roemer (ed.), *Analytical Marxism* (Cambridge: Cambridge University Press).

Holloway, J. and Picciotto, S. (eds.) (1978) *State and Capital: A German debate* (London: Edward Arnold).

Jay, M. (1973) *The Dialectical Imagination* (London: Heinemann).

Laclau, E. (1977) *Politics and Ideology in Marxist Thought* (London: New Left Books).

Laclau, E. and Mouffe, C. (1985) *Hegemony and Socialist Strategy* (London: Verso).

Lukes, S. (1983) 'Can the base be distinguished from the superstructure?', in D. Miller and L. Siedentop (eds.), *The Nature of Political Theory* (Oxford: Oxford University Press).

Miliband, R. (1982) *Capitalist Democracy in Britain* (Oxford: Oxford University Press).

Nove, A. (1983) *The Economics of Feasible Socialism* (London: Allen & Unwin).

O'Connor, J. (1973) *The Fiscal Crisis of the State* (New York: St Martin's Press).

Offe, C. (1984) *The Contradictions of the Welfare State* (London: Hutchinson University Library).

Parkin, F. (1979) *Marxism and Class Theory: A bourgeois critique* (Oxford: Oxford University Press).

Pashukanis, E. B. (1979) *Selected Writings on Marxism and Law* (London and New York: Academic Press).

Polan, A. (1984) *Lenin and the End of Politics* (London: Methuen).

Poulantzas, N. (1973) *Political Power and Social Classes* (London: New Left Books).

Poulantzas, N. (1978) *State, Power, Socialism* (London: New Left Books).

Renner, K. (1949) *The Institutions of Private Law and Their Social Functions* (London: Routledge & Kegan Paul).

Sharpe, L. J. (1984) 'Functional allocation in the welfare state', *Local Government Studies*, January–February, pp. 27–45.

Therborn, G. (1978) *What Does the Ruling Class Do When It Rules?* (London: New Left Books).

Thompson, E. P. (1975) *Whigs and Hunters* (Harmondsworth: Penguin).

Trotsky, L. (1971) *The Struggle Against Fascism in Germany* (New York: Pathfinder).

Wolfe, A. (1977) *The Limits of Legitimacy* (New York: Free Press).

| Bringing the state back in

Theda Skocpol

The autonomy and capacity of states

States conceived as organizations claiming control over territories and people may formulate and pursue goals that are not simply reflective of the demands or interests of social groups, classes, or society. This is what is usually meant by "state autonomy." Unless such independent goal formulation occurs, there is little need to talk about states as important actors. Pursuing matters further, one may then explore the "capacities" of states to implement official goals, especially over the actual or potential opposition of powerful social groups or in the face of recalcitrant socioeconomic circumstances. What are the determinants of state autonomy and state capacities? Let us sample the arguments of a range of recent studies that address these questions.

States as actors
Several lines of reasoning have been used, singly or in combination, to account for why and how states formulate and pursue their own goals. The linkage of states into transnational structures and into international flows of communication may encourage leading state officials to pursue transformative strategies even in the face of indifference or resistance from politically weighty social forces. Similarly, the basic need of states to maintain control and order may spur state-initiated reforms (as well as simple repression). As for who, exactly, is more likely to act in such circumstances, it seems that organizationally coherent collectivities of state officials, especially collectivities of career officials relatively insulated from ties to currently dominant socioeconomic interests, are likely to launch distinctive new state strategies in times of crisis. Likewise, collectivities of officials may elaborate already established public policies

From T. Skocpol, 'Bringing the state back in: current research', in P. B. Evans, D. Reuschemeyer and T. Skocpol (eds.), *Bringing the State Back In* (1985), Cambridge: Cambridge University Press, Chapter 1.

in distinctive ways, acting relatively continuously over long stretches of time.

The extranational orientations of states, the challenges they may face in maintaining domestic order, and the organizational resources that collectivities of state officials may be able to draw on and deploy—all of these features of the state as viewed from a Weberian–Hintzean perspective can help to explain autonomous state action. In an especially clear-cut way, combinations of these factors figure in Alfred Stepan's and Ellen Kay Trimberger's explanations of what may be considered extreme instances of autonomous state action—historical situations in which strategic elites use military force to take control of an entire national state and then employ bureaucratic means to enforce reformist or revolutionary changes from above.

Stepan's book *The State and Society: Peru in comparative perspective* investigates attempts by state elites in Latin America to install "inclusionary" or "exclusionary" corporatist regimes.[1] A key element in Stepan's explanation of such episodes is the formation of a strategically located cadre of officials enjoying great organizational strength inside and through existing state organizations and also enjoying a unified sense of ideological purpose about the possibility and desirability of using state intervention to ensure political order and promote national economic development. For Brazil's "exclusionary" corporatist coup in 1964 and for Peru's "inclusionary" corporatist coup in 1968, Stepan stresses the prior socialization of what he calls "new military professionals." These were career military officers who, together, passed through training schools that taught techniques and ideas of national economic planning and counterinsurgency, along with more traditional military skills. Subsequently, such new military professionals installed corporatist regimes in response to perceived crises of political order and of national economic development. The military professionals used state power to stave off or deflect threats to national order from nondominant classes and groups. They also used state power to implement socioeconomic reforms or plans for further national industrialization, something they saw as a basic requisite for improved international standing in the modern world.

Ellen Kay Trimberger's *Revolution from Above* focuses on a set of historical cases—Japan's Meiji restoration, Turkey's Ataturk revolution, Egypt's Nasser revolution, and Peru's 1968 coup—in which "dynamically autonomous" bureaucrats, including military officials, seized and reorganized state power. Then they used the state to destroy an existing dominant class, a landed upper class or aristocracy, and to reorient national economic development.[2] Like Stepan, Trimberger stresses the formation through prior career interests and socialization of a coherent official elite with a statist and nationalist ideological orientation. She also agrees with Stepan's emphasis on the elite's concern to contain any possible upheavals from below. Yet, perhaps because she is in fact explaining a more thoroughly transformative version of autonomous state action to reshape society, Trimberger places more stress than Stepan on the role of foreign threats to national autonomy as a precipitant of "revolution from above." And she highlights a structural variable that Stepan ignored: the relationship of the state elite to dominant economic classes. As Trimberger puts it, "A bureaucratic state apparatus, or a segment of it, can be said to be relatively autonomous when those who hold high civil and/or military posts satisfy two conditions: (1) they are not recruited from the dominant landed, commercial, or industrial classes; and (2) they do not form close personal and economic ties with those classes after their elevation to high office."[3] Trimberger also examines the state elite's relationship to dominant economic classes in order to predict the extensiveness of socioeconomic changes a state may attempt in response to "a crisis situation—when the existing social, political, and economic order is threatened by external forces and by upheaval from below."[4] State-initiated authoritarian *reforms* may occur when bureaucratic elites retain ties to existing dominant classes, as, for example, in Prussia in 1806–1814, Russia in the 1860s, and Brazil after 1964. But the more sweeping structural changes that Trimberger labels "revolution from above," including the actual dispossession of a dominant class, occur in crisis situations only when bureaucratic state elites are free of ties or alliances with dominant classes.[5] As should be apparent, Trimberger has given the neo-Marxist notion of the relative autonomy of the state new analytical power as a tool for predicting the possible sociopolitical consequences of *various* societal and historical configurations of state and class power.

State autonomy in constitutional polities
Stepan and Trimberger deal in somewhat different, though overlapping, terms with extraordinary instances of state autonomy—instances in which nonconstitutionally ruling officials attempt to use the state as a whole to direct and restructure society and politics. Meanwhile, other scholars have teased out more circumscribed instances of state autonomy in the histories of public policy making in liberal democratic, constitutional polities, such as Britain, Sweden, and the United States.[6] In different forms, the same basic analytical factors—the international orientations of states, their domestic order-keeping functions, and the organizational possibilities for official collectivities to formulate and pursue their own policies—also enter into these analyses.

Hugh Heclo's *Modern Social Politics in Britain and Sweden* provides an intricate comparative-historical account of the long-term development of unemployment insurance and policies of old-age assistance in these two nations.[7] Without being explicitly presented as such, Heclo's book is about autonomous state contributions to social policy making. But the autonomous state actions Heclo highlights are not all acts of coercion or domination; they are, instead, the intellectual activities of civil administrators engaged in diagnosing societal problems and framing policy alternatives to deal with them. As Heclo puts it:

> Governments not only "power" (or whatever the verb form of that approach might be); they also puzzle. Policy-making is a form of collective puzzlement on society's behalf; it entails both deciding and knowing. The process of making pension, unemployment, and superannuation policies has extended beyond deciding what "wants" to accommodate, to include problems of knowing who might want something, what is wanted, what should be wanted, and how to turn even the most sweet-tempered general agreement into concrete collective action. This process is political, not because all policy is a by-product of power and conflict but because some men have undertaken to act in the name of others.[8]

According to Heclo's comparative history, civil service administrators in both Britain and Sweden have consistently made more important contributions to social policy development than political parties or interest groups. Socioeconomic conditions, especially crises, have stimulated only sporadic demands from parties and interest groups, argues Heclo. It has been civil servants, drawing on "administrative resources of information, analysis, and expertise" who have framed the terms of new policy elaborations as "corrective[s] less to social conditions as such and more to the perceived failings of previous policy" in terms of "the government bureaucracy's own conception of what it has been doing."[9] Heclo's evidence also reveals that the autonomous bureaucratic shaping of social policy has been greater in Sweden than in Britain, for Sweden's premodern centralized bureaucratic state was, from the start of industrialization and before the full liberalization and democratization of national politics, in a position to take the initiative in diagnosing social problems and proposing universalistic solutions for administering to them.

Heclo says much less than he might about the influences shaping the timing and content of distinctive state initiatives. He does, however, present evidence of the sensitivity of civil administrators to the requisites of maintaining order in the face of dislocations caused by industrial unemployment. He also points to the constant awareness by administrators of foreign precedents and models of social policy. Above all, Heclo demonstrates that collectivities of administrative officials can have pervasive direct and indirect effects on the content and development of major government policies. His work suggests how to locate and analyze autonomous state contributions to policy making, even within constitutional polities nominally directed by legislatures and electoral parties.

Along these lines, it is worth looking briefly at two works that argue for autonomous state contributions to public policy making even in the United States, a polity in which virtually all scholars agree that there is less structural basis for such autonomy than in any other modern liberal capitalist regime. The United States did *not* inherit a centralized bureaucratic state from preindustrial and predemocratic times. Moreover, the dispersion of authority through the federal system, the division of sovereignty among branches of the national government, and the close symbiosis between segments of the federal administration and Congressional committees all help to ensure that state power in the twentieth-century United States is fragmented, dispersed, and everywhere permeated by organized societal interests. The national government, moreover, lacks such possible underpinnings of strong state power as a prestigious and status-conscious career civil service with predictable access to key executive posts; authoritative planning agencies; direct executive control over a national central bank; and public ownership of strategic parts of the economy. Given such characteristics of the U.S. government, the concept of state autonomy has not often been used by scholars to explain American policy developments.

Nevertheless, Stephen Krasner in his *Defending the National Interest* does use the concept to explain twentieth-century continuities in the formulation of U.S. foreign policy about issues of international investments in the production and marketing of raw materials.[10] A clever heuristic tactic lies behind Krasner's selection of this "issue area" for systematic historical investigation: It is an issue area located at the intersection of properly geopolitical state interests and the economic interests of (often) powerful private corporations. Thus, Krasner can ask whether the short-term push and pull of business interests shapes the definition of the U.S. "national interest" with respect to raw materials production abroad or whether an autonomous state interest is consistently at work. He finds the latter pattern and attributes it to actors in a special location within the otherwise weak, fragmented, and societally permeated U.S. government:

> For U.S. foreign policy the central state actors are the President and the Secretary of State and the most important institutions are the White House and the State Department. What distinguishes these roles and agencies is their high degree of insulation from specific societal pressures and a set of formal and informal obligations that charge them with furthering the nation's general interests.[11]

Unfortunately, Krasner does not expand on the concept of "insulated" parts of the state. In particular, he does not tell us whether various organizational features of state agencies make for greater or lesser insulation. Instead, Krasner primarily emphasizes the degree to which different parts of the federal executive are subject to Congressional influences.[12] And he cannot fully dispel the suspicion that the Presidency and the State Department may simply be subject to class-based rather than interest-based business influences.[13] Nevertheless, he does show that public policies on raw materials have been most likely to diverge from powerful corporate demands precisely when distinctively geopolitical issues of foreign military intervention and broad ideological conceptions of U.S. world hegemony have been involved. Thus, Krasner's study suggests that distinctive state-like contributions to U.S. policy making occur exactly in those instances and arenas where a Weberian–Hintzean perspective would insist that they should occur, no matter how unpropitious the overall governmental potential for autonomous state action. As J. P. Nettl once put it, "Whatever the state may or may not be internally, . . . there have . . . been few challenges to its sovereignty *and* its autonomy in 'foreign affairs.' "[14]

My own work with Kenneth Finegold on the origins of New Deal agricultural policies also suggests that autonomous state contributions to domestic policy making can occur within a "weak state." Such autonomous state contributions happen in specific policy areas at given historical moments, even if they are not generally discernible across all policy areas and even if they unintentionally help to create political forces that subsequently severely circumscribe further autonomous state action.[15] Finegold and I argue that, by the period after World War I, the U.S. Department of Agriculture was "an island of state strength in an ocean of weakness."[16] We attribute the formulation of New Deal agricultural interventions—policies that responded to a long-standing "agrarian crisis" but *not* simply in ways directly demanded by powerful farm interest groups—to the unique resources of administrative capacity, prior public planning, and practical governmental experience available to federal agricultural experts at the dawn of the New Deal. Our argument resembles Hugh Heclo's findings about innovative civil officials in Britain and Sweden. Essentially, we found a *part* of the early-twentieth-century U.S. national government that allowed official expertise to function in a restricted policy area in ways that were similar to the ways it functioned in Sweden, or in Britain between 1900 and 1920.

In addition, however, we trace the political fate of the New Deal's administrative interventions in agriculture. We show that, in the overall context of the U.S. state structure, this initially autonomous state intervention inadvertently strengthened a particular lobbying group, the

American Farm Bureau Federation, and gave it the final increments of electoral and administrative leverage that it needed to "capture" preponderant influence over post-1936 federal agricultural policies. Subsequent state planning efforts, especially those that implied redistribution of economic, racial, or social-class power, were then circumscribed and destroyed by the established commercial farming interests championed by the Farm Bureau.

In short, "state autonomy" is not a fixed structural feature of any governmental system. It can come and go. This is true not only because crises may precipitate the formulation of official strategies and policies by elites or administrators who otherwise might not mobilize their own potentials for autonomous action. It is also true because the very *structural potentials* for autonomous state actions change over time, as the organizations of coercion and administration undergo transformations, both internally and in their relations to societal groups and to representative parts of government. Thus, although cross-national research can indicate in general terms whether a governmental system has "stronger" or "weaker" tendencies toward autonomous state action, the full potential of this concept can be realized only in truly historical studies that are sensitive to structural variations and conjunctural changes within given polities.

Are state actions "rational"?
An additional set of comments must be made about the rationality of autonomous state actions. Often such actions are considered more capable of addressing "the capitalist *class* interest" or "society's general interests" or "the national interest" than are governmental decisions strongly influenced by the push and pull of demands from interest groups, voting blocs, or particular business enterprises.[17] In such perspectives, state officials are judged to be especially capable of formulating holistic and long-term strategies transcending partial, short-sighted demands from profit-seeking capitalists or narrowly self-interested social groups. But scholars skeptical about the notion of state autonomy often respond that state officials' own self-legitimating arguments, their claims to know and represent "general" or "national" interests, should not be taken at face value. State officials have no privileged claims to adequate knowledge of societal problems or solutions for them, argue the skeptics. Besides, their legitimating symbols may merely mask policies formulated to help particular interests or class fractions.

Surely such doubts about the superior rationality of state actions deserve respectful attention; yet we need not entirely dismiss the possibility that partially or fully autonomous state actions *may* be able to address problems and even find "solutions" beyond the reach of societal actors and those parts of government closely constrained by them. Partly, the realization of such possibilities will depend on the availability and (even more problematically) the appropriate use of sound ideas about what the state can and should do to address societal problems. Partly, it will depend on the fit (or lack thereof) between the *scope* of an autonomous state organization's authority and the scale and depth of action appropriate for addressing a given kind of problem. Planning for coordinated systems of national transportation, for example, is unlikely to be achieved by state agencies with authority only over particular regions or kinds of transportation, no matter how knowledgeable and capable of autonomous official action those agencies may be. In sum, autonomous official initiatives can be stupid or misdirected, and autonomous initiatives may be fragmented and partial and work at cross-purposes to one another. Notwithstanding all of these possibilities, however, state actions may sometimes be coherent and appropriate.

Still, no matter how appropriate (for dealing with a given kind of crisis or problem) autonomous state activity might be, it can never really be "disinterested" in any meaningful sense. This is true not only because all state actions necessarily benefit some social interests and disadvantage others (even without the social beneficiaries' having worked for or caused the state actions). More to the point, autonomous state actions will regularly take forms that attempt to reinforce the authority, political longevity, and social control of the state organizations whose incumbents generated the relevant policies or policy ideas. We can hypothesize that one (hidden or overt) feature of all autonomous state actions will be the reinforcement of the prerogatives of collectivities of state officials. Whether rational policies result may depend on how "rational" is defined and might even be largely accidental. The point is that policies different from those demanded by societal actors will be produced. The most basic research task for those interested in state autonomy surely is to explore why, when, and how such distinctive policies are fashioned by states. Then it will be possible to wonder about their rationality for dealing with the problems they address—and we will be able to explore this issue without making starry-eyed assumptions about the omniscience or disinterestedness of states.

Can states achieve their goals?
Some comparative-historical scholars not only have investigated the underpinnings of autonomous state actions, but have also tackled the still more challenging task of explaining the various *capacities* of states to implement their policies. Of course, the explanation of state capacities is closely connected to the explanation of autonomous goal formation by states, because state officials are most likely to try to do

things that seem feasible with the means at hand. Nevertheless, not infrequently, states do pursue goals (whether their own or those pressed on them by powerful social groups) that are beyond their reach. Moreover, the implementation of state policies often leads to unintended as well as intended consequences, both when states attempt tasks they cannot complete and when the means they use produce unforeseen structural changes and sociopolitical reactions. Thus, the capacities of states to implement strategies and policies deserve close analysis in their own right. [. . .]

A few basic things can be said about the general underpinnings of state capacities. Obviously, sheer sovereign integrity and the stable administrative–military control of a given territory are preconditions for any state's ability to implement policies.[18] Beyond this, loyal and skilled officials and plentiful financial resources are basic to state effectiveness in attaining all sorts of goals. It is not surprising that histories of state building zero in on exactly these universal sinews of state power.[19] Certain of these resources come to be rooted in institutional relationships that are slow to change and relatively impervious to short-term manipulations. For example, do state offices attract and retain career-oriented incumbents with a wide array of skills and keen motivation? The answer may well depend on historically evolved relationships among elite educational institutions, state organizations, and private enterprises that compete with the state for educated personnel. The best situation for the state may be a regular flow of elite university graduates, including many with sophisticated technical training, into official careers that are of such high status as to keep the most ambitious and successful from moving on to nonstate positions. But if this situation has not been historically established by the start of the industrial era, it is difficult to undo alternative patterns less favorable to the state.[20]

Factors determining a state's financial resources may be somewhat more manipulable over time, though not always. The amounts and forms of revenues and credit available to a state grow out of structurally conditioned, yet historically shifting political balances and bargains among states and between a state and social classes. Basic sets of facts to sort out in any study of state capacities involve the sources and amounts of state revenues and the degree of flexibility possible in their collection and deployment. Domestic institutional arrangements and international situations set difficult to change limits within which state elites must maneuver to extract taxes and obtain credit: Does a state depend on export taxes (for example, from a scarce national resource or from products vulnerable to sudden world market fluctuations)?[21] Does a nonhegemonic state's geopolitical position allow it to reap the state-building benefits of military aid, or must it rely on international bankers or aid agencies that insist on favoring nonpublic investments and restrict the domestic political options of the borrower state?[22] What established authority does a state have to collect taxes, to borrow, or to invest in potentially profitable public enterprises? And how much "room" is there in the existing constitutional–political system to change patterns of revenue collection unfavorable to the state?

Finally, what authority and organizational means does a state have to deploy whatever financial resources it does enjoy? Are particular kinds of revenues rigidly "earmarked" for special uses that cannot easily be altered by official decision makers?[23] Can the state channel (and manipulate) flows of credit to particular enterprises and industrial sectors, or do established constitutional–political practices favor only aggregate categorical expenditures? All of these *sorts* of questions must be asked in any study of state capacities. The answers to them, taken together, provide the best general insight into the direct and indirect leverage a state is likely to have for realizing any goal it may pursue. A state's means of raising and deploying financial resources tell us more than could any other single factor about its existing (and immediately potential) capacities to create or strengthen state organizations, to employ personnel, to coopt political support, to subsidize economic enterprises, and to fund social programs.[24]

State capacities to pursue specific kinds of policies
Basic questions about a state's territorial integrity, financial means, and staffing may be the place to start in any investigation of its capacities to realize goals; yet the most fruitful studies of state capacities tend to focus on particular policy areas. As Stephen Krasner puts it:

> There is no reason to assume *a priori* that the pattern of strengths and weaknesses will be the same for all policies. One state may be unable to alter the structure of its medical system but be able to construct an efficient transportation network, while another can deal relatively easily with getting its citizens around but cannot get their illnesses cured.[25]

Those who study a comprehensive state-propelled strategy for change, such as a "revolution from above" or a major episode of bureaucratically sponsored reforms, may need to assess the overall capacity of a state to realize transformative goals across multiple spheres. Moreover, as Krasner points out, it may be useful to establish that "despite variations among issue areas within countries, there are modal differences in the power of the state among [for example] the advanced market-economy countries."[26] Nevertheless, such overall assessments are perhaps best built up from sectorally specific investigations, for one of the most important facts about the power of a state may be its *unevenness* across policy areas. And the most telling result, even of a far-reaching revolution or reform from above, may be the *disparate* transformations produced across sociopolitical sectors.

Thus, in a provocative article, "Constitutionalism, class, and the limits of choice in the U.S. foreign policy," Ira Katznelson and Kenneth Prewitt show how U.S. policies toward Latin America have been partly conditioned by the uneven capacities of the American national government: strongly able to intervene abroad, yet lacking the domestic planning capacities necessary "to direct the internal distribution of costs entailed by a less imperialist foreign policy."[27] [. . .]

Many studies of the capacities of states to realize particular kinds of goals use the concept of "policy instrument" to refer to the relevant means that a state may have at its disposal.[28] Cross-national comparisons are necessary to determine the nature and range of institutional mechanisms that state officials may conceivably be able to bring to bear on a given set of issues. For example, Susan and Norman Fainstein compare the urban policies of northwest European nations with those of the United States. Accordingly, they are able to conclude that the U.S. national state lacks certain instruments for dealing with urban crises that are available to European states, instruments such as central planning agencies, state-controlled pools of investment capital, and directly administered national welfare programs.[29]

Analogously, Peter Katzenstein brings together a set of related studies of how six advanced industrial-capitalist countries manage the international trade, investment, and monetary involvements of their economies.[30] Katzenstein is able to draw fairly clear distinctions between the strategies open to states such as the Japanese and the French, which have policy instruments that enable them to apply policies at the level of particular industrial sectors, and other states, such as the British and U.S., which must rely on aggregate macroeconomic manipulations of fiscal and monetary parameters. Once again, as in the Fainstein study, it is the juxtaposition of different nations' approaches to a given policy area that allows relevant policy instruments to be highlighted. Neither study, however, treats such "instruments" as deliberate short-term creations of state managers. Both studies move out toward macroscopic explorations of the broad institutional patterns of divergent national histories that explain why countries now have, or do not have, policy instruments for dealing with particular problems or crises.

States in relation to socioeconomic settings
Fully specified studies of state capacities not only entail examinations of the resources and instruments that states may have for dealing with particular problems; they also necessarily look at more than states as such. They examine states *in relation* to particular kinds of socioecono-

mic and political environments populated by actors with given interests and resources. One obvious use of a relational perspective is to investigate the power of states over domestic or transnational nonstate actors and structures, especially economically dominant ones. What capacities do states have to change the behavior or oppose the demands of such actors or to transform recalcitrant structures? Answers lie not only in features of states themselves, but also in the balances of states' resources and situational advantages compared with those of nonstate actors. This sort of relational approach is used by Stephen Krasner in his exploration of the efforts of U.S. policy makers to implement foreign raw materials policy in interactions with large corporations, whose preferences and established practices have frequently run counter to the state's definition of the national interest.[31] [. . .]

In Peter Katzenstein's *Between Power and Plenty*, [. . .] (as indicated earlier) the object of explanation is ultimately not state *power over* nonstate actors, but nations' strategies for managing "interdependence" within the world capitalist economy. One notion centrally invoked in the Katzenstein collection is that of a "policy network" embodying a patterned relationship between state and society. In Katzenstein's words:

> The actors in society and state influencing the definition of foreign economic policy objectives consist of the major interest groups and political action groups. The former represent the relations of production (including industry, finance, commerce, labor, and agriculture); the latter derive from the structure of political authority (primarily the state bureaucracy and political parties). The governing coalitions . . . in each of the advanced industrial states find their institutional expression in distinct policy networks which link the public and the private sector in the implementation of foreign policy.[32]

Katzenstein argues that the definition and implementation of foreign economic policies grow out of the nexus of state and society. Both state goals and the interests of powerful classes may influence national policy orientations. And the implementation of policies is shaped not only by the policy instruments available to the state, but also by the organized support it receives from key societal groups.

Thus, policy objectives such as industrial reorganization might be effectively implemented because a central state administration controls credit and can intervene in industrial sectors. Yet it may be of equal importance that industries are organized into disciplined associations willing to cooperate with state officials. A complete analysis, in short, requires examination of the organization and interests of the state, specification of the organization and interests of socioeconomic groups, and inquiries into the complementary as well as conflicting relationships of state and societal actors. [. . .]

Bringing the state back in to a central place in analyses of policy making and social change does require a break with some of the most encompassing social-determinist assumptions of pluralism, structure–functionalist developmentalism, and the various neo-Marxisms. But it does not mean that old theoretical emphases should simply be turned on their heads: Studies of states alone are not to be substituted for concerns with classes or groups; nor are purely state-determinist arguments to be fashioned in the place of society-centered explanations. The need to analyze states in relation to socioeconomic and sociocultural contexts is convincingly demonstrated in the best current research on state capacities.

Notes

1. Alfred Stepan, *The State and Society: Peru in comparative perspective*, Chaps. 3 and 4. See also Alfred Stepan, "The new professionalism of internal warfare and military role expansion," in *Authoritarian Brazil*, ed. A. Stepan (New Haven, Conn.: Yale University Press, 1973), pp. 47–65.
2. Ellen Kay Trimberger, *Revolution from Above*.
3. *Ibid.*, p. 4.
4. *Ibid.*, p. 5.
5. Thus, in commenting on Stepan's work, Trimberger argues that he could have explained the repressive and "exclusionary" nature of the Brazilian coup (in contrast to Peru's "inclusionary" reforms, which included mass political mobilization and expropriation of hacienda landlords) by focusing on the Brazilian military's ties to Brazilian and multinational capitalists. In fact, Stepan does report ("The new professionalism," p. 54) that Brazilian military professionals received their training alongside elite civilians, including industrialists, bankers, and commercial elites, who also attended the Superior War College of Brazil in the period before 1964.
6. For France, there is an especially rich literature on state autonomy, its consequences and its limits. I am deliberately leaving it aside here, because France is such an obvious case for the application of ideas about state autonomy. See, however, Stephen Cohen, *Modern Capitalist Planning: The French experience* (Berkeley: University of California Press, 1976); and Richard F. Kuisel, *Capitalism and the State in Modern France: Renovation and economic management in the twentieth century* (Cambridge and New York: Cambridge University Press, 1981).
7. Hugh Heclo, *Modern Social Politics in Britain and Sweden*.
8. *Ibid.*, p. 305.
9. *Ibid.*, pp. 305–6, 303.
10. Stephen Krasner, *Defending the National Interest*.
11. *Ibid.*, p. 11.
12. See also Krasner, "United States commercial and monetary policy", pp. 51–87.
13. Thus, Krasner has the most difficulty in distinguishing his argument for

"state autonomy" from the structural Marxist perspective according to which the state acts for the class interests of capital as a whole. His solution, to stress "nonrational" ideological objectives of state policy as evidence against the class-interest argument, does not strike me as being very convincing. Could an imperialist ideology not be evidence of class consciousness as well as of state purpose? One might stress, instead, the perceived geopolitical "interests" at work in U.S. interventions abroad. "Free-world" justifications for such interventions are not obviously irrational, given certain understandings of U.S. geopolitical interests.

14. J. P. Nettl, "The state as a conceptual variable," *World Politics* 20 (1968), 563–4.

15. Kenneth Finegold and Theda Skocpol, "Capitalists, farmers, and workers in the New Deal – the ironies of government intervention" (paper presented at the annual meeting of the American Political Science Association, Washington, D.C., August 31, 1980). Part of this paper was subsequently published as Theda Skocpol and Kenneth Finegold, "State capacity and economic intervention in the early New Deal," *Political Science Quarterly* 97 (1982): 255–78.

16. Skocpol and Finegold, "State capacity," p. 271.

17. In contrasting ways, both Krasner's *Defending the National Interest* and Poulantzas's *Political Power and Social Classes* exemplify this point.

18. Or perhaps one should say that any state or state-building movement preoccupied with sheer administrative–military control will, at best, only be able (as well as likely) to implement policies connected to that overriding goal. This principle is a good guide to understanding many of the social changes that accompany state-building struggles during revolutionary interregnums.

19. See Tilly, ed., *Formation of National States*; Michael Mann, "State and society, 1130–1815: an analysis of English state finances," *Political Power and Social Theory* (Greenwich, Conn.: JAI Press, 1980), vol. 1, pp. 165–208; and Stephen Skowronek, *Building a New American State: The expansion of national administrative capacities* (Cambridge and New York: Cambridge University Press, 1982).

20. See Bernard Silberman's important comparative-historical work on alternative modes of state bureaucratization in relation to processes of professionalization: "State bureaucratization: a comparative analysis" (Department of Political Science, the University of Chicago, 1982).

21. Windfall revenues from international oil sales, for example, can render states *both* more autonomous from societal controls and, because social roots and political pacts are weak, more vulnerable in moments of crisis. I argue along these lines in "Rentier state and Shi'a Islam in the Iranian Revolution," *Theory and Society* 11 (1982): 265–83. The Joint Committee on the Near and Middle East of the American Council of Learned Societies and the Social Science Research Council currently has a project entitled "Social Change in Arab Oil-Producing Societies" that is investigating the impact of oil revenues on state–society relationships.

22. See Robert E. Wood, "Foreign aid and the capitalist state in underdeveloped countries," *Politics and Society* 10(1) (1980): 1–34. Wood's essay

primarily documents and discusses the anti-state-building effects of most foreign aid, but it also notes that "the 'overdeveloped' military institutions fostered by aid can provide a springboard for statist experimentation unintended by aid donors" (p. 34). Taiwan and South Korea would both seem to be good examples of this.

23. See John A. Dunn, Jr., "The importance of being earmarked: transport policy and highway finance in Great Britain and the United States," *Comparative Studies in Society and History* 20(1) (1978): 29–53.

24. For "classic" statements on the social analysis of state finances, see especially Lorenz von Stein, "On taxation," and Rudolf Goldscheid, "A sociological approach to problems of public finance," both in *Classics in the Theory of Public Finance*, ed. Richard A. Musgrave and Alan T. Peacock (New York: Macmillan, 1958), pp. 202–13 and 28–36, respectively.

25. Krasner, *Defending the National Interest*, p. 58.

26. *Ibid.*

27. Ira Katznelson and Kenneth Prewitt, "Constitutionalism, class, and the limits of choice in U.S. foreign policy," in *Capitalism and the State in U.S.–Latin American Relations*, ed. Richard Fagen (Stanford, Calif.: Stanford University Press, 1979), p. 38.

28. This concept is discussed by Peter Katzenstein in *Between Power and Plenty*, pp. 16, 297–8.

29. Susan S. and Norman I. Fainstein, "National policy and urban development," *Social Problems* 26 (1978): 125–46; see especially pp. 140–1.

30. Katzenstein, ed., *Between Power and Plenty*.

31. Krasner, *Defending the National Interest*, especially Parts 2 and 3.

32. Katzenstein, ed., *Between Power and Plenty*, p. 19.

Part III

Bureaucracy and the state

Introduction

The last part raised the issues about the importance of going beyond the classic debate between pluralism and Marxism to focus upon the character of the state. The German sociologist Max Weber was concerned to show the limitations of Karl Marx's sociology. One area in which this is particularly evident is in his contribution to the analysis of the state, which in many ways provides the crucial starting point for the examination of state autonomy. He was one of the first theorists to draw attention to the importance of the state apparatus, the bureaucracy, for the modern state. The extract from Weber included here starts with a section which locates Weber's theory of bureaucracy in his wider theory of types of authority structures. Weber postulated that the characteristic authority system of the modern state was a 'rational-legal' one, providing thereby a framework of rules to regulate complex institutional life. Within specific organisations, and particularly within state organisations, Weber saw this order as manifested in his concept of bureaucracy. The characteristics of the ideal-typical bureaucracy are set out in the rest of the extract from Weber.

Elsewhere in his work Weber worried about the extent to which bureaucracy offered a device which facilitated democratic government. It might alternatively be a device to reinforce the domination of a dictator or the basis for autonomous state power (rule *for* bureaucracy as opposed to rule *by* bureaucracy). It is this last perspective which inspires the view of bureaucracy set out in the chapter which has been reproduced from a polemical pamphlet by Tullock. Here is a view from the Right of bureaucracy as the very basis for domination by an autonomous state.

As suggested in the extract from Clegg's *Modern Organizations*, Weber's model of bureaucracy has contributed not only to discussion of issues about bureaucratic autonomy but also to consideration of issues about bureaucratic efficiency. Clearly a concern with efficiency is present in Tullock's analysis of the behaviour of bureaucrats. Clegg goes on from the Weberian model to show how this has been contrasted with the classical economic concern with competition as the guarantor of efficiency. But while Tullock seems to approach this issue as one of ideological choice, Clegg offers a sociological analysis which shows how concerns about control have influenced private entrepreneurs to act to replace markets by hierarchies.

Notice once again how analytical issues and normative issues become mixed together. The New Right attacks state bureaucracies for their autonomy and their inefficiency, but a sociological analysis of trends towards bureaucratic organisation in the private sector suggests that there may be economic imperatives which influence this. One of the more paradoxical ingredients in New Right thinking is the extent to which theorists want the state to be weak yet able to counteract monopolistic tendencies in the private sector. The brief excursion into the analysis of private organisations by Clegg has been included here because of the extent to which there is today a concern, extending beyond the ranks of the New Right, to try to introduce into state bureaucracies some of the characteristics of markets. This is attempted either through the breaking up of monolithic organisations, or through the creation of situations in which tasks can be put out to tender to private organisations. This development is examined in the article by Dunleavy in which he looks at the New Right theory used to justify these moves, but then goes on to argue that if we are to give attention to the motivation structures of bureaucrats we are likely to find that they are more complex than is suggested in Tullock's analysis. He offers us a model which sees bureaucrats as 'bureau-shapers' but not necessarily 'bureau-maximisers'. Dunleavy's analysis has been developed further in his book *Democracy, Bureaucracy and Public Choice*.

This part, therefore, is an introduction in general terms, and in terms of the contrast which has been drawn between the bureaucracy as the typical and perhaps the ideal model for state activities and the market alternative, which has been presented as preferable to state bureaucracy and increasingly recently as potentially introducible within the public sector. What must finally be emphasised, regardless of the stand taken on this argument, is that the policy-making process in the modern state is one which takes place within and between complex organisations, all of which may be loosely described as bureaucracies. For this reason we return to issues about the impact of organisations and about behaviour within organisations throughout the rest of this reader.

References

Dunleavy, P., *Democracy, Bureaucracy and Public Choice* (Hemel Hempstead, Harvester Wheatsheaf, 1991).

Rational-legal authority and bureaucracy

Max Weber

The three pure types of legitimate authority
There are three pure types of legitimate authority. The validity of their claims to legitimacy may be based on:

1. Rational grounds—resting on a belief in the 'legality' of patterns of normative rules and the right of those elevated to authority under such rules to issue commands (legal authority).
2. Traditional grounds—resting on an established belief in the sanctity of immemorial traditions and the legitimacy of the status of those exercising authority under them (traditional authority); or finally,
3. Charismatic grounds—resting on devotion to the specific and exceptional sanctity, heroism or exemplary character of an individual person, and of the normative patterns or order revealed or ordained by him (charismatic authority).

In the case of legal authority, obedience is owed to the legally established impersonal order. It extends to the persons exercising the authority of office under it only by virtue of the formal legality of their commands and only within the scope of authority of the office. In the case of traditional authority, obedience is owed to the *person* of the chief who occupies the traditionally sanctioned position of authority and who is (within its sphere) bound by tradition. But here the obligation of obedience is not based on the impersonal order, but is a matter of personal loyalty within the area of accustomed obligations. In the case of charismatic authority, it is the charismatically qualified leader as such who is obeyed by virtue of personal trust in him and his revelation, his heroism or his exemplary qualities so far as they fall within the scope of the individual's belief in his charisma. [. . .]

From M. Weber, *The Theory of Social and Economic Organization* (1947), edited and translated by T. Parsons, New York: The Free Press.

Legal authority with a bureaucratic administrative staff

Legal authority: the pure type with employment of a bureaucratic administrative staff
The effectiveness of legal authority rests on the acceptance of the validity of the following mutually inter-dependent ideas.

1. That any given legal norm may be established by agreement or by imposition, on grounds of expediency or rational values or both, with a claim to obedience at least on the part of the members of the corporate group. This is, however, usually extended to include all persons within the sphere of authority or of power in question—which in the case of territorial bodies is the territorial area—who stand in certain social relationships or carry out forms of social action which in the order governing the corporate group have been declared to be relevant.

2. That every body of law consists essentially in a consistent system of abstract rules which have normally been intentionally established. Furthermore, administration of law is held to consist in the application of these rules to particular cases; the administrative process in the rational pursuit of the interests which are specified in the order governing the corporate group within the limits laid down by legal precepts and following principles which are capable of generalized formulation and are approved in the order governing the group, or at least not disapproved in it.

3. That thus the typical person in authority occupies an 'office.' In the action associated with his status, including the commands he issues to others, he is subject to an impersonal order to which his actions are oriented. This is true not only for persons exercising legal authority who are in the usual sense 'officials,' but, for instance, for the elected president of a state.

4. That the person who obeys authority does so, as it is usually stated, only in his capacity as a 'member' of the corporate group and what he obeys is only 'the law.' He may in this connexion be the member of an association, of a territorial commune, of a church, or a citizen of a state.

5. In conformity with point 3, it is held that the members of the corporate group, in so far as they obey a person in authority, do not owe this obedience to him as an individual, but to the impersonal order. Hence, it follows that there is an obligation to obedience only within the sphere of the rationally delimited authority which, in terms of the order, has been conferred upon him.

The following may thus be said to be the fundamental categories of rational legal authority:

(1) A continuous organization of official functions bound by rules.

(2) A specified sphere of competence. This involves (a) a sphere of obligations to perform functions which has been marked off as part of a systematic division of labour. (b) The provision of the incumbent with the necessary authority to carry out these functions. (c) That the necessary means of compulsion are clearly defined and their use is subject to definite conditions. A unit exercising authority which is organized in this way will be called an 'administrative organ.'

There are administrative organs in this sense in large-scale private organizations, in parties and armies, as well as in the state and the church. An elected president, a cabinet of ministers, or a body of elected representatives also in this sense constitute administrative organs. [. . .] Not every administrative organ is provided with compulsory powers. But this distinction is not important for present purposes.

(3) The organization of offices follows the principle of hierarchy; that is, each lower office is under the control and supervision of a higher one. There is a right of appeal and of statement of grievances from the lower to the higher. Hierarchies differ in respect to whether and in what cases complaints can lead to a ruling from an authority at various points higher in the scale, and as to whether changes are imposed from higher up or the responsibility for such changes is left to the lower office, the conduct of which was the subject of complaint.

(4) The rules which regulate the conduct of an office may be technical rules or norms. In both cases, if their application is to be fully rational, specialized training is necessary. It is thus normally true that only a person who has demonstrated an adequate technical training is qualified to be a member of the administrative staff of such an organized group, and hence only such persons are eligible for appointment to official positions. The administrative staff of a rational corporate group thus typically consists of 'officials,' whether the organization be devoted to political, religious, economic—in particular, capitalistic—or other ends.

(5) In the rational type it is a matter of principle that the members of the administrative staff should be completely separated from ownership of the means of production or administration. Officials, employees, and workers attached to the administrative staff do not themselves own the non-human means of production and administration. These are rather provided for their use in kind or in money, and the official is obligated to render an accounting of their use. There exists, furthermore, in principle complete separation of the property belonging to the organization, which is controlled within the sphere of office, and the personal property of the official, which is available for his own private uses. There is a corresponding separation of the place in which official functions are carried out, the 'office' in the sense of premises, from living quarters.

(6) In the rational-type case, there is also a complete absence of appropriation of his official position by the incumbent. Where 'rights' to an office exist, as in the case of judges, and recently of an increasing proportion of officials and even of workers, they do not normally serve the purpose of appropriation by the official, but of securing the purely objective and independent character of the conduct of the office so that it is oriented only to the relevant norms.

(7) Administrative acts, decisions, and rules are formulated and recorded in writing, even in cases where oral discussion is the rule or is even mandatory. This applies at least to preliminary discussions and proposals, to final decisions, and to all sorts of orders and rules. The combination of written documents and a continuous organization of official functions constitutes the 'office' which is the central focus of all types of modern corporate action.

(8) Legal authority can be exercised in a wide variety of different forms [. . .]. The following analysis will be deliberately confined for the most part to the aspect of imperative co-ordination in the structure of the administrative staff. It will consist in an analysis in terms of ideal types of officialdom or 'bureaucracy.'

In the above outline no mention has been made of the kind of supreme head appropriate to a system of legal authority. This is a consequence of certain considerations which can only be made entirely understandable at a later stage in the analysis. There are very important types of rational imperative co-ordination which, with respect to the ultimate source of authority, belong to other categories. This is true of the hereditary charismatic type, as illustrated by hereditary monarchy and of the pure charismatic type of a president chosen by plebiscite. Other cases involve rational elements at important points, but are made up of a combination of bureaucratic and charismatic components, as is true of the cabinet form of government. Still others are subject to the authority of the chief of other corporate groups, whether their character be charismatic or bureaucratic; thus the formal head of a government department under a parliamentary regime may be a minister who occupies his position because of his authority in a party. The type of rational, legal administrative staff is capable of application in all kinds of situations and contexts. It is the most important mechanism for the administration of everyday profane affairs. For in that sphere, the exercise of authority and, more broadly, imperative co-ordination, consists precisely in administration.

Legal authority: the pure type with employment of a bureaucratic administrative staff—(continued)
The purest type of exercise of legal authority is that which employs a bureaucratic administrative staff. Only the supreme chief of the orga-

nization occupies his position of authority by virtue of appropriation, of election, or of having been designated for the succession. But even *his* authority consists in a sphere of legal 'competence.' The whole administrative staff under the supreme authority then consists, in the purest type, of individual officials who are appointed and function according to the following criteria:

(1) They are personally free and subject to authority only with respect to their impersonal official obligations.

(2) They are organized in a clearly defined hierarchy of offices.

(3) Each office has a clearly defined sphere of competence in the legal sense.

(4) The office is filled by a free contractual relationship. Thus, in principle, there is free selection.

(5) Candidates are selected on the basis of technical qualifications. In the most rational case, this is tested by examination or guaranteed by diplomas certifying technical training, or both. They are *appointed*, not elected.

(6) They are remunerated by fixed salaries in money, for the most part with a right to pensions. Only under certain circumstances does the employing authority, especially in private organizations, have a right to terminate the appointment, but the official is always free to resign. The salary scale is primarily graded according to rank in the hierarchy; but in addition to this criterion, the responsibility of the position and the requirements of the incumbent's social status may be taken into account.

(7) The office is treated as the sole, or at least the primary, occupation of the incumbent.

(8) It constitutes a career. There is a system of 'promotion' according to seniority or to achievement, or both. Promotion is dependent on the judgement of superiors.

(9) The official works entirely separated from ownership of the means of administration and without appropriation of his position.

(10) He is subject to strict and systematic discipline and control in the conduct of the office.

The economic theory of bureaucracy

Gordon Tullock

Bureaucracy

Bureaucrats are like other men. This proposition sounds very simple and straightforward, but the consequences are a radical departure from orthodox economic theory.

If bureaucrats are ordinary men, they will make most of (not all) their decisions in terms of what benefits them, not society as a whole. Like other men, they may occasionally sacrifice their own well-being for the wider good, but we should expect this to be exceptional behaviour.

Most of the existing literature on the machinery of government assumes that, when an activity is delegated to a bureaucrat, he will either carry out the rules and regulations or will make decisions in the public interest regardless of whether it benefits him or not. We do not make this assumption about businessmen. We do not make it about consumers in the market. I see no reason why we should make it about bureaucrats.

Bureaucrats and businessmen
A businessman, in an environment that is reasonably competitive and without severe externalities, will normally make a decision which is more or less in accord with the well-being of society, but not because he is consciously *aiming* at the public good. His general aim is simply to make as much money as he can, and he makes the most by doing what is in the social interest. The bureaucrat will also do what is in the social interest if the constraints to which he is subject are such that his own personal interest is identical to the social interest.

The theory of bureaucracy should be based upon the assumption that bureaucrats are as self-seeking as businessmen, and it should concern

From G. Tullock, *The Vote Motive* (1976), London: Institute of Economic Affairs.

itself with the design of constraints which will make the bureaucrats' self-interest identical with the interests of society. We should not expect the identity to be perfect – we do not have perfection in the market – but we should expect at least a high correlation. Unfortunately it is harder to arrange such a high correlation in a bureaucratic context than in the market [. . .]. To return to the main theme of this paper, since we have no perfect solution we must choose among imperfect instrumentalities. What, then, are the imperfections of the bureaucratic process?

Bureaucrats and elected representatives
In most modern countries, an immense number of decisions are taken by bureaucrats. They are supposedly in accord with the decisions of the elected representatives in democracies (or of the dictator in despotisms); but often the influence of these representatives is in practice modest. Indeed there seems now to be developing a mystique under which the bureaucrats are not even supposed to be under the control of elected officials. [. . .] The view that many decisions should be separated from political control by being put solely under the control of bureaucrats (sometimes in that oldest branch of the bureaucracy, the judiciary) is wide-spread.

Motives of bureaucrats
What does happen in a bureaucracy? What are the motivations of bureaucrats? Like everyone else, bureaucrats presumably try to improve their own utility. Their utility, again like everyone else's, is partly based upon their immediate ability to consume goods and partly on their appreciation of good things happening to other people. In other words, they are partly selfish and partly public-interested.

In most business activities, the approximation that the businessman is trying to maximise his money income turns out to work rather well, although seldom perfectly. In the bureaucracy, we would like a somewhat similar approximation. If we look over aims in which a bureaucrat might be interested, we can begin by listing those which are of primary concern to him: his salary, his conditions of work – office furniture, etc. (strictly apportioned according to rank in most bureaucracies), his power over other people, his public respect and reputation. In addition to these self-regarding values, let us assume he is also interested in the public good and consciously wants to accomplish something in his job. We can easily think of circumstances in which the two would be in clear conflict. Mr James Smith, for example, is due for promotion to department head, a job which will lead in due course to his becoming Sir James; but Mr Charles Brown is the best man for the job. It is, on the whole, doubtful whether Mr Smith will bring that truth firmly to the attention of his superiors.

On the other hand, we will easily find circumstances where Mr Smith would, for purely *selfish* reasons, be motivated to serve the interest of society. If we assume in this example that he is much abler than Mr Brown, his *selfish* motives would point in the correct direction.

(One of the advantages of the simple profit-maximising assumption in business is that it permits us to assume a single 'maximand' and make calculations. If we consider the businessman as maximising his utility . . . we no longer have as easy a problem. His utility is, to him, a simple 'function' which he can maximise; but, to us as outsiders, what is observed is a number of different elements, such as his income, respect in his profession, the beauty of his secretary, other aspects of his office, etc. We would have to work out a complex function of all those variables and them attempt to maximise it; and this complex function would have to be identical to the one he uses in utility maximising. In general, economists have abandoned this problem, and assume a simple, single goal: the profit. The loss in accuracy is fortunately slight.)

What does the bureaucrat try to maximise?
Is there a similar maximand we can use for bureaucracies? The answer is, unfortunately, 'No', if we want to be completely general. Bureaucrats tend to maximise different collections of activity. But it is true that if we confine ourselves to the type of bureaucracy found in most Western countries, there is a 'not bad' approximation: *size*.

As a general rule, a bureaucrat will find that his possibilities for promotion increase, his power, influence, and public respect improve, and even the physical conditions of his office improve, if the bureaucracy in which he works expands. This proposition is fairly general. Almost any bureaucrat gains at least something if the *whole* bureaucracy expands. He gains more, however, if *his* Ministry expands, and more yet if the *sub*-division in which he is employed expands.

I have confined this proposition to *most* bureaucracies in *modern Western democracies*. It is not necessarily true of all these bureaucracies, or of bureaucracies in other political systems. The real issue here is whether the reward structure in the bureaucracy is such that people gain when their burden expands. This is not necessarily true everywhere. Further, there is one important limitation on profit-maximisation which also applies to size-maximisation for bureaucrats: in general, people do not like hard work!

A bureaucrat ordered to do research on, say, improving the bid process for North Sea oil is presumably not totally uninterested in discovering a better method of letting the bids; but he is apt to give more consideration to the opportunity this project gives him to expand the size of his office, and hence improve his probability of promotion, prestige, etc. However, it is by no means certain that he will work hard to achieve either of these goals. Indeed, in the pathological case, he will devote the bulk of this time to essentially leisure activities (some of which, like reading history or solving crosswords, may be located in his office), and time he devotes to work will be solely devoted to an effort to expand his office with no concern at all for its ostensible object. In the more normal non-pathological case, although he may not engage in what we would normally refer to as hard work, he will devote a good deal of attention both to improving the bid process and to using the project to expand his office.

Assume the bureaucrats are simply attempting to maximise the size of their bureaucracies and leave aside, for the time being, their desire to consume leisure (technically described as 'shirking' in the management literature). Economists have gone a long way with their simple, one-argument 'utility function' for businessmen (profit-maximisation); if we cannot get as far with our one-argument utility function for bureaucrats (size-maximisation), at least we should make some progress.

Improving the bureaucracy
One way of improving the size of a bureaucracy is to do a good enough job so that people want more of the activity it is producing. [. . .]

To examine the matter a little more formally, assume that a government activity, say police protection, is produced at constant cost, represented by the horizontal line on Figure 1. The demand for it (DD) should slant downward as in Figure 1, and can be thought of as a demand of the citizenry, or of the higher level of government, i.e. the legislature or, perhaps, of the cabinet.

The usual way of organising and supplying the police is to create a series of regional monopolies, all the police in, say, Liverpool being organised under one control. It has its own decision-making process and its own ends (although much writing on administration implicitly assumes otherwise).

If it were somehow possible to buy police services competitively, individuals buying it and competing companies supplying it, the optimum amount would be obtained at point O, the cost would be the rectangle below and to the left of point O, and the consumer surplus generated for the citizenry shown by the triangle DCO.

If we assume the citizenry continue to buy police services independently (we are assuming this is technologically feasible), but they are supplied by a profit-maximising monopoly, it would provide M units of police service at a price of M', and make a profit equivalent to the rectangle above the cost line and to the left of line M. There would still be some consumer surplus, but clearly the consumers would be in a much worse situation than with competitive suppliers.

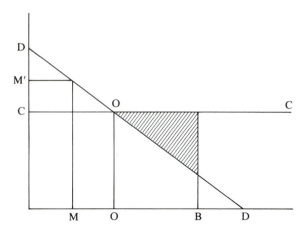

Figure 1 Supply and demand for police services

Let us now more realistically assume that the individuals are not
purchasing the police services as individuals but through a governmental
agency which has a demand for police services derived from the demand
of the individual citizens. The supplier is also a monopoly: there is only
one police force in Liverpool; and let us assume that the police attempt
to maximise the size of their bureaucracy. What is the likely outcome?

Single buyer v. single seller
First, we have a monopsony (single buyer) against monopoly (single
seller), and this is always a difficult situation for economists to analyse.
What would happen if one or the other of the two had everything his
own way? If the legislature is in complete control of the situation and
has a perfect idea of the cost structure facing the police, they could offer
the rectangle left of and below O to the police in return for the police
producing O amount of police protection, and we would have the same
solution as in free competition.

If the police have everything on their side, which means they are able
to conceal their own cost from the legislature, they can misrepresent the
cost of providing various amounts of police services, and the legislature
will not be able to discover their true 'production function'. We then get
a most extraordinary situation. The police will provide B police services
and charge the amount of the rectangle under the cost line and to the
left of B. This means that for the marginal police services they are
charging more than they receive and there is a net social waste shown by
the shaded triangle. They are able to get away with this, however,
because the size of the shaded triangle is the same as DCO. As a
perfectly discriminating monopolist always will, they have squeezed out

the entire consumer surplus, but have spent it on providing additional police services.

How do we reach this conclusion? The police department is not assumed to be profit-maximising (it is not possible for the policemen simply to pocket any profit they make), but they are benefited in various ways by the expansion in the size of the force. Since we assume that they are exploiting the demand curve to the maximum, they are also maximising their size by this socially wasteful expansion.

This situation is the ultimate result which could be expected if the bureaucracy worked hard at expanding its budget and was able to exploit the full monopoly gains in all-or-nothing bargaining from the legislature. The taxpayer would be indifferent to having the existing police force or no police force at all, which, of course, also makes possible much lower taxes. It seems doubtful whether any existing bureaucracy has reached this position. Many bureaucracies, from the standpoint of the citizen-taxpayers as a whole, may be beyond this point; but that is because they are satisfying the demands of some persistent and voluble minority. In these circumstances, a true demand curve would be that of the minority and, once again, I doubt whether many real-world bureaucracies have succeeded in exploiting their monopoly positions to the full.

There are a number of reasons why bureaucracies would not be able to reach this goal with any degree of regularity. First, and obviously, the legislature or purchaser of the services from the bureaucracy characteristically has at least some information about the production function of the bureaucracy and is not subject to what we might call 'complete' exploitation. Secondly, since the members of the bureaucracy among other things want leisure, they are unlikely to put in the concentration and hard work required to exploit the legislature to the theoretical maximum.

Ironically, the desire for leisure – what we normally call laziness – has a net benefit for society. Suppose the individuals in the bureaucracy work hard enough to get only 80 per cent of what they could if they devoted full force to achieving it. The cost level line in the diagram would be adjusted upward to indicate that you have to hire more policemen to get a given amount of protection. This clearly would be a disadvantage for the taxpayer-citizen. On the other hand, the bureaucracy in negotiating with the legislature would not get all of the welfare triangle; it would leave 20 per cent of it to the citizen. The citizen would therefore derive some benefit from the service, although if the policemen were energetic and hard-working in both 'policing' and exploiting the legislature, the consumer surplus would be entirely consumed in producing 'efficiently' police services not worth their cost. The citizen-taxpayer is better off with lazy servants than with diligent ones here, but this results simply because the diligent ones will use their diligence to extract surplus value from him.

Odds with the bureaucracy

Does the bureaucracy in practice extort its entire theoretically possible gain from the legislature? This is the classic monopoly-against-monopsony problem, and economists normally say it is insoluble. But there are good reasons for believing the odds will be heavily on the side of the bureaucracy. It will have a good idea of the legislative demand for its services, which is essentially derived from the voters' demand. The bureaucracy has access to the newspapers, television, etc., and therefore has a good idea of the popular demand. In the circumstances, the legislature is not able to keep its demand curve a secret.

These factors are exaggerated by two special characteristics of governmental demand. First, most government demands are organised by special interest pressure groups, like the farmers, who normally are intimately connected with the bureaucracy which will carry out the policy, the Ministry of Agriculture, which, in turn, is therefore very well informed about the political pressures that can be brought to bear upon Parliament and the government. Secondly, a good part of the demand for bureaucratic services comes not from the people who will *receive* them but from those who will be paid to *supply* them. The bureaucrat who works for the Minister of Agriculture, or the policeman who works for the chief constable, is also a voter. In voting, he (and his family) have two demands for their bureaucracy's service. First, they, like other citizens, gain whatever benefits it generates; but, secondly, they gain privately from the payments made to them.

They are part of the demand for their own services, and a particularly important part. They combine very good information about their bureau with strong motivation. And, indeed, they seem to represent a larger percentage of the voting population than of the total population, because they are more likely to vote. Rough estimates in the United States indicate that about one out of five Americans derives his support from a government job in the family, but about one out of four voters does so.

If the bureaucracy has a good idea of the demand for the service, the government has difficulty determining the cost of providing it. In general, the only source of such information is the bureaucracy, which is apt not only to say that economies are impossible but also, if economies are imposed, to act so as to maximise their cost instead of attempting to do the best job it can in the new circumstances.

Bureaucrats resist 'cuts' by superior knowledge

Three examples readily come to mind. The first occurred when I was serving on the council of the American Political Science Association.

We were in one of the budget crises which afflict learned societies from time to time. The APSA maintains in Washington, DC, a large office, engaged in not too well defined activities. It was suggested that one of the ways we could escape from our budget problem was to reduce expenses in this office. The permanent secretary of the society, who had been responsible for building up the office after he was appointed, immediately said that 'Yes, that could be done'; it would be possible for him to lay off two or three of the employees in the subscription service branch, i.e. those who took care of seeing to it that everyone got their *American Political Review, P.S.*, and other documents circulated to members. The result clearly would be that members were inconvenienced. He did not suggest that any of the 'policy officials' might be dispensed with, although it was never clear what the bulk of them were doing.

My second example involves the Federal Customs Service. Its budget was reduced. The civil servant in charge laid off every Customs Inspector in the United States but not one person in any other part of the Customs Service. This was too extreme, and he was transferred in a burst of unfavourable publicity; but he was not fired.

The third case, more recent, concerns newspaper reports that the Immigration Service is deliberately investing its resources in office staff rather than in Inspectors to make it necessary for Congress to increase its budget.

This kind of behaviour is common with bureaucracies; and, in general, congressmen have found it difficult to prevent. Professor William Niskanen, whose book *Bureaucracy and Representative Government*[1] rigorously develops the size-maximising principle, spent most of his life before writing it as an economist in the Department of Defense, attempting to improve its efficiency. Immediately after writing the book, he moved to a higher-level agency, the Office of Management and Budget, the general control agency of the United States government, and found that there, too, it was impossible for him to outmanoeuvre the bureaucrats because they simply knew more about their departments than he did.

Solutions: more information? – reducing bureau monopoly?
What can be done? First, an attempt to develop expertise at the upper layer is required to which the whole development of cost-benefit analysis is directed. More information would help, but it is not obviously going to lead to much improvement. What is needed is some way of lowering the bargaining potential of the monopoly bureaus.

In the market place we do not try to discover the cost structure of companies from whom we buy products or service. All we do is compare the prices and services offered by organisations and choose the one that suits us best. The existence of a monopoly, of course, makes it hard for us to do this, and we tend to feel disadvantaged. Is there some way in which we could provide for Parliament or Congress the same ability to select the lowest price rather than putting upon it the burden of determining the operating efficiency of the bureaucracy? The answer, fortunately, is that such possibilities often exist, and as far as we can tell they improve efficiency.

First, although most government services are produced under monopoly conditions, some are produced with varying degrees of competition. It is very hard to get measures of efficiency, but something can be done. Examining the data,[2] we find that the least efficient bureaus are those which have perfect monopolies.

Second, where, although the individual bureau has a monopoly in one area, several bureaus operate in different areas, the legislature can at least compare cost curves. The police forces, which in both the United States and Britain are organised as a series of local monopolies (except for privately supplied police services) rather than as a national service, are an example. There are, of course, many others, such as refuse-collection, fire-fighting, education, sewerage, etc.

Third, still more efficient are government bureaus which provide a service that is also supplied by private companies. Waste removal in the United States, for example, is sometimes a government activity and sometimes carried out by private companies charging a contract fee. So far as we can tell, the government bureaus, although not as efficient as the private companies (as measured by price and service), are neverthe-less markedly more efficient than government bureaus which do not face private competition.

Government bureaus, even in this final negative situation, are almost never as efficient as private companies in a competitive industry.

The question of the efficiency of private industry in monopolistic situations, of course, is not at issue here, since no one (so far as I know) regards this as a particularly desirable organisation of the economy. The reason is simple (Figure 1). If one company protected by a high tariff has a monopoly in motor-car production in its home market, the demand curve is for motor-cars in total. If there are two companies, the motorist who is thinking whether or not to buy a car also has the alternative of buying it from the other company. Similarly with a bureaucracy: the more the competition, the more it is forced to produce close to the optimum output and productive efficiency one would anticipate in a competitive industry.

Introducing competition into the bureaucracy

(a) COMPETITION WITHIN BUREAUS
Can we introduce competition into bureaucracy? First, we could simply stop enacting cartel legislation. Most 'efficiency' studies of government

have attempted to root out competition (called 'duplication'). In the United States' automobile market, not only is General Motors 'duplicated' by Ford, Chrysler and American Motors, but a lot of odd foreigners like British Leyland, Fiat, Volkswagen, and Toyota are also 'duplicating activity'. Wouldn't we be much more efficient if we abolished 'duplication'?

The absurdity of this proposition would not in any way be reduced if we substituted a government service for production of motor-cars. In the United States, highways are characteristically constructed by a large number of private companies. Their repair and maintenance, however, is normally done by monopolistic government enterprises. In some areas – Blacksburg, Virginia, where I live, is an example – a good deal of the maintenance is let out on bids to competing private companies. We pay lower repair prices than we would if a monopolistic agency was doing all the repairing. Furthermore, the competing companies ready and willing to replace bureaucracies in other cities and counties also make the road repair bureaucracies there careful about prices.

Thus one way of increasing the competitiveness of government services is simply to contract them out. Many services are contracted out in various places in the world. The entire line of public utilities – telephone, telegraph, radio and television transmission, water supply, sewage removal, electricity, and gas – are sometimes provided privately and sometimes publicly. Usually the private companies are given some kind of government monopoly, which sharply reduces their efficiency; but sometimes one or more of the utilities are generated by competing private companies. It is not obvious that this arrangement is ideal, but it would certainly be worth careful investigation. The mere act of looking into this possibility would probably lead to very sharp improvements in efficiency in the corresponding government agencies.

There are also many other government activities which can be performed by private agencies on contract. Fire protection is, in general, a government activity, but for some obscure reason a private fire protection industry has developed in the state of Arizona. The private fire protection companies enter into contracts with the smaller cities to provide them with fire protection, and also offer their services to private individuals. Comparative studies[3] seem to indicate that the private companies provide fire protection for about *half* the cost of public fire departments serving similar communities. Further, the private companies – tiny though they are – have been the cutting edge of scientific progress in the fire protection industry. They have invented an entirely new technology which, granted the extraordinarily small funds they have for research, is a remarkable achievement. This technology is beginning to spread through the United States government fire departments, but only very slowly, since there are few fire commissioners who really want to cut their budgets in half.

(b) COMPETITION BETWEEN BUREAUS

A second way to impose competition on bureaucracies is to retain
bureaucratic control but permit competition within it. The area served
by a bureaucracy might simply be divided into smaller areas with
separate budgets. It would help efficiency if Parliament made a habit of
changing the geographic scope of the small bureaucracies handling, say,
police protection. If, for example, the Commander in charge of division
I seems to have done better one year than the Commander in charge of
neighbouring division II, 15 per cent of II might be added to I, the
Commander of I promoted, and the Commander of II reduced. In the
following year, at the very least a good deal of thought on methods of
improving efficiency by both might be expected. Perhaps the 15 per cent
could be shifted back at the end of the next year.

Notes

1. Aldine-Atherton, New York, 1971; the argument is summarised in
   Bureaucracy: Servant or master?, Hobart Paperback No. 5, IEA, 1973.
2. Thomas E. Borcherding (ed.), *Budgets and Bureaucrats: The origins of
   government growth*, Duke University Press, Durham, NC, 1976.
3. A popular account of this phenomenon is William C. Wooldridge, *Uncle
   Sam, the Monopoly Man*, Arlington House, New Rochelle, NY, 1970, pp.
   124–7. For a more scholarly account, Roger Ahlbrandt, 'Efficiency in the
   provision of fire services', *Public Choice*, XVI, Fall 1973, pp. 1–15.

Efficiency rules, OK?

Weber and the economic enterprise alternatives

Stewart Clegg

Weber and efficiency

How and why did bureaucracy become dominant? To answer this question we have to step outside the framework of descriptive analytical theories of organizations [. . .] which tell us *how* organizations are. If we want to know *why* they are like that, another framework is required altogether, it would seem.

In what are probably the most frequently cited words that Weber ever wrote on the subject of organizations, it seems as if the 'why?' question is answered unambiguously in terms of efficiency:

> The fully developed bureaucratic mechanism compares with other organizations exactly as does the machine with the non-mechanical modes of production . . . Precision, speed, unambiguity, unity, strict subordination, reduction of friction and of material and personal costs – these are raised to the optimum point in the strictly bureaucratic administration, and especially in its monocratic form. (Weber 1948: 214)

Certainly, Weber has often been interpreted in this passage as offering a eulogy to bureaucracy (for example, Blau and Scott 1963). However, as Albrow (1970: 63) points out, 'It would be quite misleading to equate Weber's concept of formal rationality with the idea of efficiency.' What Weber realized only too clearly was that 'technical formal rationality' was not necessarily the equivalent of 'efficiency'. Not only was 'efficiency' a 'foreign' term to Weber (see Albrow 1970: 64), but, even in those terms he made his own, its achievement would have

From S. R. Clegg, *Modern Organizations* (1990), London: Sage Publications.

required more than sheer technique alone. It also required a normative, moral context of value which could only be given culturally, rather than instrumentally. Rather than the spread of bureaucracy being due solely to its instrumental efficiency, according to Weber, it would be more correct to point to the cultural conditions of 'rationalization' as the appropriate explanation. Such a cultural explanation points to the *institutionalization* of value as the overarching factor in interpreting the rise of particular types of organization. The iron cage is a cultural construct rather than a rational constraint.

Had Weber wanted to make an argument linking efficiency to bureaucracy he would certainly have found it easy to do so. He was, after all, thoroughly familiar with the tradition of Austrian marginalist economics (Therborn 1976: 290–5) in which such connections had been drawn. However, had he followed this path it is doubtful that the linkage would have been a positive one. Had Weber embraced an argument which linked bureaucracy to the achievement of efficiency it would have been necessary to mount a counter-argument to the marginalist position. From the perspective of marginalism what was most striking about bureaucracy was its inefficiency rather than its efficiency. Simply stated, this position regarded voluntary and reciprocally oriented transactions between individuals to be the maximally efficient form of exchange. Bureaucracy, rather than facilitating the market in these, instead interposes the heavy hand of centralized authority which overrides freely contracting individuals.

Hayek, markets and efficiency

From a marginalist economic perspective, order does not have to be organized: it is something which can emerge spontaneously, if it is not subject to interference. As Friedrich Hayek (1944: 21) argues, 'the commands as well as the rules which govern an organization serve particular results aimed at by those who are in command of the organization', as opposed to that 'spontaneous order' which the market can provide. Organizations, whether public or private bureaucracies (but particularly those of organized labour), distort the spontaneous order of the market (Hayek 1967). Against the necessity of organization which Weber argues for, Hayek would favour decentralization and de-authorization of action to aid the spontaneous formation of coalitions entered into by freely contracting subjects, untrammelled by the hands-on authority of any organizations.

For Hayek the market is a source of spontaneous order. It is the market which resolves the Hobbesian mystery. Social order is possible because of the myriad free and independent decisions to buy and sell on the market which the price mechanism allows. No system of central planning could achieve the same effects, he argues. Thus, organizations, as such systems, must be a second-best alternative to markets (and their very existence, of course, destroys 'fair' markets). The emergent basis of market order is premised upon the free decisions of many disconnected individuals, often based upon the most tacit and implicit of knowledge, who are brought into a relationship with each other simply through decisions to buy and sell, decisions effected through the 'price mechanism'. Planning could not hope to replicate the implicit, tacit and differentiated bases of this order. It could only ever be a stage on *The Road to Serfdom* (Hayek 1944).

Where planning fails, Hayek believes that a vicious cycle will set in, unless things are then left to markets. Otherwise, ever grander and more ambitious plans will seek to compensate for the failures of earlier ones. Such a fetish of planning will be doomed to failure. Planning fails because of the impossibility of any omnipotence capable of centralizing and synthesizing all the data necessary for decision-making. Besides, such omnipotence is unnecessary. According to Hayek the market can do whatever a plan can do so much more effortlessly and economically. The order which it produces does not need to be contrived. This uncontrived order is not purely a result of the serendipitous 'hidden hand' of the market: a moral order is involved as well. Hayek (1960: 62) writes that the freedom which is the market 'has never worked without deeply ingrained moral beliefs . . . coercion can be reduced to a minimum only where individuals can be expected as a rule to conform voluntarily to certain principles' (cited by Hindess 1987: 130).

Interestingly, Hayek, the advocate of freedom through the market, does not oppose the existence of enterprise organization *per se*. Hayek recognizes the existence of organizations as goal-oriented systems, at least where they are profit-oriented corporations. Whatever other goals an organization has ought to be rigorously subordinated to 'the profitable use of the capital entrusted to the management by the stockholders' in order to secure 'the single aim' of obtaining 'the largest return in terms of long-run profits'. Without this dedication 'the case for private enterprise breaks down' (Hayek 1967: 300, 312). Hayek makes an exception to the rhetoric extolling the pleasures of unbridled liberalism and the purity of the market as the most sacred of institutions. Large organizations are allowable as long as every aspect of their functioning is subordinated to the market principle of profit raised to an over-arching goal.

Hindess (1987: 127) notes that the central concept buttressing the market in Hayek's thought is that of 'liberty'. It is because planning reduces liberty that it is to be avoided; yet he does not regard the organizational basis of most enterprise calculation in the modern world as such a reduction of liberty. In this respect, as Hindess (1987: 129) observes, he is a far less astute and realist commentator than was Weber (1978):

> The fact that employees are not legally prevented from resigning and seeking alternative employment does not mean that they are not subject to coercion by their employers. The extension of freedom of contract in a society may well go hand in hand with the development of highly authoritarian relationships in the sphere of employment.

Exactly so. A certain blindness as to this issue is a peculiar affliction of all 'market' premised approaches to organization analysis in their delimitation of a sphere of efficiency other than the market.

Market perspectives on organizations

Hayek, as the most notable proponent of the 'market', is the patron saint of a panoply of theoretical approaches which have been enormously influential in 'New Right' advocacy in the past decade. They have done much to prepare an ideological climate more than just a little receptive to accounts constructed in terms of 'markets' and more than just a little mistrustful of organizations. One should not think, however, that all contemporary market-oriented accounts are necessarily convinced that organizations represent something akin to the devil's work. Some strive to 'explain' organizations, rather than dismiss them entirely as illegitimate entities. Chief amongst these have been some economists whose innovation has been to realize that the fictive phenomenology of the market, with its free, boundless and perfect rationality, makes a less than convincing account of the majority of economic transactions. An idea which corresponds rather less to the idea of free exchange and rather more to the idea of organized transactions is needed for these. Efficiency is the key concept for these theorists in a way in which it never was for Weber.

One thing should be clear about these economic approaches to organizations. These frameworks operate with a particular set of a priori values: these are that organizations are an aberration from a more natural form of economic activity. This more natural form is that of exchange on the market, conceptualized as both an economic primitive and, in principle, as an 'essential' category of analysis (Hindess 1987). The market is regarded as a fundamental principle. The beneficial effects of this principle, it is maintained, should be evident in any transactions which transmit and conform to this essential principle. These benefits, it is argued, are those of economic efficiency and personal liberty, virtues which markets maximize.

In this view there were markets before organizations. Markets need not be explained. The classic statement of this is Adam Smith's (1961) statement in *An Enquiry into the Nature and Causes of the Wealth of Nations* that the market exists as a result of inherent propensities of human nature. Above all, these propensities are oriented towards 'regard' for 'self-interest':

> It is not from the benevolence of the butcher, the brewer or the baker that we expect our dinner, but from their regard to their own self-interest. We address ourselves not to their humanity, but to their self-love, and never talk to them of our own necessities but of their advantage. (Smith 1961: 15)

Smith also says that where butchers, brewers or bakers get together to organize the restraint of trade, they are far more likely to do so in order to erect organizational barriers to free trade in collusion rather than to plan how best to maximize the market. From Smith's perspective economic action is not a natural phenomenon. Instead, the nature of this phenomenon is self-interested action by rational actors; these actors are individuals. This is a perspective which stresses 'an atomized, *under*-socialized conception of human action' (Granovetter 1985: 483) which has been iterated endlessly in the classical and neoclassical traditions in economics (also see the critiques in Clegg 1989b; Clegg, Boreham and Dow 1986). From this perspective the deviation of organization from the market principle, as a principle based on 'hierarchy', is something to be explained. Among contemporary theorists it is Oliver E. Williamson (1975) who has done most to elevate an essentialist belief in the market to an axiom of organization analysis. This has been done by addressing the existence of organizations from a perspective which stresses the priority of markets. Where markets fail then organizations may triumph. [. . .]

From a perspective with these priorities it should be evident why organizations present an analytical problem. In the vast majority of the advanced industrial societies economic transactions take place either in or between organizations. The greatest volume in monetary terms is controlled by the very small number of very large organizations. Given this then the existence of organizations rather than markets as the major loci of economic action is a major embarrassment for the economics of neoclassicism. For one thing, where economic action occurs in organizations then the 'freedom' of the market as a solution to malfeasance or mistrust disappears. While one can easily transfer one's action from one horse-trader to another in a country fair or a bazaar, it is somewhat more complex (particularly under the labour market conditions of 'deregulation' favoured by neoclassical economists) as easily to reorder one's employment relations or to choose not to buy some essential from some monopoly or oligopoly supplier. Perhaps it is for this reason, amongst other more evidently ideological ones, that the public policy prescriptions of schools of theory such as 'public choice analysis' should so often consist of the nostrum that there should not be any *public* policy as such: instead what is public should be privatized, with decision-making left to the celebrated 'invisible hand' of 'market forces'. For the same sort of reasons the 'artificial' nature of organization generally, as opposed to the assumed 'naturalness' of the market, predisposes this school to regard the existence of organizations as a problem to be explained. Starting from the premise of the superiority and naturalness of the market, *the* problem of organization analysis for market-oriented theorists is why organizations should exist in the first place, when markets are self-evidently the most efficient means of ordering transactions.

There are two major specifications, from a market-oriented perspective, which seek to explain why it is that bureaucratized organization structures preponderate where and when they do. One derives from the economic historian Alfred DuPont Chandler (1977; 1984) and stresses the way in which organization was an efficient response to market pressure, while the other is derived from the 'transaction cost economics' of Oliver E. Williamson (1975; 1981; 1985), which stresses how organization is a response to market failure.

Contemporary market theorists: Williamson and Chandler

In Williamson's (1975) work the thrust of the essentialist assumptions which explain the shift from 'market' to 'hierarchy' turns out to be, in fact, a formal specification of the efficiency argument which has been wrongly attributed to Weber. There are large organizations, and thus there is bureaucratization, because 'efficiency is the main and only systematic factor responsible' (Williamson 1983: 125). It is only where markets fail that organizations should emerge. (Note the normative 'should': the more empirically neutral 'will' really does not capture the tone of liberal zeal which pervades this analysis.)

Chandler begins by looking at how pre-industrial, small scale, family owned and rudimentarily managed enterprises were transformed into large scale, impersonally owned and bureaucratically managed multi-divisional structures in the twentieth century United States of America. The story is that up until the advent of the continental railway system in America, business organizations remained typically small, usually under the control of merchants. The coming of the railway system from the middle of the nineteenth century changed this. The first change was due to the enormous geographic diversity of the railways themselves. The possibilities of control through the personal surveillance of an ownercontroller were dissolved by the great spread of the operations of the organization. The railways had to develop some alternative if they were to prosper. The alternative was found in the adoption of military models of bureaucracy and a modern 'multi-unit' corporate form. The second change was occasioned by the markets that the railways opened up. The possibilities of a mass market could now be entertained, at least by those organizations which were able to increase the volume of their production.

Chandler argued that as businesses enlarged they found it more efficient to incorporate under one framework the multiple services which they had previously bought from commission agents on the market. These were services such as the purchase of raw materials, debt financing, marketing and distribution. Administrative co-ordination began to replace market exchanges as the major mechanism of control because it was a technically more efficient way of doing *a greater volume* of business. Productivity and profits were higher and costs were lower where organization through rudimentary bureaucratization replaced the fragmentation of markets.

Some other detail gives us an insight into how this growth was achieved. Although it takes place continuously – each time a firm hires more labour or buys out a competitor – it has been established that there are, in fact, distinct patterns of growth achieved through mergers (Aglietta 1979). Organizations don't just 'grow' into bigness: they frequently get there by virtue of assertive action *vis-à-vis* other organizations; they take them over. Thus, large organizations often acquire their bigness through takeovers. Aglietta (1979: 222–3) suggests that there have been several periods of heightened merger activity in the United States, with the initial peak occurring at the end of the nineteenth century. It was out of this wave of mergers that bureaucratized structures were to be consolidated.

At the end of the nineteenth century there occurred a wave of both horizontal, diversificationary mergers and vertical mergers which incorporated suppliers, marketing outlets and so on. The upshot of these was that what had been distinct family businesses were reconstituted under one centre of organizational control. Past family owners were often retained as more or less independent managers in the new organizations (Edwards 1979: 18). Their intimate knowledge of the local business was invaluable to the new owners, who frequently knew little of the specifics of the businesses they now controlled. Such people were able to exercise power personally on the basis of close technical knowledge of the work performed. Moreover, unlike the new owners, they had been in sufficient physical proximity to the workforce to be able to have an effective 'surveillance' (Foucault 1977) of the organization. It was a surveillance based on both technical knowledge and spatio-visual proximity. Frequently, these conditions were replicated within newly merged organizations by incorporating elements of an internal market into the larger organizations. The system for doing this is variously known as 'internal contracting' (Littler 1980) and as 'inside contracting' (Clawson 1980). [. . .]

The internal contract system was widely used by organizations in the nineteenth century, and into the twentieth century, in the major capitalist nations of Britain, Japan and the United States (Littler 1982). Essentially the system comprised an employer and owner of capital hiring a number of internal subcontractors. These individual subcontractors would negotiate a lump sum payment with the capitalist in a contract in which they would agree to provide a specific number of goods, by a specified date or on a specified basis, by hiring labour to work within the organization, using its technology, raw materials and so on to produce commodities only for the organization.

The internal contract may be defined in terms of what Williamson (1985) regards as the basic unit of economic analysis: an economic transaction, defined as an exchange of goods and services across technological boundaries. The costs of the transaction were fixed by the capitalist in the initial contract negotiated with the inside contractor. After that it was left up to the internal contractor to determine how, by whom, at what profit or loss to the contractor and in what way the transaction was accomplished. In Williamson's terms, all the costs of the transaction seem to have been displaced by the capitalist on to the internal contractor. Typically, this person would manage through rudimentary direct surveillance of the work.

The system solved by default the problem of surveillance which was likely to occur as the size of organizations grew beyond the spatio-visual grasp of a single individual. We can conceptualize this readily (see Figure 1). A number of separate organizations in an industry, such as the steel industry, might have been related to each other through a series of market transactions. The product of organization A becomes the material for transformation and fabrication by organization B, and so on. The exchanges are connected through the market as organization A contracts with organization B, using money as the medium of exchange and the contract as the medium of co-ordination. Subsequent to their horizontal integration through takeover the distinct organizations are subsumed within the framework of an encompassing organization, in which the medium of co-ordination is the internal contract (see Figure 2). It reproduced within single ownership organizations the exact possibilities for simple, personal control which had always characterized smaller organizations. It instituted the profit motive in the internal contractor: it was up to this individual, acting under the discipline of the contract and profit expectation, to achieve the transaction transforma-

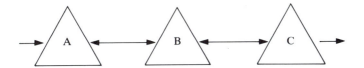

Figure 1 Organizational co-ordination through external market contract

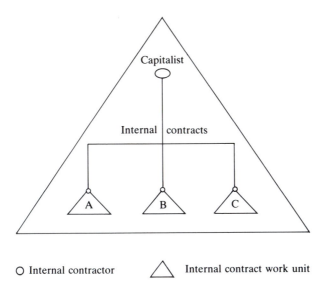

Figure 2 Organizational co-ordination through internal contract

tion. Exactly how this was done was up to the discretion of the internal contractor and the negotiation of the members of the 'work unit'. Sometimes the relationships were familial, under patriarchal authority; sometimes they would be highly exploitative, sometimes less so, under the informally hierarchical relationships of a 'gangerman' and 'gang'; occasionally they might be collectivist, under the rubric of what we might term 'self-management'.

From the capitalist's point of view the internal contract had a number of attractions as a system. It was flexible in terms of demand fluctuations and their impact on employment. It displaced risks inherent in the organization of work, quality of labour, raw materials and plant on to the contracting agent. It absolved the capitalist from detailed capital accounting through the mechanism of the fixed payment lump sum contract. It opened up possibilities for advancement by workers who might become contracting agents and it generated a mechanism whereby innovation might flourish in methods of work design and organization internal to the contract.

None the less, despite these evident advantages, internal contracting began to decline from the last quarter of the nineteenth century in both Britain and the United States, and in Japan from the early twentieth century. In Williamson's terms the costs of the transactions began to outweigh their benefits. These costs were those associated with the monitoring of the contracts. They offered little control over quality or pilferage, for instance. Some of the internal contractees acted 'opportunistically with guile', that is they did not do exactly what the capitalist and the contractor expected of them. This should hardly be surprising to anyone familiar with that large literature in industrial sociology which demonstrates how the rationality of action by different economic actors in the same firm is invariably constructed situationally (for example, Taylor and Walton 1971). One person's 'rationality' may well be another person's 'guile'. Resistance is quite normal behaviour in organizations (Clegg 1989b: 207-9). Some people may even be sufficiently guileful to the extent that they will join trade unions in order to try to improve their collective situation!

There was a situation – whether a problem of guile or not – in which were displayed resistant 'modes of rationality' on the part of workers in early twentieth-century organizations. In addition, other rationalities, such as those of 'scientific management', were being developed by other agents in order to achieve a more efficient utilization of these workers' labour power. Such a utilization required a more regulated contractual relationship between the individual worker and the organization than the internal contract typically provided, particularly as the market conditions in the environment changed. It was the development of various types of 'rationalization' movement, such as scientific management, which led to the widespread bureaucratization of employment relations in organizations (Clegg and Dunkerley [1980: 84–6] go into this in some detail). Thus, for these various reasons strategically placed agents in organizations sought to replace the uncertainties of the internal marketplace through creating governance structures which internalized transactions, reduced their costs and thus, from the capitalist point of view, increased efficiency (Williamson 1985: 68–162). They also sought to avoid the uncertainties of external markets by buying out competitors, suppliers, marketers and so on.

Translating the specifics of economic history into the abstractions of economics, bureaucratization occurs when transaction costs can be minimized by internalizing them within firms rather than mediating them through markets. In this perspective, first there were markets and then there were organizations which grew as a response to market failures. The probability of market failure is higher the more complex and uncertain is the market – that is, the more it diverges from the ideal of perfect competition. All this is elegantly if occasionally somewhat unrealistically expressed by Williamson in terms of a few key concepts: the 'uncertainty' of markets, the 'opportunism' of economic agents, sometimes based upon their 'bounded rationality' (the fact that they have 'strategically contingent' [Hickson *et al.*, 1971] skills with which to bargain), the 'asset specificity' of organization information about operating environments and so on. Different kinds of transactions will give rise to different kinds of organizations. Those that are most uncertain in their foreseeable outcomes, and which are substantially specific, as well as frequently recurring are the transactions most likely to find expression in organizations. The nature of organization diversity is to be explained through the complexities of markets. The organizations we have are, on the whole, the most efficient there can be, otherwise they wouldn't exist: this is the conclusion which this Panglossian logic draws us inexorably to. How else could the perfect fiction of the perfectly competitive market have been replaced in the first place?

Organizations derive from markets where contracts tend to be longer rather than shorter term; where the environment is more rather than less certain (actually a tautology, as the key variable affecting the certainty of the market is its perfectly competitive status – that is, its lack of organization; once organization is admitted, then the uncertainty of the environment begins to accrue, by definition); and where the barriers to entry for new agents are high (again, implicitly, these barriers are frequently organizational in that they concern the capacity to hire labour, raise credit, secure supplies and so on; these are less matters of individual ability and more of organizational contacts, networks and environmentally available resources). So the thrust of Williamson's theory is to argue that organizations grow when markets fail. However, in a sense what he is describing is a situation where markets fail because organizational conditions have begun to develop. Markets fail either because of the 'bounded rationality' which agents display when confronted with decisions which are contingent on complex long-term transactions or where agents display 'opportunism' – rational self-interest expressed in terms of a tendency to cheat on the conditions which have been contracted. While the latter conditions are not necessarily organizational, the former seem to be so. Where an argument proposes that markets fail because of organizational growth, then it would be injudicious simultaneously to hold that this failure should also serve as an explanation of the emergence of organizations. The effect would also be the cause.

Granovetter (1985: 494) identifies the transition from markets to hierarchies in terms of the mix of 'under- and over-socialized assumptions' which Hobbes deployed in *Leviathan*. The market, as we have seen, is conceptualized as if it were a natural state; the organization is regarded as a moral community in which hierarchical diktat (or 'fiat') can play a backup role if the moral order fails and agents act 'opportunistically with guile'. Organization thus functions in a way which is similar to the mythical Hobbesian community and monarch in political theory more generally (Clegg 1989b): it internalizes conditions of both organic unity and hierarchical authority. One may find that it aids one in interpreting this argument if one keeps one's metaphorical tongue firmly in one's metaphorical cheek. Otherwise, one might conclude that the nature of 'membership' in organizations has nothing to do with that economic necessity to endure 'the dull compulsion to labour' of which both Marx and Weber wrote. For the majority of people the key calculus would seem to be which, if any, organizational employer they can hawk themselves to. Whether or not the transaction is then bathed in an ethos of morality is entirely an empirical question, depending in large part on the institutional framework within which the exchange is constructed. The same might also be said of recourse to hierarchy: no necessity adheres to either. In fact, the recourse to hierarchy in Williamson begs the whole issue of how it is that obedience is produced in organizations (see Biggart and Hamilton 1985; Clegg 1989a) as well as the 'embeddedness' of all organizational action within institutional frameworks (Granovetter 1985).

Williamson's approach is to argue that organizations grow when markets fail due to increased transaction costs. Note that structural failures, due to the growth of concentration, are excluded here. By contrast, Chandler, as we have seen, argues that they grow where they are market-driven. Both accounts tend to underplay the possibility that organizations are conduits, arenas and opportunities for power (Clegg 1989a). Organizations might better be understood as sites of power built from the *bricolage* of whatever materials might be available, including rational knowledge about their functioning, by whatever agents have an interest in and around them. Contracts are not incidental to this, as has been demonstrated empirically (Clegg 1975) and argued theoretically (Clegg 1989a) elsewhere.

References

Aglietta, M. (1979), *A Theory of Capitalist Regulation*, London, New Left Books.
Albrow, M. (1970), *Bureaucracy*, London, Pall Mall.
Biggart, N. W., and G. G. Hamilton (1985), 'The power of obedience', *Administrative Science Quarterly*, 29, pp. 540–9.

Blau, P. M., and W. R. Scott (1963), *Formal Organisations: A comparative approach*, London, Routledge & Kegan Paul.

Chandler, A. D. (1977), *The Visible Hand: The managerial revolution in American business*, Cambridge, Mass., Harvard University Press.

Chandler, A. D. (1984), 'The emergence of managerial capitalism', *Business History Review*, 58, pp. 473–502.

Clawson, D. (1980), *Bureaucracy and the Labour Process: The transformation of US industry 1860–1920*, New York, Monthly Review Press.

Clegg, S. R. (1975), *Power, Rule and Domination*, London, Routledge & Kegan Paul.

Clegg, S. R. (1989a), 'Radical revisions: power, discipline and organisations', *Organisation Studies*, 10(1), pp. 97–115.

Clegg, S. R. (1989b), *Frameworks of Power*, London, Sage.

Clegg, S. R., P. Boreham and G. Dow (1986), *Class, Politics and the Economy*, London, Routledge & Kegan Paul.

Clegg, S. R., and D. Dunkerley (1980), *Organisations, Class and Control*, London, Routledge & Kegan Paul.

Edwards, R. (1979), *Contested Terrain: The transformation of work in the twentieth century*, New York, Basic Books.

Foucault, M. (1977), *Discipline and Punish: The birth of the prison*, Harmondsworth, Penguin.

Granovetter, M. (1985), 'Economic action and social structure: the problem of embeddedness', *American Journal of Sociology*, 91, pp. 481–510.

Hayek, F. A. (1944), *The Road to Serfdom*, London, Routledge & Kegan Paul.

Hayek, F. A. (1960), *The Constitution of Liberty*, London: Routledge & Kegan Paul.

Hayek, F. A. (1967), *Studies in Philosophy, Politics and Economics*, London, Routledge & Kegan Paul.

Hickson, D. J., et al. (1971), 'A strategic contingencies theory of intra-organizational power', *Administrative Science Quarterly*, 16, pp. 216–29.

Hindess, B. (1987), *Freedom, Equality and the Market*, London, Tavistock.

Littler, C. R. (1980), 'Internal contract and the transition to modern work systems: Britain and Japan', pp. 157–85 in D. Dunkerley and G. Salaman (eds.), *The International Yearbook of Organization Studies 1979*, London, Routledge & Kegan Paul.

Littler, C. R. (1982), *The Development of the Labour Process in Capitalist Societies*, London, Heinemann.

Smith, A. (1961), *An Enquiry into the Nature and Causes of the Wealth of Nations*, Indianapolis, Bobbs-Merrill.

Taylor, L., and P. Walton (eds.) (1971), *Images of Deviance*, Harmondsworth, Penguin.

Therborn, G. (1976), *Science, Class and Society*, London, New Left Books.

Weber, M. (1948), *From Max Weber: Essays in sociology*, trans. and ed. H. H. Gerth and C. W. Mills, London, Routledge & Kegan Paul.

Weber, M. (1978), *Economy and Society: An outline of interpretive sociology* (2 vols.), eds. G. Roth and C. Wittich, Berkeley, University of California Press.

Williamson, O. E. (1975), *Markets and Hierarchies*, New York, Free Press.

Williamson, O. E. (1981), 'The economics of organization', *American Journal of Sociology*, 87, pp. 548–77.
Williamson, O. E. (1983), 'Organisational reform, residual claimants and corporate control', *Journal of Law and Economics*, 36, pp. 25, 351–66.
Williamson, O. E. (1985), *The Economic Institutions of Capitalism*, New York, Free Press.

Explaining the privatization boom

Public choice versus radical approaches

Patrick Dunleavy

By 'privatization' I mean strictly the permanent transferring of service or goods production activities previously carried out by public service bureaucracies to private firms or to other forms of non-public organization, such as voluntary groups. [. . .]

New right explanations

The rapid development of a privatization boom in Britain, and its more protracted evolution in the USA, pose a number of crucial explanatory problems for new right accounts of public policy making in liberal democracies. Using public choice approaches, a range of influential new right thinkers, such as Tullock (1975), Niskanen (1975), Breton (1974) and Buchanan (Buchanan *et al.*, 1978), have constructed quite detailed and apparently plausible models of how the public sector budget is *necessarily* inflated under pluralist political arrangements. Politicians and parties are driven by the logic of party competition to bid up voters' expectations of what governments can do to improve their lot. Once in office, political leaders and representatives manipulate public policy in ways informed by a 'political cost/benefit analysis' (Wilson, 1973, Ch. 16). Log-rolling coalitions push up the state budget by endorsing packages of issues which would fail if voted on individually, while

From P. Dunleavy, 'Explaining the privatization boom: public choice versus radical approaches', *Public Administration*, **64**, 1986, pp. 13–34.

pork-barrel tactics write into national budgets the funding for multiple local private goods. Medium-level politicians have short time spans in which to make an impact; for them, policy initiatives are valuable in attracting external interest group support, even if they later turn out not to be worth while or implementable. The ratchet effect in state activities tends to keep programmes and agencies in being once they have been created. Central political figures (such as the US president or the Prime Minister/cabinet in Britain) are supposed to provide important centralizing checks on overall budgetary growth. In fact their influence and motivation are both limited, since they are also concerned to manipulate the economy along a path set by the political business cycle so as to recreate favourable economic conditions in election years.

Bureaucratic behaviour adds a further powerful twist to this process. Rational officials foster their own self-interest in making policy decisions. State agencies exercise a monopoly control over information on the pattern of costs and benefits in different output ranges. For the annual budget, agencies submit a block bid for overall funding to the legislature or other 'sponsor' body. Sponsors are usually internally fragmented into committees or departments, which are staffed or headed-up by politicians whose interests are closely convergent with those of the bureau, especially because they have an above-average demand for agency outputs. Bureaucrats best serve their own welfare by pushing continuously for budgetary growth, which increases their numbers, improves promotion prospects, allows the bureau to be more easily managed, creates areas of discretionary patronage or possibly perks-fiddling, and generally builds up organizational slack and improves job security (Niskanen, 1973a and 1973b; Breton, 1974, Ch. 9; Borcherding, 1977). Because agencies are so weakly controlled by sponsors, and because the budget-maximization goal is open-ended, bureaucracies *inherently* over-supply outputs, establishing a budget which delivers up to twice the socially optimal level of services – that which would be provided by private firms operating in perfect competition conditions.

Privatization is a central prescriptive maxim of new right and public choice authors for three major reasons. First, it subjects state agencies to competition from contractors, forcing them to reveal information to sponsors which they would otherwise keep secret under the block budget system – such as the relationship between varying levels of service and total costs. For example, school cleaning may normally be treated as an indivisible good. But going out to tender automatically projects decisions about the trade-off between different cleaning standards and costs into sharp focus. The contract specification has to go into great detail about the service standards required. And contractors may very well query the specification, arguing that small reductions in cleaning standards would offer disproportionate savings, or that a minor funding increase would permit improvements in the service achieved. Second, these authors generally assume that contracting firms are more efficient in meeting well-defined functions, since they are single-purpose organizations and can operate more flexibly than public agencies. Third, privatization is recommended as a way of breaking up the restrictive practices and monopoly control over innovations exercised by trade unions and professions in the heavily unionized and professionalized public sector.

It follows that if the budget-maximization account of bureaucracies is correct, government officials in all kinds of agencies should oppose privatization. The introduction of competition, and its concomitant forced revelation of additional information, shifts power away from bureaux to their sponsor bodies. It should drastically reduce agencies' capacity to go on over-supplying outputs, and accordingly could produce major budget reductions. It greatly increases uncertainty and risk for budget-maximizing officials, and creates a more turbulent environment for them to operate in. If privatization reduces agency costs then it lowers the funding totals controlled by top officials, and may adversely affect their status ranking *vis-à-vis* other departments. The shift of staff away from the agency to contractors reduces the manpower and organizational resources controlled by managers, potentially undermining their existing salary and seniority ratings, and cutting back on their ability to divert public resources towards satisfying private goals. Finally, privatization attacks the integrity of public sector organizations, particularly eroding the strong protective ideologies which bureaux build up to insulate their over-supply behaviour from external scrutiny or criticism. The salience of these ideologies in organizations such as the social welfare services, the police or the army needs little emphasis.

The response of legislators or ministers to privatization will be more variable. Obviously those whose preferences lie outside a given policy area X will tend to favour the introduction of contracting there if this liberates spare resources for developing non-X programmes. But committee members or political department heads most directly involved in exercising the sponsor function in the X policy area should oppose privatization for much the same reasons as budget-maximizing bureaucrats. If politicians perceive an overall public good potential in privatization, it might be rational for them to try to overcome this difficulty by binding themselves to a general agreement to introduce competitive tendering. Such a 'contract' is obviously quite feasible in Britain where political department heads are few in number and have well-developed institutions for co-ordinating their actions (the cabinet and the strong national party organizations) (Hardin, 1982, Ch. 10). In addition, ministers share a common ideology and have common electoral interests in their party political roles. Indeed, the potential for 'contractarian' collective action to succeed in British cabinet government may be so strong that a real danger of substantially inappropriate or counter-productive adherence to a general agreement exists (see the section on 'Explaining "inappropriate" privatization' below). By contrast, in the US Congress, legislators on committees come from opposing parties, their party ties are anyway of low salience, co-ordinating institutions for budget-setting within Congress are still relatively weak, and individual legislators have a lot to gain in electoral terms by free-riding on any general agreement. Consequently even if there is general Congressional assent to the principle of privatization, this is likely to be combined with resistance to its application in 'our area' inside committees and sub-committees.

The problem for public choice and new right accounts is to explain why the privatization boom has taken off so fast and met with such low-level resistance from the public service bureaucracies. This difficulty is far more acute with contracting-out forms of privatization than with other activities often labelled by the same term. For example, it might be feasible to explain why managers have complied so readily with selling equity stakes in public corporations in terms of the behaviour of rationally self-interested bureaucrats anticipating a switch to the less restrictive salaries and perks conditions of the private sector. But public service privatizations are a different matter, since the potential for existing senior bureaucrats to cross over fruitfully into the private sector will be very low indeed. Accordingly, it seems that public choice and new right accounts must explain the rapid growth of privatization with only subdued resistance or non-compliance from policy-level bureaucrats, in one of the following ways:

1. Previous new right estimations of the power of budget-maximizing officials *vis-à-vis* sponsor bodies were greatly overstated. The privatization boom demonstrates that there is nothing inherent about the success of supply-side pressures for budgetary growth. At least in the UK, sponsor bodies clearly have (and by implication always have had) the ability to assert their priorities over the state apparatus. However, it was not until the advent of new right governments in London and Washington that political leaders have had the appropriate preference structures required to exercise sponsor power on behalf of curtailing budget growth and improving efficiency. Because of its high estimate of leadership influence on the parameters of state behaviour, I term this view the *heroic variant* of a new right approach.

2. The apparent importance of the privatization boom is deceptive. In fact only incremental changes have been implemented. Privatization

most resembles previous management innovations [. . .] in having once-for-all impacts in the early years of its introduction, without any broader or continuing impact on public policy formulation. I term this view the *fatalist variant* of a new right approach.

Either of these alternatives positions achieves consistency at the cost of damaging a large part of the current appeal of new right views. If the heroic argument is true then past accounts of bureaucracy which claimed to use deductive techniques to uncover their inherent modes of operation turn out to have reasoned inductively from a purely contingent state of affairs. There cannot be any necessary quality about bureaucratic over-supply and budget-maximization behaviour if a simple change of political will at the helm of representative institutions is enough to make the state apparatus operate in a basically different way. I am reminded rather forcefully of the new right's past critique of conventional public administration in which they complained of the lack of realism in assuming that public servants were somehow more dedicated to the public interest than ordinary mortals. The heroic variant seems susceptible to the same attack, since it relies on the 'special virtue' of the Thatcher or Reagan administrations to explain how previously ineluctable trends or tendencies have apparently been reversed.

By contrast, if the fatalist argument is correct, then the new right/public choice approach retains its empirical analysis in the shape it was, but at the cost of jettisoning one of its key policy prescriptions, which have made it so attractive as a model for 'practical men'. There is the same potential for infinite regress away from empirical refutation present in new right policy analysis as in monetarist economic prescriptions. Friedman declines to accept that evidence from British economic performance since 1979 represents a critical test of monetarism, since the Thatcher governments have not 'really' put the doctrine into practice. Similarly the new right may retreat into the claim that the current Conservative administration or the Reaganauts have suffered from 'weakness of will' on privatization. The empirical model survives via such disclaimers, but at the cost of moving rapidly closer to prescriptive utopianism.

Radical explanations

By a 'radical explanation' I denote primarily a socialist but basically non-Marxist account of public administration in liberal democracies. There are a number of schools of thought which might qualify for such a label, including some variants of contemporary neo-Marxism and work in a more Weberian tradition. The precise qualities to be looked for in such a tradition remain the subject of debate (Dunleavy, 1982a; O'Leary, 1985; see also Grey, 1984, for an orthodox Marxist view). But it is agreed that a radical public administration must both be applied and connect directly with prescriptive reasoning. I confine my attention here to my own recent work developing a thorough-going critique of public choice theories of bureaucracy, which develops and exemplifies (at least for the purposes of this paper) the characteristics of a radical approach (Dunleavy, 1985).

The radical critique of public choice views argues that rational officials in government agencies will not systematically pursue budget-maximization. All large agencies involve substantial numbers of officials in policy making and require a considerable mobilization of effort in a competitive and potentially hostile environment before collective goods (such as a budget increment) can be attained. Rational bureaucrats will put their efforts primarily into individual rather than collective forms of welfare maximization. There is likely to be a collective action problem in policy-level officials collaborating to advocate budgetary expansion, since the net utilities accruing to senior bureaucrats will be small, and discounted by the probability that their involvement will be decisive in securing extra funding. Unless this side of the equation exceeds their probably substantial personal advocacy costs, rational officials would do best to free-ride on other bureaucrats' efforts rather than actively to budget-maximize.

There are anyway very substantial grounds for doubting that officials' welfare is positively or continuously associated with budgetary expansion in the way which Niskanen assumes. Only that part of an agency's overall appropriation which is spent on its own administrative activities (the *core budget*) is highly correlated with lower officials' welfare. Policy-making officials might take an interest in a broader range of spending, so long as it remains under the agency's own control without passing to other public sector bodies for implementation (a category known as the *bureau budget*). Advocacy costs, however, attach to the overall flow of funds passing through the department (the *programme budget*), even if much of this expenditure flows on to subordinate agencies for service delivery. There are some very important differences between agencies in the inter-relationship of core, bureau and programme budgets.

I distinguish at least five common types of agency roles (Dunleavy, 1985, pp. 310–13):

Delivery agencies directly produce goods or supply services or implement policy at a grass roots level;
Regulatory agencies supervise firms, individuals or other agencies, via

inspections, mandatory requirements, policy-sensitive taxation or subsidies, without directly producing goods or services themselves.

In both these types of agency I expect growth in the programme, bureau and core budgets to be very closely related to each other, since the bulk of spending goes on the agency's own activities. The main difference between them is that delivery agencies will typically by much larger than regulatory agencies.

Transfer agencies pay out money in grants, pensions, welfare benefits, or other forms of transfer payment to the public or sections of it or to client interest groups;
Contract agencies put work out to commercial tender with private corporations or other governmental agencies.

In both these types I expect the core budget to be only loosely related to the bureau and programme budgets, since their activities involve passing on the bulk of their overall budgets to private sector clients or contractors.

Control agencies route money to subordinate public sector agencies, without being directly responsible for final implementation. Consequently growth in either their bureau or core budgets is only loosely related to changes in the programme budget.

For example, a police force is a delivery agency. All its funding goes on supporting its own activities (rather than out to other agencies); so that the programme and bureau budgets are identical. Most of the bureau budget goes on manpower, so that the core and bureau budgets are nearly the same. Hence overall programme budget expansions correlate quite highly with welfare gains for policemen. By contrast, if the DHSS supplementary benefits side (a transfer agency) prints higher values on giro cheques for the unemployed, their programme budget goes up massively, but how has the welfare of officials who staff the agency been changed? Similarly, why should rationally self-interested officials in the DES (a purely control agency) worry if school or university funding is cut back? Their programme budget will show a decline admittedly, but how has their own welfare suffered?

Attention to these sorts of questions demonstrates that there is a very variable relationship between overall programme budgets and officials' welfare across delivery, regulatory, transfer, contract and control agencies. Basically where policy is administered by large line bureaucracies there is a close connection. But where policy is administered by *systems* of bureaux, then the connections at the policy and budget-setting top levels become very remote indeed (Dunleavy, 1984a). In this context it is significant that in both Britain and the USA there has been a very marked shift in the balance of public spending since 1980, away from social welfare services run by systems of bureaux with only control agencies at the federal or central government levels, and towards the defence sector – almost the only area of government where very large, centrally run delivery agencies still operate.

Finally, the class and gender interests of senior bureaucrats in all agencies (but especially in central departments) can be advanced far more directly and successfully by bureau-shaping strategies rather than by budget-maximization. Rationally self-interested officials are empirically more likely to be interested in work-related utilities rather than in income-maximization – since many aspects of public service employment systems make them infertile ground for diverting agency resources to individual ends. Officials want to work in small, elite and centrally placed staff agencies (such as the Treasury or the Cabinet Office), not in large-budget but routine, troublesome and conflict-prone line agencies (such as the DHSS computer centre in Newcastle). The bureau-shaping model predicts that policy-level staff will try to shift their agency as far as possible towards the ideal type of a pure control agency, hiving off implementation functions to quasi-governmental agencies or subnational governments, automating routine jobs in order to liberate resources for new posts at the policy levels, and creating dual state structures to insulate key decision centres from public scrutiny or participation. Here representative political inputs are concentrated on low-level delivery agencies, while the central government becomes a non-executant, money-moving administration, retaining tight strategic controls, especially over funding levels to the constituent parts of the state apparatus (Cawson and Saunders, 1983; Dunleavy, 1984b).

In this model some types of extensive public service privatization should be welcomed and facilitated by senior bureaucrats. It is perfectly consistent with the general bureau-shaping motivation that policy-level staffs in almost all types of agency should co-operate in shedding low-level or routine functions to contractors. After all, what does it matter to senior bureaucrats who changes the towels in the office washrooms, so long as they do get changed and they do not have to engage in delicate industrial relations negotiations with the washroom attendants? Similarly why should a Director of Technical Services in a local authority care if refuse collection is privatized, thereby removing the need for her to manage some of the best-organized and most militant public service workers as well as listening to endless debates amongst councillors on the timing of refuse collections runs? The class interests of senior bureaucrats are simply not engaged in these decisions on behalf of preserving the status quo.

On the contrary, the pursuit of privatization affords unprecedented opportunities for policymakers in delivery agencies to effect radical transformations in their agency's character and status. An increasing shift to a control agency format effectively insulates policy-level staff from reliance on continued high levels of budget appropriations in order to maintain their welfare levels. The costs of privatization are borne overwhelmingly by rank-and-file state workers, whose job security, hours of work, working conditions, access to union protection, and wage rates may all come under drastic downward pressure. Equally, policy-level bureaucrats have little to lose if there are qualitative changes in service provision, service standard reductions or decreased public or consumer control over the format of service provisions as a result of privatization. These costs are borne chiefly by consumers and service recipients.

Explaining 'inappropriate' privatization

A number of possible explanations of the blanket character of the privatization 'boom' have been discussed at various points above. A new right author might say that the United Kingdom's central executive machinery is organized in such a way that contractarian joint action by political department heads is the only way of ensuring that the collective benefits offered by the privatization of services are realized, even if this engenders some inappropriate adoption of privatization. [. . .] A radical could claim that the class interests of policy-level bureaucrats lead them to pursue privatization, even when its by-product effects in immiserizing state workers or reducing services to consumers mean that the strategy is at odds with the 'public interest'.

But in my view the 'boom' character of recent changes requires some additional explanation, especially to show why legislators confronted with substantial evidence that privatization will not advance social welfare may none the less push ahead with change. I suggest that this phenomenon of *inappropriate privatization* highlights a problem almost completely neglected in public choice accounts of bureaucracy – namely, that there may be quite large differences between the 'internal' and the 'social' costs of public service provision being undertaken by a government agency. Like private firms, government agencies' activities create 'externality' effects. A reasoned allocation of externality effects between the 'benefits' and the 'costs' of agency activity is essential before we can understand how they will operate.

In demand terms, government agencies differ from private firms in facing a legislature whose purchasing (sponsoring) behaviour is guided by *social* demand for the agency's output, rather than the direct or specific market demands of individuals. In principle, then, the legislature is able to take account of the external benefits and disbenefits of an agency's formally proclaimed programme – reacting to overall social demand for all aspects of its budget-funded activity. Any 'by-product' benefits or disbenefits *specifically* produced by this activity will be taken into account in drawing up the legislature's marginal social benefit curve.

It is conceivable that in principle *all* the externality implications of any agency's activity could be incorporated into the analysis solely by altering the shape or position of the legislature's demand curve. After all, 'costs' are arbitrarily and subjectively defined in most macro-economic analysis simply as foregone utilities (McCormich *et al.*, 1974, pp. 201–18). So any externalized costs, or externalized benefits with private cost implications, could perhaps be classified as detracting from or contributing to the net benefits of an agency's programme. This seems to be the position implicitly adopted by Niskanen, who considers only the legislature's (social) demand curve and agency's (private) internal cost curve.

But there are a number of powerful reasons why this strategy of sublimating all externalities (positive or negative) in the positioning of the marginal social benefit curve may be misleading and may obscure fruitful areas for the analysis of bureau behaviour. There are five main arguments for accommodating some kinds of externality effect on the cost side of agency behaviour:

(i) Some of the positive and negative externalities we wish to analyse would normally and even invariably be included on the cost side of the analysis in looking at private firms' behaviours. If our account of public agencies' behaviour is to be at all comparable we should follow suit.

(ii) Some of the negative externalities analysed will be included by individuals and firms in *their* cost curves directly, rather than simply viewed as reductions from net benefit received.

(iii) It seems useful to distinguish between positive externalities specifically attributable to agency activity, and those general externality benefits which may follow from having a government bureau rather than some other type of organization responsible for an area of social activity. In particular, the legislature will relatively easily be able to perceive programme-specific positive externalities and to incorporate them in its marginal social benefit curve. But where these benefits are very general they may not be perceived or incorporated, even if achieving the benefits in question has the effect of raising the agency's cost curves artificially above those which a private firm would experience. This sort of effect seems better accommodated by looking at the marginal social costs of agency activity, rather than trying to fit such an effect into the positioning of the marginal social benefit curve.

(iv) Where the sponsor body is itself internally divided into programme-specific sections or committees (a central feature of Niskanen's analysis of the demand conditions for bureau outputs), then the rationale for distinguishing between the specific and the very generalized externality effects of agency activity is greatly strengthened. Since the programme committee defines demand, it may well fail to take into account generalized external benefits and costs affecting activities outside its purview. Although the virtually complete fragmentation of sponsor demand which Niskanen assumes is undoubtedly one of the most ethnocentric and time-specific features of his analysis (Goodin, 1982), some lesser measure of sponsor fragmentation will normally occur.

(v) Finally, we need to recognize that the legislature's ability to appreciate the incidence of positive externalities and external costs is unlikely to be the same. Negative externalities of an agency's activities impinging upon individuals, groups, firms or other organizations give rise to complaints of which the legislature will be made aware, perhaps forcefully. But diffused positive externalities may not be very visible to the public, and certainly may not be concentrated enough to show up in additional levels of public support for particular programmes, although they may show through in other ways, such as overall satisfaction with government or trust in officials. Hence legislatures or sponsors differentially perceive external costs more than external benefits. This asymmetry reinforces the arguments for attributing some of these effects at least to a separate marginal social cost curve for bureau output, rather than simply incorporating them into the legislature's marginal social benefit curve.

Two kinds of externalization by public agencies are possible: one where net costs are exported and the other where the agency externalizes benefits.

Externalized costs: some agencies project a large part of the costs of their activities onto other social actors. For example, regulatory agencies which are relatively low-budget operations externalize very substantial compliance costs onto individuals, firms or other agencies by requiring them to complete forms, compile statistics, report infringements or accidents, observe legal requirements, answer correspondence, etc. Some estimates of US federal government regulatory activity suggest that the 'compliance costs' of regulation in 1976 were of the order of between two and twenty times as great as the administrative costs directly attributed to such activity by government agencies (Bennett and Johnson, 1980, pp. 45–51). Transfer agencies may also externalize considerable costs onto other groups. For example, the DHSS in Britain has constructed such a complex web of welfare entitlements that a large amount of time and expertise may be necessary for people to claim their due. However, unless these externalized costs begin to offset very substantially the benefits being transferred, people are less likely to complain about them.

We can envisage agencies which externalize costs as having a marginal social cost curve which is *higher* than their marginal internal cost curve. In this case, if the agency succeeds in persuading a sponsor to fund up to the point where its internal costs are being covered by social returns on the expenditure, this is still bound to cause over-supply when measured against the social cost curve. In fact the legislature will usually take account of cost externalities since constituents will complain about them and data about their incidence will be in the public domain. Certainly, the bureau in question will not be able to monopolize information about externalized costs; indeed for regulatory agencies they may not even be any more visible to officials than to the legislature. So it seems likely that legislators will take the higher marginal social costs of regulatory agency activities into account when fixing the bureau's budget.

Given this framework of an agency externalizing costs, we can examine a situation in which privatization will clearly be inappropriate, producing results which reduce social welfare. Figure 1 shows a government agency where the social cost curve lies above the internal cost curve with a social cost optimal level of output of Q1. For argument's sake we none the less suppose that the government agency was in the past able to mislead the legislature so as to oversupply output as Q2, with a consequent sub-optimal reduction of overall original consumers surplus equal to the area ARB of extra production where social costs outweigh social benefits.

Privatization in this situation will only make the over-supply problem worse, since it will typically coincide with, or depend upon, or have the effect of achieving a reduction in scrutiny by the legislature. If the firm taking over the function has a profit rate tied to production – i.e. assuming the legislature's control remains just stringent enough to deny the firm super-normal profits – then it will use its ability to externalize costs to push up the level of output to Q3, enlarging the area of net socially wasteful production to ASC, at which point total (normal) profits are maximized.

This kind of effect may not be confined simply to privatization. Institutional changes which tend to insulate sections of the state apparatus [. . .] from effective control by the legislature or other generalized political control mechanisms, may well have similar effects

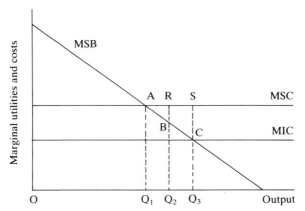

Figure 1 The effect of privatization where an agency externalizes costs

in pushing output up to a level justified in internal but not social cost terms (Dunleavy, 1982b).

Externalized benefits: many agencies externalize net social benefits as a result of their activities, benefits which are not taken into account by the legislature in positioning its demand curve, but which can be displayed as a marginal social cost curve lying *below* each agency's internal cost curve. What happens here is that a series of general public opinion expectations and political requirements about the ways in which government agencies should operate cause agencies to be involved in directing social development in optimal ways, even when these developments have little if anything to do with agencies' specific policy objectives. Examples of these general requirements (see Pitt and Smith, 1981, Ch. 2), which might raise bureaux' costs of production well above those of private firms of comparable size and activity levels, include:

— paying 'a living wage' or above-minimum wage levels
— using regular salaried staff, not casual labour
— encouraging proper pensions development
— practising rigorous meritocratic recruitment and promotion
— operating good health-and-safety-at-work measures
— recognizing trade unions and practising 'good industrial relations'
— encouraging racial and sexual equality of opportunity
— positively helping handicapped clients or employees
— using above minimum numbers of professional staff in appropriate contexts
— assessing cases fairly and acting reasonably
— operating fail-safe and double-check procedures against mistakes
— thoroughly investigating grievances and complaints
— thoroughly respecting confidentiality

— treating people (whether workers or clients) with respect and giving advice on their rights
— always acting in the letter and spirit of the law
— consulting the public on issues affecting them
— accepting political interference and guidance
— generally observing 'good practice' rather than cutting corners.

Whether the legislature always or even usually improves social welfare by imposing these requirements on social welfare institutions is clearly a matter for debate (Le Grand and Robinson, 1984; Heald, 1983). However, for the purposes of this paper I *assume* that the legislature does indeed advance the public interest by such provisions. The expectations generated about public agency operations bear most heavily in cost terms on bureaux with a lot of staff and direct contact with the public. Consequently delivery agencies are the most seriously affected, followed after a large gap by transfer agencies and perhaps contract agencies. (Transfer agencies may also externalize substantial costs, however, both to businesses and to clients.) Control and regulatory agencies are little affected because of their small staff and absence of large-scale implementation responsibilities. Because delivery agencies are such large employers of staff they have tended to be used as a leverage point, a sector of the labour market or of social life generally where the government can 'give a lead' or set an example for other large organizations to follow. Normally these objectives have little to do with the agency's specific functions (those which the legislature has in mind when setting its budget level) but are imposed on it by central control or regulatory agencies, backed in turn by the legislature as a whole acting in a non-budgetary role. Key examples have been the ability of the labour movement and of ethnic groups to secure practices favourable to their members' interests. All of these changes and concessions raise the bureau's internal cost curve, and yet (assuming they advance social welfare) the marginal social cost curve is markedly below the agency's internal costs.

The extent to which an agency is internalizing the costs of achieving social development objectives unrelated to its specific delivery functions will commonly go unrecognized by the legislature. Both they and the public may miss these generalized benefits only when they are *not* in place. A classic example of this phenomenon occurred after 1979 when the new Conservative government compelled the Central Electricity Generating Board (CEGB) to change their existing policy on disposing of power stations (see *Sunday Times*, 26 June 1983, p. 17, and 24 July, p. 3; *The Times*, 1 July 1983, p. 3; 23 July, p. 23; 29 July, p. 2). Instead of the CEGB knocking down its old plant and selling the cleared site to a developer, the government decided that it was cheaper (indeed even profitable) to dispose of unwanted plant by selling it off to private demolition firms, who would pay good money for the copper and other scrap metal the buildings contained. However, old power stations also contain enormous quantities of lethal asbestos, and fierce complaints were soon voiced that the private contractors were ripping buildings apart to get at the valuable scrap in ways which exposed both their workforce and nearby communities to hazardous levels of asbestos dust. In mid-1983 the Conservative government was forced by public pressure in Fulham to ask the CEGB to strip out asbestos itself before disposing of power stations to private firms, at an additional cost of some £40 million a year. Although a regulatory system supposedly exists to force private firms to strip asbestos safely, in practice the government has acknowledged that only if the operation is retained in a public agency would there be an effective control over handling. This kind of problem – a contrast between good practice in the public sector and corner-cutting in private firms – is particularly acute where the industrial structure of an industry is highly fragmented (as in demolition), since generalized public opinion influences have less impact on small (cowboy) contractors than on larger firms.

If legislators do not perceive the reduced social costs of having a function carried out by a public agency, they will use what they know of the agency's internal cost curve in fixing the budget. The delivery agency may find it relatively easy to budget-maximize against its internal cost levels, but the extent to which this behaviour results in over-supply against the social cost optimal level remains unclear. Indeed a degree of over-provision against the internal cost optimum may increase the social welfare by bringing about a level of production activity closer to the social cost optimum – an effect which delivery agency staff may be best placed to appreciate.

Inappropriate privatization is most likely to occur where a government agency is externalizing benefits, because where its marginal social cost (MSC) curve lies below its internal costs level there is every likelihood that the agency's internal costs are higher than those of private sector firms with comparable kinds of activity or function. If the legislature becomes aware of this financial costs differential, and is unaware of the agency's externalized benefits, then a potentially attractive case for contracting-out may be perceived. [. . .]

Conclusion and discussion

Table 1 presents the central arguments of the paper in summary form. This presentation should bring out the close theoretical inter-dependence between judgements of the significance of the privatization boom

Table 1 Summary of new right and radical views of privatization

New right views	
Heroic variant	Fatalist variant

1. Basic premises

Bureaucrats are open-ended budget-maximizers. Political sponsor bodies are fragmented and susceptible to log-rolling and pork-barrel pressures for greater spending. Sponsors normally have little detailed control over budgeting because of bureaux' monopoly control of information about marginal costs and benefits, in particular output ranges.

2. Significance of the privatization boom

A major reversal of past trends and a key innovation in changing state agency practices.	Small-scale, incremental and probably once-for-all impact (e.g. in rolling back the worst cases of union restrictive practices).

3. Origins of this effect

New political will of Thatcher/Reagan governments, backed by a sea-change in public attitudes.	Undented high level of bureaucratic power, the involvement of vested interests in agency programmes, union veto powers.

4. Explanation of apparent low bureaucratic resistance to privatization

Bureaucratic power has been successfully attacked by new right governments and undermined by declining public faith in the 'nanny state'. In addition, new policy technologies have a particular bite in an era of generalized fiscal strains.	The bureaucracy has never been more than marginally inconvenienced by new right governments. Hence they have not had to fight very hard to water down the core projects of the Thatcher and Reagan governments.

5. Explanation of 'inappropriate' privatization

Some small-scale instances of welfare-reducing privatization might follow as a by-product of a contractarian form of collective action in the sponsor body. In order to realize the overall collective benefits, sponsor members adhere to a universalized privatization norm designed to prevent departmental 'backsliding'.	Since only minimal privatization can succeed against bureaucratic and interest-group resistance, there is little 'inappropriate' privatization.

Radical account

1. Basic premises

Policy-level officials have strong bureau-shaping goals, subject to a contingent budget constraint. Major trends in state growth have reduced their dependence on high budget appropriations to maintain their welfare, e.g. bureau-shaping can be advanced by creating decentralized networks of state agencies, deconcentrating to QGAs, creating 'dual state' structures, and by internal bureau reorganizations, such as automation/computerization.

2. Significance of the privatization boom

Major accentuation of past trends with new policy technology adapted to foster more rapid bureau-shaping changes.

3. Origins of this effect

Strong interaction between a political/corporate privatization campaign and the congruent interests of policy-level bureaucrats.

4. Explanation of apparent low bureaucratic resistance to privatization

Privatization advances the (class) interests of central and policy-level officials at the expense of job losses and worsened conditions for rank-and-file state workers. It also produces a qualitative and quantitative reduction of services to recipients, especially the poor and the working class.

Table 1—*contd.*

5. Explanation of 'inappropriate' privatization

Main model	Social costs variant
The coincidence of partisan, corporate and bureaucratic pressures over-determines a privatization boom similar to those preceding earlier 'policy booms'.	There is a marked divergence of social and internal costs in state agency operations. Legislators do not take account of the externalized benefits of agency activities, especially in fiscal crises. Hence they push ahead with welfare-reducing privatization.

and reasoning about its origins. I have argued that from a radical perspective the shift to contracting-out forms of privatization must be seen as a continuation of the strategies already well developed by senior policy-level bureaucrats for advancing their class (and frequently gender) interests against those of rank-and-file state workers and service consumers. By contrast, the divergence in new right interpretations reveals a fundamental contradiction inherent in the most widely disseminated public choice models of political processes.

References

Bennett, J. and M. Johnson. 1980. *The Political Economy of Federal Government Growth.* College Station, Texas: Centre for Research and Education in Free Enterprise, Texas A & M University.

Borcherding, T. E. 1977. *Bureaucrats and Budgets.* Durham, North Carolina: Duke University Press.

Breton, A. 1974. *The Economic Theory of Representative Government.* Cambridge: Cambridge University Press.

Buchanan, J. *et al.* 1978. *The Economics of Politics.* London: Institute for Economic Affairs.

Cawson, A. and P. Saunders. 1983. 'Corporatism, competitive politics and class struggle', in R. King (ed.) *Capital and Politics.* London: Routledge & Kegan Paul.

Dunleavy, P. J. 1982a. 'Is there a radical approach to public administration?', *Public Administration*, 60, 215–33.

Dunleavy, P. J. 1982b. 'Quasi-governmental sector professionalism', in A. Barker (ed.) *Quangos in Britain.* London: Macmillan.

Dunleavy, P. J. 1984a. 'Bureaucrats, budgets and the growth of the state, Part I: Existing public choice approaches'. Unpublished paper, LSE: available on request from author.

Dunleavy, P. J. 1984b. 'The limits to local goverment', in M. Boddy and C. Fudge (eds.) *Local Socialism: Labour councils and new left alternatives.* London: Macmillan.

Dunleavy, P. J. 1985. 'Bureaucrats, budgets and the growth of the state: reconstructing an instrumental model', *British Journal of Political Science*, 15, 299–328.

Goodin, R. E. 1982. 'Rational bureaucrats and rational politicians in Washington and Whitehall', *Public Administration*, 60, 23–41.

Grey, C. 1984. 'Marxism and public administration.' Paper to the Annual Conference of the Political Studies Association, University of Southampton, 10 April.

Hardin, R. 1982. *Collective Action*. Baltimore: Johns Hopkins University Press.

Heald, D. 1983. *Public Expenditure*. Oxford: Martin Robertson.

Le Grand, J. and R. Robinson, (eds.). 1984. *Privatizing the Welfare State*. London: Allen & Unwin.

McCormich, B., P. Kitchin, G. Marshall, A. Sampson and B. Sedgwick. 1974. *Introducing Economics*. London: Penguin.

Niskanen, W. A. 1973a. *Bureaucracy and Representative Government*. New York: Aldine-Atherton.

Niskanen, W. A. 1973b. *Bureaucracy: Servant or master?* London: Institute for Economic Affairs.

Niskanen, W. A. 1975. 'Bureaucrats and politicians', *Journal of Law and Economics*, 18, 617–43.

O'Leary, D. B. 1985. 'Is there a radical public administration?', *Public Administration*, 63, 345–52.

Pitt, D. and B. Smith. 1981. *Government Departments*. London: Routledge.

Tullock, G. 1975. *The Vote Motive*. London: Institute for Economic Affairs.

Wilson, J. Q. 1973. *Political Organizations*. New York: Basic Books.

Part IV

Applying policy-making theories

Introduction

This part contains only two, fairly long, extracts. They are included here to pull together some of the ideas about the policy process which have been covered so far, exploring the way different theoretical approaches may be related to each other. Very often contrasting theoretical approaches may be used together, either by pulling out pieces from each or by comparing and contrasting explanations to see how they illuminate the policy process in different ways. Policy analysis is not an exact science. It involves trying to understand and explain events in situations in which we never have complete information about what happened and why it happened, and our interpretations are influenced by our frames of reference and our ideologies.

In the article by Blowers two perspectives – the pluralist and the political economy perspective – are contrasted. The second perspective is the one which derives from Marxist theory and emphasises structured economic determinants of action. Blowers subsequently examined this story at much greater length, and with even more elaborate use of the theories, in his book *Something in the Air: Corporate power and the environment*. In this article he ends by stressing the way in which two explanations may stand side by side, illuminating the story in different ways. In his book he goes further, to suggest ways in which the theories may be differentially used to illuminate different parts and different phases in the long saga of pollution control policy in the brickfields he studied.

The second extract comes from Chris Ham's book on British health policy. He explicitly contrasts Marxist and pluralist perspectives but takes us on to the sort of structuralist perspective adopted by Alford which, whilst having more in common with Marxism than with pluralism, recognises interests which extend beyond simple economic ones. Two crucial interests are identified, called by Alford those of 'professional monopolists' and 'corporate rationalisers', which, whilst they have links with wider economic interests, have an autonomy of their own – in the British case, embedded within the autonomous state. Hence we are reminded of the need to look within the state, but also see that we have to recognise that the state may be no more a unitary concept than are the 'capital' and 'labour' of simplistic Marxist theory. In looking within the state to the interests of two specific groups, in this case doctors and managers within the health service, we need to bear in mind Dunleavy's injunction to consider carefully the 'bureau-shaping' activities which such groups may pursue, and to recognise the implications of these for health policy outputs.

Reference

Blowers, A., *Something in the Air: Corporate power and the environment* (London, Harper & Row, 1984).

Master of fate or victim of circumstance

The exercise of corporate power in environmental policy-making

Andrew Blowers

Introduction

The debate about corporate power has tended to polarise around two theoretical perspectives. One, the *pluralist* view, argues that business is an interest group competing with other interests for access to decision makers in a relatively open political framework. In this view, business pursues its economic objectives but also reacts to social pressures for control over its activities exerted by the interests of consumers, labour and the environment. Strategies of cooperation, concession and compromise are arbitrated through a responsive, representative and democratic policy which engages in consultation with the interests involved, promoting policies which seek to balance economic, social and technological factors. The other view, the *political economy* perspective, defines business as a dominant force engaged in the control of large sectors of economic and political life. Business is 'not simply another interest group: its role [is] actually more akin to that of a ruling class or dominant elite' (Vogel, 1981, pp. 1–2). Business power is all pervasive, controlling the nation's technology, pattern of work organisation,

From A. Blowers, 'Master of fate or victim of circumstance – the exercise of corporate power in environmental policy-making', *Policy and Politics*, **11**, 1983, pp. 393–415.

location of industry, market structure, resource allocation and income distribution. Business is able to penetrate all levels of political decision making and, by strategies of manipulation, information control and sanctions, is able to define the political agenda and resist controls or financial penalties that threaten its continued prosperity.

The debate about corporate power has suffered in that it has been conducted at a largely abstract level and where specific evidence is used it is often transposed into grand generalisations which may be inapplicable across different societies. Temporal and spatial factors have often been neglected. Viewed over time it is possible to conceive different periods during which business was on the defensive, followed by periods when it was able to exert power more aggressively. 'Instead of endlessly debating the power of business in the abstract or focusing on the outcomes of particular policy disputes, political scientists need to pay more attention to the processes by which the power of business as a whole varies over time' (Vogel, *op. cit.*, p. 3). Similarly, the power of business varies according to place. Some countries, or regions within countries, provide a more propitious environment for business expansion than do others. Disadvantages (climate, wage and union structure, resource availability, infrastructure) can be partly overcome by various forms of concession (subsidies, incentives, state spending on services for industry etc.). The question that needs to be answered is how business responds to these temporal and spatial differences. On the one hand it may seek to accommodate to the pressures exerted upon it or, alternatively, it may exploit its power by seeking to undermine constraints or extract concessions which favour its interests.

One way in to understanding the exercise of corporate power is to focus on an aspect of business interaction with government. The environmental problems created by business activity—air and water pollution, dereliction and resource depletion—impose costs on the community which have provoked government intervention in the form of controls, regulations and standards. In support of the pluralist case it can be argued that this intervention reflects the power of environmental groups able to restrain industry by exploiting the available legal and political opportunities. Against this it can be argued that the success of government intervention is more apparent than real. Businessmen may accept certain restrictions but only to the point where business efficiency will be impaired. 'Hence they often predict dire consequences when a new regulation is imposed on them, yet thereafter quickly find ways to prosper under it' (Lindblom, 1977, p. 179). Technological and economic changes have had a far more profound impact on environmental improvement than has been achieved through regulation. For example, changes in fuel type, in housing design and in population density were already reducing the incidence of pollution from smoke and sulphur dioxide when the Clean Air Act was introduced in Britain in 1956 (Waller, 1982). It is possible to conclude that, 'even when policy making and state intervention have appeared to play a part this merely acts to reinforce the economic interests of the polluter and the polluted' (Sandbach, 1982, p. 3). In many cases industry simply claims that pollution control is neither technically nor economically feasible and so little progress is made.

In trying to establish whether or not business has been able to sustain its objectives in the face of environmental pressures we need to define what exactly constitutes the exercise of power. There are various definitions, each stressing a particular outcome of the exercise of power. One definition sees power in terms of dominance in decision making. 'The power of a group or class is a function of its ability to define the political agenda, to win political victories, and to benefit disproportionately from policy outcomes' (Vogel, *op. cit.*, p. 4). The strategies deployed by industry in the environmental field are similar to those outlined by Kimber and Richardson (1974). They include the use of advance intelligence and information, privileged access to officials and decision makers, and raising public consciousness by rational argument on the merits of the case. The control by industry of information sources about the technological and economic implications of control and its superior resources for employing expertise and influencing decisions are critical weapons in defending its cause. But it may be felt these resources have been matched by environmentalist groups using their access and deploying countervailing command of information and expertise, often sufficient to neutralise the power of business.

Another definition of power focuses on its impact. 'By "power" I mean the ability to make decisions having effects upon a substantial portion of the community, or a considerable impact upon a smaller public' (Reagan, 1963, p. 74). Industry may impose costs of pollution and dereliction on a wide public, which stimulates antagonism and organised opposition. But it also confers jobs on a smaller section of that same public and is able to build powerful coalitions of workers and capital to defy environmental groups. And it can also exploit territorial divisions by threatening to remove its activities (and their economic benefits) to more welcoming locations. This threat of investment withdrawal, if it can be carried out, remains the most powerful weapon of business. It suggests a third definition of power, 'the ability of a class or group to realise its own specific objectives' (Sandbach, 1980, p. 135). The objectives of industry are to maintain its productive capacity at least cost in order to achieve maximum profitability. The extent to which it succeeds will determine whether business is dominant, or merely an interest group having to accommodate its objectives in the face of opposing interests.

Environmental issues provide a good test bed for examining the exercise of corporate power. In particular they enable us to confront the alternative versions proffered by pluralists and exponents of political economy. These alternatives can be posed in the form of two propositions,

—*corporate power can be defined as an interest in conflict with other interests (such as environmental interests) each with different objectives. The outcome of this conflict is uncertain and depends on changes in circumstances which favour certain interests against others.*

—*corporate power may be conceived as a class interest able to achieve its objectives in the face of opposition from other interests (such as environmental groups) by adopting strategies that best exploit the circumstances. The outcome in this case is predictable, only the means for achieving it are uncertain.*

By examining a particular case I shall show how both positions can contribute to our understanding of the exercise of corporate power. This example covers a period during which circumstances changed (sometimes dramatically) and in which alternative locations played a part in influencing decisions.

There are, of course, problems in offering generalisations from individual cases but the lack of empirical evidence on this question needs to be remedied. 'Case studies leave to their readers the task of determining how findings add to previous knowledge . . . A hypothesis (which sets forth conditions and consequences) even though incorrect is easier to relate to new experience than are collections of unexceptionable but unorganised anecdotes' (Polsby, 1980, pp. 122–3). With this in mind I offer this case study to demonstrate that both the above propositions may prove valid—it is merely a question of how the evidence is interpreted.

London Brick Company

The London Brick Company, by a process of mergers and takeovers conducted over several decades, had achieved by 1974 a monopoly of fletton brickmaking (Hillier, 1981; Cox, 1979). The fletton process is based on the thick Oxford Clay deposits of Buckinghamshire, Bedfordshire and Cambridgeshire. The clay produces bricks of consistent quality and contains a high organic content which enables the bricks virtually to fire themselves. Fletton bricks are, therefore, cheap to produce and can bear transport costs, giving London Brick access to a national market taking about 40% of the total brick output. Demand for bricks is linked to the fortunes of the construction industry. Booms in production (such as in 1973 when London Brick produced over 3,000 million bricks) are followed by slumps and, in the current recession, the company's output is less than half its 1973 figure. London Brick's dominant position in the market and in the Oxford Clay area provides it with support from national interests concerned with construction and from local interests concerned with employment and the local economy. But the fletton brick industry gives rise to major environmental problems. One is the dereliction caused by the excavation of clay; the other is air pollution which results from the emission of sulphur oxides, fluorides and organic substances known as mercaptans which give rise to the offensive smell characteristic of the brickfields. Over time, as dereliction has increased and public sensitivity to environmental issues has developed, these problems have provoked opposition calling for restoration of the clay pits and control of air pollution.

The conflict between economic and environmental interests came to a head in 1979 when the company applied for planning permission to rebuild its major brickworks in the Marston Vale in Bedfordshire. It proposed to build two new 'superworks', one at Stewartby in the centre of the Vale and the other to the south of Ridgmont near the M1. Each works would be built in two phases, each phase having a capacity of 5 million bricks per week, totalling 10 million per week for the works. Effluent gases would be emitted through tall chimneys, one for each phase (two for each works) 400 feet above ground level. Thus four new chimneys would replace the 98 smaller chimneys at existing works and were accepted by the Alkali Inspector as the best practicable means of pollution control. In the Inspector's view the pollutants would be dispersed and diluted and rendered harmless through the tall stacks. He shared the industry's view that pollution abatement was neither technically nor economically feasible but that provision for a third flue should be made during construction of the works in the event of appropriate technology being discovered. These proposals were met with resistance from environmentalists, farmers, local residents and some politicians. Although they accepted the principle of new works for the future prosperity of the industry and the local economy they maintained that permission should be withheld unless pollution control measures were installed.

The environmentalists seized the opportunities afforded them by the dispersal of powers over pollution control. Formally, the control of emissions is a matter for either district councils or the Alkali Inspectorate. The districts (Environmental Health Departments), operating under the Clean Air Acts (1956, 1968), are responsible for the control of smoke emissions from domestic and commercial premises and from furnaces. The districts also have controls (under the Public Health Act,

1936) over industries which cause a nuisance or which are designated as 'offensive trades'. There remain many industrial processes 'which are not subject to any prospective or anticipatory controls' (Wood, 1982, p. 3). But major processes which, because of the quantity of emissions or technical problems of control, cannot be dealt with locally are registered under the Alkali Acts. They are subject to the control of district Alkali Inspectors with prospective powers over new works and retrospective powers over existing works, who apply the concept of 'best practicable means' for abatement. 'The Chief Inspector . . . lays down the broad national policies and, provided they keep within their broad guidelines, inspectors in the field have plenty of flexibility to take into account local circumstances and make suitable decisions' (Hill, p. 13). Inspectors thus work in a negotiating role with industry in reaching decisions (Vogel, 1980). Although the agency is well versed in technical criteria it also considers economic aspects and its lack of formal competence in this area must, according to Bennett, 'cast doubt on the soundness of its decisions' (1979, p. 95).

The close relationship between the Inspectorate and industry excludes environmentalist pressures. This has led environmentalists to encourage the use of planning powers to exert greater control over polluters. Planning authorities can influence the source and impact of emissions through their control over location and land use. They may also use discretionary powers in the form of planning conditions, agreements and policies. The possible duplication of powers between authorities has led the Department of the Environment (1981) to remind local planning authorities that 'planning conditions should not be used to regulate pollution where appropriate specific powers can be used'. Nevertheless, the tendency to employ such powers has led to increasing conflict between the environmentalists, applying pressure through planning conditions and policies, and industry, resisting any controls which go beyond those required by the Alkali Inspector. Both sides may be prepared to negotiate and achieve compromise through planning agreements though, as in the following case, this may be insufficient to prevent conflict.

The conflict did not suddenly erupt but had a long period of gestation. It is possible to trace four stages in the development of the conflict. The first, a long period during which environmental issues flared up from time to time, did not produce any significant change in the company's policies towards dereliction or air pollution. This can be described as the *non decisionmaking* phase. The issue became active once the permissions had been applied for in 1979 and, at first, there was a phase of *negotiation* between the opposing groups. Later, when negotiation failed to realise a victory for either side, the conflict deepened into a phase of *confrontation*. Finally, there was the phase of *resolution* when the conflict was settled and the issue, once more, subsided in terms of public debate. In the following account I shall focus on the changes in political and economic circumstances during the course of the conflict and the strategies employed by the company in meeting these changes. What we have to consider is whether changes in the company's strategy were deliberate, based on careful calculation of outcomes, or simply reactions to changing but unforeseen events, pragmatic adjustments rather than preconceived plans.

The phase of non decisionmaking
Throughout the post-war period there has been public concern about the visible problems of dereliction and a less palpable, but more profound, anxiety about the risks to human health, animals and crops from air pollution. From time to time this has erupted in public debate, for example at a public inquiry into a proposal to build a new brickworks at Woburn Sands (Bucks.) in 1966 (Porteous *et al.*, 1977), at a conference on the brickfields at Bedford in 1967 (Beds. County Council, 1967), and during the public consultation on the structure and minerals plans for Bedfordshire during 1976–8 (Beds. County Council, 1976a and b, 1978a and b). Despite all the argument nothing was achieved; in essence it was a period of non decisionmaking in which the company carried on its activities without serious challenge.

Just after the war the various brick companies operating in the Marston Vale were granted a series of planning permissions by the Minister at a time when the national need for bricks was an overriding concern. These permissions covered vast areas, providing the industry with sufficient clay resources to last until well into the next century. The conditions attached to the permissions were very liberal [. . .] and there was no reference to air pollution save in one permission, where the Minister 'observes that your Research Department are working to eliminate to the greatest degree the possibility of damage to the countryside from injurious fumes' (Letter to London Brick Co. Ltd., 26th May 1949). Given such relative freedom to despoil and pollute, the brick companies had no need to take any positive action except some cosmetic tree planting to assist good public relations, or to find material to fill the pits at a profit.

During the 1950s and 60s cases of fluorosis (a debilitating bone disease in cattle attributed to the ingestion of fluorides) were reported in the brickfields. Research had revealed a higher incidence of this disease in Bedfordshire than in other areas, with the clear implication that the problem was caused by the brickworks (Burns and Allcroft, 1964). London Brick tackled this problem in three ways—by buying up land for its own farming; by out of court settlements with farmers negotiated with the National Farmers' Union; and by a clause in which its tenants waived all claims for damage caused by the company's activities. In these ways farming interests were kept relatively quiet until the late 1970s, when they played a major part in the opposition to the company's redevelopment plans.

Armed with its liberal planning permissions the company had little need to stir itself to action to defend its interests. It was able to argue that restoration was only possible if massive amounts of fill could be imported at an economic cost. It could point to contracts negotiated [. . .] to import domestic waste into the brickfields to restore one of the worked out pits. And it could claim, with the support of the Alkali Inspector, that there were no processes of pollution control that were either economic or technically feasible.

However, by the late 1970s the national need for bricks was no longer overriding; new methods of construction had gained ground and construction was at a low level. Research evidence on the hazards of pollution to human health, though statistically inadequate and inconclusive (e.g. Brothwood Report, 1960) had contributed to a growing public concern about the company's activities which reflected a more general shift in values in favour of environmental concerns. The company's failure to provide adequate landscaping or to ensure restoration fuelled public antagonism. Opposition which had, hitherto, been sporadic and ephemeral began to establish a firm base as local action groups made common cause with conservationist and farming interests. They but waited an opportunity. That opportunity came with the company's redevelopment plans. London Brick found itself embattled with powerful and well-organised environmental interests able to exploit political circumstances. In this atmosphere London Brick's long established, largely low profile strategy would no longer serve as an adequate defence.

The phase of negotiation
It was clear that, initially, the company was unaware of the public hostility that could be orchestrated into strong opposition. The Managing Director reflected the mood of the company, observing, 'We thought the plans would be snatched from our hands and we'd be told to get on with it as soon as possible'. This complacent attitude had been encouraged by the lack of resistance to similar plans in neighbouring Cambridgeshire where two new superworks had already been opened. The company were simultaneously applying for permissions for a further new works in Cambridgeshire, and had plans for one in Buckinghamshire as well as the two new Bedfordshire works. Its stated priorities were to build first at Ridgmont, then at Stewartby in a long term programme of complete redevelopment of the fletton industry which would reduce the labour force, thereby increasing productivity and

enabling the company at least to maintain its share of a market which was in secular decline. Whether or not it was foreseen at the time, this blanket series of applications would enable the company later to switch its investment priorities, giving it the flexibility needed to outmanoeuvre opposition.

The company made its early approaches through the Bedfordshire planning officials and the Chairman of the Environmental Services Committee (the planning committee). During the period before an application is made companies enjoy confidential and privileged access to authorities and the opportunity to discuss their plans in confidence. This has been called the 'pre-parliamentary' phase by Knoepfel *et al.*, during which companies 'seek to define the problem in such a way that problem solving strategies are considered and ultimately selected which give the emitters a maximum degree of freedom of action and legal security while, at the same time, causing them only minimal costs' (1980, p. 45).

The planning officials had long been concerned with the problem of dereliction but had been frustrated by the permissive conditions which gave them little power to impose restoration on the company. The company recognised that concessions would need to be offered to secure the support of the planning officials and, through them, the elected members. London Brick proposed a package of environmental improvements in return for the permissions. It was agreed the package should be negotiated in the form of a Section 52 Planning Agreement legally binding on the company. Section 52 Agreements are regarded by some commentators as evidence of corporatism in town planning, 'a drift away from the taken-for-granted values and assumptions which underlie pluralist democracy, and towards the values and assumptions inherent in the philosophy of corporatism' (Reade, 1982, pp. 10–11). Such agreements are conducted in secret and bargains are struck in which 'developers and planners are likely to develop shared perspectives as to which things are in "the public interest" and which are not' (p. 13). Agreements are justified as a means of securing planning gains in return for planning permissions and this was certainly how the Bedfordshire agreement was portrayed. 'These environmental advantages amount to a very attractive package indeed and it is difficult to envisage any other circumstances in which such far reaching improvements could be achieved' (Report to Environmental Services Committee, 27th March 1980, p. 50).

The planning officials were also concerned about the siting of the new Ridgmont works. Instead of the existing site on a prominent ridge visible for miles around they preferred a site beneath ground level in an exhausted part of a clay pit. This idea provoked a local action group representing a village downwind of the site to claim that the planners were attempting 'to force a new brickworks and its obnoxious side effects onto an hitherto unaffected residential area' (Cranfield Action Committee, 5th June 1979). The short campaign they mounted was totally successful and the company withdrew the scheme in favour of the site adjacent to the existing works.

Once the application had been submitted in August 1979 the 'parliamentary' phase began. During this phase the outcome 'will depend on the balance of power among the interested actors involved . . . and the strategies they use in pursuing their objectives' (Knoepfel *et al.*, *op. cit.*, p. 14). It soon became evident that pollution rather than dereliction was the key political issue. Opponents claimed that the dangers from pollution had been underestimated and that the company had failed to pursue abatement measures or monitoring of emissions with sufficient vigour. Tall chimneys, they asserted, would only disperse the problem more widely. A cause for concern became a call for control. The pollution issue offered opponents the best prospect of a powerful coalition embracing local action groups and the farming community, already aware of the pollution hazards. Hence fluorides became the main focus of attention, though London Brick continued to stress smell as the main problem. The dangers of fluoride were less obvious but more sinister than smell or sulphur dioxide and, for that reason, became a more compelling issue.

London Brick responded to this new challenge with a predictable defence. They relied on the Alkali Inspector's view, reiterated in successive reports, that levels of fluoride were 'satisfactorily low'; that tall chimneys would virtually eliminate the problem; that pollution control equipment was neither technically nor economically feasible; and that the third flue would be installed to treat gases if it was found to be necessary and if appropriate technology could be proven. They sought to minimise the problem. 'The effluent also contains a minute amount of fluoride, the concentration measured at ground level being about one-hundredth of the threshold limit for possible effects on human health' (London Brick Company, 1978, p. 17). [. . .]

Having selected fluoride as their target the opposition began to mobilise political support. The general background of public disquiet was orchestrated by a group of powerful interests which emerged to spearhead the attack on the company. This group was called Public Review of Brickmaking and the Environment (PROBE) and was chaired by the Marquis of Tavistock, with his seat at Woburn Abbey and extensive land holdings in the county. Its membership included leading county councillors, MPs, local businessmen, medical and engineering experts and a local farmer who claimed his cattle were suffering from fluorosis. Using contacts with the local and national media, with farming interests and with government ministers, PROBE increased the political salience of the pollution issue.

The County Council had commissioned a report from consultants to investigate the effects of pollution, methods of control and monitoring, and to advise the Council on what action should be taken on the permissions. The report concluded, 'The case for fluoride removal, with respect to grazing animals, is unproven at the present time' (Cremer and Warner, 1979, p. A24). Although methods of fluoride removal were possible there was no technique for removing all pollutants. The problems of raw materials, waste disposal and production costs made the known processes unattractive. The report defined odour rather than fluoride as the main problem, recommending that planning permission should be deferred or rejected until alternative kilning techniques had been developed to remove the smell. The report appeared to confirm the company's claims, though on the subject of odour removal it was not aware 'of any practicable or proven technology which will permit the realisation of this objective' (London Brick Company, 1980, p. 1). Still the company was prepared to negotiate. It offered one further conces-sion—a part permission for the first stage of one of the new works using conventional technology and the deferral of the second stage while a research programme was undertaken to demonstrate the feasibility of pollution control measures. This concession did not satisfy the oppo-nents and marked the end of the phase of negotiation.

The phase of confrontation
The limits of negotiation were formally embodied in the Section 52 Agreement. This provided for comprehensive schemes of buffer zones around villages; demolition of old works; landscaping and tree planting; and revocation of the old permissions with much tighter conditions. It also embraced the concept of a part planning permission and participa-tion by the County Council in a research programme on pollution control. This represented an attempt to secure greater control over areas in which formal planning powers were relatively weak. Environ-mentalists regarded the Agreement as no more than the company should be expected to offer. They were sceptical about the possibility of enforcement and recognised that the restoration of the pits depended on the unlikely prospect of vast amounts of waste material becoming available. On the pollution issue, too, environmentalists questioned whether concessions had been made. All the company had agreed to do was carry out a research programme prior to the second stage of the works being built. If no techniques were found to be feasible or economic the company could go ahead using conventional technology. The company's plans had in no way been hindered by this agreement.

Conversely, London Brick regarded these concessions as the limit to which it could go—any further and its investment programme would be impeded, involving high costs and unacceptable delays. The use of a Planning Agreement to introduce a pollution research programme might be viewed, on the one hand, as an unwarranted intrusion of planning into an area under the jurisdiction of another agency, or an assertion of the local public interest in an area where it might otherwise have been unrepresented.

At this point, with an intransigent opposition matched by an unyielding company, the room for compromise had disappeared and the two sides were in confrontation. The company had exhausted its advantages of privileged access to officials and its negotiations had failed to secure an easy passage for its application. The issue now entered the political arena. On one side were supporters of London Brick, led by the Chairman of the Environmental Services Committee, who were anxious to cooperate with the company and felt a good bargain could be struck which balanced environmental needs against the jobs and wealth resulting from the investment. Opposing them were those who felt that more could be extracted from the company which was portrayed by the Leader of the Council as 'the unacceptable face of capitalism'. Politically, the 71 Conservatives, the dominant group on the Council, were split, representing two strands in the party—a conservationist wing with strong rural interests and a wing favouring private enterprise as embodied in London Brick. The small opposition groups (Labour, 9 members, and Liberal, 2 members) [. . .] opposed the company. It had been agreed that the planning permissions were so significant that they should be decided by the full Council of 83 members.

Delays had already caused the company to review its investment plans. It now wished to develop at Stewartby rather than at Ridgmont to take advantage of the need to open up clay reserves nearby. In March, 1980, the Environmental Services Committee, by a large majority, recommended the Council to grant a part permission for redevelopment at Stewartby. London Brick was confident of success but, at the April meeting of the County Council, another obstacle was encountered. A report on the pollution problem commissioned by the Department of the Environment (1980) was not ready and so a decision was deferred until the following July.

This delay was used by PROBE to undertake an extensive press campaign and lobbying among the uncommitted members of the Council. A pamphlet supporting new brickworks, 'But not at any price!', was issued and members of the Council were provided with free champagne and persuasion in the Portrait Gallery at Woburn Abbey. At the Council meeting in July London Brick's opponents, skilfully led by the Leader of the Council, by a majority of 38 to 28 with 17 absent or abstaining, applied a new condition to the permission for the first phase of the Stewartby works. This required that the brick kilns should be 'so designed as to be capable of removing the pollutants (sulphur dioxide and fluoride) and odours given off in the firing process' (County Council, 3rd July 1980, Minute 80/73). The Council also deferred a decision on the application for the Ridgmont Works, a decision which was to prove of far greater significance later.

The company had, up to this point, relied on its access to officials to persuade local politicians. Its objectives had been thwarted and so it responded by a more direct approach. Its first move was to reinterpret the condition. The Council, it was argued, having approved the new works would need to apply conditions that were 'both reasonable and not repugnant to the permission'. On legal advice the condition was interpreted to mean, 'the kilns shall be so designed as to be capable of removing the pollutants and odours to the gas treatment plant if and when an appropriate plant can be constructed'. This was followed by a direct appeal by the Chairman of London Brick at a meeting with council members. For the first time a hint was given that the company would, if necessary, withdraw its investment if it did not gain satisfaction from the County Council [. . .].

Despite the sympathy of the Environmental Services Committee the County Council was not persuaded by these new pressures. It was clear that the Council had meant that pollution control should be applied before the works were commissioned and not at some future date, if and when such measures became available. The appearance of the company Chairman at a meeting with members was criticised as an unfortunate precedent. The Council in December 1980 confirmed its original decision by 43 votes to 33. This proved to be the apogee of the opponents' cause. Events now moved swiftly in favour of the company.

The phase of resolution
Unable to gain a permission through negotiation or through political confrontation, the company precipitated a change in the political environment by announcing that it was no longer pursuing its development plans for Stewartby. In February 1981 a permission for a new superworks at Whittlesey was granted by Cambridgeshire County Council without a pollution condition and this became the company's first investment priority, implying it would be up to a decade before it revived its plans for Stewartby or Ridgmont. The initial strategy of applying for several works in different counties appeared to have paid off in that the Achilles Heel had been found in Cambridgeshire.

Meanwhile, the recession had deepened, weakening the company's outlook but, paradoxically, strengthening its hand with Bedfordshire County Council. During a recession the brick industry combines a reduction in production capacity through short-time working with an increase in stockholding. There comes a point when these measures are unable to reduce the supply of bricks sufficiently and the closure of complete works becomes necessary. The choice of which works to close is economically determined. [. . .] By the beginning of 1981 London Brick was on short-time working and stocks amounted to five months' supply, and there was no hint of improvement in the market. The company decided to close a major works and selected Ridgmont, the second largest works in Bedfordshire, to close in May 1981 with the loss of 1,100 jobs. It justified the decision on the grounds that Ridgmont was an old works producing bricks of variable quality with a high wastage, and that it was of the right size (14% of total output) to achieve the necessary reduction in production capacity. Whether fortuitous or by design the closure of Ridgmont was of major political significance.

Bedfordshire was faced with the twin prospect of no investment in new works and the closure of one of its large old works. Employment, not pollution, was now the major issue. The environmentalist case was fatally weakened and a powerful alliance of material interests—capital and labour—took the initiative. The trade unions exerted telling pressure on councillors, particularly the Labour Group, whose votes had been decisive in opposing the company's plans. With a County Council election due the following May the brickworks issue promised to be an important, and in some seats a crucial, issue.

London Brick, once again, changed their investment strategy. If an acceptable permission could be obtained in Bedfordshire it would receive priority over Cambridgeshire. Further delays had weakened the case for Stewartby and the closure of Ridgmont opened up the opportunity to develop there. Fortuitously the County Council had deferred a decision on the Ridgmont works but the company had not withdrawn its application. The way was therefore still open for the Council to permit a new works at Ridgmont. In the changed economic circumstances the Environmental Services Committee in March 1981, urged on by the councillor for the Ridgmont area and without reference to the County Council, granted permission for the Ridgmont works without any pollution condition on the first phase. It incorporated the Section 52 Agreement for a research programme to investigate pollution control measures that might be applied to later phases of the development.

In economic terms the prospect of lost investment and jobs had motivated labour interests to apply pressure. Politically, a looming election had concentrated the minds of councillors. Procedurally, the undetermined application for Ridgmont and the decision not to refer the matter once again to the Council had presented the company's supporters with the means of achieving victory. But it was a pyrrhic victory since the prospect of investment had receded and the company announced the closure of further works, including one of two remaining in Bedfordshire. A more apposite conclusion would be that everybody had lost—workers had lost jobs, environmentalists had lost the chance of enforcing pollution control measures, the company had lost its investment opportunity, and the community had lost the wealth generated by brickmaking.

Master of fate or victim of circumstance?

We can now return to the propositions reflecting alternative interpretations of corporate power to examine which better stands the test of the evidence from the London Brick case study. On the one hand, the political economy view suggests a close correspondence between economic power and political achievement. The company, in this view, possessed reserves of power so that it could manipulate circumstances in its favour. Its ultimate success was inevitable though the means for achieving it varied. Alternatively, the pluralist view perceives power allocated among competing interests. In this view the company was buffeted by circumstances, shifting from one strategy to another as it faced obstacles strewn in its path by opponents. Throughout the debate the outcome was unclear and depended on the relative power available to different participants. These views may now be compared by providing alternative versions of the conflict.

The political economy interpretation
For a long period London Brick appeared to be inactive—action was unnecessary since the company could not be challenged. The lack of sufficient opposition to influence the company's policies may be explained as a recognition of the company's power and the weakness of its opponents. It was a case of anticipated reactions, a belief that nothing could be achieved by action. In Moodie's words, 'the absence of pressure may therefore be of little significance—it could, conceivably, mean either that the potential pressure is so great that it need not be applied, or that the aggrieved group has no leverage' (1970, p. 65). The planning permissions provided the company with the freedom to avoid action. Certainly the planning officials felt there was no means by which they could force the company to achieve restoration of the clay pits. The company, by undertaking minimal tree planting, by refuting the research evidence on the hazards of pollution and by denying the possibility of pollution control, was able to defeat attempts to exercise

some control over its activities. Its largely passive strategy can be seen as a mobilisation of bias sufficient to prevent opponents from realising their common interest in seeking environmental improvements.

The period of non decisionmaking was not unlike that described by Crenson (1971) in Gary (Indiana). [See the extract from Lukes in Part II of the reader.]

There is some evidence of suppression of the air pollution issue by London Brick. When opposition did become manifest in the 1960s over the issue of cattle fluorosis the company acted decisively, buying up land, settling out of court with farmers and employing a tough tenancy clause. Thus by a combination of inaction, and, when necessary, suppression, London Brick avoided interference in its activities for three decades.

When public opposition crystallised around the redevelopment plans the company met it by adjusting its strategy. London Brick recognised that it was most likely to secure its objectives by working closely with the planning officials. Planners, it seemed, would be happy to trade some improvement in the landscape for planning permissions without air pollution controls. The company possessed a shrewd insight into the attitudes of officials.

> Yet ordinarily as new problems arise—for example, public demands for restriction on air pollution—businessmen know that government officials will understand their wishes—in this case their unwillingness or incapacity to bear without help the costs of stopping industrial discharges through the air. Businessmen will find the government official ready to acknowledge their special competence and interest, eager to welcome them into negotiation, anxious about the possible adverse effects of costly antipollution measures on prices and production. (Lindblom, *op. cit.*, p. 184.)

The company's investment strategy had an inevitable logic. By applying simultaneously for new works in three counties it would be possible to sift out the weakest point. Once this was established the company could divide and rule, achieving permissions at all locations on the terms offered by the most permissive authority, in this case Cambridgeshire. Similarly the company applied for two sites at Ridgmont when only one was required. It could accept the one which attracted the least opposition. The planners, left to choose the site, would face the opprobrium while the company would appear to be responding to public pressure. Again, the apparently perverse switch of investment priorities from Ridgmont to Stewartby and back to Ridgmont can be seen as a calculated manoeuvre to exploit changing circumstances. Delays at Ridgmont left Stewartby as an acceptable proposition. But when the Council impeded its plans London Brick was able to revert to its Ridgmont application, which it had not withdrawn and which the Council had not determined. This shows a subtle appreciation of available opportunities.

Once the pollution issue had emerged the company appeared willing to offer concessions. It was prepared to accept a part permission and to undertake research into pollution before the second stage was commissioned. In reality it had conceded nothing since its investment programme would not be interrupted and it had always accepted the possibility of pollution control if appropriate technology could be proved. Failing a technical break-through the permission enabled it to build the second stage without abatement measures. The company refused to accept fluoride as a problem, arguing that the offensive smells should be tackled first. Thus the initiative on pollution research and control remained firmly with the company.

When the company's concessions failed to convince the Council it shifted to a more ebullient strategy. It first hinted that it would withdraw its investment, usually sufficient to cause the capitulation of opposition. Businessmen 'need only point to the costs of doing business, the state of the economy, the dependence of the economy's stability and growth on their profits or sales prospects—and simply predict, not threaten, that adverse consequences will follow on a refusal of their demands' (Lindblom, *op. cit.*, p. 185). In this case the hint was not quite sufficient and was transformed into a threat with the announcement of a change in investment priorities to Cambridgeshire. Although the deepening recession made the closure of plant inevitable the selection of Ridgmont, it could be argued, happened to exert the maximum amount of pressure on the County Council. Furthermore, the alliance with the unions was another means of extracting an acceptable permission. In sum, when the possibilities of peaceful cooperation with the Council had failed to produce the goods, all the company had to do was to deploy the reserves of power which it commanded to secure a desirable outcome.

In terms of the definitions of power stated earlier it is possible to argue that London Brick had ultimately managed, in Vogel's terms, to set the political agenda and had won a political victory. There was little doubt either that it had the ability to make decisions which would have a major impact on the community in terms of pollution and jobs (Reagan, 1963). It had ample resources, possessed insight into the political process, and could play a waiting game. The acid test of its strategy was a success in realising its objectives (Sandbach, 1982) and here, too, it had gained a planning permission, different in some details, but in principle what it had originally asked for. This political economy interpretation has a neat symmetry and a plausible logic. But it can also be argued that the company failed to benefit from the conflict and that it failed above all to secure the investment, though economic circumstances were responsible for that. The flaws in this interpretation become apparent when the same evidence is examined from a pluralist viewpoint.

The pluralist interpretation

Pluralists would agree that for a long time after the original permissions had been granted action by the company was unnecessary. But they would dispute the explanation for this. Polsby, a leading pluralist, argues, 'If a issue is not raised in a community, there are at least two possible reasons why it is not: either it is being suppressed or there is a genuine consensus that it is not an issue' (*op. cit.*, p. 216). Pluralists would point to the national consensus in favour of brickmaking and the lack of any tangible disquiet about the environmental issue at local level. It is quite conceivable that during this early phase, until the dereliction issue became obvious and anxieties about cattle fluorosis were aroused, the issue was disregarded and public opinion was quiescent. This lack of interest or abstention on the part of the public should occasion no surprise. 'How does abstention differ from apathy, laziness, pessimism, or lack of interest in politics? These are all widespread; indeed they are the common condition. Most people prefer spending their time, money, and skill for purposes other than shaping public policy' (Wolfinger, 1972, p. 1071).

Once opposition was aroused the company was forced to respond and to lean heavily on the support of government bodies, notably the Alkali Inspector. Opponents challenged the company's failure to act in the spirit of the planning permissions and viewed the close relationship between the company and the Alkali Inspector with suspicion. As Bennett observes, 'the Inspectorate chooses to pursue a policy of close cooperation with industry and only rarely resorts to formal enforcement procedures' (1979, p. 95). When the fluorosis issue developed London Brick reacted pragmatically to buy off the opposition. Over the long non decision making phase the company's varied and unpremeditated responses helped to create a climate of suspicion and hostility that would eventually transform the balance of power between London Brick and its opponents.

It appears that the intensity of opposition which greeted the company's redevelopment plans in 1979 took it by surprise, resulting in a change of strategy. Pluralists would see its reaction as defensive with the company uncertain which course to follow. At first, London Brick sensed that its privileged access to the planning officials would enable it to secure the planning permissions. The company seemed to discount the fact that the advice of officials might be rejected by the politicians. Thus, when the sympathy and reassurance it received from officials was not matched by a welcome from the politicians the company was, once again, caught unawares and faced a powerful opposition it had not anticipated.

Pluralists would see little that was sinister in the company applying for several sites in different counties at the same time. The company had adopted a long term investment programme and had presumably not expected permissions to be any more difficult to gain at one site than another. Its priorities were determined by financial criteria. Bedford-shire appeared to be the company's first priority, a point that was later confirmed by the company's Chairman.

> I really cannot commit my Board at this stage to where it starts. The last thing I would like to suggest to you is that our position would be in any way influenced by the fact that we have now permissions both in Buckinghamshire and of course in Cambridgeshire. We will have to decide in terms of the total modernisation programme where we should start . . . If it is any help for you and I am talking informally . . . I personally would like to see a start in Bedfordshire, but that does not commit the decision taken by the Board. (Report to Environmental Services Committee, 9th December 1980, p. 20.)

As to the decision to apply for alternative sites at Ridgmont, this can be explained in terms of accepting the planners' advice that options should be presented for debate. When public opposition to one site developed the company reacted by agreeing to locate the works at the other site. The shift to Stewartby was again a reaction to events. The delays encountered at Ridgmont meant it was necessary to build first at Stewartby to take advantage of the new clay workings there.

As the conflict deepened the company found itself giving ground. It offered a series of concessions, the Section 52 Agreement and, later, the agreement to accept only a part permission for the first phase of the new Stewartby works. The reports of both the consultants and the Depart-ment of the Environment confirmed that smell was the major problem and so it was natural for the company to focus on this rather than the problem of fluoride.

London Brick continued to negotiate through the officials and with the Chairman of the Committee, still failing to perceive the danger to its interests of the well-organised opposition that was lobbying members of the County Council. Its lack of perception and failure to exert any pressure in a changing political environment contributed to its defeat in July 1980. At last recognising its vulnerability, the company was forced to alter its strategy yet again. It still hoped to persuade the Council by its rather feeble attempt to reinterpret the pollution condition and, then, by throwing the weight of the company Chairman into the debate. But the support it gained with the Environmental Services Committee, though crucial to later events, failed to change the Council's mind at its December meeting. This defeat appeared to leave the company with little option but to cut its losses in Bedfordshire and take its investment to Cambridgeshire. The subsequent closure of Ridgmont was a matter of commercial necessity—it was the optimum size plant needed to reduce production in a falling market. The company insisted the decision had nothing to do with the fate of its planning permissions in Bedfordshire.

London Brick had little idea of the transformation that this decision would bring about. Two quite unforeseen developments came to the beleaguered company's aid. One was the spontaneous intervention of the unions, who, facing the loss of jobs, provided the company with support and weakened the political opposition facing an election. The alliance of labour with capital is characteristic in environmental conflicts. 'On some political and economic issues it tends to identify with industry' (Engler, 1961 p. 492). The other development was pure serendipity—the recognition by a councillor that the Council's failure to determine the Ridgmont permission left the way open to the Environmental Services Committee to grant a permission without the pollution condition and without reference to the Council. Borne along by events, the company accepted the windfall and switched its priorities once again to Ridgmont since, by now, delays at Stewartby had precluded the building of new works in time to take advantage of the new clay workings.

In this version the company appears not as the masterful exploiter of events but as the creature of circumstance. It had not appreciated the force of opposition its plans would engender and was pitched into a battle of opposing interests whose outcome remained, until the end, uncertain. Its investment strategy became the prisoner of events. It was not clear where it would invest first either in terms of which county or even in terms of which specific sites within Bedfordshire. In the end London Brick not only failed to impose its will on the local authority but lost its whole investment strategy, as the delays caused by the conflict ruined its hopes of making a start on its redevelopment plan. In terms of the definitions of power identified earlier the company had not defined the political agenda nor won any political victories which enabled it to benefit. It could be argued, too, that it had failed to realise its specific objectives. It is undeniable that it took decisions which had a considerable impact on the community. The decision to close Ridgmont, though caused by economic circumstances, had a major impact. But it is equally the case that its opponents were able to take decisions which, potentially at least, could affect the company's investment plans and thus its impact on the environment.

Conclusions

The London Brick case illustrates the importance of temporal and spatial factors in corporate decision making. Over a long period the company was able to exercise power by inaction and by taking the requisite steps to thwart opposition. When it found itself in confrontation with environmental interests it sought to negotiate, and when that failed, it retaliated. More generally it is possible to perceive an oscillation in the balance of power as the successes of environmental groups are met by a resurgence of business power. It seems that when business is at its weakest in economic terms it can defend itself against environmental pressures best. When jobs and profits are on the line the business case meets with more sympathy from governments. Large multi-plant companies can also make choices between alternative investment opportunities. In this case London Brick, though tied to its Oxford Clay resource base, was able to select which plants to close and where to redevelop. To pluralists such changes in strategy underline the differences in the balance of power between corporate and environmental interests that exist at different times and in different places. The political economy perspective sees it differently, as evidence of the flexible but overwhelming opportunities for the exercise of power available to business.

This case study has, perhaps, oversimplified two alternative interpretations. It has, however, suggested that both are plausible though both are also flawed. The political economy version contends that business possesses such reserves of power that the eventual outcome is never in doubt. This requires, at some points, a willing suspension of disbelief. For example, did the company fully recognise the opportunities which lay open to it after its defeat by the Council? Perhaps it did not need to since it might have won anyway. The pluralist argument relies, typically, on taking things at their face value. It regards the company as no more than an interest group with roughly equal chances of success in a battle with other interests. It suggests, perhaps, that the company was more naive and innocent than was really the case. But the pluralist stress on the uncertainty of the outcome and the importance of changing circumstances is, at least, as compelling as the notion of the company as an omnipotent giant able to impose its will. We are left, perhaps, to conclude that both perspectives contribute to our understanding of the exercise of corporate power. As Dunleavy argues, 'it does not seem utopian to detect signs of empirically supported common ground, underlying the fundamental theoretical disputes which separate the two halves of the debate' (1981, p. 16).

References

Bedfordshire County Council (1967) *Bedfordshire Brickfield*, October.
Bedfordshire County Council (1976a) *County Structure Plan, Public Participation*, Phase 1, Report, June.

Bedfordshire County Council (1976b) *County Structure Plan, Public Participation*, Phase 2, Report, December.

Bedfordshire County Council (1978a) *Minerals, Appraisals and Issues*, March.

Bedfordshire County Council (1978b) *Minerals, Appraisals and Issues, Public Consultation*, March to July.

Bennett, G. (1979) 'Pollution control in England and Wales: a review', *Environmental Policy and Law*, 5, pp. 93–9, 190–3.

Brothwood Report (1960) *Report on Atmospheric Pollution in the Brickworks Valley*, Bedfordshire County Council, Health Department, October.

Burns, K. N. and Allcroft, R. (1964) 'Fluorosis in cattle. 1. Occurrence and effects in industrial areas of England and Wales 1954–7', Animal Disease Surveys Report No. 2. Pt. 1 Ministry of Agriculture, Fisheries and Food, HMSO.

Cox, A. (1979) *Brickmaking: A history and gazetteer*, Survey of Bedfordshire, Bedfordshire County Council, Royal Commission on Historial Monuments (England), November.

Cremer and Warner (1979) *The Environmental Assessment of the Existing and Proposed Brickworks in the Marston Vale Bedfordshire*, Main Report, prepared for Bedfordshire County Council by Cremer and Warner, Consulting Engineers and Scientists, October.

Crenson, M. A. (1971) *The Un-Politics of Air Pollution: A study of non-decisionmaking in the Cities*, Baltimore, The Johns Hopkins Press.

Department of the Environment (1980) *Air Pollution in the Bedfordshire Brickfields*, Report, Directorate of Noise, Clean Air and Waste.

Dunleavy, P. (1981) 'Alternative theories of liberal democratic politics: the pluralist-marxist debate in the 1980s', paper prepared for Social Sciences Foundation Course, The Open University.

Engler, R. (1961) *The Politics of Oil: Private power and democratic directions*, University of Chicago Press.

Hill, M. 'Air pollution control in Britain' (unpublished paper).

Hillier, R. (1981) *Clay that Burns: A history of the fletton brick industry*, London Brick Company.

Kimber, R. and Richardson, J. J. (1974) *Campaigning for the Environment*, London, Routledge & Kegan Paul.

Knoepfel, P., Weidner, H., Hans, K. and Watts, N. (1980) *The Environmental Quality Game: A proposal for an analytical model*, International Institute for Environment and Society, Berlin.

Lindblom, C. E. (1977) *Politics and Markets*, New York, Basic Books.

London Brick Company (1978) *Report and Accounts*.

London Brick Company (1980) *Brickworks Redevelopment Plan*, London Brick Company Assessment and Implications of the Cremer and Warner Report.

Moodie, G. C. (1970) *Opinions, Publics and Pressure Groups*, London, George Allen & Unwin.

Polsby, N. W. (1980) *Community Power and Political Theory*, 2nd edition, New Haven, Yale University Press.

Porteous, A., Attenborough, K. and Pollitt, C. (1977) *Pollution: The professionals and the public*, The Open University Press.

Reade, E. J. (1982) 'Section 52 and corporatism in planning', *Journal of Planning and Environment Law*, January, pp. 8–16.

Reagan, M. D. (1963) *The Managed Economy*, New York, Oxford University Press.

Sandbach, F. (1980) *Environment, Ideology and Policy*, Oxford, Basil Blackwell.

Sandbach, F. (1982) 'Pollution control: in whose interest?', paper given to Conference on Environmental Pollution and Planning, Southampton.

Vogel, D. (1980) 'Coercion versus consultation: a comparison of environmental protection policy in the United States and Great Britain', paper for the British Politics Group, American Political Science Annual Convention, Denver, Colorado.

Vogel, D. (1981) 'How business responds to opposition: corporate political strategies during the 1980s' (draft paper).

Waller, R. E. (1982) 'Air pollution and health', paper given to Conference on Environmental Pollution and Planning, Southampton.

Wolfinger, R. E. (1972), 'Nondecisions and the study of local politics', *American Political Science Review*, vol. 65, pp. 1063–80.

Wood, C. (1982) 'Local planning authority controls over pollution', paper given to Conference on Environmental Pollution and Planning, Southampton.

| Power in health services

Chris Ham

Marxist approaches

Marxists argue that medical care in societies like Britain must be seen as part of the capitalist mode of production (Doyal, 1979). Within capitalism, Marxists contend that there is an important division between the owners of the means of production – the dominant class or bourgeoisie – and those who have to sell their wage labour – the subordinate class or proletariat. It is the capitalist mode of production which gives rise to class relations of production, and Marxists go on to argue that the economically dominant class is also politically dominant. The state therefore acts in the long-term interests of the bourgeoisie, and performs a number of functions.

In O'Connor's terms, the state assists in the process of capital accumulation, and also performs the function of legitimation (O'Connor, 1973). State expenditures are directed towards these ends, and are made up of social capital and social expenses. State expenditures on health services partly comprise social capital, in so far as health services involve the reproduction of a healthy labour force, and partly they comprise social expenses, in so far as health services help to maintain non-working groups and promote social harmony. State involvement in the provision of health services stems from two sources: action by the bourgeoisie to reduce the costs of labour power and to prevent social unrest; and action by the proletariat through the class struggle to win concessions from the bourgeoisie. However, Marxists argue that there may develop a fiscal crisis for the state when the demand for expenditure on health services outstrips the ability of the state to fund that expenditure. At this point a restructuring of public expenditure may occur to the disadvantage of state health services. Marxists would interpret this as an attack on the interests of the subordinate class, even

From C. Ham, *Health Policy in Britain* (2nd edition 1985), Basingstoke: Macmillan.

though health services are seen as a form of social control (Gough, 1979).

Within this theoretical perspective, inequalities in service provision between client groups are explained in terms of the lack of productivity of the mentally ill, mentally handicapped and the elderly. It is suggested that because these groups cannot make a significant contribution to the development of the economy and of profit, they will receive a lower quality service than productive groups. Similarly, social class inequalities in health are interpreted by Marxists as evidence of the continuing influence of economic factors on health and the persistence of class divisions within society. The distribution of benefits within health services is therefore explained by reference to class conflict and the dominance of the bourgeoisie.

At a macro level of analysis Marxist theory has considerable explanatory value. Yet a convincing theory of power must also be able to explain the processes of policy-making and implementation [. . .]. Marxist approaches are much weaker at this level of analysis, and Marxist studies of particular decisions, issues or health care organisations are little developed. In contrast, pluralist theories, with their focus on the role of pressure groups and bargaining and negotiation within policy communities, offer a range of insights into the dynamics of health policy-making, and we will now consider the utility of these theories.

Pluralism

The essence of the pluralist democratic theory of power is that the recourses which contribute to power are widely distributed among different groups. [. . .] Pluralists argue that no one group is dominant, and each is able to exercise some influence (see for example Dahl, 1961). Power is in fact shared between official groups in governmental agencies and outside interests exerting pressures on these agencies. This helps to ensure there is no consistent bias in the allocation of values, although pluralists would recognise that groups vary in their ability to exercise power. Developments in health services and health policy are explained in terms of the interplay between pressure groups. Since there is no dominant interest, pluralists analyse the distribution of power in relation to particular issues, studying who wins and who loses through often detailed examinations of the preferences of different interests and the extent to which decisions match up with expressed preferences. The question of who has power is for the pluralists an empirical question, to be answered by means of careful case studies of particular policy areas. A range of factors may be important, including party manifestos, key individuals, official reports and the activities of pressure groups, but their relative influence must be studied in specific cases. Examples of studies of the NHS which have their roots in the pluralist democratic tradition are Willcocks' (1967) examination of the creation of the NHS and Eckstein's (1960) analysis of the operation of the BMA. Each author analyses the way in which decisions are arrived at in a system of pressure group politics, and each is able to show how the outcomes were the result of compromise between the various interests involved. Professional interests vie with consumer interests, and civil servants with politicians, but alliances change, leading to the fragmentation of power which pluralists observe. The strength of pluralist theory is the richness of detail provided about decision-making and the high degree of sophistication which has often been achieved in the analysis of individual, group and organisational influences on policy processes.

Like Marxism, though, pluralism does not provide a completely adequate theory of power. For example, [. . .] earlier [. . .] we noted the key position occupied by the medical profession in the organisation of health services, and our discussion of how policies are made and implemented in the NHS suggests certain inadequacies in the pluralist position. In particular, the strength of producer groups and the relative weakness of consumer groups cast doubt on the pluralists' argument that any group can make itself heard effectively at some stage in the decision-making process, and that no group is dominant (Ham, 1977). Accordingly, [. . .] attention needs to be paid to the work of Alford, who has maintained that it is important to analyse the nature of structural interests within health services. We will now examine Alford's thesis in greater detail.

Structuralist approaches

Alford argues that structural interests are those interests which gain or lose from the form of organisation of health services (Alford, 1975a). There are three sets of structural interests: dominant, challenging and repressed. Dominant interests are the professional monopolists; challenging interests are the corporate rationalisers; and repressed interests are the community population. Dominant interests are served by existing social, economic and political institutions, and therefore only need to be active when their interests are challenged. Alford argues that the medical profession is dominant in health services, but the profession may be challenged by corporate rationalisers such as health planners and administrators. Again, patient and consumer groups representing the community population may seek to move out of their repressed position by organising to articulate their interests. These struggles between structural interests are not the same as the competition for power between pressure groups. Pressure group competition may well take place within structural interests, as between, for example, different groups of doctors. These conflicts are important, but they leave unchallenged the principle of professional monopoly and dominance. Pressure group politics coexist with struggles between structural interests, and may explain how particular issues are resolved. Structural interests are, however, more significant in influencing the overall distribution of benefits, and in shaping the main contours of power relationships.

The value of Alford's framework has been demonstrated in a study of policy-making in the NHS (Ham, 1981), and the inequalities in power he points to indicate a position close to elitist interpretations of the power structure. In the health sector, professional control of knowledge, recruitment and training, as well as claims to professional autonomy over the content of work, provide the basis of the medical profession's power. Its organisation through powerful pressure groups in continuous contact with governmental agencies, coupled with involvement at all stages in the system of administration, enhance this power. In emphasising elite power based on professional position, the above analysis offers an alternative to both pluralism and Marxism. Structuralist approaches recognise the existence of pressure group politics but contend that studies which remain at the level of groups are incomplete.

Equally, while structuralists acknowledge the importance of economic and class factors, they maintain that class divisions are less important in explaining the development and organisation of health services than divisions between structural interests. The two are by no means synonymous. In particular, the growth of intermediate groups between the bourgeoisie and the proletariat requires some modification of the straightforward Marxist position, and highlights the need for a framework able to take account of the complexities of social divisions within contemporary society. This suggests that what is required is an approach which builds on the strength of each of the theoretical positions discussed here. We have argued that all three positions have some merits, but none provides an adequate account by itself. Rather than seeking to develop one theory to the point where it furnishes a complete explanation in its own right, it may be preferable to attempt to search for links between the different theories. An investment of effort in this direction holds out the prospect of high returns, not least because the three positions we have discussed tend to focus on different levels of analysis.

The key issue, then, is to develop 'mediating frameworks to connect macro-theory with specific policy issues' (Dunleavy, 1981, p. 4). One approach to this is through the examination of dominant value systems in particular policy areas and their influence on policy. More specifically, by analysing the operation of professional ideologies in health services, it may be possible to establish links between the way issues are defined and resources allocated, the nature of structural interests and the distribution of power, and macro theories of the state (Ham, 1980). The difficulties of doing this are considerable, but a start can be made by exploring the role of the medical profession and the way in which the profession's view of health has come to occupy a dominant position.

Concepts of health

There are many different concepts of health. Margaret Stacey has identified three dimensions along which these concepts vary: individual or collective; functional fitness or welfare; preventive or curative (Stacey, 1977). Stacey notes that in Western societies the individualistic concept of health tends to dominate, and it is usually associated with ideas of functional fitness and curative approaches. This concept seeks the causes of illness within the biological systems of individuals, and it attempts to provide a specific cure for illness in order to make individuals fit for work. Alongside the individualistic concept of health, Stacey notes the existence of a collective concept which emphasises the importance of prevention. The collective concept seeks the causes of illnesses within the environmental, economic and social systems in which people live, and attempts to prevent illness arising by tackling the unhealthy aspects of those systems. Stacey also notes the existence of a welfare concept of health, emphasising the importance of relieving pain and providing care.

While these concepts coexist, it is the individualistic, functional fitness, curative approach which is the most influential. This approach has been characterised as the medical model of health, a model in which doctors have a central role and hospitals play a major part. It has been suggested that the model has two components: a disease component, which holds that illness results from pathological processes in the biochemical functions of the body; and an engineering component, which sees the body as a machine to be repaired by technical means (Illsley, 1977). The medical model emphasises specific, individual causes of illness and searches for specific individual cures for these illnesses.

Acceptance of the medical model is important, first, in justifying the pre-eminent position of the medical profession in health matters, and second, in helping to explain the pattern of investment in health services. Within the NHS, the bulk of resources is allocated to personally orientated, general and acute hospital services. Much less importance has been attached to collective, preventive and welfare approaches to health. However, this may be changing as the medical model comes under increasing attack.

The attack on medical dominance in the health field has been spearheaded by writers such as McKeown (1976), who have questioned the significance of the medical contribution in bringing about improvements in health. McKeown's work has demonstrated that improved nutrition, purer water supplies, behavioural changes limiting family size and leading to the better spacing of births, and improved methods of sewage disposal have been mainly responsible for the advances in health which have occurred in the last 200 years. These factors contributed to the decline in infectious diseases, and assisted in reducing death rates and increasing life expectancy. In contrast, medical science had very little impact until the introduction of vaccines and certain drugs in the twentieth century. Yet McKeown argues that even these interventions came at a time when overall death rates were already in decline as a result of earlier environmental and behavioural changes. [. . .]

McKeown's work has had a major influence in the development of the health field concept articulated by Lalonde (1974). The health field concept analyses illness and disease in terms of four elements: human biology, the environment, life-style and health care organisation. Human biology includes aspects of health, such as ageing, which are developed within the body as a result of the basic biology of man. The environment comprises matters relating to health external to the body, over which the individual has little or no control. Life-style refers to the decisions by individuals which affect health and over which they have control. And health care organisation consists of the arrangements made to provide organised health services to individuals. Like McKeown, Lalonde suggests that while most efforts to improve health have centred on medical interventions through health care organisation, it is the other three elements which are more important in identifying the causes of sickness and death. In particular, Lalonde points to the need for people to adopt healthy life-styles in order to prevent illness arising.

This is very much in line with the policy on prevention adopted by the DHSS. [. . .] The Department has used the work of people like McKeown to argue that greater emphasis should be given to prevention, and that individuals should look after themselves by giving up smoking, adopting an appropriate diet, taking exercise, and so on. This individualistic approach to prevention does not seriously threaten the medical model, and it has been criticised for 'blaming the victim'. A growing body of research indicates that life-style may be less significant than the environment (defined in its widest sense) in influencing illness and disease, and that a collective approach to health is needed if progress is to be made in tackling contemporary health problems. [. . .]

These studies constitute a significant challenge to the medical model, not least because they imply a much reduced role for doctors. It must be added, though, that medicine has remained remarkably resilient in the face of criticism, and continues to provide the dominant explanation of health problems in contemporary Western societies.

What are the implications of this analysis for the earlier discussion of power in health care systems? What we hope to have shown is that the medical model, as the dominant (though not only) value system in the health field, exercises a key influence on the definition of issues and the allocation of resources. The question this raises is whose interests are served by the medical model? Stacey (1977) has reminded us that concepts do not stand alone, they must be understood in terms of the power of different groups. Let us then return to the examination of theories of power for help in explaining the dominance of the medical model.

Power, interests and ideology

In the pluralist framework, concepts of health and the role of medicine are not seen as having special significance. The medical profession is viewed as one interest among many, albeit in most studies a key interest; and concepts of health are implicitly assumed to have emerged out of the underlying consensus on which pluralist theories are based. Within this consensus, prevailing concepts of health are no more than a reflection of the shifting balance of power between interests. The fact that they have remained the same over time is seen by pluralists as an indication of the large measure of agreement between these interests on the meaning of health and the manner in which services should be provided. The question that needs to be asked about this interpretation is whether the consensus which pluralists observe is genuine or false. In other words, is the consensus the result of spontaneous agreement among different groups in the population, or does it derive from manipulation by dominant groups?

This question is not easily resolved. Pluralists would argue that people's expressed preferences are the only reliable guide to their interests, and the fact that these preferences demonstrate strong support for the medical profession is in itself sufficient to show that the consensus on values is genuine. In contrast, critics of pluralism would argue that people's real interests may differ from their expressed preferences, in which case the possibility of a false consensus being manipulated by dominant groups cannot be ruled out. The problem with this approach is how to establish the existence of real interests which are different from expressed preferences (Saunders, 1979). One line of analysis in the health field would be to develop McKeown's work, which, as we have noted, has suggested that society's investment in health is not well used because it is based on the medical model. What this indicates is that people's real interests might be better served by an alternative pattern of investment. That is, improved health might result from a reorientation away from personally orientated, hospital-based health care towards a system in which more emphasis was given to the social causes of illness and disease. If this could be demonstrated, then a rather different explanation of the interests served by dominant concepts of health would be needed.

Such an explanation is provided by structuralists. For structuralists, dominant concepts of health serve the interests of the medical profession because they legitimate the profession's claim to control in health services. In other words, prevailing concepts of health are explained by the position of the medical profession as a dominant structural interest and its success in getting individualistic definitions of illness and disease accepted. The dominance of medicine is in turn accounted for historically in terms of the success of physicians, surgeons and apothecaries in winning state approval for their position, and in turning their occupations into professions having exclusive control over their area of work (Wilding, 1982). Medical dominance does not imply a conspiracy against subordinate groups. Rather, it reflects the power of doctors, their control of key resources such as expertise and knowledge, and their ability to achieve acceptance for their own concept of health. This concept of health makes sense to groups in the population other than doctors, but as we have shown, it is not the only concept, and it is not necessarily the concept which best serves the interests of the population.

Like structuralists, Marxists would challenge the pluralists' position that consensus is genuine, but would see dominant concepts of health not as an indication of the power of the medical profession, but as evidence of the dominance of the bourgeoisie. In particular, Marxists argue that the individual, disease-based model of curative medicine helps to maintain the position of the bourgeoisie by masking the real causes of illness which lie within the social and economic system of capitalism. As Navarro has put it:

> the social utility of medicine is measured primarily in the arena of legitimation. Medicine is indeed socially useful to the degree that the majority of people believe and accept the proposition that what are actually politically caused conditions can be individually solved by medical intervention. From the point of view of the capitalist system, this is the actual utility of medicine – it contributes to the legitimation of capitalism. (Navarro, 1976, p. 208)

For Marxists, the medical model is a key linking concept, not only explaining how issues are defined and benefits distributed in the policy process, but also highlighting underlying class divisions within society.

The conclusion to be drawn from the Marxist analysis is that the dominant concept of health serves bourgeois interests, that power is weighted heavily in favour of those interests, and that doctors, although seemingly in a powerful position, merely administer the health care system on behalf of the bourgeoisie.

It thus emerges that Marxists and structuralists see different interests being served by dominant concepts of health. Structuralists argue that the medical profession has power in its own right, not simply power deriving from its utility to the bourgeoisie. In contrast, Marxists argue that medical power results from class power. The Marxist position is well summarised by Navarro, who criticises writers such as Alford for

> their failure to recognise that those elites (for example medicine) are in reality segments of a dominant class and that, when they are considered in a systemic and not just a sectorial fashion, they are found to possess a high degree of cohesion and solidarity, with common interests and common purposes for transcending their specific differences and disagreements. (Navarro, 1976, pp. 189–90)

The question which needs to be raised about this argument is whether all conflicts are 'in reality' class conflicts, and if so how disagreements between the state and the medical profession can be explained.

It has been suggested, for example, that it cannot be assumed that state expenditure on health services is automatically in the interests of the bourgeoisie. Saunders (1981) has criticised Marxists for ignoring the possibility that such spending may be dysfunctional for capital. The fiscal crisis of the state has illustrated the importance of Saunders's criticism, and has indicated that while expenditure on areas of collective consumption like the NHS may benefit professional interests, it may be against the interests of the bourgeoisie, whose main purpose is to maintain capital accumulation. A similar point is made by Cawson (1982) who argues that the growth of public expenditure has been fuelled by the bargaining processes between the state and producer groups. Cawson explains this in terms of the development of a corporate sector in the British political system in which producer groups like the BMA are intimately involved in both the making of policy and its implementation. Cawson predicts that expenditure cuts will be resisted by producer groups and that governments faced with a fiscal crisis will seek to reduce the burden of public expenditure by privatising services.

It can also be suggested that attempts will be made to curtail professional power. There is evidence that this is happening in the United Kingdom, with the Conservative Government elected in 1979 seeking to limit the restrictive practices of occupations such as solicitors, accountants and architects. In relation to health services, the management reforms initiated since the Griffiths Report can be seen as an attempt to strengthen the hand of planners and administrators in their challenge to medical dominance. The appointment of general managers, and the call for doctors to be more closely involved in management, were both designed to introduce greater control over the activities of the medical profession and to influence the behaviour of consultants in their position as the key controllers of resources in the NHS. What is more, the recommendation in the Griffiths Report that arrangements for consultation on decisions should be streamlined was interpreted by some observers as an attempt to maintain community interests in their repressed position. More important, a number of commentators have argued that what Griffiths was really talking about was a change in management style, with less reliance being placed on administrative and professional values and greater importance being attached to the positive management of the Service. [. . .]

To summarise this argument, it is clear that developments such as the introduction of general management into the NHS, the challenge to the professions and the privatisation of services cannot be explained simply in terms of the internal dynamics of the Service. Policies in the health field are constrained by a wider set of factors, particularly the approach taken by government to the management of the economy and public expenditure. The value of the perspective offered by writers such as Cawson is precisely that it draws attention to the economic context within which social policies are developed. Cawson's analysis of corporatism and welfare is closely linked to the structuralist analysis of power. Both Cawson and Alford recognise the significance of the process of capital accumulation in capitalist society and the role played by the state in promoting profitable economic activity. At the same time, they reject Marxist models of political analysis which reduce all conflicts to class conflicts. Alford (1975a) in particular maintains that the way in which the accumulation process influences structural interests and policy development in the health field is highly complex. While health policy cannot be adequately understood without reference to economic policy, it cannot be explained solely in terms of class analysis. As Alford has written, 'The translation of class interests (or a cultural consensus) into organisational form and then into action is problematic and contingent' (Alford, 1975b, p. 153). This again points to the need to develop mediating frameworks for linking different levels of analysis.

Conclusion and summary

At first sight, pluralist theories offer a convincing explanation of the distribution of power within health services. After all, the NHS comprises a large number of different groups competing for resources, and most decisions result from bargaining between these groups. Furthermore, health policies tend to involve small adjustments to what has gone before, and a variety of interests are often involved in policy-making. This is in part the picture which has emerged from the discussion of health policy-making and implementation in earlier chapters, and it fits the description of political activity put forward in the pluralist model.

However, Marxist theories challenge the assumptions behind pluralism and provide an alternative explanation. Instead of focusing on immediate conflicts between pressure groups, Marxists seek to relate health care systems to the economic systems within which they are located. By analysing the underlying processes at work, Marxists argue that health services are dominated by the bourgeoisie, whose interests are served by prevailing concepts of health and illness. Health services help to legitimate capitalism and to promote capital accumulation. Pluralists are unable to perceive this because they concentrate on surface struggles and neglect deeper class conflicts. Furthermore, pluralists take dominant concepts of health for granted, and do not question seriously the beneficial impact of medicine or the possibility that conflict may be limited to a narrow range of issues through ideological domination.

In contrast to both approaches, Alford's theory of structural interests looks beyond the surface politics of pressure group conflicts and finds not class struggle but professional dominance. This approach recognises that the world of everyday politics may well approximate to pluralist theories, but it goes further to identify wide discrepancies in power in relation to dominant, challenging and repressed structural interests. Alternative concepts of health are acknowledged to exist, and prevailing concepts reflect the ability of dominant groups to get their definitions accepted. Within this framework, it is possible to encompass both the strengths of pluralist theory, recognising the diversity and variety of pressure group behaviour, and some of the insights of the Marxist analysis, acknowledging that what appears to be going on may obscure underlying conflicts between key interests.

References

Alford, R. (1975a), *Health Care Politics*, Chicago, University of Chicago Press.
Alford, R. (1975b), 'Paradigms of relations between state and society', in L. N. Lindberg, R. Alford, C. Crouch and C. Offe (eds.), *Stress and Contradictions in Modern Capitalism*, Lexington, Mass., Lexington Books.
Cawson, A. (1982), *Corporatism and Welfare*, London, Heinemann.
Dahl, R. A. (1961), *Who Governs?*, New Haven, Yale University Press.
Doyal, L. (1979), *The Political Economy of Health*, London, Pluto.

Dunleavy, P. (1981), 'Professions and policy change: notes towards a model of ideological corporatism', *Public Administration Bulletin*, 36.

Eckstein, H. (1960), *Pressure Group Politics*, London, Allen & Unwin.

Gough, I. (1979), *The Political Economy of the Welfare State*, London, Macmillan.

Ham, C. J. (1977), 'Power, patients and pluralism', in K. Barnard and K. Lee (eds.), *Conflicts in the NHS*, Beckenham, Croom Helm.

Ham, C. J. (1980), 'Approaches to the study of Social Policy Making', *Policy and Politics*, 8(1), 55–71.

Ham, C. J. (1981), *Policy Making in the National Health Service*, London, Macmillan.

Illsley, R. (1977), 'Everybody's business? Concepts of health and illness', in SSRC, *Health and Health Policy: Priorities for research*.

Lalonde, M. (1974), *A New Perspective on the Health of Canadians*, Ottawa, Government of Canada.

McKeown, T. (1976), *The Role of Medicine*, London, Nuffield Provincial Hospitals Trust.

Navarro, V. (1976), *Medicine under Capitalism*, Prodist.

O'Connor, J. (1973), *The Fiscal Crisis of the State*, New York, St Martin's Press.

Saunders, P. (1979), *Urban Politics*, London, Hutchinson.

Saunders, P. (1981) *Social Theory and the Urban Question*, London, Hutchinson.

Stacey, M. (1977), 'Concepts of health and illness', in SSRC, *Health and Health Policy: Priorities for research*.

Wilding, P. (1982), *Professional Power and Social Welfare*, London, Routledge & Kegan Paul.

Willcocks, A. J. (1967), *The Creation of the National Health Service*, London, Routledge & Kegan Paul.

Part V

The debate about rationality and incrementalism

Introduction

The two articles in this part seem to take us off in a new direction, but there are in fact important connections between the debate about rationality and incrementalism in public policy making and the debate about the structure of power. Two comparatively recent contributions to a debate which has a rather longer history have been chosen. The debate goes back to an argument advanced from a very clearly prescriptive viewpoint by Herbert Simon in his *Administrative Behaviour*. He set out to recommend a rational approach to the making of policy decisions whilst nevertheless taking into account organisational and political realities. Simon recommended an approach involving careful examination of options to arrive at a decision which would 'satisfy' in terms of policy goals even if it was not the ideal or optimal decision.

This approach was challenged by Braybrooke and Lindblom on two grounds, both rooted in the pluralist analysis of politics. One was that in many circumstances the pressures upon decision-makers are such that such 'rationality' is unattainable; many decisions are 'incremental', involving small adjustments to what has been done before. This process is one of 'partisan mutual adjustment' in the light of pluralist competition to influence decisions. The other objection derived specifically from the pluralist ideal that the best kind of democratic process involves this sort of incremental adjustment. Hence to attempt rational decision making would mean engaging in the kind of social engineering in which political elites endeavoured to disregard the popular pressures upon them. Subsequently many writers tried to find the middle ground between these two positions. Of particular interest here was the evolution of the thinking of one of the main protagonists, Lindblom, who, as McLennan showed in his piece in Part II, increasingly came to recognise that pluralism was often biased. Hence, he can be seen as taking an increasingly state-centred view, in which some approach to 'rational' decision making by administrators may be important to counteract the impact of powerful interests.

The article by Smith and May seeks to help us find our way through this debate, by showing how prescriptive and descriptive positions are mixed together within it. In their view the rationalist position is particularly clearly prescriptive, whilst the incrementalist position provides a good description of what is likely to occur in the real world. However, that straightforward distinction, which is generally helpful to us in the debate, is challenged a little in the second article. Here Gregory celebrates Lindblom's important contribution to policy-making theory, emphasising a *prescriptive* point that 'good' decision making is likely to be that which is best adjusted to the political realities which require it to be incremental.

Gregory's thoughtful analysis of this subject highlights a point mentioned in the introduction to Part I. It is a peculiarity of our use of language in the study of the policy process that the word 'rationality' has been appropriated to describe a process as opposed to an outcome. It is, moreover, a process more concerned with relating means to ends than with ensuring that there is a mandate for those ends. This turns on its head a body of philosophical work which was concerned with the extent to which totalitarian regimes (see, in particular, the work of Popper, 1966) tried to practise wholesale social engineering without reference to the views, needs or interests of their subjects. This was seen as deeply irrational in terms of its outcomes, however carefully it related means to ends. It brings us back to the issues about the 'autonomous state', in which the people engaged in 'rational' planning may be Orwellian 'big brothers'.

This is not necessarily to argue that the pluralist optimism of the original Braybrooke and Lindblom work was right all along. Devastating events have occurred as a result of a chain of incremental decisions; look, for example, at the way the United States gradually moved into engagement in war in Vietnam. Moreover, a simple pluralist faith in popular mandates here may not be sufficient; some appalling human acts have been justified in terms of their popular support (here, of course, the analysis offered by Lukes in Part II indicates some of the difficulties with this notion). It is therefore not so easy to take a simplistic stance on the decision-making debate when it is set out in abstract terms. Our answers may depend upon the issues and will certainly depend upon more detailed analysis, some of which will follow later in this book, of who controls the policy outputs of the state and how they control it. This takes us into issues about policy implementation.

References

Popper, K. R., *The Open Society and its Enemies* (5th edn., London, Routledge & Kegan Paul, 1966).
Simon, H. A., *Administrative Behaviour* (2nd edn., New York, Macmillan, 1957).

The artificial debate between rationalist and incrementalist models of decision making

Gilbert Smith and David May

Introduction

As students of the formation and implementation of government policies have become dissatisfied with a predominantly descriptive and generally atheoretical approach to their subject, so more express attention to the abstract concepts and ideas which guide data collection and analysis in policy studies has become indispensable. The notion of 'decision making' is indisputably central to studying the process through which policies are both designed and effected and this paper is about the components of that idea. Such analysis may be thought redundant for 'decision' is a common enough term. But, as the already extended discussions of 'key concepts' such as poverty,[1] need,[2] justice,[3] implementation[4] or control[5] have shown, commonsense notions in everyday usage tend initially to be rather blunt instruments when pressed into service as tools for research. And as any good craftsman knows, there are few things more dangerous than using blunt tools.

In the literature on public administration[6] a debate about the relative merits of rationalistic as opposed to incrementalist models of decision making has featured for some years now and although the terms of this debate are rather well known it has had comparatively little impact upon empirical research in the area of either policy or administrative studies. However, an awareness of the limits to rational decision making in institutions has exerted a significant influence upon the direction of the more sociologically oriented work in the field of organisational analysis.[7]

From G. Smith and D. May, 'The artificial debate between rationalist and incrementalist models of decision making', *Policy and Politics*, **8**, 1980, pp. 147–61.

It is the purpose of this note to suggest that, when work from these several fields is considered together, it is apparent that (1) the components of 'decision making' in social policy are by no means obvious, (2) the rationalism versus incrementalism debate is in certain respects an artificial dispute and (3) this has implications for the design and conduct of empirical research on decision making which aspires to be policy relevant.

Two models of decision making

An essentially rationalistic approach to decision making has predominated in the study of organisations. This approach advances a definition of decision making which is described by Scott as consisting of a process with the following components:

1. A search process to discover goals.
2. The formulation of objectives after search.
3. The selection of alternatives (strategies) to accomplish objectives.
4. The evaluation of outcomes.[8]

These are the elements which are viewed as common to the making of all kinds of decisions – and rightly so. That is, good decisions are those which conform to this pattern. As Etzioni observes:

> Rationalistic models are widely held conceptions about how decisions are and ought to be made. An actor becomes aware of a problem, posits a goal, carefully weighs alternative means, and chooses among them according to his estimate of their respective merit, with reference to the state of affairs he prefers.[9]

It is important to note that the approach purports to offer a framework which is at one and the same time explanatory and normative.

The rationalistic approach, however, has been widely criticised. First, it is regarded as being too narrow. It neglects the range of political variables which limits the extent of choice available in the light of the power of relevant vested interests. Most decision makers in policy contexts do not work in an environment devoid of constraints. They are simply not free to consider all possible options and often they are compelled to shortlist, if not actually recommend, options that they would not even pretend to justify as the most appropriate in terms of a simple means–ends schema. This is the well-known process of pressure group politics. And students of the policy process are showing considerable interest in the pluralist and related theories which have been a regular part of the political science parentage of public administration.[10]

Secondly, the rationalistic approach is seen as utopian. Most policy decisions have numerous unanticipated consequences which are neither as inconsequential nor disposed of nearly as readily as the model tends to imply. The model represents, perhaps, the planner's dream but in the real world, it is argued, ends are not that clear, decisions are not that neat and evaluation is not that systematic. Indeed it has been argued[11] that ambiguity is actually a rather central feature of most policy and should be acknowledged and studied as such. Since,

> the executive's . . . task of translating ambiguous political directives into operational agency policy . . . is one which requires a far more sensitive value theory than any now available in the context of administrative scholarship,[12]

McCleery sees the rational model as appropriate only to those limited kinds of bureaucracy where the executive is given very precise guidance. But in practice policy institutions of this kind may well be the exception rather than the rule.

Thirdly, the rationalistic approach is accused of being value biased in that rationality is itself a quality prized in varying degrees. There is by no means consensus on the fact that rationality represents some universal good nor even upon the definition of rationality.[13] Particularly in an organisational context the model is accused of favouring management and senior professions to the detriment of low-ranking staff, clients and patients, whose perspectives are in practice neglected. There is a tendency to equate rationality with the smooth running of the organisation. Although clearly we need to know a great deal about the way in which claimants and clients, patients and the general public approach service agencies, there is some evidence, in studies of welfare services for example,[14] that the importance attached to the smooth running of different aspects of a service may in significant respects differs between groups associated with the agency.

Fourthly, rationalistic models are seen as too rigid in drawing sharp distinctions between ends and means, values and decisions, and facts and values. What counts as 'fact' is notoriously subject to the interests and values of the parties involved.

> Traditional conduct, like other forms of unreflected social process, does not differentiate between means and ends, nor between the criteria for truth and good conduct. What is good and what works must be true.[15]

As Lindblom,[16] in his much quoted article, points out, means and ends are often chosen simultaneously within the administrative process. The frequent absence of any clear means–ends relationship is often particularly apparent when several of the stages of implementing policy are examined together and overall. (Policy research is habitually handicapped by the fact that individual research projects can so seldom examine all stages in the process. Not infrequently it is what happens *between* major stages that is most interesting.) Cassidy and Turner,[17] for example, have used the idea of 'up stream causality' in studying systems of criminal justice to suggest, for instance, that rates of apprehension and charging may be a function of the proportion of those charged found guilty in the courts, rather than vice versa. Thus means often precede ends, become ends or even cause ends. Ends become means as one decision merges into the next. Values may rationalise rather than determine decisions and certainly actors are often unable to rank their values independently of specific choices. The ambiguity of means, ends and their relationship is substantially greater than rational models allow.

A final criticism of rationalistic models is that they are impractical. Even with the aid of computer technology a review and evaluation of all *possible* answers to a problem in order to select the optimal solution is seldom plausible and the cost of the search may well exceed the savings achieved by the solution eventually discovered. This is one of the dilemmas faced by policy makers in deciding whether or not it is worth commissioning research. The Seebohm Committee, for example, set up to examine the reorganisation of the personal social services in Britain, is only one of a number of government committees and commissions that have felt that the delay in producing their report which would be occasioned by awaiting the results of a programme of research would not be justified.[18] It is easy for supposedly rationally minded social scientists to criticise policy makers for neglecting systematic research. It is less easy actually to demonstrate its utility when weighed against the costs.[19] Even if the savings of a novel policy option do exceed the search costs there is no way of knowing about that before the search begins. Inevitably, it is argued, at least some choices must be made without reference to the relationship between means and ends.

In reaction to these criticisms Lindblom has set out the alternative approach termed, provocatively, 'muddling through', or 'disjointed incrementalism'.[20] This model posits the decision maker as starting not with some ideal goal but with the policies currently in force. Decision making entails considering only incremental change, or changes at the margins. Only a rather restricted number of policy alternatives is reviewed and only a limited number of consequences is envisaged and evaluated for any given alternative. In empirical support of this view Jansson and Taylor,[21] while commenting upon the virtual absence of studies which assess the effectiveness of planning procedures in social agencies, rank only one third of the sample of agencies which they studied, as undertaking extensive search activity for new policies. In contrast to the conventional view which sees means adjusted to ends, incrementalism promotes the opposite, allowing for a continuous and reciprocal relationship between means and ends. It is argued that in this way the problems of decision makers are rendered more manageable, for what counts as 'the problem' is constantly subject to redefinition in the light of available means to solve it. Thus the very subject of the decision may be transformed and reinterpreted through the analysis. Evaluation is thus seen not as a separate activity but as taking place in series with decision making. Braybrooke and Lindblom conclude:

> Since policy analysis is incremental, exploratory, serial, and marked by adjustment of ends to means, it is to be expected that stable long-term aspirations will not appear as dominant critical values in the eyes of the analyst. The characteristics of the strategy support and encourage the analyst to identify situations or ills from which to move *away* rather than goals *towards* which to move (original italics).[22]

Like the rationalistic model, the incrementalist approach has also been subjected to important criticisms. It is accused of being conservative in that it copes with only remedial and short-term change and reinforces inertia. Dror[23] suggests that it is a valid approach only if the results of present policies are generally satisfactory, if the nature of the problem is relatively stable and if means for dealing with that problem are continuously available. Generally, however, he regards 'its [incrementalism's] main impact as an ideological reinforcement of the pro-inertia and anti-innovation forces prevalent in all human organisations, administrative and policy making'.[24] Certainly there *are* major barriers to policy innovation. Booth,[25] for example, has described those factors in the machinery of local government in Britain which have inhibited the introduction of alternatives to residential care in the personal social services, in spite of a strong 'rational' case against the extensive supply of residential provision. Dror concludes:

> The 'rational-comprehensive' model has at least the advantage of stimulating administrators to get a little outside their regular routine, while Lindblom's model justifies a policy of 'no effort'.
> Taken together, the limited validity of the 'muddling through' thesis and its inertia-reinforcing implications constitute a very serious weakness.[26]

The incrementalist approach is also accused of being unjust since 'good' decisions are assessed not by their ranking on some objective evaluative criterion but simply by their acceptability in a particular situation. The approach is therefore thought to favour the interests of the most powerful and systemically to under-represent the interests of the underprivileged and politically unorganised. Incrementalism, too, is felt to be more narrow and more limited than the model it seeks to replace. Incremental decisions take place within the context of more fundamental decisions and the approach has little to say about how decisions of this more fundamental kind are made. While it may afford a strategy for researching some of the more detailed workings of the decision making process it is incomplete as a framework for 'macro' analysis.

Finally it is argued that although much has been made of the practicality of the incrementalist approach in fact it is extremely costly. Although the costs of rational decision making are high the costs of failing to explore radical alternatives to existing policies may be even higher. Admittedly the optimal solution is not to be preferred if the costs of discovering it are greater than the savings incurred. But the incrementalist approach is accused of offering no way of informing participants that a sub-optimal solution which has emerged is so costly comparatively as to represent an outcome that decision makers would find unacceptable if the costs were apparent. This is the situation that techniques such as cost benefit analysis[27] and planning strategies such as corporate management seek to avoid, although the few case studies available show substantial disparity between practical experience and the ideal accounts.[28] Nevertheless, Hyderbrand concludes,

> the question remains whether gradual incremental change is only a form of adaptation which leaves basically intact what *ought* to be changed (original italics).[29]

Two 'third' approaches

Now this debate has generated important criticisms of both rationalist and incrementalist approaches and the study of decision making can hardly proceed without taking them into account. Certainly neither model has survived unscathed as the basis for research in social policy, and both Etzioni[30] and Dror[31] have attempted to avoid the weaknesses of rationalist and incrementalist models by combining the strongest features of the two. Each offers a 'third' alternative. Etzioni describes the 'mixed-scanning approach' and Dror outlines what he calls the 'normative-optimum model for policy making'. But both have limitations.

Mixed scanning entails a decision making process in two phases. Initially a broad sweep is made of policy options and these are assessed against stated values in general terms. Then, within this framework, decision making proceeds incrementally in matters of detail. Etzioni claims that:

> each of the two elements in mixed-scanning helps to reduce the effects of the particular shortcomings of the other; incrementalism reduces the unrealistic

aspects of rationalism by limiting the details required in fundamental decisions, and contextuating rationalism helps to overcome the conservative slant of incrementalism by exploring longer-run alternatives.[32]

But in fact it is not clear that the unrealistic and conservative shortcomings would actually be avoided. They might merely be confined or moved to different sectors of the decision making process. There is no guarantee that within these confines they might not even be accentuated. We would need to examine mixed scanning in practice before we could judge. Other issues are sidestepped. For example, Etzioni retains the presumption that decision makers can summarise and rank their values, at least ordinally. As we have mentioned, it has been argued with conviction that values are ordered only in contexts of specific choice.

However, the central weakness of mixed scanning lies in the importance attached to a distinction between two different kinds of decision.

> It is essential to differentiate fundamental decisions from incremental ones. Fundamental decisions are made by exploring the main alternatives the actor sees in view of his conception of his goals, but – unlike what rationalism would indicate – details and specifications are omitted so that an overview is feasible. Incremental decisions are made but within the contexts set by fundamental decisions (and fundamental reviews).[33]

But just as the distinction between means and ends is flexible, as we have seen, so fundamental decisions in one context are incremental in another and vice versa. It is at least possible that decision makers would define decisions in different ways, either quoting or ignoring detail and either exploring or neglecting alternatives, as suited their purposes in particular situations. Without further empirical data the doubt remains that mixed scanning is just as utopian as rational planning and just as lethargic as 'muddling through'. The important point is that rationalism and incrementalism embody diametrically opposed principles which are not reconciled by mixed scanning's sampling of either side.

Dror also seeks a model to 'increase rationality-content' in decision making while acknowledging that, 'Extrarational processes play a significant role in optimal policy making on complex issues'.[34] Essentially his alternative consists of a recapitulation of some of the aspects of rational planning but with heavy caveats of the form, '*some* clarification of values' or '*preliminary* estimation of pay-offs' or 'explicit arrangements to stimulate creativity'. Lindblom has criticised Dror for offering no more than a series of discrete statements which do not connect and cannot be said to constitute a 'model' for decision making.[35] However, the weakest feature of Dror's statement is the role assigned to 'intuition' and 'experience'. These are disconcertingly vague variables and hardly more than residual categories for non-rational sources of information. The whole model borders on the tautologous as an extended restatement of the opening commitment to both rational and non-rational elements. Again the important point is that the central features of the dispute between rationalist and incremental models of decision making remain largely unmarred by this attempt to offer this 'third' alternative.

An artificial debate

These, then, are the terms of the argument. But in this note we are not proposing to come down in favour of one side or the other, nor indeed in favour of the attempts that have been made to construct a 'third' model of decision making as a compromise between the two. For in spite of prolonged dissension between rationalist and incrementalist models of decision making, both they and the several versions of a rapprochement have in common epistemological features the significance of which outweigh any specific points of variance. What we are proposing to do is to suggest that in certain respects the debate is somewhat artificial, firstly because it is not at all clear that the protagonists are actually arguing about the same thing and, secondly, because there is an important issue – of what it takes to act in accord with a set of rules about decision making behaviour – which is largely ignored on both sides. As policy research seeks clarification of the notion of 'decision making' it seems important initially to question some ground rules of the debate as it stands.

First, it is a mark of all the models that we have discussed that they should serve both explanatory and normative purposes. Bittner has commented on the general concept of rational organisation that, 'Even though one finds only "*is*" and "*is not*" in the substantive determination, there attaches the sense of "*ought*" to the entire scheme' (original italics).[36] In this debate that inclination is widespread and quite explicit. We have already mentioned Etzioni's observation that rationalistic models are widely held conceptions about how decisions *are and ought* to be made. It is also an important aspect of Lindblom's thesis that incrementalism both describes decision makers' behaviour and formalises an account of how they should behave. Furthermore Etzioni claims of the mixed scanning tactic that:

> Mixed-scanning provides both a realistic description of the strategy used by actors in a large variety of fields and the strategy for effective actors to follow[37]

and adds that the approach should be, 'at once *more realistic and more effective* than its components' (italics added).[38] And Dror, too, retains this commitment to a concurrently descriptive and prescriptive enterprise:

> What is needed is a model which fits reality while being directed towards its improvement, and which can in fact be applied to policy making while motivating a maximum effort to arrive at better policies.[39]

It is perhaps an indication of how deeply ingrained is this dual commitment within the disciplines of administrative and policy studies that such a statement does not immediately stand out as odd, confused and confusing as a basis for empirical research.

However, it *is* anomalous to presume *a priori* that 'is' and 'ought' in modes of decision making correlate. Certainly the authors who adopt this position do not explain at all clearly how a model is supposed to serve simultaneously as an accurate description of how decisions are made and as a description of how they might be made differently by way of improvement. Can these decision making models serve both functions? The debate which this note has been reviewing suggests not. Indeed the frequency with which current practices are criticised and changes advocated indicates precisely the opposite; namely that quite different frameworks may be required for explanatory and normative discussion. We are not of course arguing that explanatory social research can have no prescriptive policy implications. (A legitimate concern with improving both substantive policy and the way in which it is made and implemented is the *raison d'être* of much research in this field.) But to press either rationalist or incrementalist models into service for both functions at the same time is to risk what Bittner has termed 'ambiguities that defy clarification'.[40] Certainly as the debate is currently structured concepts in use for analysis and practice are utterly confused and it is hard to see how lucidity can be distilled.

One way forward may lie in the suggestion that the protagonists in the 'rationalism versus incrementalism' debate are really arguing about different kinds of things and that the term 'decision making' is thus in danger of being applied insensitively to a variety of phenomena and to confusing effect. It may be helpful to make some distinctions.

It will be apparent from discussion earlier in this note that few commentators generally doubt rationalistic models to be rather accurate pictures of widely held images about ideal decision making procedures. Criticism centres on the fact that rationalistic models are empirically inaccurate, or unrealistic. *That is not the way things are.* On the other hand there is a degree of sympathy for the view that the incrementalist approach has much validity as an empirical model of how policies are made (or, as McCleery puts it, 'more often, not made').[41] Criticism here centres on the claims of this approach to be useful normatively. *That is not the way things should be.*

Now viewed in this light it can be seen that the debate between rationalistic and incrementalist models is artificial in the sense that it is based on what Etzioni[42] elsewhere has pointed to as the confusion of comparing real with ideal states of affairs and expecting them to be the same. The two models are about different social phenomena and as such should seek to perform different functions. We should not expect them to agree. It certainly comes as no surprise to students of organisational behaviour to learn that the ideal accounts offered by organisational members of their practices are only a partial basis for explanation. As Bittner notes:

> It has been one of the most abiding points of interest of modern organisation-al research to study how well the programmatically intended formal structures of organisations describe what is going on within them, and what unintended, unprogrammed and thus informal structures tend to accompany them.[43]

And with a degree of consistency which is unusual in the social sciences, study after study has concluded that we require more than one account to describe the several facets of organisational life. The problem is not to reconcile the differences between contrasting rational and in-cremental models, nor to construct some third alternative which combines the strongest features of each. The problem is to relate the two in the sense of spelling out the relationship between the social realities with which each is concerned.

If this point is a valid one it has implications for policy related research. It means that more sophisticated accounts than those currently available are required of the impact of policy makers' ideologies, about the nature of decision making, upon the conduct and outcomes of the various stages of the policy process. In that sense what is called for is a data-based metatheory, delineating more precisely the role and functions of existing decision making models within the machinery of policy and administration. Methodologically that may be difficult for it must probably rest upon participant and other forms of observational data as well as upon interviews and records which so often reflect primarily ideological variables. But it is hard even to begin those tasks while 'is' and 'ought' remain so totally confused.

A second general feature of the debate is that both incrementalist and rationalist models, again together with the proponents of a 'third' view, largely ignore the issue of *what it takes*[44] to constitute conformity to the rules of either rationalist or incrementalist principles. That is, insuf-ficient attention has been paid to organisational members' own coding practice. For activity which may be classified by the organisational analyst in one set of terms may be described by the decision makers themselves, either prospectively or restrospectively, in another. What then is the relative status of the member's and analyst's coding manual? For instance, much apparent confusion of means and ends and objectiveless behaviour, from an incrementalist stance, may well be held by members as quite in accord with rational conduct. In the welfare services, for example, social workers are often accused by their critics of 'muddling through' yet persist in rational accounts of their own professional practices and decisions.

The point is that there is much flexibility in the way in which decision making can be described and it would be naive to suppose that members do not employ this flexibility in their own interests. For models of decision making are as much 'active elements of the concrete phenomenon of organisation' as a 'disinterested statement about it'.[45] As Turner[46] has argued, we must at least consider the possibility that social scientists have been 'set up' for their view of organisational life and thus been systematically misled about its character by presuming that the relationship of correspondence between an organisational concept and the practical activities that constitute that concept *in situ* is unambiguous. It is not. Since concepts and rules in organisations are used both prospectively and retrospectively to assign meaning to courses of action, what a scheme of ideas practically entails is a matter for empirical research. We may even find that it does not substantially affect the outcome of events whichever approach decision makers themselves claim to be following. They are likely to choose whatever is situationally most convenient and then justify their mode of choice in whatever terms appear most likely to prove acceptable.

One example of this can be seen in the field of British central government funding of applied social research. The Rothschild Report[47] recommended changes in the way in which decisions about financing projects were to be made. Although this may have altered the relationship between central government and some of the research councils, many established commissioning practices in departments' external research programmes and in relations between departments and government research units undoubtedly continued unchanged, but under the revised terminology of the 'customer–contractor principle'. Bittner has made the general point thus:

> Extending to the rule the respect of compliance, while finding in the rule the means of doing whatever need be done, is the gambit that characterises organisational acumen.[48]

Again if the point is a valid one it has implications for research. For it casts doubt upon the utility of expending any more intellectual energy in developing *a priori* 'models' of decision making. The way forward lies in producing more, and more carefully researched, data based answers to the following questions. What do relevant professionals, administrators, policy makers and laymen actually mean by 'decision making'? What activities do they include within these rubrics? What tactics do they employ? When? Where? How? And to what effects?

A concluding observation within Bittner's programmatic statement summarises the wider enterprise of which this kind of research would form a part:

> The problem that requires investigation is how various evaluations can be used as credits, and what sorts of credits have the consequence of assimilating some partial performance closer to the larger enterprise. The investigation of this problem would reveal the negotiable relationship between policy and politics.[49]

It is central to research in the field of policy and administration to understand not only how individual policy decisions are operationalised but also how decision makers at all stages of the policy process operationalise the notion of 'decision making' itself.

Conclusion

Empirical research in policy studies rightly involves the uncomfortable process of moving continually from theory to data and back again. While research in this area has sometimes been criticised for its atheoretical features, it is also important that concepts and models hastily adopted from allied fields should not be allowed to distort the phenomena under review. The concept of 'decision' is undoubtedly central both to the processes of making and implementing policy but in this note we have been suggesting that its components are by no means obvious, that this in itself constitutes a topic for enquiry and that the debate between rationalist and incrementalist models of decision making, as it is currently structured, provides an inadequate basis for policy research.

We have discussed incrementalist and rationalist models as well as attempts to provide a 'third' alternative. We have concluded that the debate is an artificial one for two reasons. Firstly, the relationship between 'is' and 'ought' is confused and there are good grounds for suggesting that whereas incrementalist models may perform an explanatory function, rationalist models are largely confined to a prescriptive role. Secondly the debate does not consider seriously the issue of what it takes to act in accord with any set of decision making rules and thus neglects the way in which policy makers and administrators may use 'decision making' as a gloss for a range of practices.

Throughout we have suggested that if these arguments are valid they have implications for policy research. They imply a commitment to an adequate explanatory account of decision making practices in the policy process as a precursor to prescriptions about how decisions ought to be made. They imply too the need for empirical studies of what decision makers mean by 'decision making' and how that varies in the varied contexts in which policy arises and gains practical effect.

Notes

1. P. Townsend (ed.), *The Concept of Poverty* (London: Heinemann, 1970).
2. A. Forder, *Concepts of Social Administration* (London: Routledge & Kegan Paul, 1974).
3. B. Davies, *Social Needs and Resources in Local Services* (London: Michael Joseph, 1968).
4. A. Dunsire, *The Execution Process. Volume 1, Implementation in a Bureaucracy, Volume 2, Control in a Bureaucracy* (London: Martin Robertson, 1978).
5. *Ibid.*
6. C. E. Lindblom, 'The science of "muddling through",' *Public Administration*, Vol. 19 (1959), 79–99. Y. Dror, '"Muddling through – "science" or inertia?', *Public Administration Review*, Vol. 24 (1964), 153–7. A contribution to 'Government decision making', a symposium with contributions from Y. Dror, C. E. Lindblom, R. W. Jones, Mickey McCleery and Wolf Hyderbrand, *Public Administration Review*, Vol. 24 (1964), 153–65.
7. G. Salaman and K. Thompson (eds.), *People and Organisations* (London: Longman for the Open University Press, 1973).
8. W. G. Scott, 'Decision concepts', in F. G. Castles *et al.* (eds.), *Decisions, Organisations and Society* (Harmondsworth: Penguin Books, 1971), 19.
9. A. Etzioni, 'Mixed-scanning: a "third" approach to decision-making', *Public Administration Review*, Vol. 27 (1967), 385. Etzioni is quoted with particular relevance to this note in K. N. Wright, 'An exchange strategy for the interface of community-based corrections into the service system', *Human Relations*, Vol. 30 (1977), 879–97.
10. See for example, P. Hall *et al.*, *Change, Choice and Conflict in Social Policy* (London: Heinemann, 1975).
11. See, for example, D. May, 'Rhetoric and reality: the consequences of unacknowledged ambiguity in the children's panel system', *The British Journal of Criminology*, Vol. 17 (1977), 209–27; G. Smith, 'The place of "professional ideology" in the analysis of "social policy": some theoretical conclusions from a pilot study of the children's panels', *The Sociological Review*, Vol. 25 (1977), 843–65; D. M. Hill, 'Political ambiguity and policy: the case of welfare', *Social and Economic Administration*, Vol. 12 (1978), 89–119.
12. M. McCleery, 'On remarks taken out of context', *Public Administration Review*, Vol. 24 (1964), 161.

13. B. R. Wilson (ed.), *Rationality* (Oxford: Blackwell, 1970).
14. J. Mayer and N. Timms, *The Client Speaks* (London: Routledge & Kegan Paul, 1970); E. Sainsbury, *Social Work with Families* (London: Routledge & Kegan Paul, 1975); S. Rees, *Social Work Face to Face* (London: Edward Arnold, 1978).
15. R. Hyderbrand, 'Administration of social change', *Public Administration Review*, Vol. 24 (1964), 164.
16. *Op. cit.*
17. R. G. Cassidy and R. E. Turner, 'Criminal justice system behaviour', *Behavioural Science*, Vol. 23 (1978), 99–108.
18. *Report of the Committee on Local Authority and Allied Personal Social Services* (The Seebohm Report), Cmnd. 3703 (London: HMSO, 1968), para. 115.
19. See A. B. Cherns, R. Sinclair and W. I. Jenkins, *Social Science and Government: Policies and problems* (London: Tavistock, 1972).
20. *Op. cit.* See also D. Braybrooke and C. E. Lindblom, *A Strategy of Decision* (New York: Free Press, 1963).
21. D. S. Jansson and S. H. Taylor, 'Search activity in social agencies: institutional factors that influence policy analysis', *Social Service Review*, Vol. 52 (1978), 189–201.
22. *Op. cit.*, 102.
23. *Op. cit.*
24. *Ibid.*, 155.
25. T. Booth, 'Finding alternatives to residential care – the problem of innovation in the personal social services', *Local Government Studies*, Vol. 9 (1978), 3–14.
26. *Op. cit.*, 155.
27. See, for example, A. Williams and R. Anderson, *Efficiency in the Social Services* (Oxford: Blackwell; London: Martin Robertson, 1975).
28. See, for example, A. P. Kakabadse, 'Corporate management in local government: a case study', *Journal of Management Studies*, Vol. 14 (1977), 341–51.
29. *Op. cit.*, 164.
30. *Op. cit.*
31. *Op. cit.*
32. *Op. cit.*, 390.
33. *Ibid.*
34. *Op. cit.*, 155.
35. C. E. Lindblom, 'Contexts for change and strategy: a reply', *Public Administration Review*, Vol. 24 (1964), 157–8.
36. E. Bittner, 'The concept of organisation', *Social Research*, Vol. 32 (1965), 250.
37. *Op. cit.*, 388.
38. *Op. cit.*, 390.
39. *Op. cit.*, 156.
40. *Op. cit.*
41. *Op. cit.*

42. A. Etzioni, 'Two approaches to organisation analysis: a critique and a suggestion', *Administrative Science Quarterly*, Vol. 5 (1960), 257–78.
43. *Op. cit.*, 237.
44. See especially on this point D. H. Zimmerman, 'The practicalities of rule use', in J. D. Douglas (ed.), *Understanding Everyday Life* (London: Routledge & Kegan Paul, 1971), Chapter 9.
45. E. Bittner, *op. cit.*
46. S. Turner, 'Complex organisations as savage tribes', *Journal for the Theory of Social Behaviour*, Vol. 7 (1977), 99–125.
47. *A Framework for Government Research and Development* (The Rothschild Report), Cmnd. 4148 (London: HMSO).
48. *Op. cit.*, 251.
49. *Ibid.*, 254.

Political rationality or incrementalism

Robert Gregory

Introduction

The name of C. E. Lindblom is synonymous with the concept of incrementalism in the academic literature on public policy making. From the early 1950s he developed an incisive critique of theoretical approaches which depicted public policy making as an exercise in means/ends rationality based on the analysis of comprehensive information. According to Lindblom, such rational-comprehensive, or synoptic, models grossly misrepresented the real practices of policy making, to which he applied his concepts of successive limited comparisons (Lindblom, 1959) and disjointed incrementalism (Braybrooke and Lindblom, 1963).

He has since developed and refined his thoughts on the role of formal analysis in policy making (Lindblom and Cohen, 1979; Lindblom, 1980); he has abandoned his earlier pluralist assumptions about the distribution of group power in liberal democracies (Lindblom, 1977, 1980); and he has also acknowledged an earlier failure to distinguish clearly enough between incremental *analysis* and incremental *politics*, and among differing types of the former (Lindblom, 1979). He has, however, remained committed to the argument that the synoptic model of policy making is an unrealistic and even morally dubious 'ideal'.

The main criticism levelled against Lindblom is that disjointed incrementalism cannot cope adequately with technical complexity and rapid change in modern society. Yehezkel Dror, Amatai Etzioni and more recently Robert Goodin have argued for the development of what they see as more integrated and comprehensive (less marginal) and

From R. Gregory, 'Political rationality or "incrementalism"? Charles E. Lindblom's enduring contribution to public policy making theory', *Policy and Politics*, **17**, 1989, pp. 139–53.

better informed (more analytical) policy strategies (Dror, 1964, 1968, 1971; Etzioni, 1967; Goodin, 1982).

The collection of ideas commonly associated with the term 'incrementalism' constitute the Lindblomian paradigm of public policy making, which embodies a particular meaning of rationality. This meaning is substantially different from the two other concepts of rationality that are central to the theoretical debate on public policy making, namely, *technical* (or formal) rationality, which is about the selection of appropriate means for achieving given ends, and *economic* rationality, which is about determining the most efficient use of resources among competing purposes (for example, Hartwig, 1978). The two latter concepts either together or separately inform the synoptic— or, as it will sometimes be called here, rationalist—model.

This review does not attempt any philosophical examination of these various concepts of rationality. Instead it concentrates on the notion of objective-setting, in which the essential differences between the Lindblomian and synoptic paradigms are located.

Incrementalism: multiple meanings

The term 'incrementalism' has become a popular shorthand symbol for one or more of several ideas progressively propounded by Lindblom, mainly since his major collaborative work with Robert Dahl (Dahl and Lindblom, 1953), and which taken collectively constitute the Lindblomian paradigm. These are:

1. That in public policy making the level of theoretical understanding of the relationships among relevant variables is low (Lindblom, 1959; Braybrooke and Lindblom, 1963).
2. That policy makers typically confine themselves to consideration of those variables, values and possible consequences that are of immediate concern to themselves and which differ only marginally from the status quo, thus greatly simplifying their analysis of possible options (Lindblom, 1959).
3. That in the face of such limited informational and theoretical input policy movements are based on trial and error interventions of an intendedly marginal kind, so that unanticipated consequences may be coped with more easily (Lindblom, 1959; Braybrooke and Lindblom, 1963).
4. That policy and/or political change occurs only marginally, that is, what will be the case tomorrow will not differ radically from what exists today. This is what Lindblom refers to as incrementalism 'as a political pattern'—its 'core meaning' (Lindblom, 1979, p. 517).

5. That policy making is a process of political and social interaction—negotiation, bargaining, etc.—among groups promoting and protecting differing and competing interests and values. This is Lindblom's (1965) 'partisan mutual adjustment', a political process that contrasts with a system in which policy is driven by centralised, information-based decision-making (either system being capable of producing incremental policy change, which thus is conceptually different from partisan mutual adjustment).

6. That political and policy change is not a function of any coherent set of transcendently guiding goals (Braybrooke and Lindblom, 1963; Lindblom and Cohen, 1979).

These meanings can be aggregated into two groups, which focus attention on two different aspects of public policy making. The first group embraces meanings 1, 2 and 3, and concerns the role of formal analysis in policy making. The second group, encompassing the fourth, fifth and sixth meanings, relates to the socio/political context of public policy making. Thus, Lindblom's central concept of 'disjointed incrementalism' is essentially an amalgam of meanings contained in the first group, in that it attempts to convey how decision-makers simplify their analytical tasks. His 'simple incremental analysis' (the second meaning stated above) is one of several elements in disjointed incremental analysis, while 'disjointed incrementalism' is in turn one of several possible forms of 'strategic analysis', that is, 'analysis limited to any calculated or thoughtfully chosen set of stratagems to simplify complex policy problems' (Lindblom, 1979, p. 518). The 'disjointed' nature of what Lindblom refers to as 'this complex method of analysis' (Lindblom, 1979, p. 517) is a function of the socio/political context in which it operates: many wills mingle in the making of policy, and consequently analysis is always both partial and partisan. This does not refer simply to any biased generation or misrepresentation of evidence, although this is frequently to be expected, but rather to the inevitability of multiple and divergent viewpoints, based on necessarily selective and incomplete information, that characterises political discourse (Lindblom and Cohen, 1979; Lindblom, 1980).

Incrementalism as analysis

Simply stated, the debate between the so-called rationalists and the incrementalists has been about how to 'improve' public policy processes and outcomes. Just what constitutes 'improvement' in public policy making is a matter of preference, and may be measured against an almost infinite range of criteria. Politicians, bureaucratic advisers, policy analysts, public employees working at the counter, and the clients, beneficiaries or victims of policy are all likely to focus on different issues. For theorists who advocate the development of more 'rational' policy, improvement has to do with the degree to which formal analysis overcomes the 'irrationalities' and limitations of political interaction. Problems of policy making are problems of intellect, in that there is seen to be not enough of it about. According to Dror (1971, p. 28), for example:

> The inadequacy of present normal sciences for the purposes of policy making improvement is the result of their basic paradigms. Therefore, in order to produce the scientific inputs necessary for policy making improvement, a scientific revolution is essential.

And Goodin (1982, pp. 37–8) concludes, *inter alia*, that:

> any responsible policy must be based on some theoretical understanding of the system into which it intervenes . . . . based on our theoretical understanding of the particular system concerned, it is sometimes appropriate to think big and sometimes appropriate to think small. Clearly, the most dangerous course, however, is to deny the need for theory and refuse to think at all.

On this issue Lindblom and his critics often seem to be talking past one another, arguing perceived differences when in fact they share common ground. To Lindblom, 'achieving impossible feats of synopsis is a bootless, unproductive ideal' (Lindblom, 1979, p. 518). He sees strategic analysis as a more productive ideal because it is practicable. But writers like Dror and Goodin are hardly unaware of the shortcomings of 'pure' rationality, while strategic analysis hardly seems different from Simon's (1947) 'bounded rationality', which is predicated upon a recognition of those shortcomings (Paris and Reynolds, 1983, pp. 124–36). To this extent the debate between Lindblom and his critics has been of very limited significance.

Their major differences over the role of analysis in policy making become apparent on a closer examination of the three meanings contained in the first group, above. Common to these is the core issue concerning the level of *theoretical understanding* in policy making. The first meaning addresses this point directly, while numbers 2 and 3 are derived as a secondary consequence of it. The issue of theoretical understanding in policy making is one to which Goodin (1982) has paid particular attention. The three forms of incrementalism that he identifies (Goodin, 1982, Ch. 2) approximate respectively the elements identified above. The first type is a small-step, trial and error, totally pragmatic process of decision-making independent of any theoretical understanding; the second is incrementalism that adapts by testing theoretical hypotheses through small changes in a limited range of variables; and the third, a 'minor theme', is where theoretically informed interventions are tested by small changes which do not foreclose future options—'the smaller the change the more likely it is to be reversible' (Goodin, 1982, p. 36). Goodin argues that incrementalism shuns 'analytical problem-solving' because 'social theories are too infirm to form the basis for policy making' (Goodin, 1982, p. 19).

If Goodin had set out to show that policy makers are, in fact, guided by theoretical assumptions, even if these are only inchoate and unsoundly based, his thesis would have been a valid elucidation of a point not clearly defined by Braybrooke and Lindblom. In other words, even purely pragmatic decision-makers, such as those depicted in Goodin's first case, are guided in their choices of action by *implicit* beliefs about possible or likely outcomes. To call these beliefs or assumptions 'theories' may be stretching a point, but only if we confine the concept of theory to formal and explicit hypotheses about cause and effect. Thus, Lindblom's (1959) decision-maker, who shapes an economic policy not on the basis of complete causal knowledge about the relationships among a range of economic variables, but in light of his or her understanding of the various trade-offs among a range of significant values that are embodied in a number of differing alternative courses of action, is guided by beliefs about the probable consequences of the choice that is made. In effect, these are inchoate 'hypotheses'. Cases where a decision-maker has absolutely *no* speculative idea about causal relationships—irrespective of how ill-founded these ideas might prove to be in practice—are probably so rare as to be insignificant.

Goodin, however, is primarily concerned with formal theory in policy making. His proposition is that incrementalists either fail to use formal theory at all; or, if they do, they do not use enough, or they use it too cautiously. Here he is much less persuasive in his criticism. This is mainly because, if Goodin is to be believed, these incrementalists—of all three varieties—somehow have an aversion to theoretical under-standing of the problems and issues they address. While not saying it explicitly, he invites the reader to conclude that this reluctance to engage theory stems from the decision-maker's stupidity, or laziness, or both. But Goodin's impatience with incrementalists reflects his own inadequate appreciation of the *political* context and nature of their work: if only politicians and their advisers ignored the political character of their work then policies would, from the point of view of those who devise them, be much more 'successful'. His example of the manage-ment of the British economy in the post-war years is an interesting one. According to Goodin, the failure of successive governments to halt the 'precipitous decline' of the British economy can be attributed to flaws in the first type of incrementalism. Governments had no shortage of theories about how to deal with the economy but, 'faced with profound disagreement among economic advisers and heavy pressure for quick results, (they) approached the decision problem in a highly incremental manner', trying a number of policies but abandoning each as it failed to produce quick results. Goodin refers to two economists who offer good reasons for believing that any of the strategies would have worked, given time, 'but governments, operating in an extremely atheoretical way, had no clear idea how long to ask insistent citizens and Zurich gnomes to wait for results' (Goodin, 1982, p. 23).

Even if Goodin's assumption about the longer-term efficacy of the chosen strategies is correct, the problem that British governments faced was surely a political one. Knowing what Goodin believes they should have known, their problem was how to convince 'insistent citizens' impatient for results in the short term. In situations of that sort the choices confronting governments are inevitably as much about maintaining electoral support as about determining the theoretical validity of alternative policies. To suggest that this ought not to be so, as Goodin implicitly does, is to depict the political context of governmental policy making as some sort of pathological impediment to 'rational' choice. That does not advance understanding very far.

Politics is not for 'curing'. It never goes away, even when governments profess or appear to be sticking to policies that have the blessing of theoretical 'experts'. The Thatcher government would seem to be more to Goodin's liking (although he does not say) since it has become known for the Prime Minister's resoluteness in sticking to macroeconomic policies that are based on Friedmanite theory intended to create conditions for sustainable, non-inflationary growth of output and employment. The Lange (Labour) government in New Zealand provides another pertinent example. In its first term of office it received widespread acclamation for its abandonment of the pragmatic and politically opportunistic policy stances of its predecessors in the post-war years, and for its commitment to the 'new laissez-faire' which is based on economic liberalism, and a belief in the primacy of inflation as the most important economic problem, to be addressed by the pursuit of firm monetary policy (Boston, 1987; Easton, 1987). After three years of massive reforms to the structure of the New Zealand economy the government was returned to office at the 1987 general election with the biggest Parliamentary majority in the country's history.

Does all this indicate that the sort of incrementalist policy making deplored by Goodin is now on the wane, that at least in the area of macroeconomic management Britain and New Zealand are seeing a new breed of analytical problem-solvers, instructed by formal theory, and impatient with practical political considerations? No. It can be argued, for example, that the Thatcher government has responded more pragmatically than many would allow to the theoretical shortcomings underpinning its policies (Boston, 1987, p. 141). Apart from that, however, while it may appear that these governments, especially the Lange one, have to a greater extent than their predecessors placed their faith in the longer-term efficacy of theoretically informed choices, they have been able to do this only by solving simultaneously their political problem—persuading their 'insistent citizens' that (a) a longer-term perspective is necessary, and (b) it will ultimately deliver.

It cannot be conceded that there is a stronger commitment to theory *per se*. Rather, what has changed has been the theoretical paradigm that policy makers have employed in informing their economic strategies. Prior to the Thatcher and Lange governments the dominant paradigm had been a neo-Keynesian one based on counter-cyclical demand management strategies. This has been replaced by the radically different paradigm of Friedmanite 'neo-conservative' market liberalism. Moreover, especially so in New Zealand, but also in Britain, radical programmes of public sector reform have been driven not by traditional public administration theory, but by the 'public choice' or 'economics of bureaucracy' theoretical framework (see, for example, Gregory, 1987; Hood, 1987; Roberts, 1987). Arguably, contrary to Goodin's belief that British (and, by extension, New Zealand) governments have been too impatient with theoretical prognostications, and have preferred to respond in a pragmatic manner to changing economic and political circumstance, it may be that the neo-Keynesian theoretical framework within which they operated gave rise to their expedient counter-cyclical macroeconomic management. Similarly, because of their radical challenge to the older order of things the reforms introduced under the 'new laissez-faire' theoretical paradigm demand a firm and continuing political commitment (or at least the appearance of it) if they are to produce the outcomes their authors promise.

Goodin claims that the incrementalists' avoidance of theoretical understanding is based on their assumption of quick and complete results which leaves them blind to policy responses that flow from 'threshold' or 'sleeper' effects, and too inclined to precipitate undesirable policy change. 'What we really need in order to anticipate threshold or sleeper effects is a fairly full set of theoretically integrated empirical generalisations' (Goodin, 1982, p. 26). But, particularly in social policy, such generalisations are extraordinarily difficult to generate, are usually inconclusive and politically contentious when they are, and offer an unconvincing 'excuse' for not proceeding on the basis of well-intentioned judgement that acknowledges the need to act until (often unforeseeable) consequences dictate a policy review. Ironically, Goodin's example of what he considers to be a non-incremental policy based on a 'comparatively full theoretical understanding' confirms the centrality of political power and opportunity that his analysis otherwise ignores. Continuing Congressional support for NASA's plan to put a man on the moon was obviously crucial to its ultimate success. But that support was based on a widely shared belief in the scientists' capacity to deliver the goods—which is quite different from 'theoretical understanding of the processes involved in a space launch' (Goodin, 1982, p. 27)—and on the perceived virtues of the plan itself. (Had they the resources most governments would find it much easier to employ theoretical understanding to fly to the moon than to determine an acceptably fair and efficient distribution of public goods and services.)

A similar response is invited by Goodin's critique of his second type of incrementalism. This is where analysts acknowledge their reliance upon theory about how a system works, but use incremental procedures for perfecting the theory (Goodin, 1982, p. 28). He offers here an orthodox statement about the difficulties faced by analysts in ensuring the internal and external validity—contamination and replicability—of social experiments that are intended to inform public policy making (see, for example, Roos, 1975; J. O. Wilson, 1974). But it is not at all clear as to what Goodin is criticising in this approach, and no alternative possibility is offered. Instead, he rests content with a statement that could well have been lifted from a practitioner's manual on 'muddling through':

> policy makers have no alternative but to plan as best they can with such information and theory as are available to them at the time. This category of cases is of tremendous importance, since the policy environment is typically highly volatile. (Goodin, 1982, p. 33)

What is at issue is a deeper understanding than that offered by Goodin of the relationships—no matter how direct or diffuse—between theory and practice, belief and action, research and application, in public policy making. For example, popular belief in the efficacy of neo-Keynesian demand management strategies was a vital factor in ensuring the success of those policies in the decades following the Great Depression. Goodin has little, if anything, to say about the subtleties of such interactions, which is surprising in light of the fact that Lindblom, the major target of his criticisms, had already offered an exploratory examination of them in his co-authored work with D. K. Cohen (Lindblom and Cohen, 1979). There, the authors argued a point that is fundamentally challenging to Goodin's analysis: that what they call 'professional social inquiry' (which includes the development and testing of theories) is seldom conclusive in its findings and even less often, if ever, 'independently authoritative' in its application (1979, pp. 41–3).

This shortcoming is evident, too, in Goodin's third concept of incrementalism, which has at its centre a belief in 'the virtues of thinking small' (Caiden and Wildavsky, 1974, p. 309), lest non-incremental decisions produce irreversible effects. Goodin rightly points out that there is no necessary relationship between the irreversibility of a policy intervention and its size: large-scale interventions may be just as reversible as small ones, while the converse may also be true. Moreover, according to Goodin, there is nothing intrinsically wrong with irreversibility in any case: 'it is enormously desirable to eradicate evils once and for all' (Goodin, 1982, p. 37).

But Goodin ignores a more compelling truth, namely, that in so many areas of governmental policy, but especially in the vast area of social policy, it is often politically difficult to agree either on what the problems to be 'eradicated' are, or on how they ought to be addressed. As Banfield (1980, p. 18) has observed:

> Social problems are at bottom political; they arise from differences of opinion and interest and, except in trivial circumstances, are difficulties to be coped with (ignored, got around, put up with, exorcised by the arts of rhetoric etc.) rather than puzzles to be solved. In coping with difficulties, formal analysis may sometimes be helpful, but it is not always so. (See, too, Blumer, 1971; Rittel and Webber, 1973.)

Such problems do not readily lend themselves to 'solutions' that are—in Lindblom and Cohen's terminology—either scientifically *conclusive* or politically, socially or morally *authoritative*. The 'Final Solution' devised by the Third Reich is a dramatic illustration. Goodin suggests that incremental policy changes are, under his third type, a function of the analyst's desire to avoid the irreversibility that is believed to result from inadequate theoretical understanding. But is it not that policy makers tend to proceed cautiously under circumstances of high political salience, incomplete and ambiguous information, and where 'reversibility' is assessed in terms of political and social cost rather than technical/experimental validity?

Albeit indirectly, however, Goodin's critique does draw attention to a major weakness in the Lindblomian paradigm; for while there is no necessary relationship between reversibility and the size of policy change, neither is there any such relationship between the latter and the degree of political benefit or cost. This will be discussed in the following section, which focuses on those incrementalist ideas contained in group 2, relating to the socio/political character of public policy making.

Incrementalism as politics

The incremental paradigm explains what it sees as the typically marginal and gradualist character of policy change in terms of processes of social and political interaction, whereby different groups and interests seek to protect and pursue their disparate purposes largely without reference to any set of overarching, common, goals. According to Lindblom (1979, p. 522), while this process of incremental *politics* is closely related to disjointed incremental *analysis* it is not to be confused with it. Nor, he points out, should the process of partisan mutual adjustment be confused with incremental politics *per se*:

> One can imagine a nation practising political incrementalism without partisan mutual adjustment, or with only a minimum of it. One can also imagine partisan mutual adjustment for non-incremental policy making. (1979, p. 523)

Notwithstanding these caveats, a reading of all Lindblom's work on incrementalism leaves the strong impression that he has over-stressed the extent to which policy change is and must be marginal. He denies that political incrementalism is, in principle, slow moving:

> A fast-moving sequence of small changes can more speedily accomplish a drastic alteration of the *status quo* than can an only infrequent major policy change. . . . One might reply of course that drastic steps in policy need be no more infrequent than incremental steps. We can be reasonably sure, however, that in almost all circumstances that suggestion is false. *Incremental steps can be made quickly because they are only incremental. They do not rock the boat, do not stir up the great antagonisms and paralyzing schisms as do proposals for more drastic change.* (Lindblom, 1979, p. 520. Emphasis added)

This may or may not be so. Apart from the fact that what constitutes incremental or radical change is a matter of subjective judgement, a seemingly radical policy change may not be considered undesirable by those affected by it, and may even be warmly welcomed. What is primarily at issue here is not, as Lindblom suggests in regard to the American political system 'a structure of veto powers [in the Constitution, in legislative procedures, and in property rights] that makes even incremental moves difficult and insufficiently frequent' (1979, p. 520). It is the exercise of political power generally—coalition building, and the fostering, maintenance and decline of support, for example (Spread, 1985)—that determines the nature, scope and focus of policy innovation and change.

Lindblom's view that policy change in the United States and Western Europe has been 'insufficiently frequent' simply expresses his own political judgement about the need for change. This in itself represents a departure from his earlier writings, in which—as many of his critics have claimed—he regarded political incrementalism as not only inevitable but desirable, seeing political democracy as being 'often greatly endangered' by non-incremental change (Braybrooke and Lindblom, 1963, p. 73).

But his argument that is is necessarily incremental not only serves to mask the subjectivity of the judgement on which that observation is based, but also obscures the much more compelling point that, whether or not policy change is incremental or radical, it is always politically driven, that is, it is always a function of extant power alignments.

This insistence on the marginality of change turned the so-called incrementalist versus rationalist debate into a blind alley. Much of the literature critical of the Lindblomian paradigm espoused the need to produce policy responses that were less incremental, more far-reaching, in scope. But in following Lindblom's lead that it is political obstacles that inhibit change the critics wrongly concluded that larger-scale policy changes could be induced by enhancing the role of formal analysis and rational techniques of calculation. This in turn drew Lindblom into pointing out the intellectual and political unrealities of synoptic analysis, while reasserting the inevitability of disjointed incremental analysis and of marginal political change. In assuming that a more synoptic style of analysis in policy making could achieve what politics could not, Lindblom's critics threw out the baby of political decision-making with what they regarded as the bathwater of gradualist change. The upshot has been an obfuscation and inter-mixing of the ideas contained in each of the two groups of incrementalist meanings. But while Lindblom has greatly over-stressed the extent to which policy change is or must be incremental, and has been rather ethnocentric in his conclusions on this point, unlike his critics he has understood very clearly that the political baby is an extremely resilient one, which, as will be shown below, has a peculiar rationality of its own.

The confusion can be removed simply by asserting that *there is no necessary relationship between the extent of any policy development or change and the degree to which professional social inquiry has informed it* (Lindblom and Cohen, 1979). The two central themes in the debate are logically, and empirically, separate: depending on whether one judges change to be marginal or radical, one can say that just as an incremental change might be guided by a more synoptic analysis with a heavy reliance on theoretical understanding, and just as a radical change might be so guided, the converse is also possible in each case. [. . .]

The reification of incrementalism

The Lindblomian paradigm illuminates the *processes* of public policy making, whereas the rationalist perspective concentrates on the *results* produced by those processes. In coining the phrase 'the science of muddling through' Lindblom sought to represent what he saw as the generic rationality of a process which, judged by the expectations of microeconomic logic, could not be relied upon to produce 'rational' results. But in insisting that disjointed incrementalism is, in fact, a method or system and 'not a failure of method for which administrators ought to apologise' (1959, p. 87), Lindblom has reified the activities and behaviour he has so ably described. In the debate spawned by Lindblom's seminal article both he and his critics tended to promote and sustain a text book illusion that incrementalist or synoptic strategies were available for adoption or rejection by persons whose business was policy making. The exchange took on the appearance of a religious crusade, in which policy makers were invited to choose either salvation or damnation. Zealous reformers preached against seduction by the easy virtues of political and analytical expediency—Goodin, for example, has decried the 'perverse and pervasive doctrine of incrementalism' (1982, p. 19)—while Lindblom sought to show that the road to a policy making hell was paved with the best of rationalist intentions.

A legacy of all this has been a common propensity to speak, often pejoratively, of a large group of people—the 'incrementalists' (a term we here place in inverted commas)—whose business is policy making, and who are said to behave in the variety of ways depicted in one or both of the two groups of meanings (above), or to talk as if 'incrementalism' were a 'thing in itself'. The literature is replete with examples, but a few will illustrate. Goodin talks of an 'incrementalist in the role of a central banker (who) might learn to raise taxes slightly every time the inflation rate creeps upward without ever bothering to try to discover what was causing the inflation' (1982, p. 20). Cates (1979, p. 528) states that 'incrementalism is an adversary process; competing values and groups reach agreement through compromise', and (echoing Lindblom) that 'incrementalism is best suited to a stable environment where fine-tuning is all that is needed'. Paris and Reynolds (1983, p. 134) argue that 'incrementalist procedures cannot be expected to provide distributive fairness'. Frohock (1979, p. 52) explains that 'an incrementalist decision-maker expects other actors, in other sections of institutions, to correct the mistakes he (sic) may make as he operates even within his limitations, and even this remedial function of in-crementalist systems depends upon the limited scope of decisions taken by everyone'. Jackson (1982, p. 148) gives standard reasons in answer-ing his own question, 'Why do decision makers use incrementalism as a decision rule?'. And finally, Lindblom himself calls incremental politics a 'suitable instrument for more effectively grappling with our policy problems', and as being 'a way of "smuggling" changes into the political system' (Lindblom, 1979, pp. 520–1).

All such usage is a form of reification: it imputes an objective, concrete 'reality' to forms of human behaviour that are properly explicable in terms of individual motivation within certain socially created contexts (Fay, 1975). Or it simply creates confusion where clarity is needed (see Smith and May, 1980, on this point). Is Goodin's banker just that—a banker, who acts in a particular way under particular circumstances, or is he or she a banker who has decided to be an 'incrementalist' (perhaps having done a university course in policy making theory)? Incrementalism is not an 'adversary process' as Cates argues (confusing, incidentally, Lindblom's concept of incremental politics with the idea of partisan mutual adjustment). It is not a process of any sort, although the term does—as noted above—focus attention on political processes. What Cates might more accurately have said is that *politics* is an adversary process which sometimes/often produces incremental change (which is to say very little). Nor is incrementalism (meaning disjointed incremental analysis) 'best suited' to anything. It just *is*. By its very nature the analysis of policy issues is inevitably partial, partisan and multi-faceted, whether or not the socio/political environment is stable or unstable. If she means that incremental *politics* is best-suited to a stable environment she is merely offering a tautology: little political change is best suited to conditions of little political change. Distributive fairness, which is the focus of Paris' and Reynolds' concern, is denied not by anyone adopting 'incrementalist procedures', but by the political capacity of some interests to prevail over others. Frohock's decision-maker is unlikely to expect other policy actors to 'correct his mistakes'; rather, he or she is much more likely to act according to the aphorism, 'where you stand depends on where you sit' (Miles, 1978), that is, to play the role of policy advocate that that person is institutionally expected (paid?) to play, alongside others playing different roles and advocating different interests. Nor are there 'incrementalist systems' which have 'remedial functions' that are 'dependent upon the limited scope of decisions taken by everyone'. Instead it is more sensible to say that in politics the pursuit of narrowly defined personal or group interests may produce policy changes which are considered by some, or all, to be an improvement on what went before. In Jackson's case it can be said that decision-makers do not 'use' incrementalism as a 'decision rule'; they do what they can with limited resources of various kinds—information, time, energy, intelligence, and so on. (The argument that disjointed incrementalism is a decision rule that can be collectively, rather than individually, applied is even more fallacious.) Finally, the 'instrument' of incremental politics, to which Lindblom refers, is nothing of the sort: rather, we should speak of a political process, which sometimes (he, of course, would say more often than not) produces small-scale change—by 'smuggling' perhaps, but also by openly declaring the goods and paying political duties on them.

It is particularly significant that in many such instances 'incrementalism' has been used in place of a perfectly good word long since available to describe the same activity: politics.

'Incrementalism' discarded: Lindblom's political rationality

In Lindblom's classical work, *Politics and Markets*, he develops his two models of the role of intellect in the social organisation of world politico-economic systems. While these models are based on the original ones set out in his earlier work, including 'The science of muddling through', in the whole of *Politics and Markets* there are but three brief references to 'incrementalism' as such. In his co-authored work with Cohen (1979) the term is referred to only once, in a footnote, as is also the case in the second edition of *The Policy-making Process* (1980). True, in each of these works Lindblom's concerns are much broader than his earlier focus on the shortcomings of rational-comprehensive policy making. Yet it is almost as if by the late 1970s he had concluded that the term was unnecessary, or that it had been the source of too much confusion. (His 1979 article, 'Still muddling, not yet through', was intended to clarify once and for all some of the differing meanings of the term.)

Whether or not that was Lindblom's own belief, his central contribution to public policy theory could better be understood if at the very least the term 'incrementalism' were used with greater discrimination, or preferably if it were dropped from usage altogether. In none of its separate meanings does it adequately capture the central point that is at the heart of virtually all Lindblom's work, but which becomes particularly explicit in his later writings, namely, that *public policy making has to be understood essentially as a political process, rather than an analytical, problem-solving, one.* [. . .]

The strength of Lindblom's work lies in the way in which, both directly and indirectly, it illuminates the nature of a rationality of collective, i.e. political, action, the crucial feature of which is its very *collectivity*. In the Lindblomian paradigm of public policy making, no one individual or group has a monopoly on truth, information or analysis. And the power to determine the ends and means of public policy is widely, though of course not equally, shared. These factors, therefore, rather than any technical limitations on the role of human intellect (as important as these might be), render futile any aspiration to the synoptic 'ideal'. While Lindblom himself may not have put it quite so bluntly, his work shows how advocates of synoptic policy making—whether they know it or not—are really presenting politically sanitised and morally dubious prescriptions for an increasingly elitist distribution of power in society. These prescriptions are disguised by a scientistic vocabulary which speaks of X-efficiency, externalities and general equilibrium, of society's inability to 'solve' (or at least develop 'optimal' policies for) its 'social problems', as if 'correct' answers are detectable by those whose proper business is to govern by virtue of their superior knowledge and intellect.

Lindblom's writing (1977, 1980) on the role of intellect in social organisation clearly illustrates that such a prospect has to be understood in terms of political power rather than scientific integrity. One may accept or reject his thesis on the 'privileged position of business' in western democracies (see Mayer, 1982; Vogel, 1987), and one might agree with Gilliatt (1987) that the Lindblomian view of politics as the search for order ignores an alternative perspective which sees it as being by nature a 'quarrelsome activity concerned with promoting conflict and disrupting order'. Nevertheless, Lindblom is surely correct in recognising that policy making is an essentially non-scientific activity (the art of the possible, no less), and that those who engage in it are not necessarily dunderheads obdurately set against theoretical insight and commitment, but are political actors who in their own 'final analysis' must measure success against a capacity to translate hopes into legitimate reality. The collective nature of political action ensures that what *is* done will depend greatly on what *can* be done, politically and socially, technically and economically, morally and culturally. [. . .]

It may also be that in many places politics has something of a bad name. It carries with it connotations of self-seeking politicians and political parties who continually subvert the collective public interest through the relentless pursuit of partisan and personal advantage. The advent of a particular government, therefore, which appears to be committed to pursuing the common good through strategies purporting to be unsullied by calculations of partisan advantage (except in so far as their 'correctness' is taken to be a measure of their political virtue) is popularly seen as a welcome relief from prevalent political cynicism. The strategies of the Thatcher government in Britain and the Lange government in New Zealand, as noted above, bring them into this category. In both countries the government's over-riding commitment to the primary objective of disinflation seems to give the lie to Lindblom's arguments that there is no one best way, and that values are determined during—not before—consideration of alternative policy options. It appears to belie the message of his initial example in 'The science of muddling through', that economic management is all about negotiating trade-offs among *marginally* differing values; and it suggests that tightly disciplined cabinets in Westminster parliamentary systems can have a unitary identity and monopoly of decision-making power far more readily than is possible in a system of 'separated institutions sharing powers' (Neustadt, 1960, p. 33). Some would say that Lindblom's representation of political decision-making might have been an appropriate description of governmental economic management at the time he presented it, that is in the 1950s and 60s, before the 'stagflation' of the 1970s disrupted the complacement application of neo-Keynesian economic policies.

The evidence for any such conclusions is illusory. As Lindblom (1980) has observed, public policy making in liberal democracies is driven by the often contradictory demands that it be subject to popular control, mindful of individual liberties, and productive of problem solutions. So while changes in economic policies may be far more sweeping in scope than the Lindblomian paradigm would suggest were possible, sooner or later conflicting demands and pressures begin to make themselves felt, and governments can ignore them only at the risk of placing other, democratic, values in jeopardy. The linear, singular strategy may even achieve its main objective—inflation, for example, might be reduced to a promised 5% per annum. The question then is, what next? The objective of retaining it at such a level has to be weighed against other, maybe more politically pressing, demands: perhaps that the exchange rate be devalued, unemployment reduced, social welfare programmes increased, and the fiscal deficit reduced. A seemingly virtuous determination to pursue objectives when sustained in the face of growing dissent becomes transformed into an arrogant authoritarianism. This is often because governments hoist themselves on the petard of their own specified objectives: a willingness to revise those objectives in the face of changing circumstances can be represented by political opponents as evidence of muddled thinking, inconsistency or lack of commitment.

Implicit in Lindblom's observations on the elusive nature of policy objectives—'(they) have no ultimate validity other than that they are agreed upon' (1959, p. 84)—is the question of whether or not the overwhelming preoccupation with talk of objective-setting and achievement in public policy making is an especially useful way of conceptualising what the process is really about. The one thinker who has made this point an explicit part of his considerable, and much underrated, contribution to public policy theory is Sir Geoffrey Vickers (for example, 1965, 1968, 1972, 1983; and Open Systems Group, 1984), who includes the idea of 'endurance through time' as one of five elements that he considers to be 'repugnant to "scientific" study' (1972, p. 265). Vickers' work shows how policy making is about the complex and continuous process of adjusting the 'value system' to the 'reality system', and vice versa, and how when viewed in this light it becomes much more relevant to talk not of goals and objectives that are achieved, once and for all, but of norms and standards that are maintained or modified over time (policy 'problems' being resolved rather than solved). For example, in the case mentioned in the preceding paragraph, the 'objective' of reducing inflation to 5% per annum should be seen instead as a means of ensuring—at least for the time being—that certain valued relationships are sustained over and above others that are valued less (say a lower trade deficit and a reduced cost of living, as against rising unemployment and lower rates of productive investment). In this, the task of governance is not to reduce inflation to a target figure, thus 'solving the problem' once and for all, but to shape and alter the standards by which policy success or failure is judged over time. (Borrowing Churchill's famous phrase, to avoid those states of affairs up with which the public will not put.)

It is ironical that these enduring insights into the nature of public policy making should have been proffered by a man whose primary intellectual training lies in economics, the discipline which has provided the theoretical foundations of the prescriptive models of policy analysis against which his own critique has been directed. But as a *political economist* Lindblom has always resisted the temptation to regard politics, in any of its multitude of forms, as a pathological obstruction to the achievement of more rational policy outcomes. As he himself has said, 'to understand policy making one must understand all of political life and activity' (1980, p. 5). He sees very clearly that while better formal analysis is always to be welcomed in policy making—'like a person in a desert who prizes the shade of any single tree he finds' (Lindblom, 1977, p. 259)—governments proceed in ways characterised by the incrementalist features contained in group 2 (above) because they are obliged to act in a socio/political arena rather than a scientific one. The essence of policy making, an iterative rather than a sequential process in which 'public policy is being formed as it is being executed, and . . . executed as it is being formed' (Friedrich, 1940, p. 6), is the search for legitimate collective action rather than the testing of scientific theories. And while not all politics is policy making, nor all policy making necessarily politics, the differences between the values of political action and scientific inquiry—that is, the differences between *advocacy* on the one hand, and *analysis* on the other—underpin the whole policy analysis enterprise, and ultimately those engaged in it must decide for themselves the extent to which they wish to sacrifice political relevance to scientific integrity or vice versa (Bulmer, 1988; Coleman, 1972; Meltsner, 1976; Price, 1965; Rein and White, 1977; J. Q. Wilson, 1981).

To suggest, as Lindblom does, that in the face of such uncertainty, ambiguity, inadequate theory and information, unintended consequences, social and technical complexity, political complicatedness, and organisational self-centredness, governments in any modern society in effect do not really know what they are doing is to invite disbelief, impatience, and not a little opprobrium. After all, who ever heard of a politician publicly admitting that he or she is not really in the business of providing 'rational' solutions? In an age when people are culturally conditioned to assume the validity of rationalistic norms there are not many votes in that. Moreover, Lindblom's political perspicacity seems to have left him with virtually nothing to say about the criteria of 'good' policy other than that it is collectively agreed upon; and it is but a short step (though one that he himself has not taken) to argue that, after the 'final analysis' has been completed, political might must be right. Yet this lacuna in his writing does not mean that, in particular, economically rational models of policy making can offer any conclusive answers (Paris and Reynolds, 1983). Nor does it compromise Lindblom's recognition that in order to understand the core of public policy making we need to pay close attention to the nature and exercise of political power.

Conclusion

Charles E. Lindblom's enduring message is that public policy making needs to be seen as an essentially political process, driven by a distinctive form of collective rationality. To understand this is to cut through the confusion created by the over-use of the term 'incrementalism', with which his name is so often closely linked. It is virtually impossible to read Lindblom without sensing his own intuitive understanding that political life is larger than technical and economic logic. While this may have led him to overstate the extent to which policy change is marginal in scope, it has also enabled him to see that formal techniques of analysis and theory-building—no matter how desirable—are inevitably mediated by processes of political interaction, and are no substitute for them.

At a time when virtually all western governments are under pressure to demonstrate the rational ordering of their objectives in the interests of enhanced efficiency, when so much public policy innovation is guided by public choice economic theory purporting to offer 'solutions' to all manner of policy problems, and when graduate schools of public policy feel a need to shape their curricula to reflect those same developments, students of public policy could do far worse than grasp what Lindblom made explicit, and left implicit, in 'The science of muddling through'. It would be a pity if they were misled into thinking that as the 'father of incrementalism', he has offered insights of only transient importance.

References

Banfield, E. C. (1980) 'Policy science as metaphysical madness', in Goldwin, R. A. (ed.) *Bureaucrats, Policy Analysts, Statesmen: Who leads?*, Washington, DC: American Enterprise Institute.

Blumer, H. (1971) 'Social problems as collective behaviour', *Social Problems*, 18, 3, pp. 298–306.

Boston, J. (1987) 'Thatcherism and Rogernomics: changing the rules of the game—comparisons and contrasts', *Political Science*, 39, 2, pp. 129–52.

Braybrooke, D. and Lindblom, C. E. (1963) *A Strategy of Decision: Policy evaluation as a social process*, New York: Free Press.

Bulmer, M. (1988) 'Social science expertise and executive-bureaucratic politics in Britain', *Governance*, 1, 1, pp. 26–49.

Caiden, G. and Wildavsky, A. (1974) *Planning and Budgeting in Poor Countries*, New York: Wiley.

Cates, C. (1979) 'Beyond muddling: creativity', *Public Administration Review*, 39, 6, pp. 527–32.

Coleman, J. S. (1972) *Policy Research in the Social Sciences*, Morristown, NJ: General Learning Press.

Dahl, R. A. and Lindblom, C. E. (1953) *Politics, Economics, and Welfare*, New York: Harper & Brothers.

Dror, Y. (1964) 'Muddling through — "science" or inertia?', *Public Administration Review*, 24, 3, pp. 153–7.

Dror, Y. (1968) *Public Policy Making Re-examined*, San Francisco: Chandler.

Dror, Y. (1971) *Design for Policy Sciences*, New York: American Elsevier.

Easton, B. (1987) 'Labour's economic strategy', in Boston, J. and Holland, M. (eds.), *The Fourth Labour Government: Radical Politics in New Zealand*, Auckland: Oxford University Press.

Etzioni, A. (1967) 'Mixed scanning: a "third" approach to decision-making', *Public Administration Review*, 27, 5, pp. 385–92.

Fay, B. (1975) *Social Theory and Political Practice*, London: Allen & Unwin.

Friedrich, C. J. (1940) 'Public policy and the nature of administrative responsibility', *Public Policy*, 1, pp. 3–24.

Frohock, F. M. (1979) *Public Policy: Scope and logic*, Englewood Cliffs, NJ: Prentice Hall.

Gilliatt, S. E. (1987) 'Being political: a quarrelsome view', *International Political Science Review*, pp. 367–84.

Goodin, R. E. (1982) *Political Theory and Public Policy*. Chicago: Chicago University Press.

Gregory, R. J. (1987) 'The reorganisation of the public sector: the quest for efficiency', in Boston, J. and Holland, M. (eds.), *The Fourth Labour Government: Radical politics in New Zealand*, Auckland: Oxford University Press.

Hartwig, R. (1978) 'Rationality and the problems of administrative theory', *Public Administration*, 56, 2, pp. 159–79.

Hood, C. (1987) 'British administrative trends and the public choice revolution', in Lane, J.-E. (ed.), *Bureaucracy and Public Choice*, London: Sage.

Jackson, P. M. (1982) *The Political Economy of Bureaucracy*, Oxford: Philip Allan.

Lindblom, C. E. (1959) 'The science of muddling through', *Public Administration Review*, 19, 2, pp. 79–88.

Lindblom, C. E. (1965) *The Intelligence of Democracy: Decision making through mutual adjustment*, New York: Free Press.

Lindblom, C. E. (1977) *Politics and Markets: The world's political-economic systems*, New York: Basic Books.

Lindblom, C. E. (1979) 'Still muddling, not yet through', *Public Administration Review*, 39, 6, pp. 517–26.

Lindblom, C. E. (1980) *The Policy-making Process*, second edition, Englewood Cliffs, NJ: Prentice Hall.

Lindblom, C. E. and Cohen, D. K. (1979) *Usable Knowledge: Social science and social problem solving*, New Haven, Conn.: Yale University Press.

Mayer, T. (1982) 'Markets and democracy: a critique of Charles E. Lindblom', *New Political Science*, 3 1/2, pp. 71–92.

Meltsner, A. J. (1976) *Policy Analysts in the Bureaucracy*, Berkeley: University of California Press.

Miles, R. E. Jr (1978) 'The origin and meaning of Miles' Law', *Public Administration Review*, 38, 5, pp. 399–403.

Neustadt, R. E. (1960) *Presidential Power: The politics of leadership*, New York: Wiley.

Open Systems Group (eds.) (1984) *The Vickers Papers*, London: Harper & Row.

Paris, D. C. and Reynolds, J. F. (1983) *The Logic of Policy Inquiry*, New York: Longman.

Price, D. K. (1965) *The Scientific Estate*, Cambridge, Mass.: Harvard University Press.

Rein, M. and White, S. H. (1977) 'Policy research: belief and doubt', *Policy Analysis*, 3, Spring, pp. 239–71.

Rittel, H. W. and Webber, M. M. (1973) 'Dilemmas in a general theory of planning', *Policy Sciences*, 4, 2, pp. 155–69.

Roberts, J. L. (1987) *Politicians, Public Servants and Public Enterprise: Restructuring the New Zealand Government Executive*, Wellington: Victoria University Press for the Institute of Policy Studies.

Roos, N. P. (1975) 'Contrasting social experimentation with retrospective evaluation: a health care perspective', *Public Policy*, 23, Spring, pp. 241–57.

Simon, H. A. (1947) *Administrative Behavior*, Glencoe, Ill.: Free Press.

Smith, G. and May, D. (1980) 'The artificial debate between rationalist and incrementalist models of decision making', *Policy and Politics*, 8, 2, pp. 147–61.

Spread, P. (1985) 'Lindblom, Wildavsky and the role of support', *Political Studies*, 33, 2, pp. 274–95.

Vickers, Sir Geoffrey (1965) *The Art of Judgement: A study of policy making*, London: Chapman & Hall.

Vickers, Sir Geoffrey (1968) *Value Systems and Social Process*, London: Tavistock Publications.

Vickers, Sir Geoffrey (1972) 'Commonly ignored elements in policy making', *Policy Sciences*, 3, 2, pp. 265–6.

Vickers, Sir Geoffrey (1983) *Human Systems are Different*, London: Harper & Row.

Vogel, D. (1987) 'The new political science of corporate power', *The Public Interest*, 87, Spring, pp. 63–79.

Wilson, J. Q. (1974) 'Social experimentation and public policy analysis', *Public Policy*, 22, Winter, pp. 15–37.

Wilson, J. Q. (1981) ' "Policy intellectuals" and public policy', *The Public Interest*, 64, Summer, pp. 31–46.

Part VI

Implementation

Introduction

To understand the policy process as a whole it is necessary to give attention to policy implementation. Thinking about implementation has evolved from a starting point in which the translation of policy into action was seen as being, under normal circumstances, an unproblematical process so long as bureaucracies were clearly subservient to their political masters. This early perspective was dominated by a view of bureaucracy as, by and large, conforming to the Weberian model, with politics as a goal-setting process, along the lines of Simon's notion of rational decision making, and by a view of the feasibility of separating administration from politics as set out in a classic essay by Woodrow Wilson (Wilson, 1887), a political scientist who became President of the United States. This view did not fail to identify administration as a creative process, elaborating policy to conform to circumstances and needs. What it was prone to disregard was the extent to which this activity would tend to transform policy, often fundamentally. Recognition of this has given implementation studies a crucial importance in the study of the policy process. Yet it is important not to see them as somehow separate from studies of the policy-making process. Rather implementation must be seen as part of policy making.

The first wave of implementation studies, of which the most influential was by Pressman and Wildavsky (1973), drew attention to this phenomenon, presenting it largely in terms of the subversion of the goals of the original policy makers. This involved a focus upon the ways in which organisational and inter-organisational phenomena would tend to transform policy. The reading from Hogwood and Gunn belongs very much in this tradition. It looks at the factors which will tend to undermine 'perfect administration' and provides a series of prescriptions to policy makers to assist them in preventing this occurrence. Implementation is interpreted in top-down terms, accepting the validity of the goals of policy makers and their capacity to make them explicit. Hogwood and Gunn offer an excellent model or yardstick against which actual implementation processes can be measured. The second wave of implementation studies, however, raises questions about how the 'implementation deficit' likely to be found should be interpreted.

235

These later studies raised three different kinds of problem about the top-down approach. First, they questioned whether top-level 'policy makers' really want to, or are able to, set clear policy goals. Second, they suggested that where goals are set they come through in such potentially contradictory ways, particularly as new policies are typically layered on top of earlier ones, that, on methodological grounds, implementation is better studied by looking at the efforts of those at the bottom to make sense of these new inputs from the top. Third, and most fundamentally, some writers challenged the normative view, embedded in the top-down approach, that goal-setting inputs *should* come from the top. This last view offered a challenge to the classical 'statist' view of democracy, suggesting that in many circumstances it is best that policy is 'negotiated' at the bottom, between those who are expected to carry it out and those who are affected by it.

All three of these criticisms have been advanced in the work of Hjern. The article by Hjern and Porter reproduced here does not outline them explicitly but rather sets out to show how policy processes occur in complex structures. They advance the view that there is a need for bottom-up analysis of administrative activities in terms of 'implementation structures'. Readers will also find this sort of view discussed in the reading in Part VII by Elmore, where the first of his models (the 'systems management model') conforms to the top-down approach whilst the other three diverge in various ways.

The last extract in this part is an article by Sabatier which explores the strengths and weaknesses of the top-down and bottom-up approaches, and aims to reach some kind of synthesis. Sabatier is particularly concerned with the methodological arguments. He is clearly not prepared to address the normative argument advanced by some of the bottom-uppers, feeling uncomfortable with a view which denies legitimacy to top-level policy makers. Accordingly he is not happy with the extent to which writers from the bottom-up perspective present the distinction between policy formulation and implementation as blurred, seeing it as precluding 'policy evaluation' (which is of course one of their main reasons for drawing attention to the issue).

Sabatier's discomfort highlights a fundamental normative concern, which many will want to resolve either by urging that policy makers should adopt explicit goals (as in the Hogwood and Gunn approach) or by interposing ideal goals which they, the analysts, believe should be present. The problem with the former is that policy makers may be adept at suggesting, for political reasons, that they have specific goals even when they know they have not provided the means to attain them (this is an aspect of 'symbolic' policy making; see Edelman, 1971). An example of the latter is an assumption that a specific social policy is concerned to advance equality. The problem with this is that it readily leads into the trap of attributing the specified goal to some of the actors, particularly those with policy-making responsibilities. Whilst both of these procedures may offer valid perspectives for evaluation purposes, they may lead, in implementation studies, to assumptions that it is the implementers as opposed to the policy makers who have subverted the postulated goal.

Whilst the three readings in this part have been selected to highlight some issues about the study of implementation, in practice all the rest of the book explores aspects of implementation and its importance for the policy process.

References

Edelman, M., *Politics as Symbolic Action* (Chicago, Markham, 1971).

Pressman, J. and A. Wildavsky, *Implementation* (Berkeley, University of California Press, 1973).

Wilson, W., 'The study of administration', *Political Science Quarterly*, 56(2), June 1887, pp. 481–506.

Why 'perfect implementation' is unattainable

Brian Hogwood and Lewis Gunn

Why 'perfect implementation' is unattainable

[. . .] In an article entitled 'Why is implementation so difficult?', Gunn (1978) drew upon Hood's analysis (1976) and those of Pressman and Wildavsky (1973), Etzioni (1976), Kaufman (1971), Bardach (1977), Van Meter and Van Horn (1975), and King (1975 and 1976) to provide for civil servants a short guide to some of the reasons why, according to these pioneering writers, any state of 'perfect implementation' was likely to be virtually unattainable in practice. Like Hood again, Gunn emphasized that 'perfection' in this context was an analytical concept or 'idea' and not, in the colloquial sense of the term, an 'ideal' to be achieved. In other words, no prescriptive model was offered and, indeed, several of the logical preconditions of perfect implementation – such as 'perfect obedience' or 'perfect control' – were identified as being morally and politically quite unacceptable as well as unattainable in a pluralist democracy.

What, then, are these preconditions which would have to be satisfied if perfect implementation were to be achieved and why are they unlikely to be achieved in practice?

The circumstances external to the implementing agency do not impose crippling constraints
Some obstacles to implementation are outside the control of administrators because they are external to the policy and the implementing agency. Such obstacles may be physical, as when an agricultural programme is set back by drought or disease. Or they may be political, in that either the policy or the measures needed to achieve it are unacceptable to interests (such as party activists, trade unions, or, in

From B. W. Hogwood and L. A. Gunn, *Policy Analysis for the Real World* (1984), Oxford: Oxford University Press.

some societies, the military) which have the power to veto them. These constraints are obvious and there is little that administrators can do to overcome them except in their capacity as advisers, by ensuring that such possibilities are borne in mind during the policy-making stage.

That adequate time and sufficient resources are made available to the programme
This condition partly overlaps the first, in that it often comes within the category of external constraints. However, policies which are physically or politically feasible may still fail to achieve stated intentions. A common reason is that too much is expected too soon, especially when attitudes or behaviour are involved (as, for example, in attempts to alter discriminatory attitudes towards the physically or mentally disabled). Another reason is that politicians sometimes will the policy 'end' but not the 'means', so that expenditure restrictions may starve a statutory programme of adequate resources. This happened in the case of the 1974 Control of Pollution Act, since it coincided with cutbacks in the public sector which denied local authorities sufficient funds to appoint the additional staff needed to implement the Act. A more unusual problem arises when special funds are made available, as in the Urban Programme, but have to be spent within an unrealistically short time, faster than the programme can effectively absorb them. It is important to realize that money is not a resource in itself but only a 'ticket' with which to purchase real resources, and there may be delays in this conversion process. The fear of having to return the 'unspent portion' of funding at the end of the financial year often leads public agencies into a flurry of expenditure, sometimes on relatively trivial items. Attempts to persuade finance officers to allow the carry-over of unspent funds to the next financial year are usually in vain, so that administrators are again quite limited in what they can do to overcome these constraints upon effective implementation. They can only advise politicians about the lead times which may be involved before a programme produces results, plan the annual cash flow to avoid any unspent portion, and seek to anticipate any blockages in converting cash into real resources.

That the required combination of resources is actually available
The third condition follows on naturally from the second, namely that there must not only be constraints in terms of overall resources but also that, at each stage in the implementation process, the appropriate combination of resources must actually be available. In practice, there is often a 'bottleneck' which occurs when, say, a combination of money, manpower, land, equipment, and building material has to come together to construct an emergency landing-strip for the RAF, but one or more of these is delayed and as a result the project as a whole is set back by

several months. As noted in [the section above], a temporary shortage of cash may be less serious in such circumstances than a blockage in the supply of some 'real' resource. The flow of additional funding for a programme can be swiftly increased, given political assent, by a turn of the fiscal 'tap', but there can be no guarantee that money can be converted into land, materials, or manpower within the time-scale of the programme. Thus a shortage in, say, the stock of seasoned timber can hold up a building programme for months. Or a dearth of skilled carpenters may seriously constrain a housing rehabilitation programme. In other words, particularly severe disruptions threaten when scarce resources are in the nature of a relatively fixed *stock* rather than a *flow*. The length of a delay in making good a deficiency in the supply of trained manpower, for example, will be determined by the minimum length of the training period involved. The main responsibility for such crises in implementation properly lies with administrative staff, including programme designers and managers, since they now have available to them a battery of techniques (often with attendant technology) such as network planning and control, manpower forecasting, and inventory control, which should help them to anticipate potential bottlenecks and take appropriate action in terms of generating or redistributing resources within the programme.

That the policy to be implemented is based upon a valid theory of cause and effect
Policies are sometimes ineffective not because they are badly implemented, but because they are bad policies. That is, the policy may be based upon an inadequate understanding of a problem to be solved, its causes and cure; or of an opportunity, its nature, and what is needed to exploit it. Pressman and Wildavsky (1973) describe any policy as a 'hypothesis containing initial conditions and predicted consequences'. That is, the typical reasoning of the policy-maker is along the lines of 'if x is done at time t(1) then Y will result at time t(2)'. Thus every policy incorporates a theory of cause and effect (normally unstated in practice) and, if the policy fails, it may be the underlying theory that is at fault rather than the execution of the policy.

Pressman and Wildavsky developed their argument from a detailed case-study of the failure of a programme in the late 1960s aimed at creating employment for members of minority groups in the Californian city of Oakland. The programme provided funds for public works and for making building and other loans available to private firms, in hopes that (a) resulting business opportunities would be taken up by investors and (b) result in the creation of new jobs which would (c) be filled by Blacks and Mexicans. Despite much initial goodwill the programme achieved very little. Few loans were taken up by firms and some proposals for public works came to nothing. Even when funds were spent as intended, the net increase in employment of members of minority groups was disappointingly small. One of Pressman and Wildavsky's conclusions was that the programme was based upon an inadequate theory of work-creation: this seeming failure of implementation was, at least in part, a failure of policy-making. A similar point is made by Bardach (1977, 251–2): 'If this theory is fundamentally incorrect, the policy will fail no matter how well it is implemented. Indeed, it is not exactly clear what "good" implementation of a basically misconceived policy would mean'.

Here, then, is one seeming problem of implementation which can only be tackled by better analysis at the issue definition and options analysis stages of the policy-making process. The difficulties of such analysis should not be underestimated, given the limits of our ability to understand and 'solve' complex social and economic problems, especially since, as Bardach (1977) reminds us, government tends to get landed with the most difficult problems with which no one else has been able to cope. However, we can attempt to improve issue definition [. . .]; we can try to test the 'hypotheses' underlying various policy options; we may be able to learn something from foreign experience (although there is little evidence that we in Britain have learned anything from the policy failures described by Pressman and Wildavsky and other American writers); and finally, we must remember that the 'moment of choice' is not the end of the policy-making process and be prepared constantly to test underlying theory against problems of practice observed at later stages in the process.

That the relationship between cause and effect is direct and that there are few, if any, intervening links
Even from the very broad outline of the Oakland programme, it will be seen that the theory underlying the policy was more complex than a simple 'if X, then Y' and extended the causal chain to 'if X, then Y, and if Y, then Z'. Pressman and Wildavsky argue that policies which depend upon a long sequence of cause and effect relationships have a particular tendency to break down, since 'the longer the chain of causality, the more numerous the reciprocal relationships among the links and the more complex implementation becomes'. In other words, the more links in the chain, the greater the risk that some of them will prove to be poorly conceived or badly executed. In the case of the Oakland programme a cruder but also more direct approach to work-creation might have had greater success. However, given the complexity of some recent British programmes – not least our own attempts to improve the employment prospects of minority groups or to regenerate our declining inner cities – we should not be too critical about American practice.

That dependency relationships are minimal

This condition of 'perfect implementation' requires that there is a single implementing agency which need not depend on other agencies for success, or if other agencies must be involved, that the dependency relationships are minimal in number and importance. Where, as is often the case in practice, implementation requires not only a complex series of events and linkages (see [above]) but also agreement at each event among a large number of participants, then the probability of a successful or even a predictable outcome must be further reduced. Pressman and Wildavsky argue that 'Adding the number of necessary clearances involved in decision points throughout the history of the program will give an idea of the task involved in securing implementation.' (A *decision point* will be reached each time an act of agreement has to be registered for the programme to continue, and *clearance* is the name given to each instance in which a separate participant is required to give his consent.) By a process of simple arithmetical calculation, Pressman and Wildavsky show that, even if there is a high chance of obtaining a clearance from a single participant at a given decision point, when all the probabilities are multiplied together the overall chances of success are extremely slender.

Such calculations are a little misleading since, as Bowen (1982) points out, the chances of success are considerably improved if there are repeated attempts at securing agreement at tricky decision points, concentration of resources on difficult clearances, parallel attempts to achieve similar results by different routes, and the beginning of a 'bandwagon' effect (see also Bardach, 1977, 242–3). Further, Pressman and Wildavsky's calculation was based on an 'all-or-nothing' concept of a favourable outcome at each decision point, whereas the chances of partial success might well be higher. That being said, it still seems likely that the greater the number of clearances required among other bodies involved in implementation, the lower will be the chances of full implementation.

It is not only in a federal system such as the USA that programmes can become overextended in terms of both causal chains and numbers of participating agencies. Anthony King (1976) argues that the capacity of British government to deal with its problems is diminishing because 'the number of dependency relationships in which government is involved has increased substantially'. Thus it is nowadays relatively rare for implementation of a public programme to involve only a government department on the one hand and a group of affected citizens on the other. Instead there is likely to be an intervening network of local authorities, boards and commissions, voluntary associations, and organized groups. An example of multi-stage, multi-agency implementation is the Glasgow Eastern Area Renewal (GEAR) project, involving as it does the Scottish Office, Scottish Development Agency, Scottish Special

Housing Association, Manpower Services Commission, Strathclyde Regional Council, City of Glasgow District Council, and several other public bodies – as well as community groups, the inhabitants themselves, and the private businesses and investors who, it is hoped, will be attracted to the regenerated area. The question of whether GEAR is a partial success story or a 'mutually non-effective group of organisations' (Booth, Pitt, and Money, 1982) is the subject of some debate in Scotland. At several points, impatience with the problems of working with so large a group of organizations has led to suggestions that an Urban Development Corporation (similar to those introduced to England) might provide a more effective basis for regenerating Glasgow's declining East End.

That there is understanding of, and agreement on, objectives
The requirement here is that there should be complete understanding of, and agreement on, the objectives to be achieved, and that these conditions should persist throughout the implementation process. (We should perhaps repeat that this 'requirement' is only in terms of the ideal-type model of 'perfect implementation': no prescriptive – far less descriptive – model is offered at this point.)

[. . .] The theory of planning is replete with references to objectives which, we are told by managerialist writers, should be clearly defined, specific, and preferably quantified, understood, and agreed throughout the organization, mutually compatible and supportive, and provide a blueprint against which actual programmes can be monitored. However, [. . .] most research studies suggest that, in real life, the objectives of organizations or programmes are often difficult to identify or couched in vague and evasive terms. Even 'official' objectives, where they exist, may not be compatible with one another, and the possibility of conflict or confusion is increased when professional or other groups proliferate their own 'unofficial' goals within a programme. Official objectives are often poorly understood, perhaps because communications downwards and outwards from headquarters are inadequate. Even if objectives have initially been understood and agreed, it does not follow that this state of affairs will persist throughout the lifetime of the programme, since goals are susceptible to succession, multiplication, expansion, and displacement. Any of these tendencies will complicate the implementation process and even – in the eyes of top management – 'subvert' it. Again we see that apparent 'implementation failures' may stem from features of other stages in the policy process.

That tasks are fully specified in correct sequence
Here the condition is that in moving towards agreed objectives it is possible to specify, in complete detail and perfect sequence, the tasks to be performed by each participant. The difficulties of achieving this

condition of perfect implementation are obvious. Also it is surely desirable as well as inevitable that there should be some room for discretion and improvisation in even the most carefully planned programme. But techniques such as network planning and control [. . .] can at least provide a framework within which projects can be planned and implementation controlled, by identifying the tasks to be accomplished, the relationships between these tasks and the logical sequence in which they should be performed. There remain, of course, the managerial problems of actually ensuring that tasks are performed correctly and on time and of taking appropriate remedial action if they are not.

That there is perfect communication and co-ordination

The precondition here is that there would have to be perfect communication among and co-ordination of the various elements or agencies involved in the programme. Hood (1976) argues that for perfect implementation to be achieved it would be necessary to have a completely unitary administrative system – 'like a huge army with a single line of authority' – with no compartmentalism or conflict within. He is not, of course, advocating such a system. Even to state this condition of perfect co-ordination is to know that, leaving aside questions of desirability, its attainment would be all but impossible within and among real-life organizations which are characterized by departmentalism, professionalism, and the activities of many groups with their own values, goals, and interests to protect.

Communication has an important contribution to make to co-ordination and to implementation generally. However, perfect communication is as unattainable a condition as most of the others we have examined. While management information systems (MIS) can assist in matching information flow to needs, they cannot ensure that the resulting data, advice, and instructions are understood as intended by the senders, or indeed, understood at all. Co-ordination is not, of course, simply a matter of communicating information or of setting up suitable administrative structures, but involves the exercise of power, and this leads to the final condition for perfect implementation.

That those in authority can demand and obtain perfect compliance

Hood's phrase is 'perfect obedience' and he expands it to mean 'no resistance to commands at any point in the administrative system'. If there were any potential for resistance it would be identified (in Hood's model of 'perfect administration') by the system's 'perfect information' and forestalled by its 'perfect control'. In other words, the final and perhaps least attainable condition of perfect implementation is that those 'in authority' are also those 'in power' and that they are able to secure total and immediate compliance from others (both internal and external to the agency) whose consent and co-operation are required for the success of the programme. In practice, within an agency there may be compartmentalism, between agencies there may be conflicts of interest and status disputes, and those with the formal authority to demand co-operation may lack the power to back up these demands or the will to exercise it. Every administrative practitioner knows how difficult it would be to achieve the condition of perfect compliance. Most of us would add that we would not want to live or work in such a system.

When implementation involves, as it sometimes does, innovation and the management of change – with major departures from previous policies and practices – there will be particularly high probability of suspicion, recalcitrance, or outright resistance from affected individuals, groups, and interests, especially if insufficient time has been allowed for explanation and consultation or if any previous experience of change has been unfortunate. We cannot (and should not) hope ever to be free from such resistance, but we can learn a good deal about its nature and about the responses open to administrators from the study of individual, group, organizational, and political behaviour. Thus the psychologist, sociologist, and political scientist have at least as much to contribute to our understanding of implementation as have the programme designer, network planner, and information systems analyst. [. . .]

A 'top-down' perspective?

The language, concepts, and approach employed to this point would be regarded by some more recent writers on implementation – or, in their language, 'the policy–action relationship' – as biased and limiting. Barrett and Fudge (1981) argue that much of the literature to which we have so far made reference demonstrates a 'managerial' perspective, reflecting a 'policy-centred' or 'top-down' view in which implementers are seen as 'agents' of those who claim to make policy. They argue that:

> rather than treating implementation as the transmission of policy into a series of consequential actions, the policy–action relationship needs to be regarded as a process of interaction and negotiation, taking place over time, between those seeking to put policy into effect and those upon whom action depends.

From our previous comments on the interdependence of policy-making and implementation, on the scope for officials to initiate and influence policy, and on the limits to centrally imposed objectives, co-ordination, and demands for compliance, it will be obvious that we can agree with much of the above statement as a *description* of what happens in real life. We also agree – indeed, is there anyone who does not? – on the importance of understanding the contribution to 'the complexity of the policy process' of 'environmental, political, and organizational' factors. Thus, in seeking to criticize some at least of the so-called 'top-down' writers, Barrett and Fudge are creating a straw man and sometimes appear to confuse ideal-type models of perfect implementation with a normative or prescriptive model.

Barrett and Fudge themselves often seem to drift between descriptive and prescriptive styles of argument. Hierarchy and the 'chain of command' are clearly out of favour and the term 'top-down' is used virtually as an epithet throughout. They appear not only to argue against but actively to dislike any suggestions that 'politics and adminis-tration' might be viewed as separate, though such an argument has the curious effect of not only politicizing administration, but also, more worryingly, of de-politicizing politics. There is, of course, an important area of overlap between politics and administration but there are also more substantial areas of relatively independent functioning which are worth preserving, both analytically and in practice.

If pressed, we must plead guilty to a measure of sympathy with the top-down view, if only on the grounds that 'those seeking to put policy into effect' are usually elected while 'those upon whom action depends' are not, at least in the case of civil servants and the staff of health services, nationalized industries, etc. In the case of local authorities, of course, we have competing democratic legitimacies, since local councils, too, are elected, and we need not elaborate upon the controversy which has been created in the early 1980s by central government's unusually assertive attitude towards, and attempts to exercise dominance over, local authorities. Even in the case of central–local relations, however, we find it difficult to see why the view from the top is necessarily less valid than that from other levels. Of course, anyone can think of favourite examples of national policies so misconceived that they deserved to be stifled at birth and we have already indicated our view that 'implementation failures' can often be traced to inadequate policies. Choose different examples, however, and the 'bottom-up' view looks less attractive. If a Home Secretary is committed to better relations between policemen and black youths, should we view with equanimity the persistence of 'street level' police attitudes and actions which are openly racist? If the central health departments were to take a stronger line on the need for preventive medicine, would it not be a matter of legitimate concern if many clinicians and health authorities continued to direct resources towards 'heroic' medicine which, in terms of lives saved (and the quality of some of those lives), often seem less than good value? If Parliament decided to move from left-hand to right-hand drive on our roads, would we be happy to leave to 'negotiation' between road-users, local authorities, and the central government such questions as when, how, and whether the change-over should take effect?

We do not disagree with Barrett and Fudge when they argue that on many occasions 'lower level actors take decisions which effectively limit hierarchical influence, pre-empt top decision-making, or alter "policies"', but we find it difficult to agree with their ready acceptance of, let alone their seeming acquiescence in, all these aspects of the 'policy/ action continuum'. Implementation must involve a process of interaction between organizations, the members of which may have different values, perspectives, and priorities from one another and from those advocating the policy. Much of this interaction can and should take place before policy formulation (e.g. in the form of consultation of local authority associations by central government departments), although there is no guarantee that such prior consultation will produce prior consent. While attempts will subsequently be made by unconvinced local authorities and others 'upon whom action depends' to modify and redirect the policy's thrust, there are surely limits – if only legal and constitutional limits – to how far such post-legislative guerrilla skirmishing should be taken. Finally, we would argue that the prescriptive aspects of policy analysis are concerned precisely with rescuing 'policy' from mere 'action'.

References

Bardach, E. (1977), *The Implementation Game*, Cambridge, Mass., MIT Press.

Barrett, S. and C. Fudge (eds.) (1981), *Policy and Action*, London, Methuen.

Booth, S. A. S., D. C. Pitt and W. J. Money (1982), 'Organisational redundancy? A critical appraisal of the GEAR project', *Public Administration*, 60, pp. 56–72.

Bowen, E. R. (1982), 'The Pressman–Wildavsky paradox', *Journal of Public Policy*, 2, 1–22.

Etzioni, A. (1976), *Social Problems*, Englewood Cliffs, NJ, Prentice Hall.

Gunn, L. (1978), 'Why is implementation so difficult?', *Management Services in Government*.

Hood, C. C. (1976), *The Limits of Administration*, London, Wiley.

Kaufman, H. (1971), *The Limits of Organizational Change*, Alabama, University of Alabama Press.

King, A. (1975), 'Overload: problems of governing in the 1970s', *Political Studies*, 23, pp. 284–96.

King, A. (1976), 'The problem of overload', in *Why is Britain becoming Harder to Govern?*, London, BBC Publications.

Pressman, J. I. and A. Wildavsky (1973), *Implementation*, Berkeley, University of California Press.

Van Meter, D. and C. E. Van Horn (1975), 'The policy implementation process, a conceptual framework', *Administration and Society*, 6 (4).

Implementation structures
A new unit of
administrative analysis

Benny Hjern and David O. Porter

Introduction

The scope of the public sector in Western democracies has dramatically expanded since the late 1940s as it has tried to keep pace with ever more pervasive externalities, the increasing uncertainties facing industry, and demands by citizens for more social services. Revenues and expenditures have risen, but so has a perception of an 'implementation deficit'. Under the auspices of, first, political science and public administration, and, subsequently, policy studies, a vast literature has focussed on this 'problem'. It would seem public programmes are never adequately implemented. From the perspective of most of these analyses, the modern state has promised programmes which it cannot deliver.

In this article we look at the findings in implementation and interorganizational studies in a somewhat different light. We suggest that perceptions of deficits in programme implementation are distorted and exaggerated by analytic frameworks which use organizations or individuals as the basic unit of analysis. A universal finding in studies of programme implementation is that clusters of public and private actors are involved. To cope with this condition, a theory is needed which bridges the gap between the atomistic theories in economics and comprehensive planning and management theories in public administration. We suggest an administrative theory with 'implementation structures' as the core units of analysis to fill this gap.

The article begins with a critique of administrative and economic theories when applied to programme implementation. It proceeds with

From B. Hjern and D. O. Porter, 'Implementation structures: a new unit of administrative analysis', *Organization Studies*, **2**, 1981, pp. 211–27.

an analysis of the administrative imperatives of programmes, and ties these imperatives to the identification of a potential pool of organizations from which localized implementation structures are formed. We then distinguish between organizations and implementation structures, and follow with an analysis of how complexity is reduced in implementation structures without recourse to hierarchy. Implementation structures and organizations are then contrasted as units for analysing the administration of programmes. The final sections present a phenomenological analysis of the formation of implementation structures, a summary of the observed characteristics of implementation structures, and some of the theoretical and normative implications of using these structures as units for analysis.

Hierarchy and markets

Many themes in the theory of administration were rationalized in the last decades of the 19th century by Max Weber and Woodrow Wilson (see Ostrom 1973:22–33, for an analysis of these rationalizations). Based on these earlier theories, public administration theorists and practitioners have tried to design comprehensive, functionally uniform, and hierarchical organizations. There should be strong executives who are democratically responsible, and a neutrally competent civil service selected on merit principles (Kaufman 1956). A Lonely Organization Syndrome – 'bring all related functions in "X" (i.e. education, housing, or manpower) together under one roof' – is still the most powerful idea in public administration.

Political economists, seeing the futility of guiding many public sector programmes through bureaucracies, have offered an alternative to the Lonely Organization Syndrome (Ostrom 1973:74ff). They have observed that, as in markets, many public services are being provided by numerous and often overlapping governments. Rather than urge consolidation of these governments into ever more comprehensive jurisdictions, the political economists encourage the proliferation of even more of them. Competition among governments, combined with improved techniques for citizens to express their individual preferences, will increase the economic efficiency of government (Bish 1974; Niskanan 1971; Tullock 1970).

Both the Lonely Organization Syndrome and the political economy approach are anachronisms. The social structures on which they were based have changed radically. Once, public organizations prospered in sparsely populated environments. Private firms were, however, more numerous and competitive. With the maturing of industrial society, political democracy, and the social welfare state, the density and interconnectedness of public and private organizations increased. Since World War II in Scandinavia, for instance, the number of organizations has increased at a faster pace than the population (Berrefjord 1978; Elvander 1973). The result has been the emergence of an 'organizational society' in which many important services are provided through multi-organizational programmes. There are interconnected clusters of firms, governments, and associations which come together within the framework of these programmes – implementation structures.

In this setting, programmes are neither implemented by the invisible hand of markets nor with the heavy hand of large government bureaucracies. Programmes are implemented through multiorganizational clusters of organizations, some of which are part of markets and others of government bureaucracies. Actors in implementation structures may concurrently have to operate in markets and hierarchies. In policy analysis, few analytical frameworks can.

Observations on implementation

One of the most pervasive findings in studies of programme implementation is that many actors are involved in what outwardly appears to be a confounding set of relationships (Altenstetter and Bjorkman 1978; Friend et al. 1974; Lovell 1978; Metcalfe 1978; Pressman and Wildavsky 1973; Scharpf 1977; Welsh 1977 to cite only a few of these studies).

In the implementation of manpower training programmes in Sweden and Germany, we found a bewildering array of organizations and actors. Among the trainees there were the unemployed, those threatened with unemployment, youth, the aged, women, the handicapped, and the hardcore unemployed. Participating in planning, financing, and offering courses were specialized training centres, municipality schools, county or state training directors, union officials, firms, social welfare agencies, county planning departments, vocational training specialists, placement officers, teachers, chambers of commerce, craft-guilds, and a score of local, regional, and national agencies.

It seemed improbable that anything could be produced in such a muddle. But we observed large numbers of students in classes. There were graduations, and the graduates often went on to better jobs than they had previously held. Employers found workers with adequate skills.

But there were problems. Certain types of students systematically dropped out of courses, or never enrolled. Many students were 'trained for unemployment' in occupations which were already overcrowded or where the skills were obsolete. Employers complained about the quality or content of the training. Courses which local actors unanimously agreed were needed were not approved, or were approved only after long delays. New plants opened to find no appropriately trained workers to operate their production lines, even though the firm had announced their plans long in advance and may even have received public financial support to locate in the area.

How can these processes be analysed? Public administration theories, grounded in the Lonely Organization Syndrome, were not sufficient if used alone. No single, comprehensive organization can command all the needed resources. Conventional market analyses were also insufficient. There was a similarity of markets in the actions of many firms, agencies, and other actors. But there were significant 'market failures' too. All actors pursuing their individual interests did not produce a programme which satisfied what participating actors thought were the collective interests. A new formulation was needed which bridged the gap between the atomistic theories in economics and the comprehensive planning and management theories in conventional public administration. What is needed is a strategy for analysing purposive action within a framework where *parts of many public and private organizations* cooperate in the implementation of a programme. We suggest not only the use of *implementation structures* as a new unit of analysis, but also that this unit is the core of a strategy for administering multiorganizational programmes.

Programme and administrative imperatives

As a first step in using implementation structures as units of analysis, we analysed the 'administrative imperatives' behind the legislation authorizing a programme. A brief examination of the programme of labour market training demonstrates the inherent multiorganizational composition of the implementation structures within its imperative. To meet the objective of 'training the unemployed for employment' in a training programme, cooperation among national, regional, and local actors is required. At the national level it is necessary to create an overall framework of regulations and resources. Regional and local actors are involved in providing actual services. Training programmes rely on a 'local presence' (Porter 1980) to provide the essentially local and personal services of training and work creation. The implementation of training programmes at regional and local levels includes the planning of courses to be offered in specific localities; assembling the teachers, equipment, and facilities to teach the courses; and recruiting, teaching, and placing participants. To offer training which will lead to employment, planners must know the employers and occupations within a region. They are dependent on employers, unions, and other public authorities for information. Training facilities have relations with other educational institutions in the region to obtain properly prepared teachers; with employers in the design of up-to-date courses; with other public authorities for facilities and resources. In recruiting students, training institutions and labour exchanges have relations with each other, and with a variety of social service and private organizations. Placement of graduates involves interactions with employers.

Starting from an analysis of the administrative imperative of a programme it is possible to define reasonably accurately the *pool of organizations* within the task environment of a programme. The programme is implemented by members from such pools.

Pools of organizations

With a little imagination it is easy to name the main corporate actors in the pool of organizations which will *potentially* be involved in implementing a manpower training programme. The pool for a manpower training programme includes national, regional, and local labour market agencies, training centres, public and private employers, unions, general county and municipal governments, planning departments, and a variety of social agencies. The regional composition and local presence of organizations with a potential interest in manpower training varies considerably, even in a 'homogeneous' country such as Sweden.

More important, the pools of organizations are not administrative entities. They are the raw materials out of which the operating implementation structures are formed, almost irrespective of mandates from the central levels for one or another agency to implement the programme. Even so, organization pools provide essential information on the background and rules of implementation within a particular locality. However, before examining the processes through which implementation structures are formed out of a pool of organizations, it is necessary to distinguish between organizations and implementation structures as analytic units and administrative entities.

Organization rationales and programme rationales

In providing social services as diverse as housing, education, health, and manpower programmes in countries as varied as the FRG, Sweden, and the United States, we have found two general orientations towards administration and implementation – an organization rationale and a programme rationale (Porter 1980). These rationales are associated with two different administrative entities, which scholars have tried to analyse as if they were a single unit. Organization rationales are embedded within organizations. As purposive entities, organizations are comprised of *parts* of several programmes. Goal structures in organizations have long resisted being reduced to a consistent and clear set of objectives (Perrow 1978), in part because different clusters of goals are associated with each group of activities or programmes.

A *subset* of the members of the organization, usually those associated with general administrative activities, follow an organization rationale. They adapt the goals of the programmes within the organization to fit a 'holistic' strategy which conforms with their perception of the niche the organization fills within its environment. Programmes, in this context, are treated as instruments for insuring the overall survival of an organization.

A Swedish labour exchange, for instance, administers programmes in placement, training, and job creation. As an entity, the exchange is sensitive to pressures from the firms, unions, and local governments in its particular locality. It defines a niche for its activities within this context, continuously moulding the parts of the placement, training, and job creation programmes it participates in to an organizationally sensible rationale which meets the expectations of these surrounding organizations and communities. High performance in any one programme area is subordinated to high performance of the organization as a whole.

But almost no programme is fully implemented by a single organization. Programmes are implemented by a cluster of *parts* of public and private organizations, i.e. implementation structures. An implementation structure is comprised of *subsets* of members within organizations which view a programme as their primary (or an instrumentally important) interest. For these actors, an implementation structure is as much an administrative structure through which purposive actions are taken as the organizations in which they are employed.

The major differences in how actions are taken in organizations and implementation structures are that in the latter:

- there is less formal structure and fewer authoritative relations;
- the social structures which exist are more dynamic and shifting. The cluster of actors does not represent a legally defined entity with its own building and corporate charter; and
- decisions to participate in a programme are 'fuzzy', based on consent and negotiation.

Implementation structures are more likely to be *self-selected* than *designed* through authoritative relationships. They are formed by the initiative of individuals in relation to a programme. These individuals do not necessarily belong to the organization formally charged with programme implementation. Further, much information about implementation structures can only be obtained by identifying their individual members. Put another way, 'the nature of self-organization consists of a self-referential process. . . .A self-organizing system, that is to say, is first and foremost, a problem-posing system, not merely a problem-solving system' (Sahal 1979:140).

Actors following organization and programme rationales, respectively, interact in similar patterns to those described by scholars of matrix organizations (Davis and Lawrence 1978; Galbraith 1971). These matrix elements are highlighted in Figure 1. Organizations (O_1, O_2, O_3 in Figure 1) participate in *parts* of several programmes (P_1, P_2, and P_3). Persons from within a single organization attempt to adjust these parts of programmes to meet overall organizational objectives. The vertical oval enclosing the parts of the three programmes implemented by O_1 is the area within which an organization rationale is practised. Persons identifying with a programme (P_1) pursue a programme rationale within the horizontal oval, trying to adjust the contributions of the parts of a number of organizations to meet the needs of the programme. Persons occupying positions at any of the nine points of intersection shown in the figure have to serve 'masters' both in programmes and in organizations. Failure to identify implementation structures as administrative entities distinct from organizations has led to severe difficulties in administering the implementation of programmes. When a new programme is enacted, it is assigned to a single organization, and everyone walks away secure in the belief that somehow it will be implemented. If there is a failure, the programme is assigned to another organization, or the department head is fired, or both. Since programmes are im-

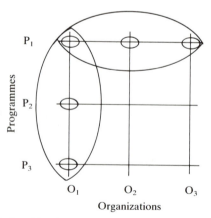

Figure 1 Matrix relationships between organization rationales and programme rationales

plemented by an implementation structure, and not a single organization, such reactions may be inappropriate and dysfunctional.

Complexity and hierarchy

Scholars and bureaucrats complain about what they perceive to be a
complexity of relationships within implementation structures, and the
seeming intractability of this complexity. In this section, it is suggested
that this perception of complexity is rooted primarily in the concepts
used to analyse programme implementation, and is unwarranted by the
actual situation. Programme implementation is complex, to be sure, but
mechanisms operate within these programmes to reduce complexity. If
implementation structures are used as the unit for administrative
analysis, more effective use of these mechanisms can be made.

One of the acknowledged strengths of hierarchy in organization
theory is that it helps to make possible the accomplishment of complex
tasks (Simon 1947; Weber 1922:223ff). A task is subdivided into a
number of small pieces and assigned to different units in an organization. The process of dividing up the tasks and recombining the
subsequent work is authoritatively coordinated through a hierarchy. The
overall goals or objectives (but not necessarily how the tasks are to be
performed [Stinchcombe 1959–60]) are determined by persons at the top
of the hierarchy. This mind-set is deeply embedded in what we have
characterized as the Lonely Organization Syndrome.

For someone guided by this mind-set, the processes of implementing
programmes are a nightmare. To administer a programme leads to
splitting headaches and feelings of powerlessness. No one is in charge.
There are few formal mechanisms for dividing up tasks. Enforcing
decisions is rendered ineffectual because the workers in the field are
employed by other organizations. There is so much happening that it is
an impossible task to try to comprehend it all.

Complexity is reduced in implementation structures in an entirely
different way than is rationalized by this variant of organization theory.
In a critique of hierarchically based theories, Ostrom (1973) observed
that the implementation of programmes by government often resembles
a market. Complexity in markets (i.e. decisions about quantity and
quality of production by firms, and decisions about consumers' needs) is
reduced by many individual consumers and firms making decisions, via a
calculus based on individual self-interest (Knight 1933).

Programme implementation structures are similar to and different
from markets in several important ways. They are similar in that there is
a need for independent, discretionary action in order to cope with the

complexity inherent in so many interdependent actions. As with markets it is difficult within implementation structures to devise a set of rules that authoritatively direct the behaviour of the clusters of relatively autonomous public and private actors. Discretion and independent actions (sometimes encouraged on normative grounds in democracies) are required to cope with the diverse situations.

But, unlike markets, implementation structures are administrative entities. They are organized around specific programmes. In markets, goods and services are moulded by households into a package which satisfies their diverse demands, rather than the objectives of a public programme. The public choice approach has overlooked this crucial difference between programme implementation structures and markets, and therefore has had difficulties suggesting how to guide public industries (Bish and Ostrom 1973).

The existence of commitments separates a rationalization of structures from others using a strictly competitive and individualistic theory of exchange. To the extent that an individual takes notice of a commitment, i.e. does what he *ought* to, rather than what he *wants* to, microeconomic approaches lose much of their applicability. A distinction between commitment and preference is meaningless in a purely individualistic calculus (cf. Hirsch 1976:14; Sen 1977:329). Microeconomic theory postulates competitive (i.e. uncommitted) action within a *given* institutional arrangement (i.e. a market or even a hierarchy). To rationalize the behaviour of members of an implementation structure, this postulate must be reversed, i.e. implementation entails commitment to programme objectives by actors who are relatively uncommitted regarding institutional arrangements.

In summary, implementation structures are *allocative and administrative* entities. They fall between market and bureaucratic rationalizations. Goods are allocated through clusters of autonomous and semiautonomous actors – as in a market but unlike a bureaucracy. Objectives are set, plans are formulated, resources made available at the right place and time, services are provided, performance evaluated – as in a bureaucracy but unlike a market.

The processes through which implementation structures are formed may be a guide to assessing how they reduce complexity. Actors self-select or are committed to participate as there are tasks to be accomplished. Thus, complexity may be reduced without recourse to hierarchy. A rationalization of implementation structures, therefore, cannot rely upon the rationalizations and methodologies offered under the Lonely Organization Syndrome or markets. But implementation structures are administrative entities, and to improve their performance they should be treated as administrative entities in a conventional way. Can strategies be developed to improve the planning, budgeting, performance, and evaluation of implementation structures (cf. Fayol 1916; Gulick 1937; Hanf, Hjern, and Porter 1978)?

Alternative units of analysis

We have found it impossible to rationalize observations on the processes of programme implementation and administration using single organizations as the unit for analysis. Such an approach would have forced us to ignore the *cognitions* of practitioners and descriptive researchers. In some organizationally grounded research the perceptions and relations of people in one section of an organization, for instance, are aggregated and compared with the perceptions and relations of people in another section. The boundaries of the sections, as legally defined, are accepted *a priori* as the proper basis for aggregation and comparison, even though the people in each section are more influenced by relationships across section, programme, or organization boundaries. *A priori* decisions on the appropriate principle for aggregation destroy much of the meaning of the data collected. Decisions on the proper unit for aggregation should be solved empirically, not *a priori* (cf. Bachrach 1977).

Lately, through the concept of domain consensus, the same mistake has been made in research on interorganizational fields (see, for example, Benson 1975: 235–8). A 'focal organization' is picked *a priori* as the unit for analysis. The focal organization *and* its domain become a unit. All interactions are treated as if they contribute to an organization rationale because the unit of analysis – the focal organization – was chosen *a priori*, not empirically. We argue that this methodological decision may lead to lumping several different administrative entities together, and treating them as one. Much of the meaning of the data is thus destroyed.

Formation and dynamics of implementation structures

We argued above that implementation structures are formed from within pools of organizations and that they are formed through processes of consensual self-selection. In contrast to other theories that deal with the forming of groups of collective action we postulate that several motives are concurrently at play when implementation structures develop.

Attempts in interorganizational theory to determine *the* motive for participation in multiorganizational networks are instructive but give no conclusive evidence on why such collectivities as implementation structures are formed. (A broader treatise on participation is found in Dachler and Wilpert 1978.) Two interrelated motivational assumptions have been developed in the interorganizational literature. One uses an exchange perspective. Relations are formed when members of two or more organizations perceive mutual benefits from interacting (cf. Bish 1978; Levine and White 1961; Tuite 1972; White 1974). Another orientation – the power dependency approach – maintains that the motive for interaction is asymmetrically defined. Relationships are formed when the motivated party is powerful enough to force or induce the other to interact (cf. Aldrich 1972, 1976; Kochan 1975; Yuchtman and Seashore 1967).

The formation of implementation structures cannot be fully described with only one of these approaches. Both exchange and power dependency motives are often found in the formation of the same implementation structure. (This is in line with other pieces of empirical research, see Schmidt and Kochan 1977.) Further, the existence of asymmetrically defined, or power dependent, motives prohibits the application of Olson's (1965) classic formulation of collective action in rationalizing the formation of implementation structures. More than a pursuit of individual self-interest is involved (see also Stigler 1975; Chamberlin 1978).

To review, within the same implementation structure there are many different motives for participation. Arbitrarily selecting one motive for participation will not solve the problem of defining and assessing implementation structures. Neither organization theory, with its emphasis on finding a single goal (Simon 1947:42–3), nor economics, with its focus on individual self-interest maximization (Downs 1967; Niskanen 1971; Tullock 1965), nor interorganization theory, with its emphasis on exchange or power dependency, has been successful in defining and assessing organizations or interorganization fields using an analysis based on a single motive. Why follow the same path in defining and assessing implementation structures? The question of motives for participation should be open to empirical assessment. A phenomenological approach to defining implementation structures is a device to analyse motives for participation without being forced into accepting untenable assumptions. Motives for participation are not the primary concern in a phenomenological approach, rather we are interested in the *use* made of the resources brought together within implementation structures. There is not necessarily a connection between the motives for entering an implementation structure and the use made of resources in an existing one (cf. Simon 1964:18–19 on this topic).

Another reason for a phenomenological approach is that the cognition and behaviour of individual members or organizations are important for understanding how resources are mobilized and used in implementation structures. As other researchers, we found 'entrepreneurs' operating within implementation structures. It has even been argued that without the reticulist or network management skills of individuals, the implementation of many programmes would grind to a halt (Friend *et al.*

1974; Lovell 1978; O'Toole 1979; Seidman 1970:170). In rationalizations of 'organization behaviour', such individual skills are largely unaccounted for. The cognitions and behaviours of individuals are compartmentalized and filtered through 'objective' group measures.

This argument for our phenomenological approach is not based on an assumption about the unique situation of individuals. Individual cognitions and behaviour, to a degree, are structured and controlled by groups and cliques within organizations, professions, or programmes. The participants in implementation structures follow a rationale which is sanctioned, but not determined, by the organizations of which they are members as well as by their more general environments. Indeed, in order to make sense of sometimes conflicting and uncertain situations of decision making, we have to assume that the participants draw upon the moral and social conventions and institutions surrounding them. We take issue with some systems analysts who stress the complexity which environments impart on the system or organization. [. . .]

A third, and more practical, reason for using a phenomenological approach is that it provides a cheap and easily understood *methodology* for identifying implementation structures for purposes of administrative analysis. In our research on the local implementation of labour market programmes we focused on mapping implementation structures as they are understood by participants. Administrators in labour market programmes often intuitively seek to identify the implementation structure within which they are, or could be, operating. We have found open-ended interviews the best technique for obtaining this information from participants.

Our interviews were structured to assess interactions in four different aspects of a programme – planning, mobilization of resources, effectuation, and evaluation. (A similar set of administrative processes is identified by Gowler and Legge 1978:202–4.) This technique yields four 'subimplementation structures', with partly different and partly overlapping members within each substructure. The starting point for defining implementation structures was the pool of organizations in a local labour market, but the participants were not confined to the local setting. We have observed interactions among local, regional, and national actors in implementing a programme at local levels (see Hanf *et al.* 1978 for a report on these specific implementation structures).

The implementation structure approach: a summary

An acronym, PIPIS, summarizes what may become a process for administering programmes. An analysis of the objectives of a *programme* suggests an administrative *imperative*. This imperative points to a potential *pool* of organizations, from which an *implementation structure* is formed.

Implementation structures are not organizations. They are comprised of parts of many organizations; organizations are comprised of parts of many programmes. As analytic constructs, implementation structures are conceptualized to identify the units of purposive action which implement programmes. They are 'phenomenological administrative units', partly defined by their participating members.

We found a number of elements which implementation structures seem to have in common. The actors and organizations in implementation structures have a *variety of goals and motives*. There may be a general interest in education, manpower training, or housing, but each actor and organization is participating in the programme partly for its own reasons. The intensity of interest in the programme varies substantially from one actor to another.

There is a *programme rationale* within which purposive action takes place. Programme-oriented actors view the resources of the various organizations in their implementation structures as a field within which they practise the familiar 'budgetary strategies'. Monetary and non-monetary resources are mobilized. Calculations are made to determine which actors within the structure offer a better potential for providing resources, and which resources could best be moulded to the priorities of the programme.

Authority relationships often focus on professional status, coordinative competence, potential or real power, and resource control. Traditional hierarchical authority tends to be of limited influence. Heads of one organization interact nonauthoritatively with midlevel managers or service providers in another.

There is a great deal of *local discretion*. Regional and national organizations may attempt to influence this discretion, particularly in such programmes as selective labour market policies, but control strategies are of very limited efficiency.

There is no single implementation structure for a national programme; rather there is a *collection of localized implementation structures*, each comprised of a distinctive array of public and private actors.

Within implementation structures, *subgroups of actors and organizations perform specialized roles*. There are substructures *for policy making, planning and intelligence, resource provision, intermediary and coordinating roles, services provision, and evaluation*. Coordination of roles within and among substructures varies considerably from one implementation structure to another.

Finally, implementation structures *differ in their relative cohesiveness*. The state of interrelatedness within particular implementation structures varies both geographically and over time. Some structures are highly *developed and regular*, others are *undeveloped and ad hoc*. The more developed and regular structures can be accurately described as *networks* of relationships in which participants have rather settled expectations about each other's actions. They relate in patterns not unlike the interactions within a cohesive organization. In the more undeveloped and *ad hoc* structures, expectations among the actors are not settled. Patterns of mutually beneficial interaction are poorly understood or have not been negotiated.

Implications and future research

The implications of accepting implementation structures as units for analysis are numerous. When implementation structures are accepted as distinct administrative entities, new lines for research open up in the more positive disciplines of sociology, political science, and psychology. Behaviours and institutions must be described, categorized, and analysed. Phenomena which have been described as anomalous or deviant when analysed within the context of organizations become explicable within implementation structures.

In more normative areas of inquiry, such as administration, democratic theory, accounting, information systems, evaluation, and law, new orientations will be needed to rationalize activities within implementation structures.

The old debate surrounding politics and administration takes on new dimensions when viewed from the analytical perspective of implementation structures. Democracy and pluralism go together, as do pluralism and discretion. Democracy has always been considered a cornerstone in the discipline of public administration, but pluralism and discretion have been troublesome. Perhaps a 'post-Weberian administration' will centre on a strategy for guiding multiorganizational programmes where negotiation, consent, and persuasion replace the biases towards control, command, and aggregate measures enforced through a unified chain of command (cf. Landau and Stout 1979). The basic administrative framework will need to resemble the responsibility centre and matrix administrative formats more than the hierarchical formats now dominant in public administration (Porter 1980).

Further, there have been few theories for intranational and cross-national comparisons of local administration. Subnational administration has been neglected or treated in a series of case studies. The implementation structure approach permits comparisons of the general features of programme administration at the subnational levels. Given the importance of evaluating the provision of social services (which rely on a local presence), such a comparative theory is much needed.

Democratic theory will also need adjustments beyond its applications to public administration. Concepts of political responsibility must be recast to take into account that many key actors in implementation derive their positions and legitimacy from nongovernmental sources. Notions of elective responsibility and corporatism do not have the breadth to cover these phenomena in programme implementation structures.

The areas of accounting, information systems, and evaluation will need to be expanded to consider financial and nonfinancial data from more of the actors within the clusters which comprise implementation structures. With the exception of some limited experience in PPBS (Schick 1980), these fields have used organizations as their units of analysis and considered the multiorganizational characteristics of programme implementation in an unsystematic fashion.

Many legal institutions and procedures also need to be reconsidered. In the absence of clear institutional lines of authority, the formulation and enforcement of legal obligations in the implementation of programmes is more problematic than in a situation where organizations are assumed to be responsible. Investigations will need to examine experiences in setting legal norms within implementation structures (e.g. Ostrom 1962) and attempt to extend principles and practices from these experiences to programme implementation generally.

References

Aldrich, H. 1972 'An organization–environment perspective on cooperation and conflict in the manpower training system' in *Conflict and Power in Complex Organizations*. A. Negandhi (ed.). Kent, Ohio: CARI, Kent State University.

Aldrich, H. 1976 'Resource dependence and interorganizational reactions: local employment service offices and social service sector organizations'. *Administration and Society* 7:419–54.

Altenstetter, C., and J. W. Bjorkman 1978 *Federal–state Health Policies and Impacts: The politics of implementation*. Washington, D.C.: University Press of America.

Bachrach, S. 1977 'From morphology to political cognitions: toward a status group model of intra-organizational analysis'. Cornell University Working Paper.

Benson, K. J. 1975 'The interorganizational network as a political economy'. *Administrative Science Quarterly* 20:229–49.

Berrefjord, O. 1978 'Fra embetsmannsstat til embetsmannsstat?' in *Forhandlingsokonomi og Blandningsadministrajon*. G. Hernes (ed.). Oslo: Universitetsforlaget.

Bish, R. L. 1974 *The Public Economy of Metropolitan Areas*. Chicago: Rand McNally/Markham.

Bish, R. L. 1978 'Intergovernmental relations in the United States: some concepts and implications from a public choice perspective' in *Interorganizational Policy Making: Limits to coordination and central control*. K. Hanf and F. W. Scharpf (eds.). London and Beverly Hills: Sage.

Bish, R. L., and V. Ostrom 1973 *Understanding Urban Government: Metropolitan reform reconsidered*. Washington, D.C.: American Enterprise Institute for Public Policy Research.

Chamberlin, J. R. 1978 'The logic of collective action: some experimental results.' *Behavioral Science* 23:441–5.

Dachler, H. P., and N. Wilpert 1978 'Conceptual dimensions and boundaries of participation in organizations: a critical evaluation'. *Administrative Science Quarterly* 23:1–39.

Davis, S. M., and P. R. Lawrence 1978 'Problems of matrix organizations'. *Harvard Business Review* May–June: 131–42.

Downs, A. 1967 *Inside Bureaucracy*. Boston: Little, Brown.

Elvander, N. 1973 *Naringslivets 900 Organisationer*. Malmo: Naringliv och Samhalle.

Fayol, H. 1916 *General and Industrial Administration*. London: Pitman. Reprinted 1949.

Friend, J. K., J. M. Power, and C. J. L. Yewlett 1974 *Public Planning: The inter-corporate dimension*. London: Tavistock.

Galbraith, J. R. 1971 'Matrix organization design'. *Business Horizons* February: 29–40.

Gowler, D., and K. Legge 1978 'The evaluation of planned organizational change: the necessary art of the possible'. *Journal of Enterprise Management* 1:201–13.

Gulick, L. 1937 'Notes on the theory of organization' in *Papers on the Science of Administration*. L. Gulick and L. Urwick (eds.). New York: Institute of Public Administration, Columbia University.

Hanf, K., B. Hjern, and D. O. Porter 1978 'Local networks of manpower training in the Federal Republic of Germany and Sweden' in *Interorganizational Policy Making Limits to coordination and central control*. K. Hanf and F. W. Scharpf (eds.). Beverly Hills and London: Sage.

Hirsch, E. 1976 *Social Limits to Growth*. Boston: Harvard University Press.

Kaufman. H. 1956 'Emerging conflicts in the doctrines of public administration'. *American Political Science Review* 50:1057–73.

Knight, F. H. 1933 *The Economic Organization*. New York: Harper Torchbook, Harper and Row. Reprinted 1965.

Kochan, T. A. 1975 'Determinants of the power of boundary units in an interorganizational bargaining relation'. *Administrative Science Quarterly* 20:434–52.

Landau, M., and R. Stout, Jr. 1979 'To manage is not to control: or the folly of type II errors'. *Public Administration Review* 39:148–56.

Levine, S., and P. White 1961 'Exchange as a conceptual framework for the study of interorganizational relationships'. *Administrative Science Quarterly* 5:583–601.

Lovell, C. 1978 'Self-linking networks in local administration'. Paper presented at the Annual Meeting of the American Society of Public Administration, Phoenix, Arizona, April.

264   IMPLEMENTATION

Metcalfe, H. L. 1978 'Policy making in turbulent environments' in *Interorgani-zational Policy Making: Limits to coordination and central control.* K. Hanf and F. W. Scharpf (eds.). Beverly Hills and London: Sage.

Niskanan, W. A., Jr. 1971 *Bureaucracy and Representative Government.* Chicago: Aldine-Atherton.

Olson, M. 1965 *The Logic of Collective Action.* Cambridge, Mass.: Harvard University Press.

Ostrom, V. 1962 'The water economy and its organization'. *Natural Resources Journal* 2:55–75.

Ostrom, V. 1973 *The Intellectual Crisis in American Public Administration.* Alabama: The University of Alabama Press.

O'Toole, L. 1979 'Inter-organizational cooperation and labor market training: some cases'. IIM/79–8 in the Publication Series of the International Institute of Management. Berlin: Science Center.

Perrow, C. 1978 'Demystifying organization' in *The Management of Human Services.* R. C. Sarri and Y. Hasenfeld (eds.). New York: Columbia University Press.

Porter, D. O. 1980 'Accounting for discretion and local environments in social experimentation and programme administration: some proposed alternative conceptualizations' in *Do Housing Allowances Work?* K. L. Bradbury and A. Downs (eds.). Washington, D.C.: Brookings Institute.

Pressman, J. L., and A. Wildavsky 1973 *Implementation.* Berkeley, Calif.: University of California Press.

Sahal, D. 1979 'A unified theory of self-organization'. *Journal of Cybernetics* 9:127–42.

Scharpf, F. W. 1977 'Public organization and the waning of the welfare state: a research perspective'. *European Journal of Political Research* 5:339–62.

Schick, A. 1980 'Budgeting as an administrative process' in *Perspectives on Budgeting.* A. Schick (ed.). Washington, D.C.: American Society for Public Administration.

Schmidt, S. M., and T. A. Kochan 1977 'Interorganizational relationships: patterns and motivations'. *Administrative Science Quarterly* 22:220–34.

Seidman, H. 1970 *Politics, Position and Power.* New York: Oxford University Press.

Sen, A. K. 1977 'Rational fools: a critique of the behavioral foundation of economic theory'. *Philosophy and Public Affairs* 6:317–44.

Simon, H. 1947 *Administrative Behavior: A study of decision-making processes in administrative organizations.* New York: The Free Press. Reprinted 1965.

Simon, H. A. 1964 'On the concept of organizational goals. *Proceedings of the American Philosophic Society* 106: 18–19, 467–82.

Starling, J. D. 1975 'System constructs in simplifying complexity' in *Organized Social Complexity.* T. R. LaPorte (ed.). Princeton, N.J.: Princeton University Press.

Stigler, G. J. 1975 'Free riders and collective action: an appendix to theories of economic regulation'. *Bell Journal of Economics and Management Science* 5:359–69.

Stinchcombe, A. L. 1959–60 'Bureaucratic and craft administration of production: a comparative study'. *Administrative Science Quarterly* 4:168–87.

Tuite, M. F. 1972 'Toward a theory of joint decision-making' in *Interorganizational Decision-making*. M. F. Tuite, R. Chrisholm and M. Radnor (eds). Chicago: Aldine.

Tullock, G. 1965 *The Politics of Bureaucracy*. New York: Public Affairs Press.

Tullock, G. 1970 *Private Wants, Public Means*. New York: Basic Books.

Weber, M. 1922 *Economy and Society*. New York: The Bedminster Press. Reprinted 1968.

Welsh, W. A. 1977 'Interregional variations in public goods and services: some methodological issues and a preliminary analysis' in *Yearbook of East-European Economics* 7, 171–212. Munich and Vienna: Gunter Olzop Verlag.

White, P. E. 1974 'Intra and interorganizational studies'. *Administration and Society* 6:105–52.

Yuchtman, E., and S. E. Seashore 1967 'A system resource approach to organizational effectiveness'. *American Sociological Review* 32:871–93.

Top-down and bottom-up approaches to implementation research

Paul A. Sabatier

The last fifteen years have witnessed an enormous amount of research on policy implementation. While the early work was primarily American – motivated in part by perceived failures in Great Society programs – much of the most interesting recent work has been done in Western Europe. For general reviews, see Yin (1980), Barrett and Fudge (1981), Alexander (1982), and Sabatier and Mazmanian (1983a).

Most of the early American studies were analyses of a single case and came to very pessimistic conclusions about the ability of governments to effectively implement their programs (Derthick, 1972; Pressman and Wildavsky, 1973; Murphy, 1973; Bardach, 1974). The second generation of studies were more analytical and comparative in perspective (Goggin, 1986). They sought to explain variation in implementation success across programs and governmental units by reference to specific variables and conceptual frameworks (Van Meter and Van Horn, 1975; Sabatier and Mazmanian, 1979, 1980). But they maintained the same 'top-down' perspective as earlier writers, i.e. they started with a policy decision (usually a statute) and examined the extent to which its legally-mandated objectives were achieved over time and why.

In the late 1970s and early 1980s, however, a quite different approach emerged in response to the perceived weaknesses of the 'top-down' perspective. Rather than start with a policy decision, these 'bottom-uppers' started with an analysis of the multitude of actors who interact at the operational (local) level on a particular problem or issue. In the process, the familiar policy stages of formulation, implementation, and

From P. A. Sabatier, 'Top-down and bottom-up approaches to implementation research: a critical analysis and suggested synthesis', *Journal of Public Policy*, **6**, 1986, pp. 21–48.

reformulation tended to disappear. Instead, the focus has been on the strategies pursued by various actors in pursuit of their objectives. Such studies have shown that local actors often deflect centrally-mandated programs toward their own ends (Lipsky, 1971; Berman and McLaughlin, 1976; Hanf and Scharpf, 1978; Ingram, 1977; Elmore, 1979; Browning *et al.*, 1981; Barrett and Fudge, 1981; Hjern and Hull, 1982; Hanf, 1982).

This paper will first examine the 'top-down' and 'bottom-up' approaches in greater detail, including an analysis of the strengths and weaknesses of each. It will then suggest a synthetic framework which integrates most of the strengths of the respective approaches and applies it to a longer time frame than in most implementation studies.

Top-down approaches: a not entirely disinterested evaluation

In analyzing the two approaches, we shall focus on a representative scholar for each: Daniel Mazmanian and Paul Sabatier for the top-downers, Benny Hjern *et al.* for the bottom-uppers. While this neglects the views of other scholars, it ensures that the work of a leading proponent of each 'school' will be subjected to detailed analysis.

Presentation
The essential features of a top-down approach are that it starts with a policy decision by governmental (often central government) officials and then asks:

(1) To what extent were the actions of implementing officials and target groups consistent with (the objectives and procedures outlined in) that policy decision?
(2) To what extent were the objectives attained over time, i.e. to what extent were the impacts consistent with the objectives?
(3) What were the principal factors affecting policy outputs and impacts, both those relevant to the official policy as well as other politically significant ones?
(4) How was the policy reformulated over time on the basis of experience?

The work of Sabatier and Mazmanian serves as a useful example of the top-down approach because it has been around for several years; it has been subjected to extensive empirical testing; and it is viewed by at least a few completely disinterested observers (Alterman, 1983; Goggin, 1984) as a leading proponent of this point of view.

The Sabatier and Mazmanian framework (1979, 1980) took as its

point of departure the first generation of implementation research with
its very pessimistic conclusions (Pressman and Wildavsky, 1973; Murphy, 1973; Bardach, 1974; Jones, 1975; Berman and McLaughlin, 1976;
Elmore, 1978). Sabatier and Mazmanian first identified a variety of
legal, political, and 'tractability' variables affecting the different stages
of the implementation process (see Figure 1).

They then sought to synthesize this large number of variables into a
shorter list of six sufficient and generally necessary conditions for the
effective implementation of legal objectives:

(1) Clear and consistent objectives.
     Taken from Van Meter and Van Horn (1975), clear legal
     objectives were viewed as providing both a standard of evaluation
     and an important legal resource to implementing officials.
(2) Adequate causal theory.
     Borrowing the fundamental insight of Pressman and Wildavsky
     (1973) that policy interventions incorporate an implicit theory
     about how to effectuate social change, Sabatier and Mazmanian
     pointed to the adequacy of the jurisdiction and policy levers given
     implementing officials as a means of ascertaining those causal
     assumptions.
(3) Implementation process legally structured to enhance compliance by
     implementing officials and target groups.
     Borrowing again from Pressman and Wildavsky (1973), the
     authors pointed to a variety of legal mechanisms including the
     number of veto points involved in program delivery, the sanctions
     and incentives available to overcome resistance, and the assign-
     ment of programs to implementing agencies which would be
     supportive and give it high priority.
(4) Committed and skillful implementing officials.
     Recognizing the unavoidable discretion given implementing of-
     ficials, their commitment to policy objectives and skill in utilizing
     available resources were viewed as critical (Lipsky, 1971; Lazin,
     1973; Levin, 1980). While this could partially be determined by
     the initial statute, much of it was a product of post-statutory
     political forces.
(5) Support of interest groups and sovereigns.
     This simply recognized the need to maintain political support
     throughout the long implementation process from interest groups
     and from legislative and executive sovereigns (Downs, 1967;
     Murphy, 1973; Bardach, 1974; Sabatier, 1975).
(6) Changes in socioeconomic conditions which do not substantially
     undermine political support or causal theory.
     This variable simply recognized that changes in socioeconomic

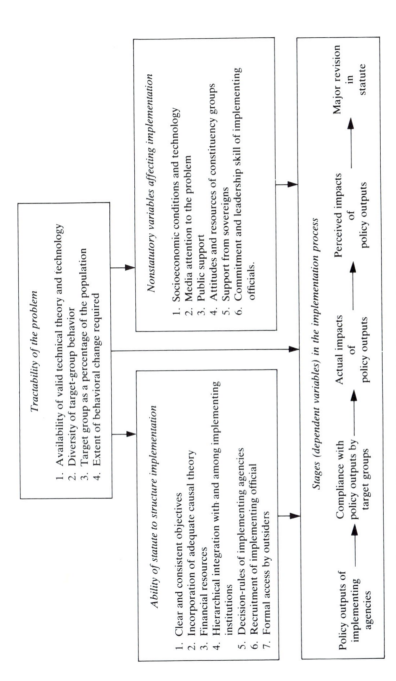

Figure 1 Skeletal flow diagram of the variables involved in the implementation process (Source: Sabatier and Mazmanian, 1980: 542)

conditions, e.g. the Arab oil boycott or the Vietnam War, could have dramatic repercussions on the political support or causal theory of a program (Hofferbert, 1974; Aaron, 1978).

In short, the first three conditions can be dealt with by the initial policy decision (e.g. a statute), whereas the latter three are largely the product of subsequent political and economic pressure during the implementation process.

Although Sabatier and Mazmanian took seriously the arguments of Lipsky (1971), Berman (1978; 1980), and Elmore (1978) concerning the substantial limitations of programmed/hierarchical control, they did not accept the pessimists' conclusion concerning the inevitability of 'adaptive' implementation in which policy-makers are forced largely to acquiesce to the preferences of street-level bureaucrats and target groups. Instead, they sought to identify a number of legal and political mechanisms for affecting the preferences and/or constraining the behavior of street-level bureaucrats and target groups both in the initial policy decision and then subsequently over time. For example, policy-makers normally have some ability to select one set of implementing officials over another; to affect the number of clearance points; to provide appropriate incentives and sanctions; to affect the balance of constituency support; etc. And, as Pressman and Wildavsky (1973) clearly showed, policy-makers can strongly affect the implementation process by basing a program on a valid causal theory rather than a dubious one. In short, while Sabatier and Mazmanian rejected hierarchical *control* – in the sense of tightly constrained behavior – as impossible, they argued that the behavior of street-level bureaucrats and target groups could be kept within acceptable bounds over time if the six conditions were met (Sabatier and Mazmanian, 1979: 489–92, 503–4).

Over the next five years, Sabatier and Mazmanian sought to have the framework tested – by themselves and others – in a variety of policy areas and political systems. The results, summarized in Table 1, indicate that the framework has been applied over twenty times. These cases have involved ten policy areas, including strong representation from land use control, education, and environmental protection. While a majority of cases have been American, many of these have focused on state or local policy initiatives rather than on the implementation of federal policy. In addition, there have been eight cases, primarily in higher education, involving six European countries.

It is now time to assess the results of this research program. This will be done, first, from the standpoint of one of the authors and then from the perspective of their 'bottom-up' critics.

Table 1 Empirical applications of the Sabatier and Mazmanian framework

---

I. Original research by Sabatier and/or Mazmanian
1. California Coastal Conservation Act, 1972–80 (Sabatier and Mazmanian, 1983b)
2. San Francisco Bay Conservation and Development Act, 1965–72 (Sabatier and Klosterman, 1981)
3. French Coastal Decrees of 1976 and 1979 (Sabatier, 1984)

II. Secondary analysis of others' research by Sabatier and/or Mazmanian
1. British Open University, 1969–79 (Cerych and Sabatier, 1986)
2. French Instituts Universitaires de Technologie, 1967–79 (Cerych and Sabatier, 1986)
3. Norwegian Regional Colleges, 1970–9 (Cerych and Sabatier, 1986)
4. University of Tromsø (Norway), 1969–79 (Cerych and Sabatier, 1986)
5. German Gesamthochschulen, 1970–9 (Cerych and Sabatier, 1986)
6. Swedish 25/5 Scheme (Cerych and Sabatier, 1986)
7. Polish Preferential University Admissions (Cerych and Sabatier, 1986)
8. 1970 U.S. Clean Air Act, 1970–9 (Mazmanian and Sabatier, 1983)
9. U.S. School Desegregation, South and North, 1955–75 (Mazmanian and Sabatier, 1983)
10. 1965 U.S. Elementary and Secondary Education Act, Title I, 1966–7 (Mazmanian and Sabatier, 1983)
11. 1970 New Towns Act (U.S.), 1970–8 (Mazmanian and Sabatier, 1983)

III. Utilization by other scholars
1. Model cities, revenue sharing, and CDBG in SF Bay Area (Browning *et al.*, 1981)
2. Variety of federal anti-discrimination programs (Bullock, 1981)
3. Evolution of U.S. welfare policy since 1935 (Goodwin and Moen, 1981)
4. 1965 ESEA, Title I, 1966–79 (Kirst and Jung, 1982)
5. Groundwater management in several New York counties (S. Jones, 1984)
6. U.S. hazardous waste policy (Bowman and Lester, 1986; Lester, 1986; Davis, 1985)
7. U.S. coastal zone management (Lowry, 1985)

A critical self-appraisal

One ought, of course, to be skeptical of self-evaluations. Authors are often tempted to select cases which fit their theories. In this instance, however, only seven of the twenty-four cases were selected by Mazmanian and Sabatier, thus affording some protection against biased case selection. That still leaves the potential for biased data selection or interpretation of results, but the reader can decide for himself after examining the case evidence.

These caveats notwithstanding, experience has demonstrated some real strengths in the Sabatier/Mazmanian framework.

First the importance it attaches to legal structuring of the implementation process – one of its major innovations – has been confirmed in numerous studies. This is particularly gratifying since one of the most frequent criticisms of the framework has been that the emphasis on structuring is unrealistic, i.e. that the cognitive limitations of policy-makers and the need for compromise at the formulation stage preclude careful structuring (Majone and Wildavsky, 1978; Barrett and Fudge,

1981). The evidence suggests that, while fairly coherent structuring is difficult, it occurs more frequently than critics realize and, when present, proves to be very important.

For example, the framework emphasized the importance of selecting implementing institutions supportive of the new program and suggested creating new agencies as a specific strategy. This turned out to be possible in six of the twenty-odd cases studied [. . .] and in many other cases formulators expressly selected sympathetic existing institutions. When this was not possible, e.g. compensatory education in the U.S., it proved to be a serious impediment to effective implementation.

Likewise, two of the major contributions borrowed from Pressman and Wildavsky (1973) – veto points and causal theory – were confirmed in many studies. In the case of the coastal commissions, for example, the agencies' greater success in protecting scenic views than in providing public access to the beach can largely be explained by reference to the number of veto points: In particular, the coastal commissions had all the legal authority necessary to protect scenic views, while actually providing public access required the cooperation of at least a half-dozen other agencies (Sabatier and Mazmanian, 1983b). The superior ability of U.S. air pollution authorities to regulate automotive emissions than to reduce vehicle miles traveled can be attributed to a greater understanding of, and control over, the factors involved (Mazmanian and Sabatier, 1983b: Chap. 4). The much greater success of the British Open University than the French IUTs in reaching projected enrollments can be partially attributed to the better theory utilized by policy formulators in the former case (Cerych and Sabatier, 1986). While Bowen (1982) rightly cautions that the analysis of veto points is more complicated than envisaged by Pressman and Wildavsky, their contributions remain of the first order.

Perhaps the best evidence of the potential importance of legal structuring is that the two most successful cases studied to date – the California coastal commissions (at least in the short run) and the British Open University – were also the best designed institutions. That is, they structured the process to provide reasonably consistent objectives, a good causal theory, relatively few veto points, sympathetic implementing officials, access of supporters to most decisions, and adequate financial resources.

Second, the six conditions of effective implementation have proven to be a useful checklist of critical factors in understanding variations in program performance and in understanding the strategies of program proponents over time. While the relative importance of specific factors has varied across cases – with implementing agency support being probably the most consistently critical one – all except clear and consistent objectives have been important in many cases. There is also some evidence that interest group support may be more critical in the U.S. than in many European countries – presumably reflecting the greater autonomy of administrative agencies in countries like Great Britain, France, and the German Federal Republic.

Third, the relatively manageable list of variables and the focus in the framework on the formulation–implementation–reformulation cycle encouraged many of our case authors to look at a longer time-frame than was true of earlier implementation studies (i.e. ten years instead of four). This, in turn, led to a discovery of the importance of learning by program proponents over time as they became aware of deficiencies in the original program and sought improved legal and political strategies for dealing with them. The best example is the American compensatory education case, where serious deficiencies revealed by early evaluation studies enabled program proponents to greatly strengthen the legal structure and constituency support over time (Kirst and Jung, 1982; Mazmanian and Sabatier, 1983). For other examples of learning over time, one can cite the supporters of the French IUTs who greatly improved their understanding of the factors affecting student choices over time (Cerych and Sabatier, 1986).

Fourth, our focus on legally-mandated objectives – particularly when combined with the ten-year time span for assessing program effectiveness – helped produce a less pessimistic evaluation of governmental performance than was true of the first generation of implementation studies. On the one hand, the focus on legally-mandated objectives encouraged scholars to carefully distinguish the objectives contained in legal documents from both the political rhetoric surrounding policy formulation and the tendency of critics to evaluate a program on the basis of what they mistakenly perceived to be its objectives – the criticism of the 'failure' of the Open University to meet the needs of working class students being a case in point. In addition, the longer time-frame used in many of these studies meant that several which were initially regarded as failures – U.S. compensatory education and the French IUTs – were regarded in a more favorable light after proponents had had the benefit of a decade of learning and experimentation (Kirst and Jung, 1982; Mazmanian and Sabatier, 1983; Cerych and Sabatier, 1986).

On the other hand, several years' experience with testing the Sabatier/Mazmanian framework has also revealed some significant flaws – quite apart from the more serious methodological criticisms of the 'bottom-uppers.'

First, the emphasis they placed on 'clear and consistent policy objectives' was a mistake. Experience has confirmed the critics' charge that very few programs meet this criterion, either initially or after a decade (Majone and Wildavsky, 1978; MacIntyre, 1985). Instead, the vast majority incorporate a multitude of partially-conflicting objectives. This does not, however, preclude the possibility of assessing program effectiveness. Instead, it simply means that effectiveness needs to be reconceptualized into the 'acceptability space' demarcated by the intersection of the ranges of acceptable values on each of the multiple evaluative dimensions involved. This can be illustrated by the case of the Norwegian regional colleges: They were supposed to serve students from the local region and to foster regionally-relevant research at the same time that they were also mandated to be part of a national educational system in which the transfer of student credits among institutions and the evaluation of faculty research by peers in other institutions had to be protected. While the institutions after a decade were receiving 'excellent' ratings on very few of these dimensions, the evidence suggests they were satisfactory on all of them (Cerych and Sabatier, 1986).

On a related point, most implementation scholars have followed Van Meter and Van Horn (1975) in assuming that, *ceteris paribus*, the probability of effective implementation of a reform is inversely related to the extent of envisaged departure from the status quo ante. In their study of European higher education reforms, however, Cerych and Sabatier (1986) provide evidence that the relationship is not linear but rather curvilinear. They suggest that very incremental reforms – e.g. the Swedish 25/5 Scheme for adult admission to universities – simply do not arouse enough commitment to get much done, while those such as the German *Gesamthochschulen* which envisage a comprehensive reform of the entire system arouse too much resistance to get off the ground. Instead, those reforms – e.g., the British Open University – which are ambitious enough to arouse intense commitment from proponents but rather limited in their effects on the entire (e.g. higher education) system stand the best chance of success.

Second, while Sabatier and Mazmanian encouraged a longer time-frame and provided several examples of policy-oriented learning over time, their framework did not provide a good conceptual vehicle for looking at policy change over periods of a decade or more (Goodwin and Moen, 1981; Browning *et al.*, 1981; Goggin, 1984; Lowry, 1985). This is primarily because, as we shall see below, it focused too much on the perspective of program *proponents*, thereby neglecting the strategies (and learning) by other actors which would provide the cornerstone for a more dynamic model.

The assessment thus far has been from the point of view of the authors or other sympathizers of a top-down perspective. It is now time to examine the more fundamental methodological criticisms raised by 'bottom-uppers,' most notably, Benny Hjern.

The bottom-up critique

The fundamental flaw in top-down models, according to Hjern and Hull (1982), Hanf (1982), Barrett and Fudge (1981), Elmore (1979), and other bottom-uppers, is that they start from the perspective of (central) decision-makers and thus tend to neglect other actors. Their methodology leads top-downers to assume that the framers of the policy decision (e.g. statute) are the key actors and that others are basically impediments. This, in turn, leads them to neglect strategic initiatives coming from the private sector, from street-level bureaucrats or local implementing officials, and from other policy subsystems. While Sabatier and Mazmanian are not entirely guilty of this – in particular, their focus on causal theory and hierarchical integration encourages the analyst to examine the perspectives of other actors – this is certainly a potential Achilles' heel of their model.

A second, and related, criticism of top-down models is that they are difficult to use in situations where there is no dominant policy (statute) or agency, but rather a multitude of governmental directives and actors, none of them preeminent. As this is often the case, particularly in social service delivery, this is a very telling criticism. While Sabatier and Mazmanian can recognize such situations – through the concepts of (inadequate) causal theory and (poor) hierarchical integration – they have very little ability to predict the outcome of such complex situations except to say that the policy they are interested in will probably not be effectively implemented.

A third criticism of top-down models is that they are likely to ignore, or at least underestimate, the strategies used by street-level bureaucrats and target groups to get around (central) policy and/or to divert it to their own purposes (Weatherly and Lipsky, 1977; Elmore, 1978; Berman, 1978). A related point is that such models are likely to neglect many of the counterproductive effects of the policies chosen for analysis. While a really skillful top-downer can attempt to deal with such deficiencies, there is little doubt that these, too, are important criticisms.

Finally, there are a whole series of arguments that the distinction between policy formulation and policy implementation is misleading and/or useless (Nakamura and Smallwood, 1980; Barrett and Fudge, 1981; Hjern and Hull, 1982; Hjern, 1982). These include the following: The distinction ignores the fact that some organizations are involved in both stages and/or that local implementing officials and target groups often simply ignore central legislators and administrators and deal directly with each other; since it is difficult to isolate policy decisions, it is preferable to talk about action and reaction (Barrett and Fudge, 1981); and because policies change as they get implemented, it is better to talk about policy evolution (Majone and Wildavsky, 1978).

This criticism strikes me as much less persuasive than the previous three. On the other hand, there are certainly cases, such as the Swedish 25/5 Scheme (Cerych and Sabatier, 1986), where there is no discernible policy 'decision' but rather a series of very incremental steps over time. But in the vast majority of the cases using the Sabatier and Mazmanian framework, it was not only possible but also highly desirable to retain the distinction between formulation and implementation. In fact, of the twenty-four cases, the 25/5 Scheme was the only one in which anyone even remotely skilled in legal analysis would find it difficult to discern an initial major policy decision. As for the arguments that some organizations are involved in both formulation and implementation, so what? The same organizations also try to influence local and central government; does this suggest that distinction between levels of government ought also to be rejected as useless? Finally, while local officials and target groups may sometimes ignore the legal authority of central officials, if such officials were really as insignificant as Hjern *et al.* suggest then why do the very same local officials and interest groups spend thousands of hours and millions of dollars every year trying to influence them?

Furthermore, obliterating the distinction between formulation and implementation will have two very significant costs (Sabatier and Mazmanian, 1983a). First, it makes it very difficult to distinguish the relative influence of elected officials and civil servants – thus precluding an analysis of democratic accountability and bureaucratic discretion, hardly trivial topics. Second, the view of the policy process as a seamless web of flows without decision points (Majone and Wildavsky, 1978; Barrett and Fudge, 1981) precludes policy evaluation (because there is no policy to evaluate) and the analysis of policy change (as there is never a defined policy at t_0 which changes into another defined policy at t_1).

In sum, while the first three criticisms are reasonably persuasive, the fourth is not. The bottom-uppers have thus been able to advance some rather telling arguments against the top-down approach. Have they also been able to accomplish the more difficult task of developing a more viable alternative?

Bottom-up approaches: the promised land?

In discussing the bottom-up perspective, the focus will be on the work of Benny Hjern and his colleagues – David Porter, Ken Hanf, and Chris Hull – who, while at the Science Center in Berlin during the period from roughly 1975 to 1983, developed a coherent methodology for conducting implementation analysis. It is this willingness to propose an intersubjectively reliable alternative to top-down approaches which distinguishes Hjern *et al.* from many bottom-up critics (e.g. Barrett and Fudge, 1981) and is one of the principal reasons their work has been chosen for analysis.

Presentation

Hjern *et al.* began with an acute awareness of the methodological weaknesses of the top-down approach, a commitment to the development of an intersubjectively reliable methodology, and a concern with policy areas – e.g. manpower training – involving a multitude of public and private organizations.

In contrast to the top-down approach – which starts from a policy decision and focuses on the extent to which its objectives are attained over time and why – the bottom-up approach of Hjern *et al.* starts by identifying the network of actors involved in service delivery in one or more local areas and asks them about their goals, strategies, activities, and contacts. It then uses the contacts as a vehicle for developing a network technique to identify the local, regional, and national actors involved in the planning, financing, and execution of the relevant governmental and non-governmental programs. This provides a mechanism for moving from street-level bureaucrats (the 'bottom') up

Table 2 Comparison between top-down and bottom-up approaches

	Top-down (Sabatier and Mazmanian)	Bottom-up (Hjern *et al.*)
Initial focus	(Central) government decision, e.g., new pollution control law.	Local implementation structure (network) involved in a policy area, e.g., pollution control.
Identification of major actors in the process	From top down and from government out to private sector (although importance attached to causal theory also calls for accurate understanding of target group's incentive structure).	From bottom (government and private) up.
Evaluative criteria	Focus on extent of attainment of formal objectives (carefully analyzed). May look at other politically significant criteria and unintended consequences, but these are optional.	Much less clear. Basically anything the analyst chooses which is somehow relevant to the policy issue or problem. Certainly does not require any careful analysis of official government decision(s).
Overall focus	How does one steer system to achieve (top) policy-maker's intended policy results?	Strategic interaction among multiple actors in a policy network.

to the 'top' policy-makers in both the public and private sectors (Hjern et al., 1978; Hjern and Porter, 1981; Hjern and Hull, 1985). Table 2 (see previous page) compares some of the central features of top-down and bottom-up approaches.

The study of Swedish manpower training programs, for example, by Hjern et al. (1978) started with the interaction of unions, governmental employment agencies, local governments, and industrial firms in several areas, and then moved from there via a networking technique to identify the people actually involved in planning, financing, and executing the relevant programs. They concluded that program success was far more dependent upon the skills of specific individuals in 'local implementation structures' than upon the efforts of central government officials.

In addition to their study of manpower training programs in Sweden and the German Federal Republic, Hjern et al. have sought to apply this technique to a variety of programs designed to foster the economic viability of small firms in the Federal Republic and several other countries (Hjern and Hull, 1985). They have also encouraged the application of their approach to Swedish energy policy (Wittrock et al., 1982), English manpower training (Davies and Mason, 1982), Dutch pollution control (Hanf, 1982), and Swiss economic development (Ackermann and Steinmann, 1982). It should be noted, however, that – with the exception of Hanf – these latter papers are more united by a bottom-up perspective than by any serious effort to employ the networking methodology first outlined by Hjern and Porter (1981).

Evaluation

The approach developed by Hjern et al. has several notable strengths.

First, they have developed an explicit and replicable methodology for identifying a policy network ('implementation structure'). In the small firms study, for example, they started with a random sample of firms in an area, and then interviewed key officials in each firm to ascertain their critical problems, the strategies developed to deal with each, and the persons contacted to execute each of those strategies. They then used those contacts via a networking technique to identify the 'implementation structure' (Hull and Hjern, 1982). In the case of financial problems, for example, the structure would include local (and perhaps regional) banks, officials in agencies with financial assistance programs, and, in the most successful case, an official in a local redevelopment agency who had extensive contacts he could direct firms to. It is this intersubjectively reliable methodology which separates Hjern et al. from the vast majority of bottom-up (and even top-down) researchers.

Second, because Hjern et al. do not begin with a governmental program but rather with actors' perceived problems and the strategies developed for dealing with them, they are able to assess the relative importance of a variety of governmental programs *vis-à-vis* private organizations and market forces in solving those problems. In contrast, a top-down approach is likely to overestimate the importance of the governmental program which is its focus. For example, Hanf's (1982) bottom-up analysis of pollution control in the Netherlands concluded that energy policies and the market price of alternative fuels had more effect on firms' pollution control programs than did governmental pollution control programs – a conclusion which would have been difficult for a top-downer to reach.

Third, because Hjern *et al.* do not start with a focus on the attainment of formal policy objectives, they are free to see all sorts of (unintended) consequences of governmental and private programs.

Fourth, this approach is able to deal with a policy/problem area involving a multitude of public (and private) programs, none of them preeminent. In contrast, such cases present substantial difficulties for top-down approaches.

Finally, because of their focus on the strategies pursued by a wide range of actors, bottom-uppers are better able to deal with strategic interaction over time than are top-downers – who tend to focus on the strategies of program proponents, while neglecting those of other actors.

For all these strengths, however, the Hjern *et al.* approach also has its limitations.

First, just as top-downers are in danger of overemphasizing the importance of the Center *vis-à-vis* the Periphery, bottom-uppers are likely to overemphasize the ability of the Periphery to frustrate the Center.

More specifically, the focus on actors' goals and strategies – the vast majority of whom are at the Periphery – may underestimate the Center's *indirect* influence over those goals and strategies through its ability to affect the institutional structure in which individuals operate (Kiser and Ostrom, 1982). For example, if Hjern *et al.* had studied the California coastal commissions, they would have taken as given that the vast majority of coastal officials were very sympathetic to environmental protection – without ever realizing that the distribution of officials' preferences was a consequence of the prior efforts of the framers of the coastal law to structure the situation in such a way – via the distribution of appointments between state and local governments – as to maximize the probability of that outcome. Likewise, Hjern *et al.* would simply take as granted that Actor A had certain resources without inquiring into the reasons s/he had them. In short, one of the most basic shortcomings of the Hjern *et al.* approach is that it takes the present distribution of preferences and resources as given, without ever inquiring into the efforts of other actors to structure the rules of the game.

Second, in a related point, Hjern *et al.* take the present participants in an implementation structure as given without examining the prior effort of various individuals to affect participation rates. For example, their networking methodology would simply have revealed that environmental groups were frequent litigants in American air pollution cases – thus neglecting the extensive efforts of drafters of the 1970 Clean Air Act to provide such groups with legal 'standing' (formal rights of intervention) to participate in such litigation.

This brings us to a third, and more fundamental, limitation with the Hjern *et al.* approach: Its failure to start from an explicit theory of the factors affecting its subject of interest. Because it relies very heavily on the perceptions and activities of participants, it is their prisoner – and therefore is unlikely to analyze the factors *indirectly* affecting their behavior or even the factors directly affecting such behavior which the participants do not recognize. Hjern *et al.* suffer from all of the limitations – as well as the advantages – of 'grounded theory' (Glaser and Strauss, 1967). Their networking methodology is a useful starting point for identifying many of the actors involved in a policy area, but it needs to be related via an explicit theory to social, economic, and legal factors which structure the perceptions, resources, and participation of those actors.

Scharpf (1978) and Thrasher (1983) have attempted to use exchange theory toward this end, but that hasn't been followed by Hjern *et al.* Likewise, Barrett and Fudge (1981) and Barrett and Hill (1984) have toyed with a number of approaches – mostly related to bargaining – but thus far haven't come close to an explicit conceptual framework. Until they do, the implicit assumptions which are guiding their data collection will remain difficult to discern.

Finally, it is worth observing that top-downers and bottom-uppers have been motivated by somewhat different concerns and thus have developed different approaches. Top-downers have been preoccupied with (a) the effectiveness of specific governmental programs and (b) the ability of elected officials to guide and constrain the behavior of civil servants and target groups. Addressing such concerns requires a careful analysis of the formally-approved objectives of elected officials, an examination of relevant performance indicators, and an analysis of the factors affecting such performance. Bottom-uppers, on the other hand, are far less preoccupied with the extent to which a formally enacted policy *decision* is carried out and much more concerned with accurately mapping the strategies of actors concerned with a policy *problem*. They are not primarily concerned with the implementation (carrying out) of a policy *per se* but rather with understanding actor interaction in a specific policy sector.

Where do we go from here?

Having identified the strengths and weaknesses of the two approaches, there are at least two strategies which can be pursued. The first is to indicate the conditions under which each is the more appropriate approach. The second is to develop one or more syntheses of the competing approaches.

Comparative advantage
The top-down approach is useful, first, in cases where there is a dominant public program in the policy area under consideration or where the analyst is solely interested in the effectiveness of *a* program. In cases like the California coastal commissions or the Open University – where a single public agency clearly dominated the field – the top-down approach is appropriate. On the other hand, in policy areas such as manpower training and employment development – which necessarily involve a multitude of public and private actors – the bottom-up approach is more appropriate. One might in fact be tempted to demarcate entire policy areas – e.g. highways, social security, income taxation – where there is a dominant public agency, but this should only be done with caution as unions and other private actors may turn out to be more important than anticipated.

On a more general note, the top-down approach is more useful in making a preliminary assessment of which approach to use: To the extent that the scores on the six conditions of effective implementation are relatively high and the investigator is primarily interested in the *mean* policy outputs and outcomes, then the top-down approach is appropriate. On the other hand, in cases where the scores on the six conditions are relatively low and one is interested in inter-local variation, then the bottom-up approach should be employed. When scores on the six conditions are moderate or mixed, the appropriate methodology depends on whether one is primarily interested in mean responses or in assessing inter-local variation. The top-down is more appropriate for the former because it focuses on the extent to which the overall system is structured/constrained. The bottom-up focuses on local implementation structures, and thus is better for assessing the dynamics of local variation. One could, of course, aggregate across numerous bottom-up studies to obtain a mean response, but this would normally be prohibitively expensive.

The top-down approach is more useful for making these preliminary assessments because of its greater theoretical development. The identification of specific variables and causal relationships makes predictions possible. On the other hand, the bottom-up approach of Hjern *et al.* (or

Barrett and Fudge) has not yet developed much of a substantive theory and thus is poorly equipped to make predictions.

In summary, the top-down approach appears to have a comparative advantage in situations in which (1) there is a dominant piece of legislation structuring the situation or (2) research funds are very limited, one is primarily interested in mean responses, and the situation is structured at least moderately well. In contrast, the bottom-up approach is more appropriate in situations where (1) there is no dominant piece of legislation but rather large numbers of actors without power dependency, or (2) one is primarily interested in the dynamics of different local situations.

Syntheses
A preferred alternative to these either-or choice situations is to synthesize the best features of the two approaches. To date, there have been at least three such efforts.

The most ambitious has been the study of the implementation of programs designed to reduce sulfur dioxide emissions in several European countries directed by Peter Knoepfel and Helmut Weidner. The conceptual framework for the study was explicitly designed to be a synthesis (Knoepfel and Weidner, 1982). [. . .]

A second approach, developed by Richard Elmore (1985), attempts to combine his previous work on 'backward mapping' – one of the bottom-up classics – with what he terms 'forward mapping', essentially a top-down perspective. He argues that policy-makers need to consider both the policy instruments and other resources at their disposal (forward mapping) *and* the incentive structure of ultimate target groups (backward mapping) because program success is contingent on meshing the two. Elmore's paper is primarily concerned with aiding policy practitioners by indicating the need to use multiple perspectives in designing and implementing policies. At that very practical level, it is excellent. It does not purport, however, to provide a model of the policy process which can be used by social scientists to explain outcomes in a wide variety of settings.

The third approach, to be outlined below, explicitly attempts to develop such a general model of the policy process which combines the best features of the bottom-up and top-down approaches, while also applying them to a longer time-frame than is the case in most implementation research.

An advocacy coalition framework of policy change

One of the major contributions of Mazmanian and Sabatier (1983) was their contention that the relatively short time span (4–5 years) used in most implementation studies not only led to premature judgments concerning program failure but also missed some very important features of the policy process, namely the extent of policy-oriented learning.

For example, early studies of Federal compensatory education programs (Title I of ESEA) concluded that the program was bringing about very little change because of ambiguous objectives, dubious causal theories, resistance of implementing officials, and the inability of proponents to organize at the local level (Murphy, 1973). But later studies incorporating a 10–15-year time span portrayed a fair amount of improvement on the part of both school officials and students' educational achievement (Kirst and Jung, 1982; Mazmanian and Sabatier, 1983: Chap. 6). Over time, objectives were clarified; research resulted in more adequate causal theories; and supportive constituencies were fostered at both the state and local levels. This suggested a process of policy learning by program proponents, as they discovered deficiencies in the existing program and then developed a series of strategies to deal with them.

While this approach did a good job of illustrating learning by proponents, its top-down assumptions made it difficult to focus equally on learning by opponents. This deficiency can be addressed, however, by incorporating bottom-uppers' techniques for ascertaining the strategies – and, by extension, the learning from experience – of a wider variety of actors concerned with a program. This points to a synthesis which combines top-down and bottom-up approaches in the analysis of policy change over periods of a decade or more.

Elements of the synthesis
The elements of such a conceptual framework are at hand. Consistent with the bottom-uppers, one needs to start from a policy *problem* or subsystem – rather than a law or other policy *decision* – and then examine the strategies employed by relevant actors in both the public and private sectors at various levels of government as they attempt to deal with the issue consistent with their objectives. The networking technique developed by Hjern *et al.* can be one of the methods for determining the actors in a subsystem, although it needs to be combined with other approaches indicating the actors who are indirectly (or even potentially) involved.

Likewise, the concerns of top-down theorists with the manner in which legal and socioeconomic factors structure behavioral options need to be incorporated into the synthesis, as do their concerns with the validity of the causal assumptions behind specific programs and strategies. This leads to a focus on (1) the effects of socioeconomic (and other) changes external to the policy network/subsystem on actors'

resources and strategies; (2) the attempts by various actors to manipulate the legal attributes of governmental programs in order to achieve
their objectives over time; and (3) actors' efforts to improve their
understanding of the magnitude of and factors affecting the problem – as
well as the impacts of various policy instruments – as they learn from
experience.

Attention thus shifts from policy implementation to policy change
over periods of 10–20 years. The longer time span creates, however, a
need to aggregate actors into a manageable number of groups if the
researcher is to avoid severe information overload. After examining
several options, the most useful principle of aggregation seems to be by
belief system. This produces a focus on 'advocacy coalitions,' i.e. actors
from various public and private organizations who share a set of beliefs
and who seek to realize their common goals over time.

In short, the synthesis adopts the bottom-uppers' unit of analysis – a
whole variety of public and private actors involved with a policy
problem – as well as their concerns with understanding the perspectives
and strategies of all major categories of actors (not simply program
proponents). It then combines this starting point with top-downers'
concerns with the manner in which socioeconomic conditions and legal
instruments constrain behavior. It applies this synthesized perspective to
the analysis of policy change over periods of a decade or more. This
time-frame is required to deal with the role of policy-oriented learning –
a topic identified as critical in several top-down studies, although by no
means inherent to that approach. Finally, the synthesis adopts the
intellectual style (or methodological perspective) of many top-downers
in its willingness to utilize fairly abstract theoretical constructs and to
operate from an admittedly simplified portrait of reality. It is primarily
concerned with theory construction rather than with providing guidelines for practitioners or detailed portraits of particular situations.

Overview of the framework
The advocacy coalition framework starts from the premise that the most
useful aggregate unit of analysis for understanding policy change in
modern industrial societies is not any specific governmental organization
but rather a policy subsystem, i.e. those actors from a variety of public
and private organizations who are actively concerned with a policy
problem or issue such as higher education or air pollution control
(Heclo, 1978; Jordan and Richardson, 1983; Milward and Wamsley,
1984; Rose, 1984; Sharpe, 1985).

Figure 2 presents a general overview of the framework. On the left
side are two sets of exogenous variables – the one fairly stable, the other
dynamic – which affect the constraints and resources of subsystem
actors. Air pollution policy, for example, is strongly affected by the

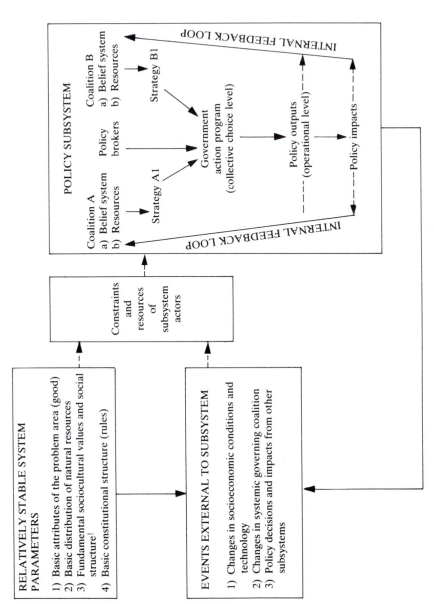

Figure 2 General overview of conceptual framework of policy change

nature of air quality as a collective good, by the geographical contours of air basins, and by political boundaries which are usually quite stable over time. But there are also more dynamic factors, including changes in socioeconomic conditions and in system-wide governing coalitions, which provide some of the principal sources of policy change. These are all features drawn from top-down models which 'structure' policy-making.

Within the subsystem, the framework draws heavily upon the bottom-up approach. It assumes, however, that actors can be aggre-gated into a number of advocacy coalitions – each composed of politicians, agency officials, interest group leaders, and intellectuals who share a set of normative and causal beliefs on core policy issues. At any particular point in time, each coalition adopts a strategy(s) envisaging one or more changes in governmental institutions perceived to further its policy objectives. Conflicting strategies from different coalitions are mediated by a third group of actors, here termed 'policy brokers,' whose principal concern is to find some reasonable compromise which will reduce intense conflict. The end result is legislation or governmental decrees establishing or modifying one or more governmental action programs at the collective choice level (Kiser and Ostrom, 1982; Page, 1985). These in turn produce policy outputs at the operational level (e.g. agency permit decisions). These outputs at the operational level, mediated by a number of other factors (most notably, the validity of the causal theory underlying the program), result in a variety of impacts on targeted problem parameters (e.g. ambient air quality), as well as side effects.

At this point the framework requires additional elements not normal-ly central to implementation studies. Some aspects of public policy clearly change far more frequently than others. In order to get a conceptual handle on this, the framework distinguishes the *core* from the *secondary* aspects of a belief system or a governmental action program. Recall the coalitions are seeking to get their beliefs translated into governmental programs, so the two concepts can be analyzed in similar categories. The extent to which a specific program incorporates the beliefs of any single coalition is, however, an empirical question and will reflect the relative power of that coalition within the subsystem.

Table 3 represents a preliminary attempt to identify the principal topics addressed in the Deep Core, the Near Core, and the Secondary Aspects of a belief system. (Only the latter two are relevant to governmental action programs.) It suggests that coalitions will be very reluctant to alter their beliefs concerning core issues such as the proper scope of governmental vs. market activity; their orientation on basic policy conflicts; the relative distribution of authority among different levels of government; or their identification of social groups whose

Table 3 Structure of belief systems of policy elites[a]

	Deep (normative) Core	Near (policy) Core	Secondary Aspects
Defining characteristics	Fundamental normative and ontological axioms.	Fundamental policy positions concerning the basic strategies for achieving normative axioms of deep core.	Instrumental decisions and information searches necessary to implement core policy positions.
Susceptibility to change	Very difficult; akin to a religious conversion.	Difficult, but can occur if experience reveals serious anomalies.	Moderately easy; this is the topic of most administrative and even legislative policy-making.

Illustrative components	1) The nature of man
	  i) Inherently evil vs. socially redeemable
	  ii) Part of nature vs. dominion over nature
	  iii) Narrow egoists vs. contractarians
	2) Relative priority of health, love, beauty, etc.
	3) Basic criteria of distributive justice: Whose welfare counts? Relative weights of self, primary groups, all people, future generations, non-human beings, etc.
	4) Ability of society to solve problems
	  i) Zero-sum competition vs. potential for mutual accommodation
	  ii) Technological optimism vs. pessimism
		1) Proper scope of governmental (vs. market) activity
		2) Proper distribution of authority among various units (e.g. levels) of government
		3) Identification of social groups whose welfare is most threatened/critical
		4) Orientation on basic policy conflicts e.g. environmental protection vs. economic development
		5) Basic choices concerning policy instruments, e.g. coercion vs. inducements vs. persuasion
		6) Desirability of participation by various segments of society
		7) Perception of relative seriousness of this problem area.
			1) Most decisions concerning administrative rules, budgetary allocations, disposition of cases, statutory interpretation, and even statutory revision
			2) Information concerning program performance, the seriousness of the problems, etc.

[a] The Near Core and Secondary Aspects also apply to governmental action programs.

welfare is most critical. For example, federal air pollution policy in the U.S. – which essentially reflects the beliefs of the environmental coalition – accords government a very important role in this policy area; places greater priority on public health than on economic development; gives the federal government an unusually preeminent role over states and localities; and places a high priority on protecting the welfare of susceptible health populations, e.g. people suffering from emphysema. These are topics on which neither the environmental coalition nor federal law have changed very much since 1970 (Mazmanian and Sabatier, 1983: Chap. 4).

On the other hand, there has been a great deal of change in the secondary attributes of federal air pollution programs which are instrumental to achieving the core aspects. These include such topics as the appropriate deadlines for meeting particular emission standards; the relative importance of various sources of pollutants affecting air quality; the most valid methods for measuring ambient air quality; the proper enforcement budget of implementing agencies; the perceived feasibility of particular pollution control technologies; and the precise effects of pollution concentrations on specific populations. While these have all been the subject of vigorous debate, they represent rather marginal, instrumental choices within the context of core beliefs.

The framework argues that the core aspects of a governmental action program – and the relative strength of competing advocacy coalitions within a policy subsystem – will typically remain rather stable over periods of a decade or more. Major alterations in the policy core will normally be the product of changes external to the subsystem – particularly large-scale socioeconomic perturbations or changes in the systemwide governing coalition. An example of the latter would be the change in Britain from Parliaments dominated by moderate socialists and conservatives to a system dominated by Mrs Thatcher's wing of the Conservative Party with a *fundamentally* different conception of the proper scope of governmental activity.

While changes in the policy core are usually the result of external perturbations, changes in the secondary aspects of a governmental action program are often the result of policy-oriented learning by various coalitions or policy brokers. Following Heclo (1974:306), policy-oriented learning refers to relatively enduring alterations of thought or behavioral intentions which result from experience and which are concerned with the attainment or revision of policy objectives. Policy-oriented learning involves the internal feedback loops depicted in Figure 2, as well as increased knowledge of the state of problem parameters and the factors affecting them. For example, a decade of experience and research in U.S. air pollution programs has indicated that efforts to reduce vehicle miles traveled by commuters through the use of, e.g., parking surcharges have only very modest effects on air quality, impose very substantial costs on commuters, and therefore are no longer a feasible policy option (Mazmanian and Sabatier, 1983). Since the vast majority of policy debates involve secondary aspects of a governmental action program – in part because actors realize the futility of challenging core assumptions – such learning can play an important role in policy change. In fact, a principal concern of the framework is to analyze the institutional conditions conducive to such learning and the cases in which cumulative learning may lead to changes in the policy core.

A more extensive exposition of the framework can be found in Sabatier (1986). This overview should, however, indicate how it synthesizes important elements from both top-down and bottom-up perspectives within the implementation literature. But the framework also borrows from a number of other literatures, including those on long term policy change (Heclo, 1974; Derthick, 1979; Browning *et al.*, 1985; Hogwood and Peters, 1983), coalition stability (Dodd, 1976; Hinckley, 1981), elite belief systems (Putnam, 1976), and the utilization of policy research (Weiss, 1977).

References

Aaron, Henry (1978). *Politics and the Professors*. Washington, D.C.: Brookings Institution.

Ackermann, Charbel and Steinmann, Walter (1982). 'Privatized policy making,' *European Journal of Policy Research* 10 (June): 173–85.

Alexander, Robert (1982). 'Implementation: does a literature add up to a theory?' *Journal of the American Planning Association* (Winter): 132–55.

Alterman, Rachelle (1983). 'Implementation analysis: the contours of an emerging debate,' *Journal of Planning Education and Research* 3 (Summer): 63–5.

Bardach, Eugene (1974). *The Implementation Game*. Cambridge: MIT Press.

Barrett, Susan and Fudge, Colin, eds. (1981). *Policy and Action*. London: Methuen.

— and Hill, Michael (1984). 'Policy, bargaining and structure in implementation theory,' *Policy and Politics* 12: 219–40.

Berman, Paul (1978). 'The study of macro- and micro-implementation,' *Public Policy* 26: 157–84.

— (1980). 'Thinking about programmed and adaptive implementation,' in *Why Policies Succeed or Fail*, ed. by Helen Ingram and Dean Mann. Beverly Hills: Sage.

— and McLaughlin, Milbrey (1976). 'Implementation of ESEA Title I,' *Teacher College Record* 77 (Feb.).

Bowen, Elinor (1982). 'The Pressman–Wildavsky paradox,' *Journal of Public Policy* 2 (February): 1–22.

Bowman, Ann and Lester, James (1986). 'Subnational policy implementation: testing the Sabatier–Mazmanian model,' *Administration and Society*, forthcoming.

Browning, Rufus, Marshall, Dale, and Tabb, David (1981). 'Implementation and political change: sources of local variation in federal social programs,' in *Effective Policy Implementation*, ed. by D. Mazmanian and P. Sabatier. Lexington, Mass.: D.C. Heath.

— (1985). *Protest Is Not Enough*. Berkeley: University of California Press.

Cerych, Ladislav and Sabatier, Paul (1986). *Great Expectations and Mixed Performance: The implementation of European higher education reforms*. Stoke-on-Trent, United Kingdom: Trentham Books.

Davies, Tom and Mason, Charles (1982). 'Gazing up from the bottoms: problems of minimal response in the implementation of manpower policy,' *European Journal of Political Research* 10 (June): 145–58.

Davis, Charles (1985). 'Perceptions of hazardous waste policy issues among public and private sector administrators,' *Western Political Quarterly* 38 (Sept.): 447–63.

Derthick, Martha (1972). *New Towns In-Town*. Washington: Urban Institute.

— (1979). *Policymaking for Social Security*. Washington: Brookings.

Dodd, Lawrence (1976). *Coalitions in Parliamentary Governments*. Princeton: Princeton University Press.

Downs, Anthony (1967). *Inside Bureaucracy*. Boston: Little, Brown.

Elmore, Richard (1978). 'Organizational model of social program implementation,' *Public Policy* 26 (Spring): 185–228.

— (1979). 'Backward mapping,' *Political Science Quarterly* 94 (Winter): 601–16.

— (1985). 'Foward and backward mapping,' in *Policy Implementation in Federal and Unitary Systems*, ed. by K. Hanf and T. Toonen. Dordrecht: Martinus Nijhoff, pp. 33–70.

Glaser, Barney and Strauss, Anselm (1967). *The Discovery of Grounded Theory*. Chicago: Aldine.

Goggin, Malcolm L. (1984). 'Book review of *Implementation and Public Policy*, Daniel A. Mazmanian and Paul A. Sabatier, eds,' *Publius* 14 (Fall): 159–60.

— (1986). 'The "too few cases/too many variables" problem in implementation research,' *Western Political Quarterly*, forthcoming.

Goodwin, Leonard and Moen, Phyllis (1981). 'The evolution and implementation of federal welfare policy,' in *Effective Policy Implementation*, ed. by D. Mazmanian and P. Sabatier. Lexington, Mass.: D.C. Heath, pp. 147–68.

Hanf, Kenneth (1982). 'The implementation of regulatory policy: enforcement as bargaining,' *European Journal of Political Research* 10 (June 1982): 159–72.

— and Scharpf, Fritz, eds. (1978). *Interorganizational Policy Making: Limits to coordination and central control*. London: Sage.

Heclo, Hugh (1974). *Social Policy in Britain and Sweden*. New Haven: Yale University Press.

— (1978). 'Issue networks and the executive establishment,' in *The New American Political System*, ed. by Anthony King. Washington, D.C.: American Enterprise Institute.

Hinckley, Barbara (1981). *Coalitions and Politics*. New York: Harcourt, Brace, Jovanovich.

Hjern, Benny (1982). 'Implementation research – the link gone missing', *Journal of Public Policy* 2(3): 301–8.

— and Porter, David (1981). 'Implementation structures: a new unit of administrative analysis,' *Organization Studies* 2: 211–27.

— and Hull, Chris (1982). 'Implementation research as empirical constitutionalism,' *European Journal of Political Research* 10 (June 1982): 105–16.

— (1985). 'Helping small firms grow,' unpublished book-length manuscript, Management Institut, Science Center, Berlin.

—, Hanf, Kenneth and Porter, David (1978). 'Local networks of manpower training in the Federal Republic of Germany and Sweden,' in *Interorganizational Policy Making: Limits to coordination and central control* ed. by K. Hanf and F. Scharpf. London: Sage, pp. 303–44.

Hofferbert, Richard (1974). *The Study of Public Policy.* Indianapolis: Bobbs-Merrill.

Hogwood, Bryan and Peters, G. Guy (1983). *Policy Dynamics.* New York: St Martin's.

Hull, Chris and Hjern, Benny (1982). 'Helping small firms grow,' *European Journal of Political Research* 10 (June): 187–98.

Ingram, Helen (1977) 'Policy implementation through bargaining: federal grants in aid.' *Public Policy* 25 (Fall).

Jones, Charles (1975). *Clean Air.* Pittsburgh: University of Pittsburgh Press.

Jones, Susan (1984). 'Application of a framework for implementation analysis to evaluate groundwater management policy in two New York counties,' unpublished master's thesis, Department of City and Regional Planning, University of North Carolina, Chapel Hill.

Jordan, A. G. and Richardson, J. J. (1983). 'Policy communities: the British and European political style,' *Policy Studies Journal* 11 (June): 60–315.

Kirst, Michael and Jung, Richard (1982). 'The utility of a longitudinal approach in assessing implementation: Title I, ESEA,' in *Studying Implementation*, ed. by Walter Williams. Chatham, N.J.: Chatham House, pp. 119–48.

Kiser, Larry and Ostrom, Elinor (1982). 'The three worlds of action,' in *Strategies of Political Inquiry*, ed. by E. Ostrom. Beverly Hills: Sage.

Knoepfel, Peter and Weidner, Helmut (1982). 'A conceptual framework for studying implementation,' in *The Implementation of Pollution Control Programs*, ed. by Paul Downing and Kenneth Hanf. Tallahassee: Policy Sciences Program.

Lazin, Frederick (1973). 'The failure of federal enforcement of civil rights regulations in public housing, 1963–71,' *Policy Sciences* 4: 263–74.

Lester, James (1986). 'Intergovernmental relations and ocean policy: marine pollution, dumping, and incineration of hazardous wastes,' in *Ocean Resources and Intergovernmental Relations*, ed. by M. Silva. Boulder: Westview.

Levin, Martin (1980). 'Conditions contributing to effective implementation and their limits,' unpublished manuscript, Brandeis University.

Lipsky, Michael (1971). 'Street level bureaucracy and the analysis of urban reform,' *Urban Affairs Quarterly* 6: 391–409.

Lowry, Ken (1985). 'Assessing the implementation of federal coastal policy,' *Journal of the American Planning Association*, 51 (Summer): 288–98.

MacIntyre, Angus (1985). 'The multiple sources of statutory ambiguity,' in *Administrative Discretion and the Implementation of Public Policy*, ed. by

IMPLEMENTATION

Hibbeln and Shumavon. New York: Praeger, pp. 66–88.

Majone, Giandomenico and Wildavsky, Aaron (1978). 'Implementation as evolution,' in *Policy Studies Review Annual – 1978*, ed. by Howard Freeman. Beverly Hills: Sage.

Mazmanian, Daniel and Sabatier, Paul (1983). *Implementation and Public Policy*. Chicago: Scott Foresman and Co.

Milward, H. Brinton and Wamsley, Gary (1984). 'Policy subsystems, networks, and the tools of public management,' in *Public Policy Formation and Implementation*, ed. by Robert Eyestone. Boston: JAI Press.

Murphy, Jerome (1973). 'The education bureaucracies implement novel policy: the politics of Title I of ESEA,' in *Policy and Politics in America*, ed. by Allan Sindler. Boston: Little, Brown.

Nakamura, Robert and Smallwood, Frank (1980). *The Politics of Policy Implementation*. New York: St Martin's.

Page, Ed (1985). 'Laws as an instrument in center–local relations,' *Journal of Public Policy* 5 (2): 241–65.

Pressman, Jeffrey and Wildavsky, Aaron (1973). *Implementation*. Berkeley: University of California Press.

Putnam, Robert (1976). *The Comparative Study of Political Elites*. Englewood Cliffs: Prentice Hall.

Rose, Richard (1984). 'From government at the center to nationwide government,' in *Centre–Periphery Relations in Western Europe*, ed. by Y. Meny and V. Wright. London: George Allen and Unwin.

Sabatier, Paul (1975). 'Social movements and regulatory agencies,' *Policy Sciences* 8: 301–42.

— (1984). 'Center–periphery relations in coastal zone regulation,' unpublished manuscript, University of California, Davis.

— (1986). 'Policy analysis, policy-oreinted learning and policy change: an advocacy coalition framework,' Manuscript submitted to *Knowledge: Creation, Diffusion, Utilization*.

— and Klosterman, Barbara (1981). 'A comparative analysis of policy implementation under different statutory regimes,' in *Effective Policy Implementation*, ed. by D. Mazmanian and P. Sabatier. Lexington, Mass.: D.C. Heath, pp. 169–206.

— and Mazmanian, Daniel (1979). 'The conditions of effective implementation,' *Policy Analysis* 5 (Fall): 481–504.

— (1980). 'A framework of analysis,' *Policy Studies Journal* 8: 538–60.

— (1983a). 'Policy implementation,' in *Encyclopedia of Policy Studies*, ed. by Start Nagel. N.Y.: Marcel Dekker, pp. 143–69.

— (1983b). *Can Regulation Work? The implementation of the 1972 California Coastal Initiative*. N.Y.: Plenum.

Scharpf, Fritz (1978). 'Interorganizational policy studies,' in *Interorganizational Policy-Making*, ed. by K. Hanf and F. Scharpf. London: Sage, pp. 345–70.

Sharpe, L. J. (1985). 'Central coordination and the policy network,' *Political Studies* 33: 361–81.

Thrasher, Michael (1983). 'Exchange networks and implementation,' *Policy and Politics* 11: 375–91.

Van Meter, Donald and Van Horn, Carl (1975). 'The policy implementation process: a conceptual framework,' *Administration and Society* 6 (Feb.): 445–88.

Weatherly, Richard and Lipsky, Michael (1977). 'Street level bureaucrats and institutional innovation: implementing special-education reform,' *Harvard Educational Review* 47 (2): 171–97.

Weiss, Carol, ed. (1977). *Using Social Research in Public Policy Making.* Lexington, Mass.: D.C. Heath.

Wittrock, Bjorn *et al.* (1982). 'Implementation beyond hierarchy: Swedish energy research policy,' *European Journal of Political Research* 10 (June): 131–43.

Yin, Robert (1980). *Studying the Implementation of Public Programs.* Boulder: Solar Energy Research Institute.

Part VII

Applications of the study of organisations to the study of the policy process

Introduction

Part III of this reader has emphasised how important it is to recognise that the policy process in modern societies occurs in a context in which the state is a complex organisation. To understand the state as an actor we saw that we must give attention to its bureaucratic character and raise questions about who controls that bureaucracy. Then in Part VI explicit attention to implementation suggested that the answer to questions about control over bureaucracy may not be a simple one. There will be a policy/action relationship in which actors at various levels within the bureaucratic system will participate. This part goes on to explore these issues further with reference to some ideas which come from organisation theory and organisational sociology.

We start by returning to managerialist thought, looking at the development of a set of ideas about the control of organisations, dominated by people who were seeking to work out the best way to do this. Pollitt, in the first extract, shows how management thought evolved, during the twentieth century, from a perspective (Taylorism) in which subordinate participants were seen as manipulable cogs in an organisational machine to one in which the needs of individuals and the complexity of the 'culture' in which they operate were recognised. This extract is, however, taken from a book in which Pollitt goes on to show that Taylorist principles continue to be asserted in the public sector. His argument on this is summarised at the end of the extract. Clearly, if public services are viewed in instrumental terms there is a justification for this, deriving, as has earlier been suggested in this book, from democratic models of the policy process.

Some radical students of organisations have suggested, particularly in relation to industrial organisations, that efforts to create more participative organisational forms may be merely a 'con', aimed at enhancing productivity through the illusion of a shared interest. However, where complex tasks are involved, in which policies have to be elaborated (or even created, as suggested in Part VI) by lower-level workers, issues about attachments to the organisation and views of the task may become of paramount importance. It is in this context that Elmore's article explores various analytic models of organisation derived from theory. Elmore uses an approach which he describes as derived from the work of Graham Allison, and which is rather like that used in the earlier extracts from Blowers and Ham. In it, various approaches to analysing the same issue are compared and contrasted for their explanatory power. In this case, however, the normative issues about **control** continuously lurk in the background, with the problems of securing control intensifying as one moves through from the first to the fourth of Elmore's models.

Of course, if one's aim is simply to understand organisational action one only needs to ask which of Elmore's models best predicts or interprets behaviour. Clearly, as already suggested, much of the implementation literature points to the limited value of the 'systems management model' in this respect. The article by Degeling and Colebatch certainly takes this view, suggesting ways in which two paradigms – a 'social action' and a 'structuralist' one – offer competing challenges to the 'instrumental' one (roughly, their name for Elmore's 'systems management model'). In their article they show how these perspectives may be integrated. Since, like so many of the contributors to this literature, they aim at having something helpful to say to managers, they end by suggesting that where appeal to 'ascribed authority' may be little use managers nevertheless can be 'active participants in the shaping of the negotiated order of which they are a part'. This view puts a very different perspective upon the concept of 'policy making' from that embedded in the top-down model.

Reference to 'negotiated order' in Degeling and Colebatch's article reminds us of a theme very clearly set out in Hjern and Porter's view of implementation structures, that the policy process involves *inter*-organisational activities as well as *intra*-organisational ones. In the last of the articles in this part, Hudson stresses the need to bear this in mind and outlines some of the theory which may be helpful in analysing inter-organisational processes.

The development of management thought

Chris Pollitt

In this [. . .] section, [. . .] the intention is to offer enough of a potted history to enable the reader to see how management thought has itself developed through several historical phases. [. . .] Those who wish for a fuller treatment of the history of management and administrative thought are advised to seek it through the more specialist references, particularly Child (1969), Dunsire (1973), Perrow (1979) and Thomas (1978).

Pushing simplification somewhere near to the point where its drawbacks begin to overtake its advantages, one may say that managerial thought grew up hastily in the final decades of the nineteenth century and has since moved through at least six broad phases. (Not too much should be made of these, since, in practice, they frequently ran side by side. The sequence here depicted is a logically neat summary of what was actually a fairly untidy process.)

In the first phase theorists struggled to come to terms with the process of industrialization, and the concomitant creation of large workforces concentrated at particular sites of production. How were these workforces to be selected, controlled, paid and prevented from endangering the increase in production and the accumulation of capital?

> Factory work involves specialization, sub division and fragmentation. Decisions about the general rules and procedures and detailed work specifications are vested in experts, managers or machinery. The speed and quality of work cannot remain with the individual workers . . . . These features required a new 'rational' work ethic on the part of the hands. (Salaman, 1981, p. 33)

Explicit theorizing on these questions was perhaps most noticeable in the US, which industrialized later and even faster than Germany or the

From C. Pollitt, *Managerialism and the Public Services* (1990), Oxford: Blackwell.

UK. In the US in the 1870s and 1880s doctrines of Social Darwinism were widely expounded. Ideas of competition and natural selection suggested that entrepreneurs and owners need have little regard for the active welfare of their workers. Nature's 'laws' would in any case ensure the survival of the fittest, and the sensible employer should therefore go with the grain of this 'legislation' by retaining the healthiest, strongest workers and not paying too much attention to the rest (Perrow, 1979, pp. 60–1).

By the beginning of the twentieth century, however, fresh theories were beginning to suggest that far more initiative lay in the hands of the owners and managers themselves. In the US the New Thought Movement emphasized not biology but the power of positive thinking. It spawned advisory texts with what now sound preposterously exhortatory titles such as *Your Forces and How to Use Them* or *Pushing to the Front* (Perrow, 1979, pp. 61–2). The emphasis was on willpower and mental energy – if individuals applied themselves keenly enough then wealth and success lay within reach (one can detect echoes of this in many popular expressions of contemporary 'new right' political and economic thought, for example Michael Heseltine's *Where There's A Will* (1987), or the Conservative Party's 1987 slogan 'The resolute approach').

Hard on the heels of the New Thought Movement came the considerably more detailed and practical body of thought most commonly associated with the name of Frederick Winslow Taylor. His *Principles of Scientific Management* (1911) became enormously influential, and its basic approach remains with us to this day. Though countless social scientists have subsequently criticized or scorned Taylor's techniques:

> A successful and durable business of management consulting and an endless series of successful books rest upon the basic principles of the classical management school. These principles have worked and are still working, for they addressed themselves to the very problems of management, problems more pressing than those advanced by social science. (Perrow, 1979, p. 59; see also Merkle, 1980)

Taylor's work was so seminal that it is worth quoting from it at some length:

> This paper has been written:
> FIRST. To point out through a series of simple illustrations, the great loss which the whole country is suffering through inefficiency in almost all of our daily acts.
> SECOND. To try to convince the reader that the remedy for this inefficiency lies in systematic management, rather than in searching for some unusual or extraordinary man.

THIRD. To prove that the best management is a true science, resting upon clearly defined laws, rules and principles, as a foundation. And further to show that the fundamental principles of scientific management are applicable to all kinds of human activities, from our simplest individual acts to the work of our great corporations, which call for the most elaborate co-operation. (Taylor, 1911, pp. 5–7)

Taylor is perhaps best known as a pioneer of time and motion techniques, and for his studies of the detailed movements of workers dealing with particular, well-defined tasks. As the above manifesto clearly shows, however, his ambitions ran far beyond this [. . .]. Scientific management constituted: 'a clearly-marked complex that ties together patterns of technological innovation with techniques of organization and larger designs for social change, unifying its entire structure with an ideology of science as a form of puritanism' (Merkle, 1980, p. 11).

Two of his claims are of particular importance. First, there is the assertion that management can be a 'true science' (with all the connotations of discovering precise, impersonal laws). Second, a parallel claim is made for universality of application – *all* human activities are subject to the laws thus discovered. Both these claims, but perhaps especially the second one, can still be heard today – *anything* can, and should, be managed.

Taylor's ideas had considerable influence on both sides of the Atlantic, and in both private and public sectors. The notion that management could be divided off as a separate and scientific field of study combined very neatly with what was by the 1920s a popular view of public administration in the US. As long ago as 1887 Woodrow Wilson had written what later became an influential paper, 'The study of administration'. Here Wilson urged that 'administrative questions are not political questions' (Wilson, 1887). This had been widely interpreted as marking out a distinct sphere of 'administration' in which politics constituted an unwelcome and improper intrusion (Dunsire, 1973, pp. 87–94). Within this sphere, therefore, 'scientific' methods could be applied. Various attempts were made to do just this, especially among the 'progressive' reformers of municipal government (Schliesl, 1977, especially pp. 163–5).

In Britain the impact of Taylorism was less pervasive, but its spirit was nevertheless clearly present in some influential quarters. The Haldane Committee report on the machinery of government espoused the general idea of a set of functional principles by which the optimal pattern of government departments could be determined (Cd 9230, 1918). In 1922 the first issue of *Public Administration*, journal of the newly founded Institute of Public Administration (now RIPA), carried an article entitled 'Public administration: a science', and editorialized in favour of this stance. Then, as now, it was supposed that, if only management and administration could be established as a scientific discipline, then public officials would be better protected against the irrationalities of 'political interference'. [. . .]

From Taylorism flowed many attempts to identify and enumerate the correct principles for the design of organizations. This extensive literature, much of it published during the 1920s and 1930s, has become known as 'classical management theory'. Among its exponents was Luther Gulick, best known for the list of chief executive functions (POSDCORB) [. . .]. However, scientific management was not without its rivals. From the early 1930s a new perspective was developed, one which has been retrospectively dubbed the 'human relations school'. The key difference from Taylorism was the advancement of a considerably more sophisticated model of the individual worker. Whereas in early scientific management the worker was treated as an individual unit responding directly to some fairly simple incentives and punishments, the human relations school substituted a model of rather a complex being who responded to a much wider variety of environmental factors, including behavioural norms created and sustained by informal groups of fellow workers. Whilst Taylor had been aware of work group solidarity he seems to have seen it as an obstacle to be overcome rather than as a phenomenon which needed to be understood and turned to management advantage. For human relations theorists, however, what was required for a smoothly functioning organization was no less than a rational assessment of the whole person, set in a context of the social relations of the workplace (Perrow, 1979, p. 49).

The human relations approach grew from roots in the work of industrial psychologists during the First World War, but the investigations which established it as a major force in management were the 'Hawthorne Studies', carried out between 1926 and 1932. The classic text, *The Human Problems of an Industrial Civilisation*, was published by the leading researcher, Elton Mayo, in 1933 (Mayo, 1933). The significance of this work for managerialist ideologies today is that it established the idea that *informal* relations within and without the organization are of considerable importance. It is not only the formal organization chart, distribution of functions and systems of work measurement which are important, but also the feelings, values, informal group norms and family and social backgrounds of workers which help determine organizational performance. 'Man is not merely – in fact is very seldom – motivated by factors pertaining strictly to facts or logic' (Roethlisberger and Dickson, 1969, pp. 54–5). Subsequently this general message has been developed in many and various detailed applications – modern techniques of job enrichment, participative management styles and 'self-actualisation' (Argyris, 1960) are part of the intellectual heritage of the human relations school.

It should be noticed, however, that the genuinely 'humanizing' tendencies of the human relations movement have their limits. Many critics of the approach: 'point to the excessive concern of the authors with consensus and co-operation . . . . Conflict is given little attention, such instances as are noted being attributed to worker irrationality' (Salaman, 1981, p. 149).

Furthermore:

> whereas management like [a company] have a definite interest in recognizing more fully that production is social production – i.e. in recognizing that men are not simply commodities but thinking, social beings, with potentially valuable contributions to make, and with the potential to work together more productively – they also have an interest in limiting the development of these human potentials. And this is because, though it would suit workers to act as if there were really socialism inside work, managers themselves have to operate in a world in which market forces reign and impede the development of the very unstinted co-operation they wish to bring about. (Nichols, 1980, p. 298)

One might add that, in a contemporary public-sector context, one could substitute, without diminishing the accuracy of Nichols' generalization, the words 'cash limits, performance indicators and staffcuts' for 'market forces'.

The fifth main phase in the development of management thought is even harder to summarize than the first four. One problem here is that the sheer volume of material grew enormously during the three decades after 1945. This was in large part due to the rapid growth of management-related disciplines (social psychology, sociology, organization theory etc.) in universities and business schools. This growth was itself related to the emergence of new dominant organizational forms, especially the large multinational corporation in the private sector, and to the appearance in the UK of very large nationalized industries (mainly created by the 1945–51 Labour government) which greatly enlarged the public sector. In the face of this flood of ideas I have decided to term the period up to the mid 1970s the 'decisions and systems' phase. I do this because, alongside continuing work in the scientific management and human relations traditions, two major new foci emerged: first, a concern with the cognitive processes of individual and group decision making in organizational contexts and, second, attempts to understand the macro-features of organizational performance by characterizing them as 'open, socio-technical systems' (Sayles, 1958).

The decision-making focus is most closely associated with the name of

Herbert Simon, although it has now diversified into dozens of sub-approaches (Simon, 1947). The 'systems approach' enjoys many well-known advocates, but none quite so pre-eminent. Both perspectives share a concentration on goal-directed activity (Bourn, 1974). They are centrally concerned with the processes of objective setting, the review of alternative courses of action, the weighing and selection of these alternatives, the implementation of choices once made and the feedback (or lack of it) the decision makers receive about the consequences of the strategies which have been implemented. The decision-making approach concentrates more on the detailed cognitive and emotional processes at the individual and small-group levels, whereas the systems approach typically operates at the level of the organization as a whole, its major inputs and outputs, and the nature of the wider environment in which it is set. Neither approach denies the importance of the formal structures and behavioural processes which interested the Taylorists, nor do they ignore the social processes which were highlighted by the human relations school. Rather they incorporate and modify these insights, claiming to provide a more dynamic (action-oriented) synthesis.

For our purposes the nature of these modifications is of particular significance. Instead of searching for a timeless 'one best way' of structuring any organization, the decisions and systems perspective attempts to relate structures to organizational objectives, to the nature of the organizational environment (stable, unstable, highly competitive, oligopolistic etc.) and to the particular productive technologies employed within the organization. Thus, instead of arriving at a set of fixed 'administrative proverbs', as the classical school/Taylorists tended to do, decisions and systems writers were likely to adopt a much more relativistic stance. They say, in effect, 'If your objectives are so-and-so, and the environment you face is like this, and the technology you use is of type x, *then* you should design your organization as follows'. Because of this, one sub-school of the systems approach (which became particularly prominent in academic circles during the 1970s) is known as 'contingency theory', reflecting the idea that the optimal internal structure for an organization will be determined by the 'setting' of key environmental contingencies (Clark, 1975; Pugh and Hickson, 1976).

Nevertheless, some broad features of the classical school are still discernible. The decisions and systems paradigm is usually assumed to be universal in its applicability. All organizations are systems, with inputs, outputs etc. All set goals and then need to shape decision processes to serve those goals. Figure 1, or something similar, has appeared in dozens, probably hundreds of publications, some aimed at corporate executives, some at chemical plant managers, some at local government managers, some at hospital administrators and so on.

The second common feature with the classical school is a seeming

ENVIRONMENT   THE ORGANIZATION   ENVIRONMENT

Technical sub-system

Inputs
(resources,
demands etc.)

Psycho-social sub-system

Outputs
(decisions,
products,
services)

Structural sub-system
(the formal organization)

feedback

Figure 1 Typical systems diagram

distaste for any analysis of politics and power struggles. Systems and decisions can, it is usually assumed, be discussed in a detached, rational, scientific manner. Values, of course, have their place, but they enter the analysis preformed, from 'outside'. Once there, they can be slotted into the decision calculus, but – with a few honourable exceptions, including Simon himself – most writers in this genre do not spend much time discussing the origins, formation or substance of the values which provide fuel for the whole decision process. Furthermore, 'systems theorists, whether functionalist or not, have . . . failed to provide a theoretically satisfactory framework for the satisfactory analysis of power relations' (Martin, 1977, p. 19). Clearly, therefore, if one regards the institutions of the welfare state as being imbued with a distinctive set of social and political values, values which are crucial to their modes of operation, then the decisions and systems corpus may be limited in its explanatory and diagnostic strengths.

Decisions and systems ideas, like scientific management, extensively penetrated government and the public sector, as well as the world of business and commerce. Like Taylorism, however, they influenced some parts of the public sector more than others. Their presence was probably most noticeable in the training of general administrators, especially in central government/federal departments, and in the general administrative, planning and policy formulation units of state, local and city government. The language of systems – 'feedback', 'inputs', 'environment', 'interface' etc. – was widely learned and used, even where the impact of these concepts went little beyond rhetoric. In some areas, however, the influence of 'decisions and systems' went considerably further. [An important example was] the introduction of planning, programming and budgeting systems (PPBS) in the federal government (from the early 1960s) and, later and on a smaller scale, in Whitehall (for brief summaries, see Patten and Pollitt, 1980; and Wildavsky, 1979, pp. 32–4). When British central government was restructured by Edward Heath's incoming government in 1970 the white paper *The Reorganization of Central Government* was redolent of this brand of thought. Its first aim was:

> To improve the quality of policy formulation and decision-taking in government by presenting ministers, collectively in cabinet and individually within their departments, with well-defined options, costed where possible, and relating the choice between options to the contribution they can make to meeting national needs. (Cmnd 4506; for a detailed discussion see Pollitt, 1984, pp. 82–106)

[. . .] Elaborate planning systems and data requirements were installed at the top of government but they made little change to the operating agencies and, it soon appeared, were not necessarily regarded as terribly interesting even by the ministers in whose departments they had been installed. In local government, too, new management systems were more likely to be found in the departments of the new (post-1972) chief executives than in social services or education. [. . .] The limited penetration of the operating arms of the welfare state by decisions and systems ideas seems to have been connected to both limitations in the ideas themselves and resistance (actual or anticipated) from the professional service deliverers. Doctors, teachers and social workers had their own practices, and their own professional cultures. The prospect of 'outsiders' refining *their* goals, streamlining *their* professional decision procedures and inspecting *their* 'feedback' was not an overwhelmingly attractive one.

If, however, specific borrowings could be made from this body of thought, and those borrowings could be kept under the control of the profession concerned, then that would be a different matter. Thus decision theory techniques have begun to be employed to assist doctors with problems in medical diagnosis. In other professions, too, the spread of computer-based 'expert systems' is widely predicted (for a survey of the techniques and their implications, see Dowie and Elstein, 1988).

From the beginning of the 1970s the decisions and systems perspective came under heavy attack. Criticisms centred on 'the incapacity of the dominant systems paradigm to deal with the inherent complexity of social action and the intellectual paralysis which this had produced within the field' (Reed, 1988, p. 36). An alternative 'social action' perspective was advanced which espoused a voluntaristic epistemology, emphasized the importance and legitimacy of differing perceptions of organizational 'realities' and rested 'on a moral philosophy which asserts the primacy of individual ethical choice over the normative imperatives entailed in institutions' (Reed, 1988, p. 37; for an influential early example see Silverman, 1970). Subsequently a more overtly 'political' critique directly attacked these normative imperatives by attempting to show that, far from being 'necessary' or unavoidable, they constituted a central element in a process of systematic domination by particular social groups (Burrell and Morgan, 1979). These methodological and ideological criticisms effectively dethroned the systems and decisions perspective (at least within the academic world) but they largely failed to provide a coherent new orthodoxy. Since the mid 1970s the field of organizational studies has been particularly kaleidoscopic – and therefore extremely hard to characterize in a brief summary such as this. Reed describes the situation as one in which there was a 'melee of competing theoretical perspectives that jockeyed for intellectual "poll position"' (1988, p. 40).

There has, however, been one special recent trend which merits particular mention. This – my sixth and final key development in management thought – emerged during the 1970s, and became very fashionable in the 1980s. I am going to call it 'culture management', because it borrowed the concept of 'culture' from anthropology and sociology and attempted to make it central to the study of organizations. Just as the human relations school had reacted against the mechanistic model of the individual deployed by the Taylorists, so the culture management advocates believed that most decision-theoretic and systems analyses neglected the importance of symbolism and ritual in organizational life (see, e.g., March and Olsen, 1984; Meyer and Rowan, 1977; Pettigrew, 1985; Westerlund and Sjostrand, 1979). They aired this view in both academic journals such as *Dragon*, and in more popular formats such as *In Search of Excellence* (Peters and Waterman, 1982). A comprehensive and widely read text which integrated cultural aspects with other salient issues in management thought was Charles Handy's *Understanding Organizations* (1976).

There are almost as many alternative definitions of 'culture' as of 'ideology' (indeed the two concepts are often used in overlapping ways). One useful and influential one was that offered by Donald Schon, who said that culture was the theoretical dimension of an organization which met the need for the 'inhabitants' of the organization to gain 'a view of itself, its role within some large system, the nature of its environment, its own operation and the norms which govern its behaviour' (Schon, 1971). Handy, similarly, refers to 'sets of values and norms and beliefs', and points out that, far from there being 'one best culture', cultures may legitimately vary both between and within organizations (Handy, 1976, p. 176). Peters and Waterman tended to be more prescriptive. They argued that the successful companies they studied were 'value-driven' – that their staffs were motivated by carefully maintained cultures of excellence. The task of shaping the organizational culture was seen as one for senior management. 'Even management's job becomes more fun. Instead of brain games in the sterile ivory tower, it's shaping values and reinforcing through coaching and evangelism in the field – with the worker and in support of the cherished product' (Peters and Waterman, 1982, p. xxv).

Subsequently this cry was taken up in the public-sector context, and writers in the field of public management began to argue that one of the tasks of top public officials was to change the old culture of advice and regulation in favour of a much more responsive and proactive style. Thus Metcalfe and Richards claimed that: 'The values round which public management cultures should develop include learning, experimentation, adaptability and flexibility. The need for these values arises from the rate of change with which governments will have to cope in future' (Metcalfe and Richards, 1987, p. 85).

One problem with this approach is the generality of its key concepts. It is hard to derive very specific prescriptions for action from something as vague and elusive as 'culture'. Yet despite this vagueness the emphasis on culture also has its sinister side. For in crude or unscrupulous hands it is not hard to see how this line of thinking could be used to suppress dissent and harass staff who did not appear to have 'appropriate attitudes'. In the 'culture' movement one can see how Taylor's original attempt at direct, stick-and-carrot control of the workforce has long since given way to a much more subtle and indirect approach. Managers now work to create the right 'climate', to encourage identification with corporate goals, high motivation, internalization of 'constructive attitudes'. Those who can comply with these blandishments may be granted not simply higher pay but also discretion, status and other privileges (Salaman, 1981, pp. 172–4). Ultimately they may even cease to *see* contradictions or injustices within their employing organizations, to become what in political science terms might be termed the willing victims of the 'third dimension' of managerial power (Lukes, 1974).

Subtle managerial manipulations of organizational cultures may thus become a focus for growing concern. As yet, however, it is not clear that management possesses either the kinds of reliable theories or the kinds of inducements that would allow them to remould a given culture 'to order'. [. . .] Such attempts as have been recently mounted in British and American public services have been either crude or contradictory or largely ineffective or some combination of all three. Part of the difficulty lies in the oft-made assumptions that management somehow 'owns' an organization's culture, and that the culture can be spread homogeneously throughout the various vertical and horizontal sub-divisions of the department or agency in question (Lynn Meek, 1988). Such assumptions are contradicted by much empirical work which, by contrast, reveals that large organizations are usually honeycombed with different and contrasting cultures, many of which are deeply embedded in the belief systems of the staff concerned and are unlikely to be substantially altered by short-term management campaigns to promote a new 'image'. In sum, the cultural perspective can be of considerable value as a complement to more instrumental, goal- or decision-oriented approaches. It reminds managers (and academics) of the general importance of the symbolic dimension of organizational life, but it may never be able to furnish a practical 'toolkit' for producing new, 'management-designed' cultures on demand. Even if it could, there would remain a whole set of further questions concerning the nature of the links between belief systems and actual behaviours. Many studies have shown that staff are often involved in actions which do not appear to 'fit' their ostensible values and preferences. The links between culture and action are not straightforward.

Finally, I want to draw attention to a recently emerging analysis which sets distinct limits to the practical usefulness which managers may hope to derive from *any* general theory of management. Whitley notes that 'the goal of an integrated, coherent and practical "science of managing" seems, if anything, further away than it did in the 1950s' (1988, p. 48). This apparent failure he attributes to the fact that: 'managerial skills differ considerably from other sorts of expertise in their limited standardization across industries, their susceptibility to change, their specificity to situations rather than problems and their diffuse, varied knowledge base' (Whitley, 1989a).

[. . .] To the extent that we find the same, generic model of management being applied across a variety of non-standardized situa-tions and tasks within the public services it will be appropriate to enquire how 'appropriate' or 'realistic' this appears to be to the 'locals' who actually run these services. Note that Whitley is *not* taking the extreme position that there are no common factors; rather he is arguing that these are of limited provenance, and that effective management will require a lot of local and particular knowledge besides:

> there are general and political skills which are common to all managerial jobs insofar as these involve working with people, and indeed are probably required for all those jobs where tasks are interdependent. However, where judgement and discretion are involved in complex tasks which are highly context-dependent, skills are much more specific to particular situations and

organizational fields. Here industry knowledge and personal networks are often crucial to effective management and skills are often not readily transferable. (Whitley, 1989b)

[. . .]

Summary

Even in such a compressed history as this it is plain that management thought has bequeathed to the modern manager a rich and varied armoury of theories, concepts and techniques. Various tensions are visible – for example between the desire for a hard-edged 'science' and the fascination with evidence of idiosyncratic leadership, the strength of informal processes or the existence of exotic organizational symbolism. Yet behind all these variations lies the broader, unifying set of [. . .] assumptions concerning the growing social importance of management and the special roles and responsibilities of managers. There may also be corresponding assumptions, often hidden, to the effect that other forms of social co-ordination and integration, such as political activity, voluntary co-operation or friendship, are less efficient and probably of relatively diminishing social significance.

Though most of the major developments in management thought had their origins in the private sector (Taylorism, the Hawthorne experiments, PPBS, culture management), many of them also left their mark in the public sphere. Yet this was not a uniform influence. It was more noticeable in those parts of public sector organizations dominated by general administrative or clerical work, and in 'industrial' type areas such as nationalized industries or local authority direct labour forces. The specialist, professionalized welfare services were among the least affected. But from the mid 1970s, in both the US and the UK, this began to change. By the mid 1980s these same services were at the focus of a major movement for management change. The driving force behind this movement was a generic model of management, that is to say one which minimized the difference between private-sector business management and the running of public services. What is more [. . .] the particular species of genericism which was dominant tended to be of a neo-Taylorian character.

References

Argyris, C. 1960: *Understanding Organizational Behaviour*. London: Tavistock.
Bourn, J. B. 1974: 'The administrative process as a decision-making and goal attaining system'. Block 2, Part 2 of *D331 Public Administration*, Milton Keynes, Open University Press.

Burrell, G. and Morgan, G. 1979: *Sociological Paradigms and Organizational Analysis*. London: Heinemann.

Child, J. 1969: *British Management Thought*. London: Allen & Unwin.

Clark, P. A. 1975: 'Organizational design: a review of key problems'. *Administration and Society*, 17 (2), August, 213–56.

Cmnd 9230 1918: *Report of the Machinery of Government Committee* (the Haldane Committee). London: HMSO.

Cmnd 4506 1970: *The Reorganization of Central Government*. London: HMSO.

Dowie, J. and Elstein, A. 1988: *Professional Judgement: A reader in clinical decision making*. New York: Cambridge University Press.

Dunsire, A. 1973: *Administration: The word and the science*. Oxford: Martin Robertson.

Handy, C. B. (1976), *Understanding Organizations*, Harmondsworth: Penguin Books.

Heseltine, M. 1987: *Where There's a Will*. London: Hutchinson.

Lukes, S. 1974: *Power: A radical view*. London: Macmillan.

Lynn Meek, V. 1988: 'Organizational culture: origins and weaknesses'. *Organization Studies*, 9 (4), 453–73.

March, J. G and Olsen, J. P. 1984: 'The new institutionalism: organizational factors in political life'. *American Political Science Review*, 78, 734–49.

Martin, R. 1977: *The sociology of power*. London: Routledge & Kegan Paul.

Mayo, Elton, 1933: *The Human Problems of an Industrial Civilization*. New York: Macmillan.

Merkle, J. 1980: *Management and Ideology: The legacy of the international scientific management movement*. Berkeley: University of California Press.

Metcalfe, L. and Richards, S. 1987: 'Evolving public management cultures' 65–86. In J. Kooiman and K. A. Eliassen (eds.), *Managing Public Organizations: Lessons from contemporary European experience*, London: Sage.

Meyer, J. W. and Rowan, B. 1977: 'Institutionalized organizations: formal structure as myth and ceremony'. *American Journal of Sociology*, 83, 340–64.

Nichols, T. 1980: 'Management, ideology and practice', 279–302. In G. Esland and G. Salaman (eds.), *The Politics of Work and Occupations*, Milton Keynes: Open University Press.

Patten, J. and Pollitt, C. 1980: 'Power and rationality: theories of policy formulation'. Paper 8, Block 2, *D336 Policies, People and Administration*, Milton Keynes: Open University Press.

Perrow, C. 1979: *Complex Organizations: A critical essay*, 2nd edn., London: Scott, Foresman and Co.

Peters, J. and Waterman, R. H. 1982: *In Search of Excellence: Lessons from America's best-run companies*. New York: Harper and Row.

Pettigrew, A. 1985: *The Awakening Giant: Continuity and change in ICI*. Oxford: Blackwell.

Pollitt, C. 1984: *Manipulating the Machine: Changing the pattern of ministerial departments, 1960–83*. London: Allen & Unwin.

Pugh, D. S. and Hickson, D. J. 1976: *Organization Structure and its Context: The Aston programme*. Farnborough: Saxon House.

Reed, M. I. 1988: 'The problem of human agency in organizational analysis'. *Organisation Studies*, 9 (1), 33–46.

Roethlisberger, F. J. and Dickson, W. J. 1969: 'On organizational goals', 51–62. In J. A. Litterer (ed.), *Organizations*, 2nd edn., Vol. 1, New York: Wiley.

Salaman, G. 1981: *Class and the Corporation*. Glasgow: Fontana.

Sayles, L. R. 1958: *Behaviour of Industrial Work Groups*. New York: Wiley.

Schliesl, M. 1977: *The Politics of Efficiency*. Berkeley: University of California Press.

Schon, D. A. 1971: *Beyond the Stable State*. New York: Norton

Silverman, D. 1970: *The Theory of Organizations*. London: Heinemann.

Simon, H. A. 1947: *Administrative Behaviour: A study of decision-making processes in adminstrative organization*. New York: Macmillan.

Taylor, F. W. 1911: *The Principles of Scientific Management*. New York: Harper & Brothers.

Thomas, R. 1978: *The British Philosophy of Administration: A comparison of British and American ideas, 1900–1939*, London/New York, Longman.

Westerlund, G. and Sjostrand, S.-E. 1979: *Organizational Myths*. London: Harper & Row.

Whitley, R. 1988: 'The management sciences and managerial skills'. *Organizational Studies*, 9 (1), 47–68.

Whitley, R. 1989a: 'On the nature of managerial tasks: their distinguishing characteristics and organisation'. *Journal of Management Studies*, May.

Whitley, R. 1989b: personal communication with the author, 22 March.

Wildavsky, A. 1979: *Speaking Truth to Power: The art and craft of policy analysis*. Boston: Little, Brown.

Wilson, W. (1887): 'The study of administration'. *Political Science Quarterly*, 2, 197–222.

Organizational models of social program implementation

Richard E. Elmore

Concern about the implementation of social programs stems from the recognition that policies cannot be understood in isolation from the means of their execution. A large collection of carefully documented case studies—in education, manpower, housing, and economic development—points consistently to the same basic pattern: grand pretensions, faulty execution, puny results.[1] A reasonably broad consensus has developed among analysts of social policy that the inability of government to deliver on its promises derives only in part from the fact that policies are poorly conceived. In some instances, policies are based on poor and incomplete understandings of the problems they are supposed to address. But in the largest number of cases it is impossible to say whether policies fail because they are based on bad ideas or because they are good ideas poorly executed.[2] Increasingly, policy analysts have begun to focus on the process by which policies are translated into administrative action. Since virtually all public policies are implemented by large public organizations, knowledge of organizations has become a critical component of policy analysis. We cannot say with much certainty what a policy is, or why it is not implemented, without knowing a great deal about how organizations function. [. . .] The translation of an idea into action involves certain crucial simplifications. Organizations are simplifiers; they work on problems by breaking them into discrete, manageable tasks and allocating responsibility for those tasks to specialized units. Only by understanding how organizations work can we understand how policies are shaped in the process of implementation.

From R. Elmore, 'Organizational models of social program implementation', *Public Policy*, **26**, 1978, pp. 185–228.

The utility of organizational models

If knowledge of organizations is central to the analysis of implementation, then how do we go about putting that knowledge into a form useful for analysis? The single most important feature of organizational theory is its conceptual anarchy. When we look to the literature on organizations for guidance in the analysis of an important practical problem, such as implementation, we find a collection of conflicting and contradictory theories. This diversity of theories is a sure sign that knowledge in the field is "soft." This is not to say that it should be, or ever will be, "hard," but only that it is extremely difficult to use knowledge of this sort as the basis for analysis. Richard Nelson captured this difficulty nicely in his discussion of the intellectual underpinnings of policy analysis. "The problem of making sensible organizational changes," he argues, "is beyond the present capacity of the various organizational analysis traditions." He adds,

> [We] presently lack [a] . . . normative intellectual structure capable of guiding us effectively regarding organizational choice or modification. . . . [We] lack even a language that will enable us to list, and talk about, the organizational alternatives in a helpful manner.[3]

So on this point we're stuck. Having established that analysis of the implementation problem requires knowledge of organizations, we find that there is no single, coherent body of organizational theory that will serve as the basis for analysis. There are two ways of coping with this impasse. One is to make an heroic attempt to synthesize all organizational theory into a tidy set of analytical precepts useful in the analysis of implementation. The other is to acquiesce in the present diversity of thought about organizations and try to distill from that diversity a finite number of distinguishable models that can be used to analyze the implementation problem. I've chosen the latter strategy, largely because I believe the former to be impossible. This approach does not speak to Nelson's plea for an "effective normative intellectual structure," since it doesn't result in a single set of prescriptions about how implementation should be organized, but it does speak to his plea for a language that supports the discussion of organizational alternatives.

Those familiar with Graham Allison's study of the Cuban missile crisis[4] will recognize that I have cribbed the idea of alternative organizational models directly from him. His was the initial insight, and his is the credit for demonstrating its analytical utility. Readers of Allison will notice, however, that I depart considerably from his treatment. In most instances the differences are attributable to the nature of the subject matter; defense strategy, not surprisingly, raises a set of problems considerably different from the implementation of social programs. Suffice it to say that Allison is not responsible for the use that others make of his ideas.

Viewing the implementation process through a number of different organizational models allows us to be specific about the organizational assumptions we make when we offer prescriptions for improving implementation. Different models, we will see, lead to quite different perceptions and conclusions. "What we see and judge to be important," Allison argues, ". . . depends not only on the evidence but also on the 'conceptual lenses' through which we look at the evidence."[5] Neither policy analysts nor administrators have been particularly careful about specifying the organizational assumptions that shape their recommendations and actions. Analysts, by and large, have found organizational problems either uninteresting or insufficiently precise. Administrators have a direct stake in organizational problems, but can seldom indulge in the luxury of an extended analysis of organizational alternatives. The consequence of this failure to address organizational issues has been an embarrassingly large gap between the analyst's recommendations and the solutions implemented by administrators.[6] Forcing analysts and administrators to think systematically about organizational alternatives might ultimately drive policy-making in the direction of feasible, or implementable, policies.

Some models are basically normative—they're based on strongly held opinions about how organizations ought to operate. Some models are descriptive—they attempt to capture the essential objective attributes of organizations. In some instances it's difficult to distinguish normative from descriptive elements. But in all instances the model is a simplification of reality, not a surrogate for it.[7] No single model adequately captures the full complexity of the implementation process.

I will develop four organizational models representing the major schools of thought that can be brought to bear on the implementation problem. The *systems management model* captures the organizational assumptions of the mainstream, rationalist tradition of policy analysis. Its point of departure is the assumption of value-maximizing behavior. The *bureaucratic process model* represents the sociological view of organizations, updated to include recent research by students of "street-level bureaucracy" that bears directly on the analysis of social program implementation. Its point of departure is the assumption that the essential feature of organizations is the interaction between routine and discretion. The *organizational development model* represents a relatively recent combination of sociological and psychological theory that focuses on the conflict between the needs of individuals and the demands of organizational life. Finally, the *conflict and bargaining model* addresses the problem of how people with divergent interests coalesce around a common task. It starts from the assumption that conflict, arising out of the pursuit of relative advantage in a bargaining relationship, is the dominant feature of organizational life.

The most important aspect of these models, however, is not that they represent certain established traditions of academic inquiry. As we shall see, their major appeal is that each contains a commonsense explanation for implementation failures. And each explanation emphasizes different features of the implementation process.

The format of the discussion will be the same for each model. I will first present a list of four propositions that capture the essential features of each model. The first proposition states the central principle of the model; the second states the model's view of the distribution of power in organizations; the third states the model's view of organizational decision-making; and the fourth gives a thumbnail sketch of the implementation process from the perspective of the model. I will then discuss how these assumptions affect the analyst's perception of the implementation process. In Allison's words, I will develop "a dominant inference pattern" that serves to explain why certain features of the implementation process are more important than others and to predict the consequences of certain administrative actions for the success or failure of implementation efforts. Finally, I will draw some examples from the current case literature on social program implementation that demonstrate the strengths and weaknesses of each model.

Some readers will no doubt chafe at the idea that highly complex bodies of thought about organizations can be reduced to a few simple propositions. My defense is that this is an exercise in the *application* of theory, not an exercise in theory building. The premium is on capturing the insights that each model brings to the problem, not on making the theory more elegant or defensible. I have tried mightily to avoid creating straw men. Each model is offered as a legitimate analytical perspective.

Model I: Implementation as systems management

Propositions:

1. Organizations should operate as rational value maximizers. The essential attribute of rationality is goal-directed behavior; organizations are effective to the extent that they maximize performance on their central goals and objectives. Each task that an organization performs must contribute to at least one of a set of well-defined objectives that accurately reflect the organization's purpose.

2. Organizations should be structured on the principle of hierarchical control. Responsibility for policy-making and overall system performance rests with top management, which in turn allocates specific tasks and performance objectives to subordinate units and monitors their performance.
3. For every task an organization performs there is some optimal allocation of responsibilities among subunits that maximizes the organization's overall performance on its objectives. Decision-making in organizations consists of finding this optimum and maintaining it by continually adjusting the internal allocation of responsibilities to changes in the environment.
4. Implementation consists of defining a detailed set of objectives that accurately reflect the intent of a given policy, assigning responsibilities and standards of performance to subunits consistent with these objectives, monitoring system performance, and making internal adjustments that enhance the attainment of the organization's goals. The process is dynamic, not static; the environment continually imposes new demands that require internal adjustments. But implementation is always goal-directed and value-maximizing.

A frequent explanation for failures of implementation is "bad management." We generally mean by this that policies are poorly defined, responsibilities are not clearly assigned, expected outcomes are not specified, and people are not held accountable for their performance. Good management, of course, is the opposite of all these things, and therein lies the crux of the systems management model. The model starts from the normative assumption that effective management proceeds from goal-directed, value-maximizing behavior. Organizations are thought of as problem-solving "systems"—functionally integrated collections of parts that are capable of concerted action around a common purpose.[8]

Integration presupposes the existence of a controlling and coordinating authority. In the systems management model, this authority is called the "management subsystem" — "the source of binding pronouncements and the locus of the decisionmaking process."[9] It provides "a means of insuring role performance, replacing lost members, coordinating the several subsystems of the organization, responding to external changes and making decisions about how all these things should be accomplished."[10] Hierarchical control is the single most important element insuring that organizations behave as systems.

The translation of policy into action consists of a deliberate, stepwise process in which goals are elaborated into specific tasks. Robert Anthony's discussion of planning and management control gives a succinct statement of the transition from policy to operations:

Strategic planning is the process of deciding on objectives, on resources used to obtain these objectives, and on the policies that are to govern acquisition, use and disposition of these resources. . . . Management control is the process by which managers assure that resources are obtained and used effectively and efficiently in the accomplishment of the organization's objectives . . . [and] operational control is the process of assuring that specific tasks are carried out effectively and efficiently.[11]

These functions are distributed in descending order from the highest to lowest levels of the organization. Taken together, they describe a general set of decision rules for the optimal allocation of resources, tasks, and performance criteria among subunits of an organization.

For all its emphasis on hierarchical control, one would expect that the systems management model would make little or no allowance for the exercise of lower-level discretion by subordinates carrying out policy directives. In fact, this is not quite the case. The problem of subordinate discretion figures prominently in the literature of systems management. Understandably, the issue arose in a very visible way during the initial attempts to apply systems analysis to national defense planning. Defense planners found almost immediately that the ability of the management subsystem to control the performance of subunits was limited by the enormous complexity of the total system. Hence, a great deal hinged on discovering the correct mix of hierarchical control and subordinate discretion. Hitch and McKean call this process "sub-optimization," which they define as an "attempt to find optimal (or near optimal) solutions, but to sub-problems rather than to a whole problem of the organization in whose welfare or utility we are interested."[12] In organizational terms, suboptimization consists of holding subunits responsible for a certain level of output but giving subunit managers the discretion to decide on the means of achieving that level. In business parlance, these subunits are called "profit centers," in the public sector they have been called "responsibility centers." Suboptimization provides a means of exercising hierarchical control by focusing on the output of subunits rather than on their technically complex internal operations.

In practice, suboptimization raises some very complex problems— selecting appropriate criteria of subunit performance, accounting for the unintended consequences, or spillovers, of one unit's performance on another's, and choosing the appropriate aggregation of functions for each subunit.[13] But the notion of suboptimization gives the systems management model a degree of flexibility that is not often appreciated by its critics. It is *not* necessary to assume that all organizational decisions are centralized in order to assume that organizations are functionally integrated. If the outputs of delegated decisions are consistent with the overall goals of the organization, then there is room for a certain degree of latitude in the selection of means for achieving those outputs.

A great deal of behavior in organizations can be explained by examining devices of control and compliance. Some are easy to identify, some blend into the subtle social fabric of organizations. One common device is what Herbert Kaufman calls the "preformed decision." He argues that "organizations might disintegrate if each field officer made entirely independent decisions," so organizations develop ways of making decisions for their field officers "in advance of specific situations requiring choice":

> . . . [Events] and conditions in the field are anticipated as fully as possible, and courses of action [for each set of events and conditions] are described. The field officer then need determine only into what category a particular instance falls; once this determination is made, he then simply follows a series of steps applicable to that category. Within each category, therefore, the decisions are "preformed."[14]

Much of the work of high-level administrators in the implementation process consists of anticipating recurrent problems at lower levels of the system and attempting to program the behavior of subordinates to respond to these problems in standardized ways.

But not all devices of control are so obvious. In a casual aside, Robert Anthony remarks that "the system [of management controls] should be so constructed that actions that operating managers take in their perceived self-interest are also in the best interests of the whole organization."[15] An important ingredient of control, then, is to be found in the way people are socialized to organizations. Social psychologists Katz and Kahn observe that all organizations have "maintenance subsystems" for recruitment, indoctrination, socialization, reward, and sanction that "function to maintain the fabric of interdependent behavior necessary for task accomplishment."[16] [. . .] Organizations often require people to put the requirements of their formal roles above their personal preferences. The effect is to enhance the predictability and control of subordinate behavior in much the same way as preformed decisions and suboptimization. The difference is that instead of shaping decisions, it is the decision-*makers* who are shaped.

The major appeal of the systems management model is that it can be readily translated into a set of normative prescriptions that policy analysts can use to say how the implementation process ought to work. From the model's perspective, effective implementation requires four main ingredients: (1) clearly specified tasks and objectives that accurately reflect the intent of policy: (2) a management plan that allocates task and performance standards to subunits; (3) an objective means of measuring subunit performance; and (4) a system of management controls and social sanctions sufficient to hold subordinates accountable for their performance. Failures of implementation are, by definition, lapses of planning, specification, and control. The analysis of implementation consists of finding, or anticipating, these breakdowns and suggesting how they ought to be remedied.

Analysis is made a good deal easier in this model by virtue of the fact that organizations are assumed to operate as units; a single conception of policy governs all levels of an organization. Success or failure of the organization is judged by observing the discrepancy between the policy declaration and subordinate behavior. The analyst focuses on the "clarity, precision, comprehensiveness, and reasonableness of the preliminary policy," on "the technical capacity to implement," and on "the extent to which the actual outputs of the organization have changed in the expected direction after the introduction of the innovation."[17] But in order for this conception of analysis to make any sense in organizational terms, one must first assume that policy-makers, administrators, and analysts have a common understanding of policy and have sufficient control of the implementation process to hold subordinates accountable to that understanding.

A great deal would seem to depend, then, on whether organizations can actually be structured on the assumptions of the systems management model. The empirical evidence is suggestive, but hardly conclusive. Herbert Kaufman, who has made a career of studying administrative compliance and control, concludes his classic study of the U.S. Forest Service with the observation that "overall performance comes remarkably close to the goals set by the leadership."[18] This was accomplished using a set of management controls and social sanctions that closely approximate the systems management model. The net result is that "the Rangers want to do the very things that the Forest Service wants them to do, and are able to do them, because these are the decisions and actions that become second nature to them as a result of years of obedience."[19] [. . .]

The distinctive feature of [this case] is strong management control in the presence of wide geographical dispersion, which suggests that large organizations can approximate the ideal of value-maximizing units. But [. . .] in the existing literature [on implementation] there are no examples that come close to approximating the ideal. One explanation for this is that the literature records only failures. Another is that social programs are characterized by chronically bad management. If we could find successful examples of implementation, one could argue, they would manifest all the essential attributes of the systems management model. This is an empirical question that requires more evidence than we presently have.

But there are at least two other explanations for the lack of systems management examples in the implementation literature, and both point to weaknesses in the model. The first is that the model completely disregards a basic element common to all cases of social program implementation: federalism. Regardless of how well organized an agency might be, its ability to implement programs successfully depends, to some degree, on its ability to influence agencies at other levels of government. [. . .] Where more than one agency is involved in the implementation process, the lines of authority are [. . .] blurred. It is not uncommon for implementors of social policy to be responsible to more than one political jurisdiction—to the federal government for a general declaration of policy and certain specific guidelines, and to a state or local unit for myriad administrative details. These jurisdictional boundaries are a permanent fixture of the American federal system; they exist not to enhance the efficiency of implementation but to protect the political prerogatives of state and local government. [. . .] The systems management model [. . .] fails to account for the weakness of management control across jurisdictional boundaries.

The second possible explanation for the lack of systems management examples in the literature on social program implementation is perhaps that the model is not intended to describe reality. Recall that all propositions on which the model is based are normative; they describe how organizations *ought* to function, not necessarily how they actually do. The distinction is not as disingenuous as it sounds. We frequently rely on normative models to help us evaluate performance, diagnose failure, and propose remedies, even though we understand perfectly well that they have very little descriptive validity. We do so because they provide useful ways of organizing and simplifying complex problems. In this sense, the test of a model is not whether it accurately represents reality, but whether it has some utility as a problem-solving device. The major utility of the systems management model is that it directs our attention toward the mechanisms that policy-makers and high-level administrators have for structuring and controlling the behavior of subordinates.

It is dangerous, however, to focus on the normative utility of the model to the exclusion of its descriptive validity. To say that the model simplifies in useful ways is not the same thing as saying that the implementation process should be structured around the model. This is a mistake that policy analysts are particularly prone to make, and it involves a peculiar and obvious circularity. If the fit between model and reality is poor, the argument goes, then the model should be used to restructure reality. Only then, the analyst concludes triumphantly, can it be determined whether the model "works" or not. A special form of this argument claims that social programs fail because policies are poorly specified and management control is weak. To the extent that we remedy these problems we can predict a higher ratio of successes to failures. The problem with this argument is that the definition of success is internal to the model, and it may or may not be shared by people who are actually part of the process. The systems management model will almost certainly "work" if everyone behaves according to its dictates. If we could make value maximizers of all organizations, then we could no doubt prove that all organizations are value maximizers. But the point is that participants in the implementation process don't necessarily share the norms of the model. And it is this fact that leads us to search for alternative models.

Model II: Implementation as bureaucratic process

Propositions:

1. The two central attributes of organizations are discretion and routine; all important behavior in organizations can be explained by the irreducible discretion exercised by individual workers in their day-to-day decisions and the operating routines that they develop to maintain and enhance their position in the organization.
2. The dominance of discretion and routine means that power in organizations tends to be fragmented and dispersed among small units exercising relatively strong control over specific tasks within their sphere of authority. The amount of control that any one organizational unit can exert over another—laterally or hierarchical-ly—is hedged by the fact that, as organizations become increasingly complex, units become more highly specialized and exercise greater control over their internal operations.
3. Decision-making consists of controlling discretion and changing routine. All proposals for change are judged by organizational units in terms of the degree to which they depart from established patterns; hence, organizational decisions tend to be incremental.
4. Implementation consists of identifying where discretion is concen-trated and which of an organization's repertoire of routines need changing, devising alternative routines that represent the intent of policy, and inducing organizational units to replace old routines with new ones.

We reach instinctively for bureaucratic explanations of implementa-tion failures. "There was a major change in policy," we say, "but the bureaucracy kept right on doing what it did before." Or alternatively, "When the bureaucracy got through with it, the policy didn't look anything like what we intended." Bureaucracy was not always a pejorative term; for Max Weber, it was a form of organization that substituted impersonal, efficient, and routinized authority for that based on personal privilege or divine inspiration. Lately, though, bureaucracy has become an all-purpose explanation for everything that is wrong with government. We use terms like "the bureaucracy problem"[20] and "the bureaucratic phenomenon"[21] to describe behavior of public officials that is "inefficient, unresponsive, unfair, ponderous, or confusing."[22]

When we look behind these characterizations, the problems of implementing policies in bureaucratic settings can be traced to two basic elements: discretion and routine. As bureaucracies become larger and more complex, they concentrate specialized tasks in subunits. With specialization comes an irreducible discretion in day-to-day decision-making; the ability of any single authority to control all decisions becomes attenuated to the point where it ceases to be real in any practical sense. In the words of Graham Allison, factored problem-solving begets fractionated power.[23] With the growth of discretion also comes the growth of routine. Individuals and subunits manage the space created by discretion so as to maintain and enhance their position in the organization. They create operating routines in part to simplify their work but also to demonstrate their specialized skill in controlling and managing their assigned tasks. Individuals and subunits resist attempts to alter their discretion or to change their operating routines—in other words, they resist hierarchical management—because these things are a concrete expression of their special competence, knowledge, and status in the organization. The central focus of the bureaucracy problem, according to J.Q. Wilson, is "getting the front-line worker—the teacher, nurse, diplomat, police officer, or welfare worker—to do the right thing."[24] The job of administration is, purely and simply, "controlling discretion."[25]

The standard techniques of hierarchical management—budget and planning cycles, clearance procedures, reporting requirements, and evaluation systems—are the means by which high-level administrators attempt to structure the behavior of subordinates. To the front-line worker, though, these techniques are often incidental to the "real" work of the organization. The front-line worker's major concern is learning to cope with the immediate pressures of the job, and this requires inventing and learning a relatively complex set of work routines that go with one's specialized responsibility. This split between high-level administrators and front-line workers accounts for the quizzical, some-times skeptical, look one often gets from teachers, social workers, and other front-line workers when they're asked about the implementation of policy. "Policy?" they reply, "We're so busy getting the work done we haven't much time to think about policy."

The bureaucratic process model, then, traces the effect of lower-level discretion and routinized behavior on the execution of policy. The central analytical problem is to discover where discretion resides and how existing routines can be shaped to the purposes of policy. The major difference between systems management and bureaucratic process models is that the former assumes that the tools of management control can be used to program subordinate behavior, while the latter posits the existence of discretion and operating routines as means by which subordinates resist control. The systems management model assumes that the totality of an organization's resources can be directed at a single, coherent set of purposes—that organizations can be programmed to respond to changes in policy. The bureaucratic process model assumes that the dominant characteristic of organizations is resistance to change—not simply inertia (the tendency to move in one direction until deflected by some outside force), but as Donald Schon observes, "dynamic conservatism" (the tendency to fight to remain the same).[26] In the systems management model one assumes that, given the right set of management controls, subunits of an organization will do what they are told; in the bureaucratic process model, one assumes that they will continue to do what they have been doing until some way is found to make them do otherwise.

In the implementation of social programs, new policies must typically travel from one large public bureaucracy to another, and then through several successive layers of the implementing agency before they reach the point of impact on the client. Whether or not the policy has its intended effect on the client depends in large part on whether the force of existing routine at each level of the process operates with or against the policy.

It is frequently at the final stage of this process—the point of delivery from agency to client—that the forces of discretion and routine are most difficult to overcome. This problem is the central concern of students of "street-level bureaucracy." The growth of large public service agencies has created a distinguishable class of bureaucrat—one who shoulders virtually all responsibility for direct contact with clients, who exercises a relatively large degree of discretion over detailed decisions of client treatment, and who therefore has considerable potential impact on clients.[27] From the client's perspective, the street-level bureaucrat *is* the government. Clients seldom, if ever, interact with higher-level administrators; in fact, most public service bureaucracies are deliberately designed to prevent this. Because of the frequency and immediacy of the contact between street-level bureaucrats and their clients, it is usually impossible for higher-level administrators to monitor or control all aspects of their job performance. Consequently, a significant distance opens up between the street-level bureaucrat and his superiors. This distance breeds autonomy and discretion at lower levels of the organization. The distinctive quality of street-level bureaucracy is that "discretion increases as one moves down the hierarchy."[28]

But this concentration of discretion at lower levels has a paradoxical quality. For while street-level bureaucrats occupy the most critical position in the delivery process, their working conditions are seldom conducive to the adequate performance of their jobs. More often than not, they find themselves in situations where they lack the organizational and personal resources to perform their jobs adequately, where they are exposed regularly to physical or psychological threat, and where there are conflicting and ambiguous expectations about how they ought to perform their work.[29] Social service delivery jobs are among the most stressful in our society. Street-level bureaucrats are expected to treat clients as individuals, but the high demand for their services forces them to invent routines for mass processing. High-level administrators and policy-makers are preoccupied with the way policy is expressed in legislation, regulations, and guidelines. But the major concern for the street-level implementor is how to control the stress and complexity of day-to-day work. Out of this concern grows a whole set of informal routines that students of street-level bureaucracy call "coping mechanisms."

Learning to cope with the stresses of service delivery means learning to rely on simple, standardized sources of information to clients—case histories, employment records, permanent school records, test scores, eligibility forms, and the like. It means developing a facility for classifying and labeling people simply and quickly—"an alcoholic parent," "a broken family," "a history of drug abuse," "violence-prone and resistant to authority," "can't hold a job," and so on. It means developing one's "faculties of suspicion" in order to spot people who pose a threat either to oneself or to the system one is administering. And it means using the formal procedures of the organization to strike an impersonal distance between oneself, as an individual, and the client.[30] All these mechanisms have the effect of reducing and controlling the stress and uncertainty of daily work, and for this reason they figure prominently in the implementation of social policy. On the other hand, they are not typically included in the policy-maker's or the high-level administrator's definition of "policy." More often than not, they're either ignored or regarded as external to the implementation process.

Concentrating on formal declarations of policy at the expense of informal coping routines means that "even the most imaginative manipulations of goals, structure, staff recruitment, training and supervision may . . . represent only superficial changes . . . rather than the fundamental reforms hoped for."[31] From the perspective of the bureaucratic process model, major shifts in policy have little or no effect until they reach the final transaction between service giver and client. The elaborate superstructure of regulations, guidelines, and management controls that accompany most social programs tend to have weak and unpredictable effects on the delivery of social services because street-level bureaucrats and their clients develop strong patterns of interaction that are relatively immune to change. Implementation failures, from this point of view, are the result of a failure on the part of policy-makers to understand the actual conditions under which social services are delivered.

Empirical evidence demonstrating the effect of organizational routines on the implementation of social policy, while not extensive, is certainly compelling. Probably the first serious attempt to document the street-level effect of a major shift in policy was Miriam Johnson's study of how national manpower policy influenced the operation of local employment service offices in California.[32] The employment service is in some respects the archetypal social service delivery system. Initiated and largely funded by the federal government, it is totally administered by the states under broad guidelines from the federal level. The essential transactions of the employment service, however, occur at the street level, where employers and prospective employees are matched. Prior to the mid-sixties, the state employment services operated largely as labor exchanges; their purpose was simply to match the best person with the available job. During the mid-sixties, new federal manpower policies emphasized the services' responsibility to undertake remedial programs designed to get the poor and unskilled into the labor market. Then, in the early seventies, growing skepticism about the services' ability to help the disadvantaged resulted in a shift back to the original conception of the labor exchange. Johnson gives a client's-eye view of what it was like to deal with the employment service in each of these periods.

In the first phase—the labor exchange—the client's transaction with the employment service was dominated by the impersonal reception line and counter that separated client from bureaucrat. "There was no way for an applicant to bypass the line," she says, because only by waiting in line could the applicant get the required forms.

> The reception line led to the counter, which stood as a rampart, a boundary that defined the combat areas. It protected and defended the public agency from assault and harassment, from the public it served, from "they"—the enemy.[33]

When the California State Employment Service began to respond to the federal mandate to provide services for the disadvantaged, it did so by initiating small, experimental projects rather than attempting wholesale reform of the agency. The employment service workers who participated in these projects were given a great deal of latitude in designing them, and the first things they eliminated were the reception line and the counter. For Johnson, these actions were evidence that workers were just as oppressed by the routines of the old system as clients.[34] The counter was replaced by more informal, less structured interactions that often took the form of group counseling sessions. But these experimental projects "had no significant effect on the designers of new manpower programs and delivery systems."[35] The remainder of the employment service seemed largely unaffected by the experimental projects.

With the return to the labor exchange idea in the early seventies, employment service officers looked pretty much the same as they always had, but there was one interesting and seemingly minor difference in operating routines at the local level:

> There was still a counter . . . and there was still a receptionist. . . . [But] on the public side of the counter was something of value, . . . access to the jobs themselves. A Job Information Center was required in all . . . local offices by 1970. . . . The area was open to the public and it was not necessary to be registered for work in order to use the . . . Center. [It] was a self-screening operation in which the office supplied the referral information at the request of the applicant.[36]

It is ironic, after all the bombast and rhetoric of social action in the mid-sixties, that the net effect on the employment service should be something as simple as moving job information from one side of the counter to the other. But the example illustrates both the enormous resilience and the great importance of lower-level discretion and operating routines. Experimental projects had very little effect on the day-to-day operations of local offices, and the one change that did occur might easily have been overlooked by an analyst less sensitive to street-level operations.

Another important example of street-level response to high-level policy is the Weatherly and Lipsky analysis of the Massachusetts Comprehensive Special Education Law.[37] The law is a carefully conceived effort to put an end to arbitrary and discriminatory treatment of handicapped children by the public school system. Each local school district is required to provide an individualized evaluation of a child's needs by a team that includes teachers, specialists, and parents. The evaluation is to result in a plan for each child, outlining the services the school system will offer. If the school system cannot provide the services required, it must pay to have them provided elsewhere. To the extent possible, handicapped children must be included in regular classrooms.

And the traditional labels that had stigmatized children with special problems were to be eliminated.

During the first year of its implementation (1974–75), state and local administrators began to discover that the law imposed burdens "well beyond the capacity of any school system."[38] Implicit in the implemented program was a cruel dilemma. On the one hand the law required individualized treatment but on the other it created such an enormous administrative burden at the local level that educators were forced to develop routines for mass processing.[39] Local educators developed simple decision rules for differentiating more and less difficult cases: the loudest, most disruptive children were referred for evaluation first; children with easily identified, routine problems were processed perfunctorily, while those with more complex problems or "disruptive" parents were treated more circumspectly; teachers and administrators collaborated to reduce referrals when the burden became too heavy.[40] The evaluation conferences, which brought together teachers, specialists, and parents, tended to be characterized by largely negative assessments of children, the use of technical jargon, and preoccupation with the assignment of blame—all of which enhanced the position of professionals over parents and made the assessment procedure move more smoothly.[41] The traditional labels for children's problems were eliminated, but new, more euphemistic lables were invented.[42] In other words, routinization at the local level largely undermined the broad purposes of the law.

The basic problem, Weatherly and Lipsky point out, was not that local school personnel were determined to subvert the law. On the contrary, they made great personal sacrifices to make it work. The real problem was that the law reflected absolutely no understanding of how street-level bureaucrats respond to changes in policy and the increased workloads they entail. Faced with a broad legislative mandate and a large, complex new responsibility, local implementors invented operating routines that helped simplify their work but ran counter to the intent of the legislation.

The major advantage of the bureaucratic process model is that it forces us to contend with the mundane patterns of bureaucratic life and to think about how new policies affect the daily routines of people who deliver social services. Policy-makers, analysts, and administrators have a tendency to focus on variables that emphasize control and predictability, often overlooking the factors that undermine control and create anomalies in the implementation process. Bureaucratic routines operate against the grain of many policy changes because they are contrived as buffers against change and uncertainty; they continue to exist precisely because they have an immediate utility to the people who use them in reducing the stress and complexity of work. Failing to account for the force of routine in the implementation of policy leads to serious misperceptions.

Walter Williams argues that most implementation problems grow out of a division of labor between what he calls the "policy and operations spheres."[43] In the policy sphere, people tend to focus on global issues and general shifts in the distribution of power among governmental units. Consequently, when the responsibility for implementation shifts to the operations sphere there is little in the way of useful guidance for implementors. The limited case literature on the role of bureaucratic routines bears out this observation. The unresponsiveness of large public bureaucracies to new policy initiatives is more often than not attributable to a failure to connect the "big ideas" of policy-makers with the mundane coping mechanisms of implementors.

Unlike the systems management model, the bureaucratic process model does not give any clear-cut prescriptions for improving the implementation process. About the only normative advice offered by students of street-level bureaucracy is the rather weak suggestion that "bureaucratic coping behaviors cannot be eliminated, but they can be monitored and directed" by rewarding "those that most closely conform to preferred public objectives [and] discouraging objectionable practices."[44] What this prescription overlooks is that coping routines derive their appeal and resilience from the fact that they are rooted in the immediate demands of work; they are, then, almost generically immune to hierarchical control. It's difficult, within the context of the bureaucratic process model, to think of ways to change street-level behavior in a predictable fashion. But, as we shall see in the following section, it's not at all difficult to solve this problem when we adopt the perspective of another model.

The utility of the bureaucratic process model shouldn't hang entirely on its limited normative power, though, since its major advantages are descriptive: it captures a very common pattern of implementation failure, in which hierarchical controls generated by top management to alter the behavior of subordinates, or by one government agency to structure the behavior of another, simply fail to affect the important street-level transactions that determine the success of a policy.

Model III: Implementation as organizational development

Propositions:

1. Organizations should function to satisfy the basic psychological and social needs of individuals—for autonomy and control over their own work, for participation in decisions affecting them, and for commitment to the purposes of the organization.

2. Organizations should be structured to maximize individual control, participation, and commitment at all levels. Hierarchically structured bureaucracies maximize these things for people in upper levels of the organization at the expense of those in lower levels. Hence, the best organizational structure is one that minimizes hierarchical control and distributes responsibility for decisions among all levels of the organization.

3. Effective decision-making in organizations depends on the creation of effective work groups. The quality of interpersonal relations in organizations largely determines the quality of decisions. Effective work groups are characterized by mutual agreement on goals, open communication among individuals, mutual trust and support among group members, full utilization of members' skills and effective management of conflict. Decision-making consists primarily of building consensus and strong interpersonal relations among group members.

4. The implementation process is necessarily one of consensus-building and accommodation between policy-makers and implementors. The central problem of implementation is not whether implementors conform to prescribed policy but whether the implementation process results in consensus in goals, individual autonomy, and commitment to policy on the part of those who must carry it out.

Another frequent explanation of implementation failures is that those who implement programs are seldom included in decisions that determine the content of those programs. The closer one gets to the point of delivery in social programs, the more frequently one hears the complaint that policy-makers and high-level administrators don't listen to service deliverers. What grates most on the sensibilities of teachers, social workers, employment counselors, and the like is the tacit assumption in most policy directives that they are incapable of making independent judgments and decisions—that their behavior must be programmed by someone else. It's difficult for persons who see themselves as competent, self-sufficient adults to be highly committed to policies that place them in the role of passive executors of someone else's will.

The prevailing theories of organizational behavior represented by the systems management and bureaucratic process models encourage and perpetuate this pathology. Hierarchy, specialization, routine, and control all reinforce the belief that those at the bottom of the organization are less competent decision-makers than those at the top. High-level administrators can be trusted to exercise discretion while those at the bottom must be closely supervised and controlled. Policy is made at the top and implemented at the bottom; implementors must set aside their own views and submit to the superior authority and competence of policy-makers and high-level administrators.

Not surprisingly, this view has become increasingly difficult to defend as the work force has become more professionalized and better educated. It's now relatively clear that there are basic conflicts between the individual's need for autonomy, participation, and commitment and the organization's requirement of structure, control, and subordination. Concern for this conflict has led some to posit a "democratic alternative" to established theories of organization.[45] The label we will attach to this alternative is "organizational development." A number of schools of thought coexist within this tradition, but we will concentrate primarily on the work of Chris Argyris, who has spent an unusually large amount of effort specifying the assumptions on which his view is based.

Argyris begins with the observation that what we define as acceptable adult behavior outside organizations directly contradicts what's acceptable inside. On the outside, adults are defined as people who are self-motivating, responsible for their own actions, and honest about emotions and values. Inside organizations, adults are expected to exhibit dependency and passivity toward their superiors, they resort to indirection and avoid taking responsibility as individuals, and they are forced to submerge emotions and values.[46] Resolving this tension requires a fundamentally different kind of organization and a different theory of organizational behavior. Rational or bureaucratic theories of organization stress abstract, systemic properties—structure, technology, outputs—at the expense of the social and psychological needs of individuals.[47] The reasonable alternative is a theory that begins from the needs of individuals rather than the abstract properties of organizations. Such a theory leads "not only to a more humane and democratic system but to a more efficient one."[48]

The essential transactions of organizational life occur in face-to-face contacts among individuals engaged in a common task, that is, in work groups. Organizational effectiveness and efficiency depend more than anything else on the quality of interpersonal relations in work groups. Effective work groups are characterized by agreement on goals, open communication, mutual trust and support, full utilization of member skills, and effective management of conflict.[49] The cultivation of these attributes requires a special kind of skill, which Argyris calls "interpersonal competence" to distinguish it from the purely technical competence that comes from the routine performance of a task. Individuals are interpersonally competent when they are able to give and receive feedback in a way that creates minimal defensiveness, to give honest expression to their own feelings, values and attitudes, and to remain open to new ideas.[50] The trappings of bureaucracy and rational decision-making—routines, management controls, objectified accountability—undermine interpersonal competence and group effectiveness, encouraging dependence and passivity while penalizing openness and risk-taking. Hence, "the very values that are assumed to help make [an organization] effective may actually . . . decrease its effectiveness."[51]

Nowhere in the literature on organizational development is there a simple composite of the well-structured organization. It's fair to infer from the theory, though, that an effective organization would have at least the following features: most responsibility for decisions would devolve to lower levels of the organization; the focus of organizational activity would be the work group, formed of people engaged in a common task; and information—statements of purpose, evaluative judgments, and expressions of needed changes—would be readily exchanged without negative social consequences at all levels of the organization. All these features originate from the simple assumption that people are more likely to perform at their highest capacity when they are given maximum control over their own work, maximum participation in decisions affecting them, and hence maximum incentives for commitment to the goals of the group.

The organizational development model gives quite a different picture of the implementation process than either the systems management or bureaucratic process models. In the systems management model, implementation consists of the skillful use of management controls to hold subunits accountable for well-defined standards of performance. In the bureaucratic process model, implementation consists of changing the formal and informal work routines of an organization to conform with a declaration of intent. In both instances, *policy is made at the top and implemented at the bottom.* But in the organizational development model the distinction is much less clear. If major responsibility is actually devolved to work groups at lower levels of the organization, it makes very little sense to think of policy as flowing from top to bottom. More about this in a moment.

Implementation failures are not the result of poor management control or the persistence of bureaucratic routines, but arise out of a lack of consensus and commitment among implementors. The features of the implementation process that matter most are those that affect individual motivation and interpersonal cooperation, not those that enhance hierarchical control. Success of an implementation effort can be gauged by looking at the extent to which implementors are involved in the formulation of a program, the extent to which they are encouraged to exercise independent judgement in determining their own behavior, and the extent to which they are encouraged to establish strong work groups for mutual support and problem-solving.

Empirical evidence on the underlying assumptions of the organizational development model is relatively scarce, but the most important piece of evidence in the area of social program implementation comes from a large-scale study done completely outside the organizational development tradition. In 1972, the federal government contracted with the Rand Corporation to conduct a nationwide study of four federally funded education programs, each of which was designed to encourage innovation in the public schools.[52] The programs were administered by different units within the U.S. Office of Education and they used a variety of administrative strategies. Nearly 300 local projects were surveyed, so the potential for variation within and among programs was great. Yet the Rand analysts concluded that overall the "programs had approximately equal effects on project outcomes, despite their different management strategies."[53] They also concluded that "differences between programs explained only a small amount of the variation in implementation outcomes."[54] In short, the federal government's management of the programs seemed to have virtually no effect on the success or failure of implementation.

Pursuing this issue further, the Rand group analyzed 29 descriptive case studies of local project implementation, attempting to identify what distinguished successful from unsuccessful attempts at change. The characteristics that emerged from this analysis were (1) the existence of a strong local training component; (2) the use of local expertise and technical assistance in project implementation; (3) frequent and regular staff meetings; (4) local development of project materials; (5) the use of voluntary, highly motivated participants; and the like.[55] What is significant about all these factors is that federal administrators have virtually no control over them. Project success depended primarily on the existence and mobilization of local resources. "Our observations suggest," the analysts concluded, "that it is extremely unrealistic to expect a school district to do something wise with its federal money if it is not already committed to something wise when the funds are first received."[56]

Milbrey McLaughlin, a principal author of the study, looked in detail at a number of projects that were intended to change classroom organization. Discussing the importance of local materials development, she observes that it was "sometimes undertaken because the staff felt they couldn't locate appropriate commercial materials," but she concludes that "the real contribution lay . . . in providing the staff with a sense of involvement and an opportunity to learn by doing." She continues,

> Working together to develop materials . . . gave the staff a sense of "ownership" in the project. It also broke down the traditional isolation of the teacher and provided a sense of professionalism and cooperation not usually available in the school setting. But even more important, development of

materials provided an opportunity for users to think through the concepts which underlay the project in practical, operational terms. . . . Although such "reinvention of the wheel" may not appear efficient in the short run, it appears to be a critical part of the individual learning and development necessary to significant change.[57]

Here, in the concrete language of project-level implementation, are the essential elements of the organizational development model: emphasis on individual motivation and commitment (sense of involvement, ownership in the project), the centrality of strong face-to-face work groups (breaking down the traditional isolation of teachers, enhancing professionalism and cooperation), and the explicit criticism of conventional notions of organizational efficiency (the usefulness of reinventing the wheel).

The picture of implementation that emerges from these findings is one in which the ability of policy-makers and high-level administrators to manipulate the behavior of implementors using the standard devices of hierarchical control is severely limited. The critical variables are those arising out of individual commitment and motivation. The Rand analysts described the implementation process as "intrinsically" one of "mutual adaptation"; the policy or innovation is shaped by implementors and, likewise, the behavior of implementors is shaped by the policy or innovation.[58] The only way an innovation can become established in an organization, the Rand analysts argue, is for implementors to learn it, shape it, and claim it for their own.

But the full significance of the Rand findings is not adequately expressed by the plausible idea of mutual adaptation. Every defensible view of implementation contains some gesture toward adaptive behavior—in the systems management model, adaptation is a necessary consequence of feedback on the performance of subunits; in the bureaucratic process model, organizational routines evolve slowly over time in response to changing demands. So it's not the notion of adaptive behavior that distinguishes the organizational development model from other perspectives.

The real significance of the organizational development model, and the import of the Rand evidence, is that it effectively turns the entire implementation process on its head. It reverses what we instinctively regard as the "normal" flow of policy, from top to bottom. The message of the model is, quite bluntly, that the capacity to implement originates at the bottom of organizations, not at the top. In each of the two previous models the central problem was how policy-makers and high-level administrators could shape the behavior of implementors using the standard devices of hierarchical control. What the organizational development model suggests is that these devices explain almost none of the variation in implementation outcomes. The factors that do affect the behavior of implementors lie outside the domain of direct management control—individual motivation and commitment, and the interaction and mutual support of people in work groups. Hence, the closer one gets to the determinants of effective implementation, the further one gets from the factors that policy-makers and administrators can manipulate. The result is that, in terms of the effective structure of organizations, *the process of initiating and implementing new policy actually begins at the bottom and ends at the top*. Unless organizations already have those properties that predispose them to change, they are not likely to respond to new policy. But if they have those properties, they are capable of initiating change themselves, without the control of policy-makers and administrators. The role of those at the top of the system, then, is necessarily residual; they can provide resources that implementors need to do their work, but they cannot exert direct control over the factors that determine the success or failure of that work.

If one accepts this view, the important business of implementation consists not of developing progressively more sophisticated techniques for managing subordinates' behavior but of enhancing the self-starting capacity of the smallest unit. The organizational capacity to accept innovations necessarily precedes the innovations themselves, so one can't expect individuals to respond to new policies unless they are predisposed to do so. But once this predisposition exists, it is no longer practical to think of imposing changes from above. The only conception of implementation that makes sense under these conditions is one that emphasizes consensus building and accommodation between policy-makers and implementors. Mutual adaptation exists not because it is a pleasing or democratic thing to do, but because it is the only way to insure that implementors have a direct personal stake in the performance of their jobs. This is what the advocates of organizational development mean when they say that more democratic organizations are also more efficient ones.

The organizational development model focuses on those aspects of an organization's internal structure that enhance or inhibit the commitment of implementors. The chief determinants of success are the sort of microvariables identified by the Rand analysts: materials development by implementors, strong interpersonal and professional ties among implementors, non-manipulative support by high-level administrators, and explicit reliance on incentives that elicit individual commitment from implementors rather than those designed to enforce external conformity. To the extent that the implementation process actually becomes these things, it is neither accurate nor useful to think in terms of a single declaration of policy that is translated into subordinate behavior. Policy does not exist in any concrete sense until implementors have shaped it and claimed it for their own; the result is a consensus reflecting the initial intent of policy-makers and the independent judgment of implementors.

The organizational development model also forces us to recognize the narrow limits of one organization's capacity to change the behavior of another. When an agency at one level of government attempts to implement policy through an agency at another level, the implicit assumption is that the former controls factors that are important in determining the performance of the latter. The organizational development model suggests that those factors that have the greatest influence on the success or failure of implementation are precisely the ones over which external agencies have the least control. The maximum that one level of government can do to affect the implementation process is to provide general support that enhances the internal capacity of organizations at another level to respond to the necessity for change, independent of the requirements of specific policies. So, to the extent that the implementation process actually took the shape of the model, the federal government, for example, would invest most of its resources not in enforcing compliance with existing policies, but in assisting state and local agencies to develop an independent capacity to elicit innovative behavior from implementors.

The most powerful criticism of the organizational development model comes, surprisingly, from its strongest supporters. The bias of the model toward consensus, cooperation, and strong interpersonal ties leads us to ignore or downplay the role of conflict in organizations. The model, one of its advocates argues, "seems most appropriate under conditions of trust, truth, love, and collaboration. But what about conditions of war, conflict, dissent, and violence?" "The fundamental deficiency in models of change associated with organization development," he concludes, is that they "systematically avoid the problem of power, or the *politics* of change."[59] The same criticism may be levelled, to one degree or another, against each of the three models discussed thus far, because none directly confronts the issue of what happens in organizations when control, routine, and consensus fail. A wide range of implementation problems can be understood only as problems of conflict and bargaining.

Model IV: Implementation as conflict and bargaining

Propositions:

1. Organizations are arenas of conflict in which individuals and subunits with specific interests compete for relative advantage in the exercise of power and the allocation of scarce resources.

2. The distribution of power in organizations is never stable. It depends exclusively on the temporary ability of one individual or unit to mobilize sufficient resources to manipulate the behavior of others. Formal position in the hierarchy of an organization is only one of a multitude of factors that determine the distribution of power. Other factors include specialized knowledge, control of material resources, and the ability to mobilize external political support. Hence, the exercise of power in organizations is only weakly related to their formal structure.

3. Decision-making in organizations consists of bargaining within and among organizational units. Bargained decisions are the result of convergence among actors with different preferences and resources. Bargaining does not require that parties agree on a common set of goals, nor does it even require that all parties concur in the outcome of the bargaining process. It only requires that they agree to adjust their behavior mutually in the interest of preserving the bargaining relationship as a means of allocating resources.

4. Implementation consists of a complex series of bargained decisions reflecting the preferences and resources of participants. Success or failure of implementation cannot be judged by comparing a result against a single declaration of intent, because no single set of purposes can provide an internally consistent statement of the interests of all parties to the bargaining process. Success can only be defined relative to the goals of one party to the bargaining process or in terms of the preservation of the bargaining process itself.

Social programs fail, it is frequently argued, because no single unit of government is sufficiently powerful to force others to conform to a single conception of policy. With each agency pursuing its own interest, implementation does not progress from a single declaration of intent to a result, but is instead characterized by constant conflict over purposes and results and by the pursuit of relative advantage through the use of bargaining. This diversity of purpose leads some participants to characterize programs as "failures" and some to characterize them as "successes," based solely on their position in the bargaining process. Conflict and bargaining occur both within and among implementing agencies. Single organizations can be thought of as semi-permanent bargaining coalitions, and the process of moving a declaration of policy across levels of government can be understood as bargaining among separate organizations.

Bargaining can be explicit or tacit. We tend to associate the notion of bargaining only with direct confrontations between well-defined adversaries—labor negotiations, arms limitation talks, and peace negotiations, for example. But many forms of bargaining, especially those in implementation, occur without direct communication and with an imperfect understanding by each party of the others' motives and resources.[60] Seen in this light, implementation becomes essentially a series of strategic moves by a number of individual units of government, each seeking to shape the behavior of others to its own ends.

The key to understanding bargaining behavior is recognizing that conflict implies dependency. Even the strongest adversaries must take account of their opponents' moves when they formulate a bargaining strategy. "The ability of one participant to gain his ends," Schelling observes, "is dependent to an important degree on the choices or decisions that the other participant will make." Furthermore, "there is a powerful common interest in reaching an outcome that is not enormously destructive of values to both sides."[61] In implementation, as in all important bargaining problems, parties with strongly divergent interests are locked together by the simple fact that they must preserve the bargaining arena in order to gain something of value. Failure to bargain means exclusion from the process by which resources are allocated. But the mutual advantage that accrues to participants in bargaining has little or nothing to do with their ability to agree explicitly on the goals they're pursuing, or their means for pursuing them. Mutual advantage results only from the fact that by agreeing to bargain they have preserved their access to something of value to each of them.

[. . .] The common element in all forms of bargaining behavior, [Lindblom] argues, is that "people can coordinate with each other without someone's coordinating them, without a dominant purpose, and without rules that fully prescribe their relations to each other."[62] This point is essential for understanding the usefulness of the conflict and bargaining model in the analysis of social program implementation. The model permits us to make conceptual sense of the implementation process without assuming the existence of hierarchical control, without asserting that everyone's behavior is governed by a predictable set of bureaucratic routines, and without assuming that concerted action can proceed only from consensus and commitment to a common set of purposes. In short, the model provides a distinct alternative to the limiting assumptions of the previous three. Implementation can, and indeed does, proceed in the absence of a mechanism of coordination external to the actors themselves, such as hierarchical control, routine, or group consensus.

Bargained decisions proceed by convergence, adjustment, and closure among individuals pursuing essentially independent ends. Allison makes this point when he says that "the decisions and actions of governments are . . . political resultants . . . in the sense that what happens is not chosen as a solution to a problem but rather results from compromise, conflict, and confusion of officials with diverse interests and unequal influence."[63] The term "resultant," appropriated from physics, emphasizes the idea that decisions are the product of two or more converging forces. The mechanism of convergence depends on what Schelling calls "interdependence of expectations." Parties to the bargaining process must predicate their actions not only on predictions of how others will respond but also on the understanding that others are doing likewise. So bargaining depends as much on shared expectations as it does on concrete actions.

> The outcome is determined by the expectations that each player forms of how the other will play, where each of them knows that their expectations are substantially reciprocal. The players must jointly discover and mutually acquiesce in an outcome or a mode of play that makes the outcome determinate. They must together find "rules of the game" or together suffer the consequences.[64]

In concrete terms, this means that much of the behavior we observe in the implementation process is designed to shape the expectations of other actors. An agency might, for example, put a great deal of effort into developing an elaborate collection of rules and regulations or an elegant system of management controls, knowing full well that it doesn't have the resources to make them binding on other actors. But the *expectation* that the rules *might* be enforced is sufficient to influence the behavior of other actors. The important fact is not whether the rules are enforced or not, but the effect of their existence on the outcome of the bargaining process.

The outcomes of bargaining are seldom "optimal" in any objective sense. More often than not, they are simply convenient temporary points of closure. Asking "what it is that can bring . . . expectations into convergence and bring . . . negotiations to a close," Schelling answers that "it is the intrinsic magnetism of particular outcomes, especially those that enjoy prominence, uniqueness, simplicity, precedent, or some rationale that makes them qualitatively differentiable" from other alternatives.[65] In other words, the result of bargaining is often not the best nor even the second or third best alternative for any party; all parties can, and frequently do, leave the bargaining process dissatisfied with the result. As long as an opportunity to resume bargaining remains, there is seldom a single determinant result; all resolutions are temporary. So one should not expect the mechanisms of bargaining to lead teleologically from a single purpose to a result.

One is tempted to say that the conflict and bargaining model is not a model of organizational behavior at all, but a model of what happens when organizations fail. This argument is plausible. We tend to associate the term organization with a certain threshold of commonality that allows individuals to cooperate around a common set of goals. If this minimum condition isn't met, it seems reasonable to conclude that there is an absence of organization. Some time ago, though, the theory of organizations took a turn away from this assumption. Cyert and March, dissatisfied with the conventional wisdom of normative economic theory and the sociology of organizations, elaborated an alternative theory, beginning from the premise that organizations are essentially bargaining coalitions.[66] The process of organizational decision-making, they argue, involves continuous conflict among subunits over relatively specific purposes that define each subunit's interest in the organization. The overall goals of an organization, they argue, are calculatedly vague and essentially useless as guides to decision-making. Hence, organizations are not defined by agreement on overall purposes, but only by the process of conflict, bargaining, and coalition building among subunits. The absence of agreement on overall goals, then, is not a sign of organizational failure, but simply a clue directing our attention to the existence of conflict and bargaining as permanent fixtures of organizational life.

The real structure of organizations, then, is to be found in their bargaining processes, rather than in their formal hierarchy or operating routines. Notions of top and bottom have very little meaning. Formal position is a source of power, but only one of many, and it does not necessarily carry with it the ability to manipulate the behavior of subordinates. Many other sources of power—mastery of specialized knowledge, discretionary control over resources, a strong external constituency, and so on—can be used to enhance the bargaining position of subordinates relative to superiors, and vice versa. No simple rules can be set forth for determining the distribution of power in organizations. Stability, if it exists at all, is the short-term product of bargaining on specific decisions.

This view leads to a conception of implementation considerably different from any of the other models. One understands the process by focusing on conflict among actors, the resources they bring to the bargaining process, and the mechanisms by which they adjust to each others' moves. Most important, the distinguishing feature of the conflict and bargaining model is that *it doesn't rest on any assumptions about commonality of purpose.* In each of the previous models, it was possible to say that successful implementation was in some sense dependent on a common conception of policy shared by all participants in the process. In the systems management model, agreement was the product of management control; in the bureaucratic process model, it resulted from incorporation of a new policy into an organization's operating routines; and in the organizational development model, it resulted from consensus among policy-makers and implementors. But in the conflict and bargaining model, the outcomes of implementation are temporary bargained solutions—resultants—that reflect no overall agreement on purposes.

Success or failure of implementation is therefore largely a relative notion, determined by one's position in the process. Actors who are capable of asserting their purposes over others, however temporarily, will argue that the process is "successful." Those with a disadvantage in the bargaining process will argue that the process is "unsuccessful." It is entirely possible for the process to proceed even when all actors regard it as unsuccessful, because the costs of refusing to bargain may exceed the costs of remaining in a disadvantageous bargaining relationship. Under these circumstances, the only objective measure of success or failure is the preservation of the bargaining process itself. So long as all parties agree to bargain and mutual benefit is to be gained from bargaining, preservation of the bargaining arena constitutes success. Regardless of the level of conflict in social programs, all actors have an interest in maintaining the programs as long as they deliver benefits that are not otherwise accessible.

The empirical evidence on conflict and bargaining in social program implementation is abundant. The implementation of federal educational programs provides some of the best examples, because the process occurs in a system where power is radically dispersed across all levels of government. The Elementary and Secondary Education Act of 1965 was intended not simply to increase federal expenditures on education but also to change the operation of state and local educational agencies. Title I of the Act was intended to focus attention and resources on educationally disadvantaged children at the local level; Title V was designed to enhance the administrative capability of state educational agencies. In both cases, the pattern of interaction among agencies at different levels of government suggests conflict and bargaining rather than simple progression from a purpose to a result. In its first five years, Title I went from a period of "good working relationships" and "friendly assistance" between the federal government and local agencies, through a stage of aggressive federal enforcement of program guidelines, and eventually back to a relatively passive federal role. Jerome Murphy demonstrates that the critical element in these shifts was a change in the nature of the bargaining arena in Title I. In the late sixties, civil rights organizations conducted a large-scale study of local abuses of Title I, confirming a widely held suspicion that funds were not being focused on disadvantaged children, and then mounted an aggressive political campaign to force the U.S. Office of Education to take a stronger posture in enforcing program guidelines. After a flurry of enforcement activity that generated a great deal of political counterpressure from state and local agencies, federal administrators backed away from aggressive enforcement.[67] In other words, federal policy—legislation, regulations, and guidelines—served only as a point of departure for bargaining among implementing agencies. Local implementors designed their actions around expectations about the willingness of federal administrators to enforce the policy. When federal administrators were forced to take a different posture, local administrators responded in part with compliance and in part with counterpressure. The policy actually implemented lies somewhere between the literal requirements of the law and regulations and the interests of local implementors. Another flurry of federal enforcement would alter the situation again.

In the implementation of Title V, the federal government dispensed relatively unrestricted funds to state educational agencies for use in strengthening their administrative capacities. Murphy found that, in the aggregate, Title V did not significantly change the activities or functions of state agencies. The dominant pattern was that "funds were distributed to satisfy the interests of important elements in the organization" and were "expended mainly to meet pressing problems through the simple expansion of existing modes of operation."[68] In other words, the infusion of federal funds simply touched off intraorganizational bargaining in which subunits claimed their share of the bounty and proceeded to use it for their own immediate purposes. In the few cases where significant changes in state agencies did occur, they came "only after strong pressure from outside the organization."[69] As in the case of Title I, it took a shift in the bargaining arena to force a change in the behavior of implementors.

The extremely diffuse and fluid nature of organizational relationships in the field of education has led Karl Weick to characterize educational organizations as "loosely coupled systems."[70] Although conflict and bargaining do not figure prominently in Weick's model, the characteristics of loosely coupled systems that he identifies lead to the same conclusions as the conflict and bargaining model. The lack of structure and determinancy, the absence of teleologically linked events, the dispersion of resources and responsibilities, and the relative absence of binding regulation all add up to the kind of system in which concerned action is possible only through tacit or explicit bargaining among relatively independent actors.

The same pattern exists in a number of other studies of social program implementation. Pressman's analysis of the impact of federal programs on the city of Oakland concludes that action is possible in urban settings only when "effective bargaining arenas" exist to enforce "citizens'. . . demands on government and government's willingness to respond."[71] In the Pressman and Wildavsky study of the Economic Development Administration's job creation project in Oakland, a similar pattern was repeated. Federal administrators underestimated the complexity of local bargaining relationships and overestimated their ability to force a result consistent with their objectives.[72] Derthick's study of the Department of Housing and Urban Development's New Towns program concludes with the observation that federal programs succeed when "an adjustment between the federal program and local interests is worked out . . . with the net result . . . that programs are neither 'federal' nor 'local' but a blend of the two."[73] Cuomo's account of the attempt to locate a low-income public housing project in a middle-class neighborhood of Forest Hills, Queens, demonstrates how bargaining between local residents, city, state, and federal administrators converged on an outcome that satisfied no one but temporarily resolved the conflict.[74] The important characteristic of all these cases is that the participants in the bargaining process stood to gain more from bargaining than from not bargaining. A failure to bargain means a loss of access to goods that can be gained only by participation. Even the strongest of adversaries are locked together by the dependency of conflict.

The major contribution of the conflict and bargaining model to our understanding of social program implementation is the insight that parties to the implementation process needn't agree on anything except the necessity to bargain. The bargaining process, whether it occurs among individuals within organizations or among organizations at different levels of government, proceeds by convergence, adjustment, and closure rather than by hierarchical control or consensus. This feature of the model explains why it is such a powerful descriptive device; it allows us to interpret events without attributing an overall purpose to them. But this feature is also the model's greatest weakness: it does not allow us to posit an objective definition of success or failure, since all normative judgments are simply assertions of relative advantage in the bargaining process. The rationalist critique of the conflict and bargaining model is that it elevates confusion and mindless drift to the level of principle, that it provides an easy excuse for acquiescing in results that satisfy no one, and that it provides no basis for improving the implementation process. These criticisms are difficult to counter, except by observing that a failure to understand the intricacies of bargaining is sometimes more costly than a failure to agree on an objective measure of success.

Conclusion

In closing, two obvious but obligatory remarks are in order. The first is that models are necessarily constructs or ideal types. Nothing is immutable about the distinctions I have drawn here, nor do I make any pretense of having captured all that is important in the implementation process. What is useful about the models, I've argued, is that they draw on established traditions of organizational inquiry and they accord with certain commonsense explanations of why social programs fail. The second observation is that the evidence on social program implementation is skimpy; the cases I've used are intended only to suggest that modest empirical support can be found for the assumptions underlying each of the models. This is not to suggest that any of the evidence is very solid or that there is any reason to believe that the evidence favors one model or another. It does suggest a great need for descriptive studies of social program implementation.

The more interesting question is, of what use is the notion of alternative models to the analysis of implementation? Granting that certain models highlight certain features of the process while concealing others, what use could one make of this fact? I would like to suggest, briefly, two possibilities; but before I do, one possible use of alternative models about which I am very skeptical comes immediately to mind. This is the view that the models should be treated as rival hypotheses and that the gradual accumulation of empirical evidence will eventually prove some single model of the process superior to all others. This is unlikely to happen for two reasons. First, models contain not only descriptive information but normative information; in spite of empirical evidence that a process operates in a certain way, people can nevertheless persist in the belief that it *ought* to operate in another way. Second, people have the capacity to shape their behavior in response to models; a neat predictive model of an essentially political process, like implementation, invites people to behave in unpredictable ways to achieve their own ends. Given the diversity of opinion reflected in the four models presented here, it seems highly unlikely that the accumulation of evidence will lead to agreement. It will probably just reinforce the disagreement that currently exists. But, as I indicated above, two ideas about the use of alternative models are more promising.

The first is that applying different models to the same set of events allows us to distinguish certain features of the implementation process from others. In fact, every implementing agency probably has a set of management controls, a firmly entrenched collection of operating routines, some process for eliciting the involvement of implementors, and a set of internal and external bargaining relationships. The important question is not whether these elements exist or not, but how they affect the implementation process. One way of disentangling the effects of these factors is to analyze the same body of evidence from the perspective of several different models. This is the approach taken by Allison in his analysis of the Cuban missile crisis.

The second idea proceeds from the notion that certain kinds of problems are more amenable to solution when using one perspective than when using another. It is conceivable that in certain times and settings, the use of management controls is clearly appropriate, while in other circumstances only bargaining is appropriate. In some instances, wholesale delegation of discretion is the obvious course of action to follow, while in others firm control of discretion is necessary. The point is that models can help analysts and decision-makers distinguish among different kinds of problems. Using management controls in a system in which power is extremely diffuse, for example, is like using a crescent wrench to turn a phillips screw. The problem is to understand when certain tools of analysis and strategies of action are likely to pay off and when not.

Neither of these approaches requires complete agreement on the nature of the models or on the existence of a single model that captures all essential features of the process. They require only a willingness to treat certain parts of a complex process as analytically separable, plus a high tolerance for ambiguity.

Notes

1. A number of these studies are collected in Walter Williams and Richard E. Elmore (eds.), *Social Program Implementation* (New York: Academic Press, 1976). Another collection, which focuses on the role of regulation in the implementation process, is a special number of *Policy Sciences*, 7 (Winter 1976), edited by Francine Rabinovitz, Jeffrey Pressman, and Martin Rein. Two major reviews of the literature on implementation are, Donald Van Meter and Carl Van Horn, "The policy implementation process: a conceptual framework," in *Administration and Society*, 6 (1974): 445–88; and Erwin Hargrove, *The Missing Link: The study of implementation of social policy* (Washington, D.C.: Urban Institute, 1975).
2. Walter Williams, "Implementation problems in federally-funded programs," in Williams and Elmore (eds.), *Social Program Implementation*, pp. 15–40.
3. Richard Nelson, "Intellectualizing about the moon–ghetto metaphor: a study of the current malaise of rational analysis of social problems," *Policy Sciences* 5 (1974): 398. This article has been expanded into a book, *The Moon and the Ghetto* (New York: Norton, 1977), that includes a number of case studies demonstrating what Nelson means by analysis of organizational alternatives. His framework differs considerably from the one developed here.
4. Graham Allison, *Essence of Decision: Explaining the Cuban missile crisis* (Boston: Little, Brown, 1971).
5. *Ibid.*, p. 2.
6. *Ibid.*, p. 267. See also Arnold Meltsner, "Political feasibility and policy analysis," *Public Administration Review* (November/December 1972): 859–67.

7. This distinction is developed at length in Ralph Strauch, "A critical look at quantitative methodology," *Policy Analysis* 2 (1976): 121–44.
8. This account of the systems management model is drawn from the following sources: Daniel Katz and Robert Kahn, *The Social Psychology of Organizations* (New York: Wiley, 1966); William Baumol, *Economic Theories and Operations Analysis*, 3rd edn. (Englewood Cliffs, N.J.: Prentice Hall, 1972); Robert Anthony, *Planning and Control Systems: A framework of analysis* (Boston: Harvard Graduate School of Business Administration, 1965); C. West Churchman, *The Systems Approach* (New York: Delta, 1968); and Charles Hitch and Roland McKean, *The Economics of Defense in a Nuclear Age* (Cambridge, Mass.: Harvard University Press, 1963).
9. Katz and Kahn, *The Social Psychology of Organizations*, p. 79.
10. *Ibid.*, p. 203. Cf. Churchman, *The Systems Approach*, p. 44.
11. Anthony, *Planning and Control Systems*, pp. 16–18.
12. Hitch and McKean, *The Economics of Defense in a Nuclear Age*, pp. 128–9, 396–402. Their choice of the term "sub-optimization" is perhaps unfortunate because to most of us it communicates the meaning "less than optimal," which is quite the opposite of the meaning they wish to convey. It is clear from their discussion that they intend the term to mean "optimizing at lower levels." Some writers, however, insist on using the term to mean less than optimal. See, e.g., Anthony, *Planning and Control Systems*, p. 35. Two other sources in which the term is used consistently with the meaning of Hitch and McKean are, Baumol, *Economic Theories and Operations Analysis*, p. 395n, and Richard Zeckhauser and Elmer Schaefer, "Public policy and normative economic theory," in Raymond Bauer and Kenneth Gergen (eds.), *The Study of Policy Formation* (New York: Free Press, 1968), pp. 73–6. A more recent treatment of suboptimization in policy analysis may be found in E.S. Quade, *Analysis for Public Decisions* (New York: Elsevier, 1975), pp. 95–8.
13. Hitch and McKean, *The Economics of Defense in a Nuclear Age*, p. 129.
14. Herbert Kaufman, *The Forest Ranger: A study of administrative behavior* (Baltimore: Johns Hopkins University Press, 1969), p. 91.
15. Anthony, *Planning and Control Systems*, p. 45.
16. Katz and Kahn, *The Social Psychology of Organizations*, p. 40.
17. Williams, "Implementation analysis and assessment," in Williams and Elmore (eds.), *Social Program Implementation*, pp. 281–2.
18. Kaufman, *The Forest Ranger*, p. 203.
19. *Ibid.*, p. 228.
20. James Q. Wilson, "The bureaucracy problem," *The Public Interest* 6 (Winter 1967): 3–9.
21. Michel Crozier, *The Bureaucratic Phenomenon* (Chicago: University of Chicago Press, 1964).
22. James Q. Wilson, *Varieties of Police Behavior* (New York: Atheneum, 1973), p. 1.
23. Allison, *Essence of Decision*, p. 80.
24. Wilson, *Varieties of Police Behavior*, pp. 2–3.
25. *Ibid.*, p. 9; see also pp. 64ff.
26. Donald Schon, *Beyond the Stable State* (New York: Random House, 1971), p. 32.

27. Michael Lipsky, "Toward a theory of street-level bureaucracy," in Willis Hawley and Michael Lipsky (eds.), *Theoretical Perspectives on Urban Politics* (Englewood Cliffs, N.J.: Prentice Hall, 1976), p. 197.
28. Wilson, *Varieties of Police Behavior*, p. 7.
29. Lipsky, "Toward a theory of street-level bureaucracy," pp. 197–8.
30. *Ibid.*, pp. 201ff.
31. Richard Weatherly, "Toward a theory of client control in street-level bureaucracy," unpublished paper, School of Social Work, University of Washington, 1976, p. 5.
32. Miriam Johnson, *Counter Point: The changing employment service* (Salt Lake City, Utah: Olympus, 1973).
33. *Ibid.*, p. 21.
34. *Ibid.*, pp. 63–4.
35. *Ibid.*, pp. 85–6.
36. *Ibid.*, p. 109.
37. Richard Weatherly and Michael Lipsky, "Street-level bureaucrats and institutional innovation: implementing special-education reform," *Harvard Educational Review* 47 (May 1977): 171–97.
38. *Ibid.*, p. 180.
39. *Ibid.*, p. 182.
40. *Ibid.*, pp. 186–7.
41. *Ibid.*, pp. 189–90.
42. *Ibid.*, pp 192–3.
43. Williams, "Implementation problems in federally funded programs," pp. 20–3.
44. Weatherly and Lipsky, "Street-level bureaucrats and institutional innovation," p. 196.
45. See, e.g., Katz and Kahn, *The Social Psychology of Organizations*, pp. 211ff.
46. Chris Argyris, *Personality and Organization: The conflict between system and individual* (New York: Harper, 1957), pp. 53ff.
47. Chris Argyris, *The Applicability of Organizational Sociology* (London: Cambridge University Press, 1972), *passim*.
48. Warren Bennis, *Organization Development: Its nature, origins, and prospects* (Reading, Mass.: Addison-Wesley, 1969), p. 28.
49. *Ibid.*, p. 2 [quoting Douglas McGregor, *The Professional Manager* (New York: McGraw Hill, 1967)].
50. Chris Argyris, *Interpersonal Competence and Organizational Effectiveness* (Homewood, Ill.: Irwin, 1962), p. 42.
51. Chris Argyris, *Integrating the Individual and the Organization* (New York: Wiley, 1964), p. 138.
52. The results are reported in a five-volume study, *Federal Programs Supporting Educational Change* (Santa Monica, Cal.: Rand Corporation, 1975). The principal authors are Paul Berman, Milbrey McLaughlin, Dale Mann, Peter Greenwood, and John Pincus. A number of other researchers, including this author, worked on parts of the study.
53. Paul Berman and Milbrey McLaughlin, *Federal Programs Supporting Educational Change, Vol. IV: The Findings in Review* (Santa Monica, California: Rand Corporation, 1975), p. 22.

54. *Ibid.*, see also pp. 45–7.
55. Berman and McLaughlin, *Federal Programs Supporting Change, Vol. III: The Process of Change*, p. 39.
56. *Ibid.*, p. 26.
57. Milbrey McLaughlin, "Implementation as mutual adaptation: change in classroom organization," in Williams and Elmore (eds.), *Social Program Implementation*, pp. 172–3.
58. Berman and McLaughlin, *Federal Programs Supporting Educational Change, Vol. III: The Process of Change*, pp. 3, 31.
59. Bennis, *Organization Development*, p. 77: emphasis in original.
60. An elegant account of tacit bargaining and coordination is given in Thomas Schelling, *The Strategy of Conflict* (London and New York: Oxford University Press, 1963), pp. 53ff.
61. *Ibid.*, pp. 5–6.
62. Charles Lindblom, *The Intelligence of Democracy: Decision making through mutual adjustment* (New York: Free Press, 1965), p. 3.
63. Allison, *Essence of Decision*, p. 162.
64. Schelling, *The Strategy of Conflict*, pp. 106–7.
65. *Ibid.*, p. 70: Lindblom, *The Intelligence of Democracy*, pp. 205–25.
66. Richard Cyert and James March, *A Behavioral Theory of the Firm* (Englewood Cliffs, N.J.: Prentice Hall, 1963), p. 27.
67. Jerome Murphy, "The education bureaucracies implement novel policy: the politics of Title I of ESEA, 1965–72," in Alan Sindler (ed.), *Policy and Politics in America* (Boston: Little Brown, 1973), pp. 160–98. See also Milbrey McLaughlin, "Implementation of ESEA Title I: a problem of compliance," *Teachers College Record* 77 (1976): 397–415.
68. Jerome Murphy, "Title V of ESEA: the impact of discretionary funds on state education bureaucracies," in Williams and Elmore (eds.), *Social Program Implementation*, pp. 89 and 91. A more extended treatment of this case is found in Murphy's *State Education Agencies and Discretionary Funds* (Lexington, Mass.: Lexington Books, 1974).
69. *Ibid.*, p. 94.
70. Karl Weick, "Educational organizations as loosely coupled systems," *Administrative Science Quarterly* 21 (1976): 1–18.
71. Jeffrey Pressman, *Federal Programs and City Politics: The dynamics of the aid process in Oakland* (Berkeley, Cal.: University of California Press, 1975), pp. 14 and 143–4.
72. Jeffrey Pressman and Aaron Wildavsky, *Implementation* (Berkeley, Cal.: University of California Press, 1973), *passim*.
73. Martha Derthick, *New Towns in Town: Why a federal program failed* (Washington, D.C.: Urban Institute, 1972), pp. 97–8. Portions of this study are reprinted in Williams and Elmore, *Social Program Implementation*, pp. 219–39.
74. Mario Cuomo, *Forest Hills Diary: The crisis of low-income housing* (New York: Random House, 1974), *passim*.

Structure and action as constructs in the practice of public administration

Pieter Degeling and Hal Colebatch

The dominant paradigm and its critics

Until very recently the dominant paradigm in the study of organization and the teaching of administrative studies has been an instrumental one. That is, the organization is seen as an instrument for the attainment of given purposes, and both the nature of the organization and of the processes which take place in and around it are best understood in relation to its instrumental character.

Academic study of and teaching about organizations was seen as being about increasing their capacity to achieve these given purposes. Positivistic science was applied to the design of organizational processes, and to devising practices and techniques which would strengthen the scientific character of managerial decision-making, increase management's capacity to control, and hence enhance the strength of the organization as an instrument of rational purpose. The propagation of these ideas, practices and techniques then formed the content of management education.

This instrumental paradigm has, in the past two decades, been subject to question on a number of grounds. Within systems theory, research has pointed to the effects of factors outside an organization on organizational processes.[1] At the same time, the introduction into analysis of concepts such as power, dependence, coalition-formation and conflict has raised questions about the extent to which activity within organizations is and can be controlled and directed toward the rational pursuit of previously-defined goals.[2]

From P. Degeling and H. K. Colebatch, 'Structure and action as constructs in the practice of public administration', *Australian Journal of Public Administration*, **XLIII**, 1984, pp. 320–31.

It has become clear, for instance, that while presentations of the organization as a coherent entity with a clear set of goals are important in the process of organizing, they are not accurate descriptions of the process.[3] Other studies have raised questions about the presumed primacy of managers and their capacity to impose their will over organizational processes. Again it is clear that while the attribution of managerial primacy is a significant factor in the structuring of relations (that is, it is important in the exercise of managerial control), this is itself not an accurate and full description of how relations within organizations are structured and conducted.[4]

Recent studies have also questioned the presumption of managerial homogeneity implicit in the instrumentalist view of organization. Under examination, "management" turns out not to be a single entity, and certainly not a single-minded one. Managers have been shown to be participants in continuing contests, characterized by contingent power and shifting coalitions.[5] The increasing focus on the processes in which managers are engaged has led some writers to question the assumption that positivistic science will produce "efficient management". Evered, for instance, points out that management:

- is centrally concerned with action-taking . . . yet nearly all published research (on management) ignores action.
- involves making projections which are not open to empirical research but require the creation of a new paradigm of inquiry which will overcome the crucial deficiencies of positivistic science.
- deals with diagnosis, judgement and interpretation of events and as such requires pattern recognition and a different kind of knowing that logic and rationality are conceived in positivistic science.
- is a political process, in which the exercise of power and influence is dependent on the social and historical context in which the actors are located. The approaches of positivistic science have proved inadequate for a satisfactory analysis of these processes.[6]

Evered concludes that managerial decisions and actions are both a product of and a reaction to the phenomena of organization as experienced and interpreted by participants. That is, outcomes are produced by the way that participants act in terms of their perceptions, their values and their experiences rather than the limited "behavioural variables" which yield the universal categories (for example "human needs") of the positivistic approach. Thus we need to develop non-positivistic theories that incorporate "the unique experiential and phenomenal reality of the actors. We need theories in which the 'field' is defined by the organizational participants rather than categorical scientists".[7]

Social action theory and the practice of administration

Our understanding of organizations (and management processes) has been enhanced by the application of social action theory to their analysis.[8] Put simply, social action theory argues that the actions of organizational participants are only understandable in terms of the subjective meanings which actors attribute to the situations confronting them. This implies that analysis should focus on the meanings which actors attach to their own actions and attribute to the actions of others. Actors are depicted as intentional beings who, in casting their own actions and interpreting and evaluating the actions of others, make use of frameworks of meaning which are socially and historically based, are (in part) institutionalized and, in many instances, are perceived by those involved as social facts. To the extent that particular frameworks of meaning are shared by numbers of actors and provide a basis for them to cohere, and people act in terms of these frameworks, their actions contribute to both the re-affirmation of these frameworks and the maintenance of social (and hence organizational) structure.

Social action theorists focus attention on the inter-subjective dimension of organizational life: that is, how it is constructed, sustained and changed by the actors in interaction with one another. When viewed from a social action perspective, the arrangement and practices used (relating to the definition and division of work, the exercise of control over personnel and clientele, and resource allocation and decision processes within organizations) cannot be taken as given. Nor can they be seen as products of past exercises in organizational design which, once promulgated, will automatically be binding on organizational participants.

Instead, social action theorists argue that the various dimensions of organization structure and process (and the arrangements and practices which give them form) can only be understood when they are examined from the perceptions that participants hold of them, and how they act accordingly. From this basis, it is then possible to demonstrate how particular arrangements and practices come to be accepted and taken for granted; how and why previously accepted and taken-for-granted constructions come to be challenged; and how what is regarded as accepted practice is subject to negotiation and can be changed over time.

The social action perspective demonstrates that organizations can no longer be viewed primarily as goal-directed instruments: that is, to explain and evaluate an organization in terms of its presumed functions or goals is an inadequate base both for understanding the organizational process and for locating oneself within it as an actor. Rather, organizations are seen as structures of order in which outcomes (goods and services, and also the patterning of relations) emerge from continuing processes of negotiation. Furthermore, managers can no longer be seen as framing and implementing unambiguous organizational goals; rather, their activities are seen to focus on the maintenance of negotiated order within and between organizations.

In the social action perspective, then, management requires a self-awareness on the part of practitioners. They need to be aware of how prevailing organizational arrangements and practices have differing meanings and significance for those who are subject to them as well as for those responsible for their operation. They need an understanding of how frameworks of meaning, and consequent modes of discourse, are developed and propagated, and how in their use, these modes of discourse shape the terms under which organizational relationships are conducted. In studying administration, both academics and practitioners will want to increase their awareness of the inter-subjective dimensions of social and organizational life and the implications that these hold both in the casting of our own actions and in interpreting and evaluating or judging the actions of others.[9] And they need to understand that different frameworks of meaning can be in use simultaneously, and that these can have different implications for the structuring of organizational relationships. For instance, if we were to look at public administration in relation to the Sydney milk supply, we might encounter a range of abstract concepts: "market forces", or "government policy", or "orderly marketing". Each of these emerges from a different set of assumptions about the way the world works, that is a different framework of meaning. They are not simply concepts, but are statements about the relationships between participants in a complex organizational situation, the Sydney milk supply, and they are mobilized to explain and legitimate particular sorts of relationships. In so doing they underwrite the claims of some participants, and discount those of others.

Social structure and the analysis of organizational life
This perspective on organizations as systems of negotiated order is contested by others who see them as media through which relations of domination are maintained in capitalist society. They see organizations as systems of order which reflect and recreate established relations of power and social and economic advantage within a society. These theorists, whom we shall call "structuralists",[10] argue that organizational analysis should go beyond description of the behaviour of those who are involved in or affected by organizational processes, and should focus on the complexity of social and economic forces within a society which are given form and force by the actions of organizational participants. The structuralists argue that the social (and hence structural) make-up of these actions only becomes clear when analysis moves beyond the

formalized arrangements and practices used in particular organizational contexts and takes account of the social/historical factors which affect and are reflected in the structuring of relations within a society. To structuralists this means that organizational analysis should focus on the interrelationship between the economic structure of society, its class relations, its ideologies, and how these are developed over time. From this basis it will then be possible to explain the structuring of relations within and between organizational contexts and how this constrains actions on the part of some and facilitates actions on the part of others.

Structuralists have brought into sharper focus the differences in power and advantage which are inherent in the conduct of relations in capitalist society, and in so doing they have brought into question the presumed neutral instrumentality of organizational processes inherent in functionalist analysis. However, the structuralists retain an instrumental orientation. This is demonstrated by their claims that their approach clarifies the way that organizations operate as media of control and how (in facilitating the control which some exercise over others) organizations contribute to the maintenance of existing modes of domination and reproduce prevailing differences of power and advantage within a society.

The instrumentalism inherent in the structuralists' accounts of organizations leads them to relate the way we think about management to those processes through which the existing structuring of relations within a society is reproduced.[11] To structuralists, the connections between thought, action and structure can be seen in the process of management education. The vocational nature of management education means that it is concerned first with equipping a particular group (existing and prospective managers) with the ideological forms which buttress the existing relations of power among capital workers, organizations and clients; and secondly, with providing this elite group with social technologies which can be used to maintain managerial primacy, and the continued operation of organizations as media of control. The structuralists argue that these outcomes can only be avoided by denying the legitimacy of the vocational orientations of the field of study and/or casting the educational process into a form which will offer a radical critique of capitalist society, capitalist modes of production and the location and practice of management within these.

Acceptance of these findings poses dilemmas for those of us – academics or practitioners – whose activities are oriented to the critical review of, and to having an impact on, administrative practice. When viewed from a structuralist perspective, we are either knowing collaborators in the perpetuation of structures of domination and inequality in our society; or as ineffective critics of these structures, we contribute to their stability: the system of repressive tolerance absorbs contradictions within our society, and the underlying legitimacy of the existing system of domination is not shaken.[12]

Framing an alternative paradigm

Social action theorists and structuralists provide covering fire for one another in their rejection of the instrumental paradigm, but diverge on the construction of an alternative – a divergence which emerges over such questions as power, consciousness, voluntarism and causality – in fact over the relationship between structure and action.

Social action theorists, stressing the importance of actors' perceptions in the creation of organization, question analyses which rely on some imputed force ("structure") which is independent of the actors themselves. They argue that to assume such a cause-and-effect relationship denies the capacity of actors: first, to ascribe meaning to the social and organizational world which both confronts them and is of their making; secondly, to make choices in the framing of their own actions and to act strategically; and thirdly, to make judgements about their own actions and actions of others.

Structuralists, by contrast, decry the voluntarism which they see as being inherent in the social action perspective. They argue that social action theorists, in their concern to take account of the way that the occurrences of social life are mediated and given meaning by actors, have given insufficient weight, first to the social and historical context in which action is taking place; secondly to the way that organizational actors are part of continuing structures of domination; and thirdly to the way that action within organizational contexts is shaped by and recreates relations of dependence and domination.

To overcome this impasse, we need to focus our attention on the relationship between structure and action. It is misleading to see these as distinct and opposed categories, since they are, in fact, parts of the same process. Cicourel,[13] for instance, argues for the abandonment of frameworks which depend on drawing distinctions (necessarily arbitrary) between so-called macro structures and the micro episodes of everyday life. Instead, analysis should be focused on the way that everyday encounters are both shaped by social forms, and in turn re-constitute[14] these social forms, whose existence and effect transcend the time and space of individual actions.

Habermas relates structure and action by focusing attention on the way that communicative modes (defined as ways of ordering and ascribing meaning to phenomena, and related approaches to reasoning and discourse) have emerged in particular social–historical contexts.[15] He argues that these communicative modes, by their use and by their consequent effect on action, constitute structure, both in interpersonal relations, and in an individual's relations with wider collectivities. Moreover, in industrial societies, the dominant communicative mode is one which places emphasis on rational choice, known goals, and instruments for their attainment, and which denies the significance of personal relationships (and hence "inter-subjectivity") in both reasoning and social discourse. Habermas argues that the dominance of this communicative mode when combined with the stated values of a market economy, which emphasizes the necessity of continued economic growth, and the social and instrumental efficacy of calculable market relations, has led to the emergence of a system of order in which social relations are objectified and increasingly made subject to rational (calculative) and organizationally-based forms of control. With western industrial societies these outcomes are justified by the claim that rationalized forms of control ensure social and political order and expand a society's instrumental capabilities. The consequent devaluation of the significance of socially-negotiated (that is inter-subjective) meaning is seen as contributing to social and political integration and the continued growth of purposively instrumental organizations is seen as extending the society's ability to exercise control over the processes of social and economic production.

Habermas argues that the resulting rationalization of social life and the attendant denial of politics as an integral aspect of social life is self-sustaining, unless it is subjected to critique which focuses on the processes which, in western industrial societies, have led to the displacement of inter-subjective modes of discourse and which in present day society sustains the dominance of instrumentalism in social, political and economic life. The development of such a critique will first raise our awareness of both the nature of the existing structures of domination and the deleterious effects that these produce for both individuals and society; secondly, will raise our awareness of how these structures of domination are constituted and maintained by the actions of those who are subject to them; and thirdly, will demonstrate how through critique, and resulting forms of self-awareness and action, the existing structures of domination can be displaced by social forms which will allow for greater inter-subjectivity in social relations. This will lift the social (other-regarding) potential of individuals and social institutions to the mutual benefit of both individuals and society.

The importance which Habermas has attributed to instrumental modes of communication in present day society has provided a point of entry for researchers and teachers of public administration who approach their work from a perspective which has come to be called "critical theory".[16] The presumed instrumental rationality of institutional and organizational forms has been questioned. Attention has also been paid to the way that within these institutions, questions of choice involving contending values and interests are either not recognized, or translated into problems which are soluble by the application of impersonally derived rules and/or "scientifically" derived techniques. It has also been shown that such procedural and technical approaches to choice and decision mask the exercise of power and legitimate existing structures of control. Denhardt has argued that the application of critical theory in research, teaching and administration will mean that questions about public policy and the operation of public organizations will be placed in "larger normative and historical contexts in which they properly reside". He argues that this use of critical theory will lead those involved in research, teaching and practice to lay "the foundations for greater autonomy and responsibility within the bureaucracy and its interactions with others" and will raise our awareness of the ". . . essential connection between personal and social self-reflection, and personal and social development (including organizational development)".[17]

How this restructuring is to be achieved is not clear. Habermas and Denhardt seem to assume that structural factors within a society can be altered, negated or removed simply by raising the awareness of those involved – a view of change akin to a debating society's belief in the ultimate power of reason. It collapses politics to reasoned debate (or in Habermas's terms, "unfettered discourse") about preferred states of social being and does not address how and why those who are being advantaged (as well as those who are disadvantaged) by the existing structuring of relations will act to maintain or to change these. Furthermore, by locating the impetus for change in the consciousness of individual actors, this approach avoids or ignores significant aspects of the analysis (elsewhere in critical theory) of how these relations have come to be structured over time, and are restrained by continuing action in which the actors are involved.

We can see this in Denhardt's discussion of the potential for change. He argues that if they act from a critical perspective actors can change the values and frames of reference which underlie some of the existing arrangements and practices within an organization even though these changes "might be at odds with the dominant values of the bureau-cracy". Denhardt recognizes that this possibility would be slighter "if we assume that the dominant values of the bureaucracy are those of the society, but [s]ince bureaucracies take on a 'life' of their own and values of their own, we have reason to question the correspondence of organizational values and those of society at large".[18]

But this position and its underlying assumptions seem open to question on a number of grounds. Denhardt, along with Habermas and others, has pointed to the pervasiveness of instrumental communicative modes in western industrial society, which is built upon bureaucratic organizations which are seen as rational, scientific instruments of control. The instrumental mode is not some private language for bureaucrats. If it were, the gulf between the values of officials and the values of the rest of society would in itself be a focus for change. And Denhardt's presentation of the problem does not address the question of interest and hence of content implicit in a challenge to the dominant instrumental paradigm.

At this stage, it is important to make two conceptual clarifications concerning the relationship first between structure and action, and secondly between organizational processes and interests. As we have said, structure and action are closely linked in that each is constituted by, and in turn constitutes, the other. In Giddens' terms, the social world enables, constrains and invokes action, and it is reproduced as skilled performance by actors, and in this way reconstituted.[19] Bourdieu argues that action should be seen as the merging of objectified history and embodied history.[20] By objectified history, he refers to the practices, beliefs and structured relations of power which are recognized as having been developed over time, and which govern relationships between the positions which actors occupy in social and organizational life. By embodied history, he means those aspects of historical experience which have been internalized by actors as part of their own selves, and which in this way shape their dispositions in continuing relations with others. In this way objectified history becomes "historical action" (or enacted history), and the prevailing structuring of relations within a society and the position that this sets out for actors are re-formed. This means that social action cannot be seen as the product of some "structural" force outside of the actors, nor can their actions be explained simply by reference to what is needful for the accomplishment of some objectified purpose external to the actors (for example "the needs of capital" or "the goals of the organization"). Rather the positions which the actors came to occupy and their interpretations of these, and the courses of action they see as being open to them, are themselves the outcomes of the actions of others, past and present, dominant and dominated, advantaged and disadvantaged. All individuals in the course of their involvement in struggles for power and advantage "short of opting out of the game and falling into oblivion, have no choice but to struggle to keep up or improve their position in the field".[21]

In the course of the struggles which take place, relationships are "restructured", though not necessarily changed, and a society comes to be "peopled" by institutional forms "which no one designed and wanted" and which show little evidence of instrumental purpose or even of volition. The structuring of relations which results will be such that even those who are in positions of dominance, "cannot say, even with the advantage of hindsight, how the formula was found, and are astonished that such institutions can exist as they do".[22] Furthermore, in relation to the disposition of actors, Bourdieu notes "that no one (actor or group of actors) can take advantage of the game, not even those who dominate it, without being taken up and taken in by it. Thus, there will be no game without a belief in the game and without the wills, intentions and aspirations which activate the agents"[23] as they seek to protect or enhance their positions. In this way the actors occupy positions, but are also appropriated by them. Through their actions in and reactions to the struggles which take place they contribute to the production and reproduction of social and historical processes (for example social structure) which shape both their positions in society and their dispositions in action.

To say that social practices, which include organizational forms, stem from objective and embodied history rather than from the instrumental purpose of one or some of the actors is not to imply that these arrangements, like other forms of social patterning, favour all of the actors equally. Practices used in the allocation of resources, the exercise of control, the attribution of legitimacy and standing, and the determination of access, eligibility and priority are obviously an important part of the structuring of inequality within society. In other words, the activity of organizing creates winners and losers – meaning not only that some people do better out of them than others, but also that the experience of this becomes part of the embodied history of the actors, and something which they are motivated to enhance, defend or challenge.

The analysis and practice of administration

Our analysis has led us away from the study of "the organization" towards the contemplation of "organizing". There are many bases for organizing people; they emerge from historical experience rather than from some mechanical form of social engineering; and they are articulated by frameworks of interpretation of experience and modes of communication. In this way they generate order, and hence create the organization. But it is created by social action, not by the imposition of science; it is not self-sustaining, but is recreated by the experience of participants; and it is not morally neutral – it creates winners and losers.

This calls for a clearer view of both where managers stand in organizations, and the nature of the activities in which they engage. It becomes clear that managers are partisan players in the political processes which arise from and give shape to the structuring of relations.

Their position and standing in these processes depends on their reputed and demonstrated ability to shape and maintain systems of order to which sufficient significant groupings within the organization and the wider society can subscribe. The activities in which they engage (that is mobilizing, co-opting, mediating, networking, brokering and enunciating or propagating generalized value/rule frameworks) are not neutral in content and intent. Rather, these activities are oriented toward shaping and/or sustaining the existing systems of order and sustaining their own positions both within and external to an organization.

So analysis and practice must recognize that organizational processes are shaped through structured contest. There are within social and organization (that is structured) contexts different bases for cohesion and for cleavage. These bases are given form through the activities of individuals who, in their efforts to fashion and maintain systems of order which are congruent with their definitions of meaning, their interests and their constructions of how relations ought to be conducted, bargain and negotiate with one another. Analysis which proceeds from a recognition of the structured (but nevertheless negotiated) nature of organizational life highlights the political nature of managerial involvement in the construction and maintenance of ordered relations within their organizations and with the society at large. The practice of managers who understand this will reflect their recognition that statements about "managerial authority" have to be interpreted as part of a particular negotiated order rather than as descriptions of normal practice. These managers will see that an appeal to their ascribed authority is a frail basis for affecting outcomes; but that their impact on outcomes is a consequence of their activity in constructing and maintaining relationships, mobilizing frameworks of meaning, shaping discourse – in other words, being active participants in the shaping of the negotiated order of which they are a part.

Notes

1. Examples of so-called environmental factors recognized as having an influence on organizational processes include the incorporation of clients and possible opponents into organizational processes: P. Selznick, *TVA and the Grass Roots*, Berkeley, University of California Press, 1949; the penetration of wider social and economic factors into organizational contexts and their effects on the conduct of relations within primary work groups and between these groups and other segments of an organization; E. L. Trist *et al.*, *Organizational Choice*, London, Tavistock, 1963; the effect of market forces, technological change and other forms of uncertainty and relations of dependence on the practices and use in organizations; P. Katz and R. L. Kahn, *The Social Psychology of Organizations*, New York,

Wiley, 1966; P. R. Lawrence and J. W. Lorsch, *Organization and Environment: Managing differentiation and integration*, Boston, Harvard University Press, 1967; J. D. Woodward, *Industrial Organization Theory and Practice*, London, Oxford University Press, 1965; J. D. Thompson, *Organizations in Action*, New York, McGraw-Hill, 1967.
2. A. W. Gouldner, "Organizational analysis", in R. K. Merton *et al.* (eds.), *Sociology Today*, New York, Basic Books, 1959; C. Perrow, "The analysis of goals in complex organizations", *American Sociological Review*, 26 1961, pp. 854–66; J. Stelling and R. Bucher, "Autonomy and monitoring of hospital wards", *Sociological Quarterly*, 13, 1972, pp. 431–46.
3. For an overview of the notion of goals in organization theory and the sociology of organizations, see Richard Scholl, "An analysis of macro models in organizations", *Administration and Society*, 13(3), 1981, pp. 271–98.
4. In essence the central concern of much of organization theory (to develop organization designs and methods of control whose use would enhance the position of management) bears witness to the contingent nature of managerial control. For an overview of the ideological nature of organization theory and its use in buttressing managerial primacy see J. Child, *British Management Thought*, London, Allen & Unwin, 1969. See also J. Pfeffer, *Power in Organizations*, Boston, Pitman, 1981, pp. 1–31.
5. See C. I. Barnard, *The Functions of the Executive*, Cambridge, Mass., Harvard University Press, 1938; M. Dalton, *Men Who Manage*, New York, Wiley, 1959; R. M. Cyert and J. G. March, *A Behavioural Theory of the Firm*, Englewood Cliffs, Prentice Hall, 1963; A. Jay, *Management and Machiavelli*, London, Hodder and Stoughton, 1967; C. Perrow, *Organizational Analysis: A sociological view*, London, Tavistock, 1970; Leonard R. Sayles, *Management Behavior*, New York, McGraw-Hill, 1964; A. Downs, *Inside Bureaucracy*, Boston, Little, Brown, 1967; A. M. Pettigrew, *The Politics of Organizational Decision Making*, London, Tavistock, 1973.
6. Roger Evered, "Management education for the year 2000" in Gary L. Cooper (ed.), *Developing Managers for the 1980's*, London, Macmillan, 1981.
7. *Ibid.*, p. 75.
8. D. Silverman, *The Theory of Organisations*, London, Heinemann, 1970; D. Silverman, "Some neglected questions about social reality", in P. Filmer *et al.* (eds.), *New Directions in Sociological Theory*, London, Collier-Macmillan, 1972; D. Silverman, "Accounts of organisation: organisational 'structures' and the accounting process", in J. B. McKinlay (ed.), *Cases in Organisational Behaviour*, London, Holt, Rinehart and Winston, 1975.
9. An extended discussion of these dimensions in administrative studies is provided in M. Harmon, *Action Theory for Public Administration*, London, Longman, 1981.
10. V. L. Allen, *Social Analysis: A Marxist critique and alternative*, London, Longman, 1975; Stewart Clegg and David Dunkerley, *Organizations, Class and Control*, London, Routledge & Kegan Paul, 1980; J. K. Benson, "Organisations: a dialectical view", *Administrative Science Quarterly*, 22, 1977, pp. 1–21. Some writers restrict the term "structuralist" to Levi-Strauss and his close followers; we do not.

11. An account of this dilemma is provided in Rosemary Deem, "The teaching of industrial sociology in higher education: an exploratory analysis", *Sociological Review*, 29(2), 1981, pp. 237–51.

12. H. Marcuse, *One-Dimensional Man*, London, Routledge & Kegan Paul, 1964.

13. A. V. Cicourel, "Notes on the integration of micro and macro-levels of analysis", in K. Knorr-Cetina and A. V. Cicourel (eds.), *Advances in Social Theory and Methodology*, London, Routledge & Kegan Paul, 1981.

14. Literally "re-constitute"; that is, these social forms ("structure") only continue to have force to the extent that people act in this way, and in so doing, re-constitute the structure through their actions.

15. J. Habermas, *Toward a Rational Society*, London, Heinemann, 1971.

16. See Richard Bates, "Educational administration, the technologization of reason and the management of knowledge: toward a critical theory", paper presented to the Annual Conference of the American Educational Research Association, Los Angeles, April 1981; Robert B. Denhardt, "Toward a critical theory of public organisations", *Public Administration Review*, 41(6), 1981, pp. 628–35; Robert E. Denhardt and Kathryn G. Denhardt, "Public administration and the critique of domination", *Administration and Society*, 11(1), 1979, pp. 107–20; Robert B. Denhardt, *In the Shadow of Organisation*, Lawrence, Kansas, The Regent Press, 1981.

17. Denhardt, *op. cit.*

18. *Ibid.*, p. 633.

19. Anthony Giddens, *Central Problems in Social Theory*, London, Macmillan, 1979, Ch. 2.

20. Pierre Bourdieu, "Men and machines", in K. Knorr-Cetina and A. V. Cicourel, *op. cit.*, Ch. 11. For an earlier use of Bourdieu's work see Clare Burton, "Labour market strategies in public sector and private sector organisations", paper presented to APROS Colloquium on the Public/Private Dichotomy in Organisational Analysis, Kuring-gai College of Advanced Education, Lindfield, NSW, August 1982.

21. Pierre Bourdieu, *op. cit.*, p. 307.

22. *Ibid.*, pp. 311–12.

23. *Ibid.*, p. 308.

Collaboration in social welfare

A framework for analysis

Bob Hudson

Collaboration is a paradoxical concept in the field of social welfare. There can be little doubt that the notion is in vogue. The desirability of some form of collaborative activity has become a *sin qua non* of effective practice within the welfare professions, both at practitioner and policy-making levels. However, we know remarkably little about how collaborative activity works, why it may initially be developed, how it may be measured or even how it may be defined.

Social science research on organisations has tended to be principally concerned with *intra*-organisational phenomena. Psychologists have studied the individual in an organisation; social psychologists have focused on the relations amongst members of a group in an organisation, and the impact of a group on the attitudes and behaviour of group members; sociologists have studied informal groups, formal sub-units and the structural attributes of an organisation. There has been relatively little attempt to focus on *inter*-organisational behaviour, particularly in the application to welfare policies in Britain. This paper attempts to outline a framework for the analysis of collaborative activity, which may then be applied to a variety of welfare settings.

The significance of inter-organisational behaviour

At a broad level, the significance of interlocking networks of organisations has been established at least since the publication of C. Wright

From B. Hudson, 'Collaboration in social welfare: a framework for analysis', *Policy and Politics*, **15**, 1987, pp. 175–82.

Mills' *The Power Elite* in 1956, and it is now more widely accepted that it is interlocking organisations rather than individuals that are at the centre of power systems. Consumers or clients of welfare organisations are usually served, processed, changed or harassed not by a single organisation but by a number of related organisations.

One approach to this difficulty would be to encourage awareness on the part of the related organisations of the impact of their activities upon the individual client or consumer. This is premised upon certain assumptions about the motivation of principal decision-makers, most notably that a prevailing spirit of altruism will result in co-operation as soon as individual or community needs become known. However, it may be more realistic to assume not only that inter-organisational collaboration in social welfare has no qualities of spontaneous growth or self-perpetuation, but also that organisations strive to maintain their autonomy.

From an agency's viewpoint, collaborative activity raises two main difficulties. First, it loses some of its freedom to act independently, when it would prefer to maintain control over its domain and affairs. Second, it must invest scarce resources and energy in developing and maintaining relationships with other organisations, when the potential returns on this investment are often unclear or intangible. Hence it could be posited that an agency prefers *not* to become involved in inter-organisational relationships unless it is compelled to do so, and that simple appeals to client well-being may constitute an insufficient motivation.

A much more powerful motivation concerns the realisation of organisational goals. Welfare organisations do not normally possess or control the entire complement of resources needed for their goal accomplishment. Funds, facilities, personnel or other resources may be lacking in some measure, and organisations may therefore enter into exchanges with one another to acquire needed resources. Yuchtman and Seashore (1967) go so far as to define 'organisational effectiveness' as 'the ability of an organisation to exploit its environment in obtaining resources, while at the same time maintaining an autonomous bargaining position'.

In Britain, there is a small but growing empirical literature on collaborative welfare activity. Much of this stems from 'community care' policies and focuses in particular upon the relationship between health and personal social services authorities, but the collaborative theme has also been scrutinised in other diverse fields such as child abuse, the treatment of juvenile offenders and the housing/social services interface. What has been noticeably absent is a theoretical framework to bring some order to the findings. Transfers of resources among profit-making organisations are mediated by money and behaviour may be explained in terms of economic theory and market behaviour, but these concepts do not appear suitable for explaining interaction amongst welfare organisations. This paper will attempt to provide a more appropriate framework.

Modes of organisational co-existence

Not all organisational relationships are conducive to collaboration. Litwak and Hylton (1962) identify three modes of organisational co-existence, each with different implications for the likely development of collaboration—independence, interdependence and conflict.

Two organisations may be said to be *independent* of one another if neither needs the other's resources to accomplish its goals, and neither is interfering in the other's goal achievement. When this occurs, there is little need for exchange between organisations, and since agencies do not generally co-operate unless they have to, one would predict a low level of collaboration. If the presence of collaboration is to be broadly accounted for, then perhaps the most general explanation for its occurrence may be found in the notion of organisational *interdependence*, where each organisation perceives that its own goals can be achieved most effectively with the assistance of the resources of the others.

Conflict arises when the goal achievement of one or more organisations occurs at the expense of the goal achievement of others. Although conflict *per se* may constrain or block inter-organisational exchange, its presence also indicates some potential for such exchange; therefore, inter-organisational conflicts may be considered a more favourable condition for collaboration than independence. Organisations may move from interdependence to conflict or vice versa, through relatively subtle shifts in goals or available resources. Molnar and Rogers (1979) further distinguish between structural and operational conflict. *Structural conflict* occurs over the basic identities and responsibilities that define a relationship, and reflects an inability to establish or maintain the basic rules or principles that govern the relationship. *Operating conflict* represents the disagreements over task expectations or role performance within an inter-organisational relationship, and can be viewed as a continual process of mutual adjustment between interacting organisations.

Given that some scope for collaborative activity seems feasible or actually exists, how can we explain any specific linkages that develop? A threefold focus is available: upon the environmental context; upon the comparative properties of an organisational network; and upon collaborative linkages themselves. These three approaches are not in conflict, but should be viewed as complementary approaches. A total analysis of inter-organisational relations would require a thorough understanding of the interplay between the variables operating on all levels, but such an analysis is dependent upon the delineation and operationalisation of these variables.

The environmental context

External factors in the environment may create the necessary preconditions for inter-organisational relations by affecting the ability of an organisation to function independently. In 'turbulent fields', individual organisations, however large, cannot expect to adapt successfully, simply through their own direct actions. Emery and Trist (1965) identify several indicators of 'turbulence'—a field containing a relatively large number of organisations; inability of agencies to satisfy the demand for services; an unstable social situation; a new programme or piece of legislation; a retrenching economy. Much of this could apply to Britain.

Although a turbulent environment establishes a context for collaborative decision-making and perhaps creates a necessity for action, the tendency of organisations to act as closed systems and resist such pressures to adapt is still powerful. In Emery and Trist's research, it appeared that environmental pressures were great enough to induce agencies to talk together and enter a relatively loose confederative arrangement. It was not until much later, when the financial rewards for a closer relationship were tripled, that the agencies give up anything of value. Clearly the environment is important, but not of itself sufficient, to explain the existence and nature of inter-organisational relationships. More immediate factors require to be examined.

The comparative properties approach

The comparative dimension has been viewed as an initial determinant of the occurrence of collaborative activity and as a factor in its continued existence and success.

The comparative properties approach involves examining the similarities or differences of interacting groups or organisations on certain attributes or dimensions which constitute a set of conditions that continually shape the pattern of interaction. In effect, the comparative properties are seen as independent variables, and any subsequent collaborative mechanism as dependent variables. The literature identifies several comparative property prerequisites for the creation of collaborative activity.

Inter-organisational homogeneity

This variable is concerned with the degree to which the members of an interaction network exhibit functional and structural similarity. Reid (1969) takes the view that although similarity of goals is not necessary for collaboration to develop, it is likely to lead to additional cohesion, and more extensive and stable exchanges. Some of the literature on health/personal social services forums would certainly suggest that one obstacle to more fruitful collaboration is the difference in value-systems and goals amongst the participants. Whilst all may find virtue in a 'banner' goal of 'community care', the operationalisation of the goal may reveal conflicting underlying assumptions.

Hasenfeld (1972) makes a useful distinction between 'people-processing' and 'people-changing' organisations. Within the welfare field, the traditional focus has been upon the latter, whose explicit function has been to change client behaviour. Education and social work organisations are obvious examples.

'People-processing' organisations process people and confer public status upon them, and thereby shape people's lives by controlling their access to a range of settings. Examples would be Job Centres, Observation and Assessment Centres and Juvenile Courts.

'People-processing' organisations are much more likely to be involved in collaborative activity. Their *raison d'être* is the classification and disposition of clients, and the reactions to the status they confer occur mainly outside their boundaries. Staff activity will consist of transactions with clients at input, negotiations with them on a classification–disposition status at output, and exchanges with potential external recipients of the clients. 'People-changing' organisations are more likely to be insulated from the environment and from organisational boundary transactions. Hence it could be hypothesised that 'people-changing' organisations will be less attracted to collaborative activity than 'people-processing' organisations. This notion would help to explain why, for example, social work has a poor record of 'boundary transaction' activity with organisations concerned with social security and housing.

Domain consensus

There is some overlap between the notions of organisational homogeneity and domain consensus. Any discussion of inter-organisational analysis either explicitly or implicitly deals with the concepts of domain and domain consensus.

Thompson (1967) defines it as:

a set of expectations, both for members of an organisation and for others with whom they interact, about what the other organisation will and will not do . . . it provides an image of the organisation's role in a larger system, which in turn serves as a guide for the ordering of action in certain directions and not in others.

Braito *et al.* (1972) operationalised it as an organisation's statement as to whether or not a particular organisation should be involved in an agency formed for a specific purpose.

The establishment of domain consensus requires the resolution of some potentially difficult issues. First it requires agreement on specific organisational goals. Second it assumes a compatibility of organisational goals, philosophies and reference orientations. Finally, it requires some agreement amongst kindred professionals upon their position in a hierarchy of professionals. Clearly these will not be attained easily. An organisation's history and association with a particular problem should increase the possibility of the problem being within its domain, but even this may be insufficient to maintain the domain consensus. The public, political or other organisations may become dissatisfied with the progress of a particular organisation, question its domain and withdraw legitimation. The manner in which in the 1940s local government lost its responsibility for both hospitals and poor law relief may be examined within this framework.

The establishment of a consensus over domain has two important implications. The most obvious is the securing of legitimated claims. Possession of a domain permits an organisation to operate in a certain sphere, claim support for its activities and define proper practices within its realm. Moreover, the authority to conduct activities is generally assumed to imply a claim upon money adequate to attain performance in a prescribed sphere.

The other implication is for collaborative activity itself, but the literature has conflicting views on this. When organisations have similar domains, they are likely to be aware of one another and to have the resources needed to help each other achieve their respective goals, but similar domains also increase the potential for territorial disputes and competition. Van de Ven (1976) proposes a concave-shaped relationship between domain similarity and collaborative activity, in which the polar ends of high and low domain similarity are unlikely conditions for collaboration, and the intermediate ranges the most likely.

Network awareness

It has already been suggested that interdependency is the most fertile ground for collaboration, but organisations must have *awareness* of their interdependence. Not only must they have knowledge of one another's existence, but they must also perceive a possible matching of goals and resources that would result in more effective goal achievement. Collaboration will also be affected by the extent of positive evaluation—the judgement by workers in the organisation of the value of the work of another organisation.

This may be affected by the length of time that organisations have been members of a network. A history of distinct administrative divisions, separate patterns of accountability and isolated patterns of training and professional socialisation all militate against positive network awareness. It is not uncommon in the literature to find not only a poor understanding of the roles of related professions and organisations, but also an unduly critical appraisal of any potential contribution. Most of the reports of inquiries into child abuse cases provide ample evidence of this.

Organisational exchange

The concept of 'exchange' can be traced back to the work of Marcel Mauss, who proposed an explanation for the seemingly one-way transfer of resources by suggesting that receipt of the gift created an obligation in the receipt. The concept, therefore, implies that no goods or services are ever transferred without reciprocity of some kind being involved. Theorists have utilised exchange notions to provide a loose conceptual framework for their analyses, but few attempts have been made to apply these to inter-organisational relationships in welfare.

In their seminal contribution, Levine and White (1961) defined 'exchange' as 'any voluntary activity between two organisations which has consequences, actual or anticipated, for the realisation of their respective goals and objectives'.

Cook (1977) points out that the problem with this definition is that it incorporates *any* form of voluntary activity, thereby rendering the term synonymous with *interaction*. She prefers to confine the concept to those situations where interactions are based upon reciprocal reinforcement— where exchange provides for *each* actor a reduction in organisational uncertainty.

An exchange analysis is fruitful because it focuses attention upon power processes, which are fundamental to an understanding of collaboration. In exchange relationships, power is linked to dependence. It is precisely because the needs of *both* participating parties need to be fulfilled by an exchange (i.e. it must be beneficial to both) that an integrated and rational system does not always evolve. There are many cases where a transfer of resources from one organisation to another may be desirable from the viewpoint of a co-ordinated system, but may be beneficial to only one party. The reluctance of the NHS to enter into unilateral resource transfers to local authorities in pursuit of a community-based scheme for some clients is an illustration of this. An exchange relation is balanced when the actors have equal power (or equal levels of dependency), but equality is not a precondition for exchange. What is necessary is that neither party is powerless in relation to others, otherwise exchange will amount to little more than the formalisation of the clear dominance of one party over another.

Alternative resource sources

An important element in organisational exchange is the availability of alternative sources. An organisation is less dependent upon exchange relations with other organisations in its network to the extent that it has accessibility to elements it needs from 'outside' sources. In terms of Hasenfeld's (1972) 'people-processing' organisations, the availability of such alternatives will increase the discretion of personnel responsible for processing and reduce the pressure to form links with any one outlet. Without such alternatives, the organisation would be under pressure to control either its intake or its output of clients, or both. It may, for example, only accept clients for whom disposition resources are available, or it may confer a 'holding' status, linking the person to an outlet but defining him or her as unready for disposition. Hasenfeld's study of employment placement agencies found that clients for whom job opportunities were not available were more likely to be classified as requiring counselling than similar clients for whom job opportunities *were* available. In Britain, this framework could help to explain the functioning of observation and assessment centres, the availability of assessments and statements under the 1981 Education Act, and the continued high use of custodial options by juvenile courts.

In the comparative properties approach, the basic unit of analysis is the network of organisations, consisting of a number of distinguishable organisations having a significant amount of interaction with each other.

Such interaction may at one extreme include extensive reciprocal exchanges, and at the other intense hostility or conflict. [The] variables [. . .] above may help us to explain such variations. Benson (1975) puts forward the notion of 'inter-organisational equilibrium'. An inter-organisational network is said to be equilibrated to the extent that participant organisations are engaged in highly co-ordinated, co-operative interactions based upon normative consensus and mutual respect. He hypothesises that there is a tendency towards equilibrium, and argues that increases in one equilibrium component (partly covering [the variables] above) will tend to be associated with increases in the others. Similarly, decreases in one will be associated with decreases in the others.

The focus on collaborative linkages

The third and final focus is upon the actual *dimensions* of interaction or exchange between organisations. Four key dimensions tend to be used for examining linkage mechanisms.

Degree of formalisation
Several analyses have noted variations in the extent to which the requirements and characteristics of collaborative situations are made explicit. There are two main ways in which we can attempt to assess the degree of formalisation of a relationship—the existence of administrative or legislative sanction, and the existence or otherwise of an intermediary co-ordinating body.

The extent to which an interdependency is given *official sanction* by the parties involved refers to the degree to which rules, policies and procedures govern inter-agency agreements and contracts. In social welfare settings, informal tacit arrangements occur quite frequently among organisations—cases may be referred from one agency to another and ideas can be exchanged—but formal agreements are less common. This may be in part attributable to the greater commitment required of a formal agreement, and the potential threat to organisational autonomy which it poses.

Formalisation increases as an agreement is verbalised, written down, contractual and, ultimately, mandatory. Mandated interactions involve laws or regulations specifying areas of domain, information and financial obligations, the most obvious form being one externally imposed by the legal or political system. Aldrich (1976) found that these tended to be more intense, unbalanced in favour of one of the organisations studied and associated with lower perceived co-operation.

Benson (1975) hypothesised that in voluntary, non-mandated situations, domain consensus and positive evaluation were preconditions for collaboration, and the organisations attempted to exert power as the exchange occurred. However, when collaboration is mandated by law, the roles of the interacting organisations have already been defined, and domain consensus should not be an issue.

In such situations, positive evaluation becomes a key issue for the interacting organisations. In the operation of joint finance, for example, a form of mandated relationship exists, but there may continue to be professional and organisational skirmishing over the respective abilities and perspectives of health and personal social services.

The second dimension of formalisation is the existence of an *intermediary co-ordinating body*, which offers a measure of *structural* as opposed to *agreement* formalisation. An agency may be considered 'co-ordinating' if one of its important functions is to bring about exchanges amongst other organisations. Reid (1969) distinguishes between two major strategies that may be used to achieve this—the facilitation and induction of interdependence.

The 'facilitation' of interdependence rests upon the assumption that the organisations to be co-ordinated are already close to interdependence or are ready to move in this direction. The degree of facilitation required will depend upon the degree of interdependence already present. At its simplest, this strategy could be executed by the development of inter-organisational awareness of potential interdependencies in relation to existing goals and resources.

A more common and problematic circumstance arises when a co-ordinating agency is confronted with either a high degree of independence or conflict among constituent organisations.

This may require interdependency to be 'induced' by effecting major changes in their goals and use of resources. This inducement may be generated by the use of resources which the co-ordinating agency possesses or controls and which other organisations desire. In this way, for example, the Housing Corporation may be said to have brought a degree of order to the voluntary sector of housing. Alternatively, inducement may be accomplished through the use of 'power' or 'influence', whereby organisational goals are modified by external influences. For example, in the 1970s the DHSS and Department of the Environment attempted, by the use of Circular (18/74) and then legislation (1977 Homeless Persons Act), to impose collaborative activity upon local authority housing and social services departments. Such an approach may be tenuous and subject to rupture.

Degree of intensity
The level of intensity indicates the amount of *investment* an organisation has in its relations with other organisations. Aldrich (1979) identified two measures of intensity. First, the *amount of resources* involved in a relationship. Among welfare agencies, the number of services, referrals and staff support provided to another organisation are common indicators of the intensity of a relation, but measurement is much easier in the profit-orientated sector. Second, the *frequency of interaction* between organisations, although cognisance needs to be taken of the nature of contacts and the authority level at which they take place.

Most social services contacts involve boundary-spanning personnel who arrange the referral of clients, but these contacts may not be critical to organisational survival.

Rogers (1974) has attempted to develop a scale of intensity in inter-organisational relationships, ranging through director acquaintance, director interaction, information exchange, resource exchange, overlapping membership and written agreements. *Ad hoc* case co-ordination draws only minimally upon the resources of an organisation, whereas some form of 'programme co-ordination' encompasses a much larger portion. Unless the success of a venture has been clearly established, organisations will be inclined to choose the less intense situation over that which is highly demanding.

Degree of reciprocity

The reciprocal dimension to a collaborative relationship is based upon the notion of 'exchange', discussed earlier. Interactions need not necessarily be symmetrical—some parties to an exchange may have greater influence in determining the bases and conditions of the activity than others.

There are several elements of reciprocation, of which the most common is *resource reciprocity*—the extent to which the resources in a transaction (or in the longer run, a relationship) flow to both parties equally or benefit one of them unilaterally. The units of value transacted between agencies may encompass money, physical facilities and materials, and client referrals.

Information flows are also important—messages or communications about the units of exchange or the nature of the relationship. Resource and information flows constitute the bases of a social action system, but measurement within welfare settings is problematic because such transactions cannot be assigned an unambiguous value. This is even more true of an intangible such as prestige—the judgement by workers in one organisation of the value of the work of another organisation. Indeed, where such judgements are negative, self-validating ideologies may be internally generated which negate the assessment criteria used by external groups. Collaboration will be unlikely in such circumstances.

A related notion is *definitional reciprocity*—the extent to which the terms of a transaction are mutually agreed upon, with equal contributions from all participants. Interaction is not limited to situations in which both parties set the terms of the agreement. Many welfare agencies must follow regulatory or legislative guidelines in establishing collaborative relationships, therefore many of the terms are pre-set. However, an organisation may be predisposed to joint activity, but avoid a specific encounter because there is no give and take in problem definition.

Degree of standardisation

This represents another dimension taken from traditional models of bureaucratic structure. Just as internal standardisation of procedures smooths bureaucratic operations and promotes efficiency, so the standardisation of external relations is sought by cost-conscious administrators. Two aspects of standardisation can be distinguished.

First, *unit standardisation*—the extent of similarity between the individual units of the resources in a transaction. Litwak and Hylton (1962) hypothesise that the institution of formal collaborative mechanisms requires some reliable determination of the units of exchange and the repetition of the exchange. The argument implies that when the exchange elements are ill-defined and shifting, interaction is possible but formal interaction unlikely. Second, *procedural standardisation*—the degree of similarity over time in the procedures used for inter-organisational transactions. The intensity of interaction will have a positive effect on standardisation, because the larger the investment organisations have in each other, the more they are pushed into standardised modes of interaction for protecting their investments.

Standardisation does differ from formalisation. The latter refers to the extent to which there is an official agreement, but does not necessitate explicitness on details. An agreement that a relationship will be established may be found, but that agreement may leave open the nature and operation of the exchange.

Not all of the variables [above] are likely to be of equal significance. The resource indicator of intensity is particularly sensitive and likely to place constraints upon the others. In a situation involving large resources, one could anticipate formal agreements, standardisation of both units and procedures and reciprocal flow.

Marrett (1971) proposes two inter-organisational models. The first is characterised by a low degree of formalisation, standardisation and intensity and is represented by the kind of interaction that occurs among social welfare personnel over referrals. The second is highly formalised, standardised and intense, and is far less likely because it involves the kind of investments and commitments which organisations may not be inclined to make. Marrett argues that research is needed not so much on the first model as on the constraints to the realisation of the second.

Social change in inter-organisational networks

Given the preceding analysis, how might inter-organisational networks change in such a way as to promote collaboration? Benson (1975) identifies three sources of pressure.

Co-operative strategies
Change is sought through agreements and joint planning in which each affected social unit participates and exercises options, and any resultant network alterations are typically compromises agreed upon by the affected organisations. Such compromises will usually involve a process

of negotiation and exchange through which each party voluntarily relinquishes some valued condition in exchange for similar concessions on the part of others. However, despite the frequency of co-operative strategies, the conditions for their success are restricted, since each party must hold something of value for the other party and be capable of resisting the other's demands. Agreements may cover a wide variety of products or behaviour—exchanges of funds, personnel, facilities and clients are among the most obvious, but agreements to cease disruptive and harassing activities may be of equal importance.

Incentives strategies
This constitutes the purposeful alteration of environmental constraints which may be inhibiting collaborative activity, but falls short of a directive. It may be seen as analogous to government regulation of the economy through manipulation of interest rates, tax rates and the money supply. Such a strategy may involve an alteration of the total volume of resources flowing into a network (as in the case of joint finance) or an alteration of resource channels as a means of changing priorities. Tactics such as these typically belong to an executive office or a legislative body.

Authoritative strategies
Organisations with common vertical ties may be *directed* to engage in joint activities that would not ordinarily occur on a voluntary basis. Relations between agencies may be precisely specified, covering the regulation of contacts, referrals, resource sharing and so forth. This is premised upon the possibility of an executive or legislative body utilising a dominant position in the flow of resources to *specify* the nature of programmes and linkages at subordinate levels, and not merely to encourage or reward such activities. This could cover the example of a local authority taking action to prevent 'departmentalism', as in the cases of corporate planning and the fusion of social services and housing departments in several of the London boroughs. It would also encompass attempts at national government level to rearrange boundaries in the pursuit of collaboration, such as the attempt to produce coterminous boundaries between health and social services authorities in the 1974 NHS reorganisation.
    Broadly, such a strategy could cover:

1. the introduction of new programmes of agencies;
2. the formalisation of linkages which had hitherto been informal or variable;
3. the rearrangement of an entire system of inter-agency boundaries and linkages.

Conclusion: a warning

This paper has drawn upon American literature on management and the sociology of organisations to suggest an analytical framework for the analysis of collaborative activity in social welfare settings. The British approach to this important area has been unduly empirical. The usefulness of such a framework remains to be put to the test in a variety of settings. [. . .]

However, a provisional warning should be given against thinking that collaboration is likely to be a significant factor in resolving welfare dilemmas. Davidson (1976) has noted the paradox whereby:

> commentators on the effects of co-ordination are almost uniformly pessimistic, yet co-ordination continues to be promoted as a means of providing greater rationality in the delivery of services.

Warren *et al.* (1974) have also pointed to the frequent failure of structural arrangements for collaboration in attaining tangible results. They found that out of a total of 406 reports of structured co-ordination, only 125 instances of positive tangible results were obtained, and 29 of these were simply tautological references to improved communications.

The state of the art in assessing the feasibility of successful collaboration is not well enough developed to include precise operationalised measures for the variables involved, and further research is needed on operationalisation of the concepts and on testing the relationships between them. But at the end of the day, the fashioning of collaborative relationships of substance remains a job for talented practitioners.

References

Aldrich, H. (1976), 'Resource dependence and interorganisational relationships', *Administration and Society*, Volume 7.

Aldrich, H. (1979), *Organisations and Environments*, Prentice Hall.

Benson, J. K. (1975), 'The interorganisational network as a political economy', *Administrative Science Quarterly*, Volume 20, June.

Braito, R., Paulson, S. and Klongon, G. (1972), 'Domain consensus: a key variable in interorganisational analysis', in Brinkerhoff, M. and Kunz, P., *Complex Organisations and their Environments*, Wm. C. Brown.

Cook, K. (1977), 'Exchange and power in networks of interorganisational relations', *Sociological Quarterly*, Volume 18.

Davidson, S. M. (1976), 'Planning and co-ordination of social services in multi-organisational contexts', *Social Services Review*, March.

Emery, F. and Trist, E. (1965), 'The causal texture of organisational environments', *Human Relations*, 18.

Hasenfeld, Y. (1972), 'People processing organisations: an exchange approach', *American Sociological Review*, Volume 37.

Levine, S. and White, P. (1961), 'Exchange as a conceptual framework for the study of interorganisational relationships', *Administrative Science Quarterly*, Volume 5.

Litwak, E. and Hylton, L. (1962), 'Interorganisational analysis: a hypothesis on co-ordinating agencies', *Administrative Science Quarterly*, Volume 6, March.

Marrett, C. (1971), 'On the specification of interorganisational dimension', *Sociology and Social Research*, Volume 61.

Molnar, J. and Rogers, D. (1979), 'A comparative model of interorganisational conflict', *Administrative Science Quarterly*, Volume 24.

Reid, W. J. (1969), 'Interorganisational co-ordination in welfare: a theoretical approach to analysis and intervention' in Kramer, R. and Specht, H., *Readings in Community Organisation Practice*, Prentice Hall.

Rogers, D. (1974), 'Towards a scale of interorganisational relations among public agencies', *Sociology and Social Research*, Volume 59.

Thompson, J. D. (1967), *Organisations in Action*, McGraw-Hill.

Warren, R., Rose, S. and Bergunder, A. (1974), *The Structure of Urban Reform*, D.C. Heath.

Van de Ven, A. (1976), 'On the nature, formation and maintenance of relations among organisations', *Academy of Management Review*, Volume 1, Part 4.

Yuchtman, E. and Seashore, S. (1967), 'A system resource approach to organisational effectiveness', *American Sociological Review*, Volume 32, December.

Part VIII

The influence of front-line staff

Street-level bureaucracy, professionalism and discretion

Introduction

In analysing his 'bureaucratic process model', in the article in Part VII, Elmore drew upon Michael Lipsky's theory of 'street-level bureaucracy'. This has been of seminal importance for the examination of the impact of comparatively low-level actors as the *de facto* creators of policy. The central thrust of Lipsky's argument is comparatively simple; it is then very carefully elaborated in his book. Here what has been chosen is a small extract from the beginning of Lipsky's *Street-Level Bureaucracy* in which he sets out his essential ideas. This is followed by an article by Hudson in which he explores some key aspects of Lipsky's theory and draws upon a range of sources, including Lipsky's own pupils as well as some British writers, to illustrate the use of the theory.

Two key points about Lipsky's work should be emphasised. One is that he must not be taken to be saying simply that street-level bureaucrats subvert policy goals. Inasmuch as they do this it is because of a lack of clarity in those goals or a lack of resources to achieve them. The painful problem for street-level bureaucrats is that they enter employment with ideals which they cannot realise in practice. They *do* make policy, but not in the way they would really like to. Coping strategies dominate their lives. In this sense Lipsky's work is more compatible with the bottom-up than with the top-down approach to implementation. In addressing the normative issue, which we have seen that debate raises, Lipsky does not regard the process by which actual policy is determined as an ideal one. In a section towards the end of his book he does suggest that greater accountability of street-level bureaucrats to their clients may offer a way out of the 'dilemma' – which is, of course, the characteristic bottom-up solution.

The second important point about Lipsky's work is that many of his street-level bureaucrats are professional or semi-professional workers. Indeed, the latter term has been particularly applied to professional workers in organisations who lack control over their working conditions (Etzioni, 1969). Had space allowed it would have been desirable to explore the theme of professionalism in public service organisations more widely for the following reasons:

1. Professionalism has tended to involve making claims to work autonomy, arguing that responsibility to clients overrides responsibility to political policy makers.
2. Alternatively professionals have been seen as a group of bureaucratic employees particularly likely to engage in bureau-enlargement (see Tullock in Part III) or bureau-shaping (see Dunleavy in Part III) and accordingly an alternative model is advanced for public control over professionals which aims to put them in a position in which they are forced to sell their services in competition with each other (Friedson, 1970).

The issue of control over decision making is inevitably explored in terms of discretion. To what extent is the nature of the task to be performed by many street-level workers (and particularly service professionals) one in which surveillance by managers is difficult and decisions need to rest upon individual discretion? This is then often linked, and often confused, with the related normative question: to what extent is this discretion desirable? This second question obviously needs to be qualified by asking 'desirable to whom?'. The extract from the essay by Adler and Asquith, which prefaced their edited collection of articles on discretion, explores some aspects of these questions.

This part ends with an article by the editor written soon after he first encountered some of the issues about discretion, when working as a 'street-level bureaucrat'. The article predates both Lipsky and the intensive debate which developed in Britain about the desirability of the sort of discretion it describes. British social security is, in many respects, now very different. Yet some of the issues the article describes are encountered in specific corners of the British social security system and in many parts of other public administration tasks. The article offers a 'bottom-up' view of a system in which workers have views about how they should do their tasks, experience peer pressures and encounter moral dilemmas. Neither training nor managerial guidance eliminates those dilemmas. They are intrinsic to the policy framework, and as such could hypothetically be resolved in the policy-making process. That they are not is one of the essential facts about the policy process, which has been emphasised and explored throughout this reader.

References

Etzioni, A., *The Semi-Professions and their Organization* (New York, Free Press, 1969).
Friedson, E., *Professional Dominance* (New York, Atherton, 1970).

Street-level bureaucracy
An introduction

Michael Lipsky

Dilemmas of the individual in public services

This book is in part a search for the place of the individual in those public services I call street-level bureaucracies. These are the schools, police and welfare departments, lower courts, legal services offices, and other agencies whose workers interact with and have wide discretion over the dispensation of benefits or the allocation of public sanctions.

I have tried to show how people experience public policies in these important realms. Too often social analysts offer generalizations about organizational and governmental actions without concretely explaining how individual citizens and workers are affected by the actions, how the behavior of individuals, when aggregated, gives rise to the actions, or how and why the actions in question are consistently reproduced by the behavior of individuals. For example, it is suggested, persuasively, that the administration of public welfare has the effect of minimizing the extent to which people seek welfare assistance. But since welfare workers do not as a rule explicitly discourage welfare recipients from applying (although some of this does go on), we need to know what welfare workers do that results in a systemic bias affecting welfare participation. Similarly, we know that service bureaucracies consistently favor some clients at the expense of others, despite official regulations to the contrary. To understand how and why these organizations often perform contrary to their own rules and goals, we need to know how the rules are experienced by workers in the organization and to what other pressures they are subject.

This study is grounded in observations of the collective behavior of

From M. Lipsky, *Street-level Bureaucracy: Dilemmas of the individual in public services* (1980), New York: Russell Sage Foundation. Used with permission of the Russell Sage Foundation.

public service organizations and advances a theory of the work of street-level bureaucracies as individual workers experience it. I argue that the decisions of street-level bureaucrats, the routines they establish, and the devices they invent to cope with uncertainties and work pressures, effectively *become* the public policies they carry out. I argue that public policy is not best understood as made in legislatures or top-floor suites of high-ranking administrators, because in important ways it is actually made in the crowded offices and daily encounters of street-level workers. I point out that policy conflict is not only expressed as the contention of interest groups but is also located in the struggles between individual workers and citizens who challenge or submit to client-processing.

One aspect of the way workers, clients, and citizens-at-large experience street-level bureaucracies is the conflicts that they encounter in wanting their organizational life to be more consistent with their own preferences and commitments. For example, people often enter public employment, particularly street-level bureaucracies, with at least some commitment to service. Teachers, social workers, public interest lawyers, and police officers in part seek out these occupations because of their potential as socially useful roles. Yet the very nature of this work prevents them from coming even close to the ideal conception of their jobs. Large classes or huge caseloads and inadequate resources combine with the uncertainties of method and the unpredictability of clients to defeat their aspirations as service workers.

Ideally, and by training, street-level bureaucrats respond to the individual needs or characteristics of the people they serve or confront. In practice, they must deal with clients on a mass basis, since work requirements prohibit individualized service. Teachers should respond to the needs of the individual child; in practice, they must develop techniques to respond to children as a class. Police officers should respond to the implications of the presenting case; in reality, they must develop techniques to recognize and respond to types of confrontations, and to process categories of cases accordingly. At best, street-level bureaucrats invent benign modes of mass processing that more or less permit them to deal with the public fairly, appropriately, and successfully. At worst, they give in to favoritism, stereotyping, and routinizing—all of which serve private or agency purposes.

Some street-level bureaucrats drop out or burn out relatively early in their careers. Those who stay on, to be sure, often grow in the jobs and perfect techniques, but not without adjusting their work habits and attitudes to reflect lower expectations for themselves, their clients, and the potential of public policy. Ultimately, these adjustments permit acceptance of the view that clients receive the best that can be provided under prevailing circumstances.

Compromises in work habits and attitudes are rationalized as reflecting workers' greater maturity, their appreciation of practical and political realities, or their more realistic assessment of the nature of the problem. But these rationalizations only summarize the prevailing structural constraints on human service bureaucracies. They are not "true" in an absolute sense. The teacher who psychologically abandons his or her aspirations to help children to read may succumb to a private assessment of the status quo in education. But this compromise says nothing about the potential of individual children to learn, or the capacity of the teacher to instruct. This potential remains intact. It is the *system* of schooling, the organization of the schooling bureaucracy, that teaches that children are dull or unmotivated, and that teachers must abandon their public commitments to educate.

In the same way, the judicial system "teaches" that police officers must be impersonal and highly reactive to hints of disobedience among youth, and that judges are unable to make informed determinations or consign defendants to institutions that will help the offender or deter future offenses. Although the potential for thoughtful and useful determinations and interventions is not contradicted in any individual instance, the system teaches the intractability of the juvenile crime problem.

Street-level bureaucrats often spend their work lives in a corrupted world of service. They believe themselves to be doing the best they can under adverse circumstances and they develop techniques to salvage service and decision-making values within the limits imposed upon them by the structure of the work. They develop conceptions of their work and of their clients that narrow the gap between their personal and work limitations and the service ideal. These work practices and orientations are maintained even while they contribute to the perversion of the service ideal or put the worker in the position of manipulating citizens on behalf of the agencies from which citizens seek help.

Should teachers, police officers, or welfare workers look for other work rather than perpetuate unfair, ineffective, or destructive public practices? This would leave clients to others who have even less concern and interest in service ideals. It would mean giving up the narrow areas in which workers have tried to make a difference or in which some progress is foreseen.

Should they stay on, contributing to discredited and sometimes brutalizing public agencies? If current patterns repeat themselves this would mean fighting the losing battle against cynicism and the realities of the work situation, and watching as service ideals are transformed into struggles for personal benefits.

Should they struggle from within to change the conditions under which citizens are processed by their agencies? This path seems the hardest to maintain and is subject to the danger that illusions of difference will be taken for the reality of significant reform.

The structure of street-level bureaucracy confronts clients with dilemmas bearing on action. Consumers of public services, once they have decided on or been consigned to a place of residence, with rare exceptions cannot choose the public services to which they will be subject. They must accept the schools, courts, and police forces of their communities. If they are poor they must also accept the community's arrangements for health care, welfare, public housing, and other benefit programs. In approaching these institutions they must strike a balance between asserting their rights as citizens and accepting the obligations public agencies seek to place upon them as clients. As citizens they should seek their full entitlement; as bureaucratic subjects they feel themselves obliged to temper their demands in recognition of perceived resource limitations and the agencies' organizational needs. Although it is apparent that exceptions are often made and additional resources often found, clients also recognize the potential costs of unsuccessfully asserting their rights.

On matters of the greatest urgency and moment, such as health care, education, justice, housing, and income, clients passively seek the benign intervention of public agencies when evidence and experience suggest that their hopes will go unrewarded. The dilemmas of action are particularly acute if clients are poor, and racially, ethnically, or linguistically different from most of the public employees. Should I wait my turn and submit to the procedures of the agency, despite reservations? I risk being unable to gain attention to my particular needs and concerns. Should I speak out forcefully and demand my rights? I risk the antagonism of the workers by disrupting office procedures.

Clients experience similar uncertainties in attempting to obtain proper services through collective action. The parent who organizes others to protest school actions, or the welfare recipient who challenges welfare policy, even if he or she perceives the possibilities of collective responses, risks receiving a reputation as an unreliable troublemaker toward whom favorable treatment should not be extended.

A final set of dilemmas confronts citizens who are continuously, if implicitly, asked to evaluate public services. This occurs in as focused a forum as a referendum on a school budget, and as diffuse an arena as Proposition 13 and other expressions of dissatisfaction with the nature and quality of public services. Indeed, recent legislative initiatives to limit state and local spending have largely been understood as attacks on governmental performance and the ineffectiveness of social services.

What are the policy alternatives? When all the "fat" has been trimmed from agency budget and all the "waste" eliminated, the basic choices remain: to further automate, systematize, and regulate the interactions between government employees and citizens seeking help; to drift with the current turmoil that favors reduced services and more standardization in the name of cost effectiveness and budgetary controls; or to secure or restore the importance of human interactions in services that require discretionary intervention or involvement.

But how much can human intervention be eliminated from teaching, nursing, policing, and judging? The fact is that we *must* have people making decisions and treating other citizens in the public services. We are not prepared as a society to abandon decisions about people and discretionary interventions to machines and programmed formats. Yet how can one advocate greater attention to the intervening and discretionary roles of street-level bureaucrats in the face of the enormous and often well-deserved popular discontent with the effectiveness and quality of their work?

I try to address these questions in this book. I do not exonerate street-level bureaucracies, excuse their deficiencies, or urge their support as currently structured. Rather, I locate the problem of street-level bureaucrats in the structure of their work, and attempt to identify conditions that would better support a reconstituted public sector dedicated to appropriate service and respect for clients, one that would be more likely to produce effective service-providers. In developing the street-level bureaucracy framework, I identify the common elements of occupations as apparently disparate as, say, police officer and social worker. The analysis of street-level bureaucracy helps us identify which features of people-processing are common, and which are unique, to the different occupational milieux in which they arise.

Michael Lipsky and street level bureaucracy

A neglected perspective

Bob Hudson

Over the past decade in Britain, there has been renewed political and academic interest in the problem of 'policy implementation'. The concern of a right-wing government to reduce the scale and role of public service bureaucracies has left the air rife with talk of 'value for money', efficiency, effectiveness, performance review and so forth. Policy-makers find themselves under intense pressure to ensure that policy impact reflects the intended direction of change. The broad problem confronting policy-makers is that policy is rarely applied directly to the external world, but is mediated though other institutions and actors. Policy impact is therefore at risk of distortion by these mediators.

In health and welfare agencies, the traditional focus upon the individual has tended to inhibit scrutiny of the collective context within which such activity takes place (Roberts, 1982). Those research studies which have led to theoretical speculation have stemmed mainly from work within industrial organisations, and have tended to see 'implementation deficit' as a problem for top-level policy-makers (Hill and Bramley, 1986). Concerns about over-elaborate structures have been a major preoccupation of administration textbooks for both the public and private sectors and issues about hierarchical control have been the traditional concern of 'management science'. The primary technique for studying behaviour has been the case study.

This is clearly a very limited way of examining social policy implementation. A fresh avenue of inquiry has concentrated upon the

From B. Hudson, 'Michael Lipsky and street level bureaucracy: a neglected perspective', in L. Barton (ed.), *Disability and Dependency* (1989), London: Falmer Press.

behaviour of 'street level' personnel – those actors who do the 'actual' work of the agency – and the ways in which their activities affect the way the public bureaucracy fulfils its public responsibility. In particular, Michael Lipsky (1980) has attempted to synthesise much of the research done in America on the activities of such personnel, and to elaborate a new body of theory on the roles of 'street level bureaucrats'.

Lipsky's analysis has enormous potential for helping us to make sense of the relationship between service providers and service consumers, yet it has had a curiously muted impact. This may be because as Professor of Political Science at Massachusetts Institute of Technology, Lipsky is in the 'wrong' discipline for influencing those studying social welfare. Equally his Goffmanian eclecticism may not appeal to all, for somehow he does manage to address almost every question that occurs to the reader. This chapter will suggest that Lipsky's under-utilised theory has as much significance for understanding welfare service bureaucracies as Goffman's work has had for the understanding of closed institutions.

Lipsky uses the term 'street level bureaucrat' to describe those public service workers who 'interact directly with citizens in the course of their jobs and who have substantial discretion in the execution of their work'. Typical street level workers are teachers, social workers, police officers, doctors, health visitors, certain social security officers, certain housing officers and so forth. It is therefore a notion which encompasses a wide range of welfare services as well as embracing both professionals and non-professionals. By focussing upon this tier of organisational life, Lipsky gets us away from traditional analyses of legislative activity and high ranking policy-makers. By attempting to transcend the limitations of case study, he seeks to develop a body of theory on street level activity. He directs our attention to a very large class of people at the sharp end of welfare activity, who routinely behave in ways that remain essentially unexplained.

The essence of Lipsky's case is that street level bureaucrats have enormous power which is scarcely acknowledged in the literature on public administration; that this power extends not only to control over service consumers but also to a considerable autonomy from their employing agency; and that this power is accompanied by the dilemma of working at the sharp end of resource allocation in a situation where demand far exceeds supply. Street level bureaucrats therefore end up making policy in circumstances which are not of their own choosing and which impel them to devise strategies to protect their working environment. In this way, Lipsky is addressing the process whereby zeal is eclipsed and idealism corrupted. It is significant that Lipsky's title refers not to the *power* but to the *dilemma* of the street level bureaucrat.

What is the source of this power? The crucial source is the inescapable exercise of *discretion*. Inescapable, because street level bureaucracies *require* people to make decisions about other people. Indeed, in defence of their activities, organisations will frequently point to the expertise of their members rather than to the success of their endeavours. But once an agency admits that its members have special skills, it also admits to a limitation of the right to define appropriate street level behaviour.

Unlike lower level workers in most organisations, street level bureaucrats have a considerable amount of discretion in determining the nature, amount and quality of benefits and sanctions provided by their agencies. Policemen decide who to arrest and whose behaviour to overlook; teachers make subtle decisions on who is teachable; social workers on who is socially salvageable; health care workers on who has a life worth preserving; housing lettings officers on who gets accommodation; social security officers on who gets a community care grant and so on. The discretion is therefore largely brought to bear in the rationing of resources in a situation where demand for them exceeds supply.

Lipsky writes at great length, drawing widely upon evidence, to indicate the techniques used by street level bureaucrats in allocating resources between competing clients. To understand what is taking place, he emphasises the need to take a phenomenological view of street level behaviour—we need to understand the subjective states of mind of the actors. His analysis of the routines developed starts with the proposition that they contribute to control over a difficult and ambiguous work environment. He identifies three broad responses: modification of client demand; modification of job conception; and modification of client conception.

I shall look very briefly at each of these, but this does not do justice to the richness of Lipsky's analysis of modification of client demand. Although street level bureaucrats can rarely charge for their services, most other forms of demand control are open to them, such as perpetuating delay, withholding information, and stigmatising the process of service delivery. Social policy has yet to address this field effectively at an empirical level.

If necessary, street level bureaucrats can simply *control* clients, or at least obtain their cooperation with client processing procedures. Several aspects of practice contribute to the routine control of clients. First, street level bureaucrats interact with clients in settings that symbolise and limit their relationship – this may encompass such matters as uniforms, location, and the content, timing and pace of interaction. Second, clients are isolated from one another, and are therefore more likely to see themselves as responsible for their situations – indeed street level bureaucrats will tend to resist client organisation when it arises. Third, the procedures and services of street level bureaucrats are presented as benign and always in the best interests of clients.

But street level bureaucrats do not simply deal with occupational hazards by limiting client demand. They also modify their *own* activities and perceptions of their jobs and clients. Modification of job conception basically means that street level bureaucrats modify their objectives to match better their ability to perform. Lipsky gives several examples. One is 'psychological withdrawal', resulting in a workforce relatively unbothered by the discrepancy between what they are *supposed* to do and what they *actually* do. By accepting limitations as fixed rather than problematic, innovation is discouraged and mediocrity encouraged. It is a situation not unfrequently chronicled in research into the functioning of long-stay psychiatric and subnormality hospitals.

Modification of client conception is even more subtle. Lipsky argues that street level bureaucrats who are unable to provide all clients with their best efforts develop conceptual mechanisms to divide up the client population and rationalise the division, even though the consequence of this may be at variance with the formal goals of the organisation. This may involve 'creaming off' those clients who seem most likely to succeed in terms of bureaucratic success criteria; or it may simply involve differentiating between those clients deemed to be deserving and undeserving.

Even with this brief review, I hope to have conveyed something of the power exercised by the street level bureaucrat. But to what extent can the street level bureaucrat act autonomously of the employing agency? Lipsky himself argues that accountability to the organisation is virtually impossible to achieve where street level bureaucrats exercise a high degree of discretion. I shall return to the issue of accountability shortly, but for now it is worth re-emphasising that street level bureaucrats do carry out much of the difficult rationing at client level, and it is therefore often convenient for organisations to permit this discretion to continue relatively unabated. The exercise of street level bureaucrat discretion can be functional to the organisation.

Lipsky's analysis is useful for helping us to understand a wide range of public welfare activities, including services for people with a disability. Disappointingly little attempt has been made, in any field of activity, to put Lipsky's ideas to the test. I shall look briefly at some areas of provision for people with a disability which could benefit from Lipsky's work and which do at least have some data on the activities of street level bureaucrats.

First, Special Educational Needs. In the USA an attempt has been made by one of Lipsky's associates, Richard Weatherley (Weatherley and Lipsky, 1977), to apply the street level perspective to the study of the implementation of special education reform in Massachusetts, where the Comprehensive Special Education Law introduced provisions very similar to those in Britain's 1981 Education Act. Schools were required to operate much more sophisticated procedures for assessing needs and for developing individualised programmes for children, and, as in Britain, were expected to do this without significantly more resources. Weatherley shows how the realities at street level constrained and distorted the reforms hoped for by state legislators – assessments were not conducted; limits were placed on the number of assessments held; assessment schedules were biased in favour of children likely to be inexpensive; parental deference to professional authority was sought, and so forth. In short, street level bureaucrats sought to secure their work environment.

In Britain, no attempt to apply Lipsky's theory explicitly has been made, but in her study of 'statementing' under the 1981 Education Act, Nicki Cornwell (1987) does reveal some telling detail about he *modus operandi* of street level bureaucrats, which can help us to explain the wide variation in the percentage of school populations with statements. I shall take only two of her many illustrations, the first in relation to modifying demand by reducing service levels. In the London Borough she studied, she found that although administrators had to follow the advice of psychologists about placement, somehow demand and supply had to match. She writes that: 'Some negotiation might be needed with psychologists about this, and a gentleman's agreement reached about not putting the borough in an embarrassing situation.' Again, on modification of job conception, she argues that statementing amounts to little more than a continuously loaded conveyor belt in which decisions on outcomes are made as soon as the child is referred for assessment, but it is important in order to keep up the appearance of open and rational decision making. This is not only for the purpose of legality, but also for the psychological well-being of the street level bureaucrats involved. She writes: 'The appearance of negotiation can help to obscure the reality of the situation from the professionals involved, who can remain convinced that they are taking part in a rational assessment.'

In the field of social work Carol Satyamurti (1981) has written tellingly of the adoption of stereotyped responses to clients. She argues:

> In the social work literature, the client is often spoken of as though he were a fully consenting adult participant in the social work relationship. In practice, however, it often seemed that a parent–child relationship was a more powerful model, as far as the social worker was concerned, for her dealings with clients. This was true both at the level of face-to-face encounters, and at the level of decision-making affecting the client.

As illustrations of this, Satyamurti cites the way in which social workers encouraged dependent behaviour in their clients, the way in which social workers treated appointments and called without warning on clients, the terms in which social workers discussed clients and the assumptions they made about client 'irresponsibility'.

A third area which could usefully draw upon Lipsky's work is that of income maintenance policies, which affords a useful example of street level bureaucrats who do not hold professional status. Folk-lore is rich with tales of encounters between social security officers and claimants, but research is at a premium. An important exception is Cooper's (1985) detailed consideration of the former supplementary benefit scheme at a range of offices.

Much of Lipsky's theory is reflected in Cooper's findings. The impact of unmanageable demand is evident. He writes: 'In most offices, most of the time, the emphasis was on getting the work done at all, rather than on doing it well. . . . Many of the difficulties found in relationships between staff and claimants could be interpreted in part as devices used by staff for controlling the amount of work with which they were required to cope.' In the pursuit of coping practices, relatively junior staff were left pretty much to their own devices, but it is clear that much of this is delegated autonomy which it is functional for the organisation to permit. He notes: 'In keeping with the emphasis on "getting the work done", it was apparent on several occasions that the calibre of junior staff was judged by their ability to dispose of cases rapidly and without follow-up work, with scant reference to the outcome for claimants.'

One of the prime coping mechanisms described by Cooper is illustrative of Lipsky's notion of modification of client conception. Treatment of claimants was found to vary according to a judgement made about them by officers on the basis of very little information and a brief acquaintance. People with a disability tend to emerge from these encounters better than most, but sympathy is hardly the stuff of citizenship. Cooper's vignettes are illuminating. I shall take two contrasting examples, both dealt with by the same officer.

> . . . a married man in his 50's who had been out of work for a number of years owing to a chronic chest condition. He had called to drop in his latest medical certificate and to put a general enquiry about extra help with fuel costs over the winter. Mike (the officer) treated him very decently, asking after his and his wife's welfare, and thanking him pleasantly for the certificate. He then gave an outline of help available for fuel costs and passed over the relevant leaflet, saying, 'This will tell you how to apply. The form is on the back, see? If you have any doubts or queries come back in and we'll sort it out, OK?'

The next caller was less fortunate:

> . . . there followed Mr. Z., a young Pakistani who had recently been made redundant, bringing in his rent book and last three wage slips. He appeared shy and confused in the office environment. Mike's approach was abrupt. He wanted to know why Mr. Z. had come in. Mr. Z. said he had been told to

bring the documents. 'You must have heard wrong,' said Mike. 'We tell people to post them in. Why don't you leave it with the man on reception?' Mike took the papers and dismissed Mr. Z., with the words 'Right enough, we'll keep these and you'll get them back sometime in the post. There was nothing else was there?' As Mr. Z. retires, evidently disconcerted, Mike remarked 'What do you make of that one? Bloody odd. The best thing you can do is get them in and get them out when they're like him. We get quite a few Pakis like that, wandering in like lost sheep.'

It is worth emphasising that Cooper is describing the implementation of the 1980 Social Security Act which ostensibly afforded claimants legal entitlement to benefits. The 1986 Social Security Act has largely replaced entitlement with discretion and will make the street level bureaucrat–claimant relationship even more one-sided. The first set of figures on the community care grant, for example, reveals that six of the London DHSS offices spent none of their budget, and elsewhere the variation is huge.

If Lipsky's analysis has validity, then concern about the accountability of street level bureaucrats is bound to be high, for accountability is the link between bureaucracy and democracy. Lipsky himself argues that such accountability is virtually impossible to achieve where workers exercise a high degree of discretion, and since he also takes the view that discretion itself is inescapable, the likelihood of securing accountability seems slim.

This pessimistic appraisal has not diminished the zeal with which various forms of accountability are pursued. Four main types can be distinguished: accountability to the organisation; accountability to consumers; accountability to the law; and accountability to professional norms. Each is problematic.

Accountability to the organisation

Attempts to increase accountability to the organisation through administrative controls (both sanctions and incentives) is the most common effort to increase congruence between worker behaviour and agency policy. But for the street level bureaucrat, the formal rewards of agencies are likely to play only a minor role in directing behaviour.

Prottas (1978) points out that in many public service bureaucracies, the turnover of street level bureaucrats is very high, therefore the relevance of promotions, salary increases and retirement benefits is correspondingly low. The same is true when the street level bureaucrats are established professionals, as in law and medicine, and have other career alternatives.

It is, in any case, difficult for the agency to decide when it is appropriate to deploy such controls as it has available. Street level bureaucrat performance is notoriously difficult to define and measure, and much of the performance occurs in places inaccessible to supervisors. Greater demands can be made for written records to serve as an independent check, but when matters are ambiguous, they are less than useful; they either support the decision of the street level bureaucrat or do not mention it. Indeed, Prottas (1978) suggests that: 'The most striking characteristic of client files in many public bureaucracies is their sparseness'.

Organisational measures to *increase* scrutiny of street level activity are strewn with difficulty. Conceivably, someone could replicate the street level bureaucrat's interaction with clients, but this is a desperate measure, of use in inhibiting flagrant abuses, but not a practical means of assuring routine compliance. Similarly, close supervision will be resisted. Alvin Gouldner (1964) showed clearly that all workers have an idea of what constitutes normal supervision, and any attempt to exceed that norm will be identified as 'close supervision'.

Downs (1966) called it a 'law' of organisational behaviour, that 'the greater the efforts made to control subordinated officials, the greater the efforts by those subordinates to evade or counteract such control'. This is borne out by the discussion by Fox (1974) on the relationship between rule-imposition and low-trust relationships. Coming from a concern with industrial relations, he shows how a 'top-down' concern with detailed prescription creates and reinforces low-trust relationships. Subordinates therefore feel little commitment, which results in an even further tightening of control, and a further diminution of commitment. Hill and Bramley (1986) note: 'Low motivation in a rule-bound context produces restriction of output, working to rule, industrial sabotage and strikes. In public administration, there is often another person or member of the public, rather than a machine, to feel the effects of low official morale.'

Accountability to consumers

Proposals for greater client autonomy tend to suffer from the fact that clients generally remain relatively powerless, but there nevertheless remains a *potential* for contributing to changing street level relationships. There are two main variants.

One approach is to attempt to *eliminate street level workers as buffers* between government and citizens. A class of proposals utilising such an approach is represented by the voucher system, which promises to import consumer sovereignty into the production of welfare services. In

Britain, two recent major reports have come out in favour of vouchers – the Griffiths Report on community care (1988) and the Wagner Report on residential care (1988).

The debate is a complex one, but it will be very difficult to establish the conditions under which consumers of services are fully informed about the wide variety of options, and it is therefore difficult to create the rudiments of competition upon which the theory depends. Given Lipsky's argument that *agencies* find it difficult to assess the appropriateness of street level behaviour, it would clearly be difficult for *clients* to assess the appropriateness of a service.

An alternative route to consumer sovereignty is to *eliminate public workers from service contexts*, which, with proper support, might be handled by citizens with little assistance. Advocacy, and particularly self-advocacy, would fit into this route, and this represents one of the more exciting developments relating to people with disabilities. But at this stage, it would not be wise to make anything other than provisional claims for the success of such experiments. It has to be remembered that while clients seek services and benefits, street level bureaucrats seek control over the process of providing them, and they will not easily relinquish their grip.

A further possibility, and an increasingly fashionable one, is to democratise through forms of participation close to service delivery level – decentralisation. In social work in Britain, such notions have become increasingly popular since the Barclay Report (1982), but again, claims can be little more than provisional. In terms of Lipsky's analysis, if decentralisation intensifies pressure upon street level bureaucrats by making them more accessible, then they will develop new strategies for protecting themselves.

Accountability to the law

Judicial processes might be used to secure 'rights' to public benefits and services. Legal philosophers such as Dicey (1905), saw the growth of the 'collective state' as a threat to liberty, and the intervention of the judiciary as a brake upon the state. However, not only are procedures inaccessible to underprivileged citizens, but the legal system is not well equipped to deal with the problems associated with the exercise of discretion by street level bureaucrats.

Rather closer to organisational level, clients can bring information to the attention of other members of the bureaucracy. The ubiquity of appeals procedures in many welfare bureaucracies testifies to the hope that the availability of this channel will increase the compliance of street level bureaucrats. However, we still know relatively little about the actual uses to which appeals procedures are put, and about their effects upon street level behaviour.

Lipsky, with characteristic scepticism, argues that from the street level perspective, appeals procedures should exhibit three qualities. First, it must look as though the channels are open. Second, the channels must be costly to use, rarely successful and (if successful) not well publicised. Third, a single client should not be able to gain redress for a class of clients. This does seem to encompass much tribunal and appeal activity in Britain.

Accountability to professional norms

Lipsky concludes that most street level work is not open to meaningful revision by limiting discretion, removing public employees from interaction with clients, or modestly altering the bureaucratic structure. He stresses the idealism and commitment of many practitioners, but sees this idealism undermined by work situations and organisation structures.

In his concluding chapter, he seems to opt for the enhancement of professionalism as a way of coping with the problems of street level bureaucracy. The argument, he says, '. . . comes down simply to the realisation that control of occupational groups must come from within group members'. This is perhaps a rather insipid up-shot, particularly since he also recognises that: 'The problem with the "professional fix" lies in the gap between the service orientations of professionals in theory and in practice'.

Hill and Bramley (1986) take the view that '. . . it is far from certain that professional monopolies are not greater evils than the forms of discretion and "street level" behaviour they profess to bring under control'. This is broadly in line with Wilding's (1982) review of professional power, which concluded: 'Professional self-regulation is unsatisfactory. No profession has shown anything but the most luke-warm interest in monitoring and maintaining the standard of work of its members . . . There is little or no acceptance of a consumer's right to comment on, or complain about, the substance of the service offered'.

The intractability of the street-level bureaucrat

There would therefore seem to be clear limits on the extent to which the freedom of action of front-line staff can be circumscribed. Lipsky argues that a bureaucratic accountability *policy* should possess four pre-requisites. First, agencies must know what they want workers to do; where objectives are multiple and conflicting, agencies must be able to rank their preferences. Second, agencies must know how to measure workers' performances. Third, agencies must be able to compare workers with one another, to establish a standard for judgment. And finally, agencies must have incentives and sanctions capable of disciplining workers.

These preconditions tend *not* to apply to street level bureaucrats, because street level bureaucracies *require* people to make decisions about other people. To say that human interaction is required in service delivery is to suggest that the situation requires judgments to be made about potentially ambiguous situations; the requisite human judgment simply cannot be programmed.

Hill (1982) reminds us that many examples of deviation from the apparent intentions of policy can be seen as situations in which the centre has no real concern that its policy should become manifest. There is a degree of 'sanctioned unaccountability'. As Hill puts it: 'Delegation may owe more to a desire to obscure political responsibility, than to an acceptance of the need to come to terms with street level bureaucracy'. It would seem that the best that can be managed is a little reining in here and a little wing clipping there.

Changing street level behaviour: the wider context

Ultimately, the contradictory tendencies in street level bureaucracies cannot be understood without examining their role in society, and the way in which society impinges upon the character of bureaucratic relations. The main danger of Lipsky's phenomenological approach is that it can be construed as a form of ideological relativism, largely ignoring the question of *why* one 'weltanschauung' is considered more legitimate than another. Such studies usually operate at a level of analysis which is divorced from any notion of power in social relations.

Although Lipsky does not systematically attempt to link his analysis to a broader perspective, he does point us in that direction. The influence of the wider context is raised at two levels. First, that the character of client treatment at the hands of street level bureaucrats reflects and reinforces class and ethnic divisions. The extent to which the clients are prepared for the impersonalism, hierarchy and institutionalisation of bureaucracy is also a reflection of such divisions.

But he also goes beyond this, in raising an even more fundamental question – in what ways do street level bureaucracies reflect and perpetuate the values of the larger society? An adequate analysis of the actual exercise of discretion at 'face-to-face' level must be informed by an understanding of the structural position of welfare institutions and their relationship to the broader social, political and economic framework of society. Novak (1988) makes some attempt to do this in his Marxist interpretation of relief of poverty by the state, but overall there has been little attempt to connect and reconcile micro- and macro-sociological concerns.

The poorer people are, the greater the power that street level bureaucracies have over them. In the 1960s and 1970s, a typical government response to social problems was to commission a corps of street level bureaucrats to attend to them, for as Lipsky notes, '. . . it is easier to develop employment for street level bureaucrats, than to reduce income inequalities'. It is through street level bureaucracies that society organises the control, restriction and maintenance of relatively powerless groups.

Despite his focus upon intra-organisational processes, Lipsky nevertheless concludes: '. . . the reconstruction of street level bureaucracies is unlikely to take place in the absence of a broad movement for social and economic justice. . . . Isolated reform efforts cannot plausibly be expected to bear the full weight of social change'. This is not a message in mood [sic] with the political spirit of the 1980s, in Britain or the USA. It may help to explain the relative neglect of Lipsky's analysis.

What, then, is the message to come out of Lipsky? It is not that street level bureaucrats are simply malicious and cunning functionaries interested only in their own comfort. Rather, it is that in looking at the dilemmas in their working day, we can see just how problematic a role they are asked to play in the policy making system. Academically, the pressing need is to find out more about how street level bureaucrats are actually behaving. Getting at the truth would be problematic, but must be confronted. If we wish to understand policy implementation, we must understand the street level bureaucrat.

References

Barclay Report (1982) *Social Workers: Their role and tasks*, Bedford Square Press.

Cooper, S. (1985) *Observation in Supplementary Benefit Offices*, Supplementary Benefit Working Paper C, Policy Studies Institute.

Cornwell, N. (1987) *Statementing and the 1981 Education Act*, Cranfield Press.

Dicey, A. V. (1905) *Lectures on the Relation Between Law and Public Opinion in England*, Macmillan.

Downs, A. (1966) *Inside Bureaucracy*, Little, Brown.

Fox, A. (1974) *Beyond Contract: Work, power and trust relations*, Faber.

Gouldner, A. (1964) *Patterns of Industrial Bureaucracy*, Free Press.

Griffiths Report (1988) *Community Care: An agenda for action*, HMSO.

Hill, M. (1982) 'Street level bureaucracy in social work and social services departments', *Research Highlights*, 4, University of Aberdeen.

Hill, M. and Bramley, G. (1986) *Analysing Social Policy*, Blackwell.

Lipsky, M. (1980) *Street-Level Bureaucracy: Dilemmas of the individual in public services*, Russell Sage Foundation.

Novak, T. (1988) *Poverty and the State*, Open University Press.

Prottas, J. D. (1978) 'The power of the street level bureaucrat in public service bureaucracies', *Urban Affairs Quarterly*, 13, 3.

Roberts, E. (1982) 'A presentation of perspectives of organisational theory relevant to social work', *Research Highlights*, 4, University of Aberdeen.

Satyamurti, C. (1981) *Occupational Survival*, Blackwell.

Wagner Report (1988) *Residential Care: A positive choice*, HMSO.

Weatherley, R. and Lipsky, M. (1977), 'Street-level bureaucrats and institutional innovation: implementing special education reform', *Harvard Education Review*, 47, pp. 171–97.

Wilding, P. (1982) *Professional Power and Social Welfare*, Routledge & Kegan Paul.

| Discretion and power

Michael Adler and Stewart Asquith

In this chapter, we adopt Davis's usage of the term 'discretion'. According to Davis (1974: p. 4):

> a public official has discretion whenever the effective limits of his power leave him free to make a choice among possible courses of action or inaction.

In recent years, considerable concern has been expressed at the extent of the discretionary powers granted under administrative law to officials, professionals and certain forms of tribunal in the area of criminal justice and in the social services. The exercise of discretion has been largely removed from the ambit of the courts and from legal and judicial scrutiny. As a result, there have been a number of appeals that, in the interests of justice, discretionary decision-making should be made subject to judicial review and other principles associated with the 'rule of law'. This call for a 'return to legality' has become a common theme among those who wish to limit what they see as the arbitrariness and unfairness of discretionary decision-making. It is, they argue, only through a return to legality that the functioning of welfare institutions can be improved and that greater protection can be offered to individuals against the vagaries of criminal justice and the official benevolence of the social services. Only in this way, Reich argued fifteen years ago (Reich 1963, 1964 and 1965), can individual rights be protected and dangers and threats to the freedom and dignity of the individual be avoided. These arguments have been repeated many times since then. However, it is important to stress that appeals for a return to the rule of law should not necessarily be taken as indicative of a desire totally to eliminate discretion. Thus Davis argues (p. 43):

> To fix as a goal the elimination of all discretion on all subjects would be utter insanity.

From M. Adler and S. Asquith, *Discretion and Welfare* (1981), London: Heinemann.

and advocates only (p. 3):

> in broad terms, that we should eliminate much unnecessary discretionary
> power and that we should do much more than we have been doing to confine,
> structure and check necessary discretion.

We have two major, and related, objectives in this chapter. First, we wish to show that claims for greater legal control over the exercise of discretionary powers, though ideologically attractive in offering further safeguards to individuals against the vagaries of welfare institutions, frequently ignore the relationship of those institutions to the wider social, political and economic order. Second, we want to argue that an adequate analysis of the actual exercise of discretion at the 'face-to-face' level, i.e. between the providers and the recipients of particular social services, must be informed by an understanding of the structural position of welfare institutions and their relationship to the broader social, political and economic framework of society. Our position is that much research on the exercise of discretion

> is primarily concerned with the rational and efficient functioning of [welfare]
> systems as relatively self-contained entities and not, for example, with the
> structural basis of such systems, with their relation to any of the other systems
> that go to make up the complex of social institutions that is society or with any
> other questions that have traditionally pre-occupied mainstream sociology.
> (Low 1978: p. 14)

Studies of discretion have tended to focus either on the exercise of discretionary decision-making at a micro-sociological level or on the growth of discretionary powers and their relationship to particular configurations of social, political and economic arrangements at a macro-sociological level. There have rarely been any articulations between these micro- and macro-sociological concerns.

In this chapter our main focus will be on what McBarnett (1978) has referred to as the 'false dichotomy between macro and micro-studies, between abstract theorising and empiricism'. By considering the relationship between power and knowledge which, we argue, results in the domination of certain conceptions of social reality and thereby contributes to the maintenance of particular forms of social order, we identify the concept of ideology as a significant medium through which to analyse the exercise of discretionary powers. The theoretical and methodological relevance of ideology is premised upon the claim that the assumptions which inform discretionary decisions have of necessity to be located within much broader social–structural concerns.

Discretion as a macro problem

Much recent writing and research on discretionary decision-making has been motivated by a (quite legitimate) moral concern with the outcomes of decisions for those who are affected by them. Particularly in the context of administrative decision-making, excessive discretion has been seen as leading to arbitrariness, inequality and dependency and failing to meet the most basic requirements of justice (Davies *et al.* 1971; Thomas 1974). On the other hand, too rigid an adherence to rules and rule-guided procedures has been criticised for giving rise to inflexibility, insensitivity to differing needs and circumstances and impersonal treatment (Titmuss 1971). Critics have not hesitated to propose changes in the ways in which decisions are taken so as to enhance either 'proportional' or 'creative' justice (Stevenson 1973). Most of them, in particular those who have championed a return to legality and the rule of law, have sought to emphasise proportional justice at the expense of creative justice by arguing that discretion should be restricted and rights created wherever possible.

We do not wish to take issue with the merits of these proposals (indeed we are broadly in agreement with them), but we do, neverthe-less, criticise many of the critics and their proposals for failing to question who benefits (and why they do so) from the existing mode of decision-making and not merely who loses out, and for failing to consider the political obstacles involved in moving away from a prevailing mode of decision-making. Social reform generally calls for a transfer of power and this is particularly true in relation to discretion-ary decision-making. Discretionary powers are not exercised in a vacuum – they are exercised over individuals whose only protection may be their possession of certain rights. (By a right is meant simply an enforceable claim. Here we are not particularly concerned with moral rights, i.e. with those claims which can only be enforced by an appeal to morality. Rather, we are more concerned with legal rights, i.e. with those claims which can be enforced through the law since it is widely believed that strengthening such rights is an effective means of limiting the discretion of public officials.) Marshall (1963) distinguished three categories of legal rights – civil rights, political rights and social rights – which together comprised what he called citizenship, and it is with what he referred to as social rights (which include the right to a substitute income during periods of interruption or cessation of earnings, the right to health care in periods of sickness, to housing, education, social work, etc.) that we shall be largely concerned.

The three categories of rights include both 'positive' and 'negative' rights. Positive rights refer to rights of access to public welfare, i.e. as consumers of social services, to private welfare, e.g. by spouses to a share in matrimonial property, and to the law, i.e. to lawyers and the courts as a means of securing legal redress; while negative rights refer to protection from public authorities, private individuals and the criminal law. A public official's discretion may be limited in a number of ways, e.g. statutorily, administratively, professionally, politically or judicially, but the stronger the claim an individual has the greater is his power to make and enforce demands on officials. Conversely, the weaker the rights an individual has, the more he will be at the mercy of their discretion. These statements apply equally in the case of positive and negative rights. Of course, in order to limit effectively the powers of public officials in this way, the individual must both be aware of his rights and able to enforce them. In relation both to criminal justice and to the social services, even where rights do exist in theory these two conditions are frequently not met.

It follows, both from our introductory remarks and from the above, that the public official's discretion and the rights of those who are subject to it are aspects of a relationship of power between them. Moreover since discretion is conferred (or legitimated) and rights are granted by the state, the power relationships between these officials and the public must also be seen as reflections of structured power relationships in society. Thus, attempts to modify the nature of these relationships must acknowledge the social and political forces sustaining forms of decision-making which have to be overcome for the achievement of meaningful social reform. Many of the best known writers on discretion can be faulted for not doing so. Davis is clearly doubly guilty. Likewise, in advocating greater procedural safeguards for the 'new property' rights inherent in modern welfare provision, Reich is equally guilty of failing to ask who benefits from the absence of procedural protection for the rights in question and to question what political obstacles might stand in the way of the reforms he proposes (Reich 1963, 1964 and 1965). Of course both authors (and Reich in particular) could claim merely to be clarifying the objectives and thus influencing the strategies of movements for social reform which were already in existence (in Reich's case the American Welfare Rights Movement) but, by confining themselves to advocating change on moral grounds, they can be criticised for engaging in 'utopian' social engineering. By no means everyone has fallen into this trap. To give just one example, Macpherson has recently argued (like Reich) for the need to create new rights in common property but at the same time has identified those political forces which would be required to bring about such changes (Macpherson 1975).

Professional discretion

In many of the social services (most noticeably in health, education and social work) where the service providers are mainly professionals, decision-making is of an extremely discretionary kind. Although it is common to think of professional decision-making as calling for the exercise of judgement rather than discretion, except for the fact that the persons concerned are not strictly speaking public officials, professional decision-making clearly involves the exercise of discretion in Davis's sense. Professional decision-making is also subject to particularly weak forms of public accountability and control. Individuals have positive rights only in the most general sense that they have rights of access to the services concerned, e.g. to consult a doctor, go to school or college [. . .] or seek the advice of a social worker. They do not have rights to any particular forms of treatment, tuition or help nor do they have rights to any particular standard of health, education and welfare.

The growth of discretion has gone hand in hand with the growth of powerful professions which lay claim to esoteric professional knowledge and are able to support these claims through the development of powerful forms of occupational control (Johnson 1972). As government became increasingly involved in the direct provision of health, education and welfare so it has been able to enlist the support of the professions concerned. Although fearful of 'political interference' the power of the professions has been sufficient to protect them from public accountability and control. Thus, although the government is the main source of employment and remuneration for doctors, teachers and social workers, the doctors' clinical freedom, the teachers' control over what is taught in the schools and how it is taught, and the social workers' decisions about what kind of help, if any, should be given are largely immune from any form of democratic accountability and control. Partly because they are such powerful groups, partly because of their symbolic significance (public support for their activities symbolises a commitment to the enhancement of welfare for which government takes credit) and partly, as we shall see later, because of the ways in which they sustain particular conceptions of social reality which contribute to the maintenance of social order, they have been able to retain their very considerable discretionary powers.

Administrative discretion

Although the professions are probably the main carriers of welfare ideologies and are a very important means of delivering the social services, they are not the only means of so doing. Many social services,

e.g. housing and social security, are made available through large
bureaucracies staffed by administrators. The distinction between welfare
services that are staffed by professionals and those that are staffed by
administrators would seem to reflect a difference between those services
which attempt to do things to people and those that mainly attempt to
provide things for them. (We realise of course that the rather neat
distinction between professional and administrative decision-making is a
gross oversimplification and recognise that, theoretically, such a distinction is difficult to maintain. In organisational terms 'administrators' may
often be required to make decisions akin to those we have associated
with 'professionals' and vice versa. However, the ideal-typical designa-
tions we employ at least have the merit of identifying some of the more
important characteristics of the exercise of discretion in different
contexts.) In comparison with a professional, who is a member of a
powerful occupational group and is socialised into the professional
ideology through long periods of training and apprenticeship, an
administrator is often an official who has simply been assigned to a
particular administrative task. Thus, we would expect a professional to
have a considerably greater personal commitment to an ideology of
welfare than an administrator. As we have already pointed out,
professionals have largely unfettered discretion and make their decisions
by reference to a body of esoteric professional knowledge. By contrast,
administrative discretion is characteristically constrained by rules.
Administrators make their decisions by reference not only to rules but
also to guidelines which are intended to shape their decisions in
circumstances which are not covered by the rules. Although the
professions have extremely wide discretion, the power and status of the
professional groups concerned and the esoteric nature of their professional knowledge have, on the whole, ensured that professional prerogatives have gone unquestioned. There have, of course, been some
powerful and popular attacks on the welfare professions (see, for
example, Illich 1971 and 1975; Platt 1975) but, on the whole, professional discretion has been questioned less than administrative discretion.
Although administrators characteristically have less discretion than
professionals, they have fewer sources of institutional power (since they
can be replaced far more easily than their professional counterparts) and
lower status. Moreover, the more mundane nature of the imposed
welfare philosophies means that they are more easily called into
question both by administrators and the public. Administrative discretion is thus not only more open to distortion by officials when it conflicts
with their own value assumptions, it is also more readily criticised by the
public. Public criticism has been directed both at the official welfare
philosophies and at their distortions in practice. Hence the calls for
more rules and further controls on the exercise of administrative
discretion. Administrative discretion is the 'soft under-belly' of welfare.

Rules and discretion

Rules and discretion can be seen as providing alternative modes of decision-making and of allocating scarce resources. Rule-guided procedures can be more visible, are more explicit and may be preferred where they can be formulated and where the major concern is to ensure 'fair shares' for all. By comparison, discretion is inevitably less visible and more implicit but will be favoured where considerations of individual welfare are paramount. In general, rules will be introduced where the decision-makers are officials, where they have low status and/or little power, where there is dissatisfaction with the exercise of discretion by those who make the decision and/or by those for and against whom it is exercised, where there is outside political support for groups who are critical of the exercise of discretion and where it is, in principle, feasible to formulate a set of rules. Discretion, on the other hand, will be favoured where the decision-makers are professionals with high status and/or considerable power, where there is dissatisfaction with the operation of rules by those who make the rules or are subject to the rules, where there is outside political support for groups critical of the operation of rules or where it is not, even in principle, possible to formulate an acceptable set of rules.

A shift in one direction or another will thus take place in response to political pressure for change. At the present time, and especially in the context of cut-backs in public expenditure, there is considerable pressure for change directed towards the curtailment of discretion and the introduction of more rule-guided procedures. As we have seen, much of this pressure is directed at administrative rather than professional discretion. Although such moves are championed by those who argue for a return to legality, the introduction of rules is not sufficient in itself to enhance the rights of those affected by the decisions. In order to enhance the rights of those affected by the decision, the rules must be made public and those affected by them must be able to enforce those rules through the use of legal procedures. As Nonet (1969) has pointed out, this demands a level of 'legal competence'. Because legal competence, i.e. the ability to take advantage of such legal procedures as are available, is not equally distributed throughout the population, it does not follow that even legally enforceable rules will be equitably enforced.

References

Davies, B. *et al.* (1971), *Variations in Services for the Aged*, London, Bell.
Davis, K. C. (1974), *Discretionary Justice: A preliminary enquiry*, Urbana, University of Illinois Press.
Illich, I. (1971), *De-Schooling Society*, London, Calder & Boyars.

Illich, I. (1975) *Medical Nemesis*, London, Calder and Boyars.

Johnson, T. (1972), *Professions and Power*, London, Macmillan.

Low, C. M. (1978), 'The sociology of criminal justice: progress and prospects', in J. Baldwin and A. K. Bottomley (eds.), *Criminal Justice*, London, Martin Robertson.

Macpherson, C. B. (1975), 'Capitalism and the changing concept of property', in E. Kamenka and R. Neale (eds.), *Feudalism, Capitalism and Beyond*, London, Edward Arnold.

Marshall, C. H. (1963), 'Citizenship and social class' in *Sociology at the Crossroads*, London, Heinemann.

McBarnett, D. (1978), 'False dichotomies in criminal justice research', in J. Baldwin and A. K. Bottomley (eds.), *Criminal Justice*, London, Martin Robertson.

Nonet, P. (1969), *Administrative Justice: Advocacy and change in a government agency*, New York, Russell Sage.

Platt, A. (1975), 'Prospects for a radical criminology in the USA', in I. Taylor, P. Walton and J. Young (eds.), *Critical Criminology*, London, Routledge & Kegan Paul.

Reich, C. A. (1963), 'The new property', *Yale Law Journal*, 73 (5), pp. 733–87.

Reich, C. A. (1964), 'Individual rights and social welfare: the emerging legal issues', *Yale Law Journal*, 74 (7), pp. 1245–57.

Reich, C. A. (1965), 'Law of the planned society', *Yale Law Journal*, 75 (8), pp. 1227–70.

Stevenson, O. (1973), *Claimant or Client?*, London, Allen & Unwin.

Thomas, D. (1974), 'The control of discretion', in R. Hood (ed.), *Crime, Criminology and Public Policy*, London, Heinemann.

Titmuss, R. (1971), 'Welfare "rights", law and discretion', *Political Quarterly*, 42 (2), pp. 113–22.

The exercise of discretion in the National Assistance Board

Michael Hill

The National Assistance Board was buried, unmourned, in 1966. It had been the subject of a great deal of criticism throughout its short life, being often regarded as a department that was harsh in an unrealistic and inconsistent way. At the same time it had also been praised as a department that was humane and unbureaucratic in its approach to the public. Yet these two observations about the National Assistance Board are in no way contradictory: on the contrary they are but different facets of the same situation. The National Assistance Board was required to maintain people at a low subsistence level. At that level people differ markedly from each other in their basic needs. The Board was required to take into account these differences and thus it had to give discretionary powers to those of its officers who were actually meeting the public. Thus it was inevitable that in a relationship in which individual officers were required to size up the needs of individual applicants for help one would find inconsistency, so that while the annual reports would each year be able to quote successes in inter-personal relationships, the critics of the Board, such as Mrs Audrey Harvey,[1] would be able to draw attention to gross injustices. To become more consistent the Board would have had either to pay very much larger basic allowances or to have adopted a rigid line that would have created much suffering. In either case, any of the advantages gained from the largely non-bureaucratic relationship between officers and the public would have been lost. And whilst this aspect of the National Assistance Board's work is difficult to assess there seems little doubt that the Board's visitors provided a lifeline, irrespective of any

From M. J. Hill, 'The exercise of discretion in the National Assistance Board', *Public Administration*, **47**, 1969, pp. 75–90.

allowances they paid, to many people who would otherwise have been entirely missed by the other social services.

It therefore seems worthwhile to explore those aspects of the National Assistance Board's work which involved the exercise of discretion, to throw light on a classic bureaucratic problem. This is the problem of formalization. Too great a degree of formalization can create rigidity and impersonality, whilst too little inevitably means inconsistency and the personalization of relationships.[2] Several writers, amongst whom Blau[3] and Francis and Stone[4] are particularly relevant since they deal with service-oriented government organizations, have argued that subordinates will tend to resist or evade rigid bureaucratic rules. On the other hand, Gouldner[5] and Crozier[6] have shown that subordinates derive security from the existence of a recognized body of rules. The problem for those who control organizations is then to find a way of balancing these competing requirements. In the words of Bendix, 'The problem of bureaucracy lies . . . in the manner in which technical and administrative rationality are combined with the exercise of individual initiative in the accomplishment of a common task.'[7] In this study we will examine the exercise of discretion in a local office of the National Assistance Board as an example of a bureaucratic situation in which there was considerable emphasis upon individual initiative, and we will attempt to assess the consequences of this situation.

These observations are based on the author's experience as an Executive Officer in a local office of the National Assistance Board, between 1960 and 1963. [. . .]

The organizational framework

To provide a framework within which the points to be made about the exercise of discretion can be understood it is necessary to describe briefly the National Assistance Act and consequent Regulations, the way the Board sought to implement the Act, and the way the particular office under scrutiny was organized.

The National Assistance Board was responsible for the provision of payments to persons not in full-time work whose incomes from insurance benefits and other sources were inadequate to meet their needs. Their 'needs' were defined by scales laid down by Parliament, but (a) over and above these scales the Board were given a responsibility to meet need and thus could make additional payments of various kinds, and (b) in certain cases payments could be made below the levels defined in the 'scales,' again at the discretion of the Board.

The scheme was administered by a network of local offices manned by civil servants in the lower ranks. These offices were managed by Higher

Executive Officers (HEOs), or in some cases Senior Executive Officers (SEOs), individuals who were one or two rungs up the Executive 'ladder'. The day-to-day decision taking was carried out by Executive Officers (EOs), assisted by Clerical Officers. These officers interviewed applicants in their own homes, or, in cases of urgent need, in the office.

The ultimate responsibility for deciding the size of a person's grant was in the hands of the Executive Officers. To assist them in making these decisions they had a substantial body of internal instructions, mainly in the form of the 'Codes', manuals compiled at Headquarters and subject to continual review. The main instructions for day-to-day operation were found in the 'A' Code. However, these instructions left a great deal to the discretion of the Executive Officer, as we shall show below. There were additionally certain checks on the activities of Executive Officers from their superiors, and in certain exceptional circumstances Executive Officers had to submit cases to their superiors for decision. Details of these limitations on the discretionary activities of Executive Officers will be discussed later. It is, however, important to point out here that both checks upon action and limitations on decision-making powers were comparatively rare. Executive Officers were required to take discretionary decisions on their own in a very large number of cases. [. . .]

Areas of discretion

The following paragraphs will not provide an exhaustive list of the ways in which Executive Officers were required to exercise discretionary powers, but rather the most common and significant examples of discretion will be discussed.

In the straightforward case the allowance paid to an applicant for assistance was made up of (a) the 'Scale rates', specific amounts laid down by Parliament – so much for a married couple and so much for each child, varying according to age; and (b) the rent allowance – normally the full rent paid less deductions for services provided with the tenancy, but special rules existed to provide 'rent allowances' for owner-occupiers and for persons who were not householders. Any income or capital was offset against their 'needs', once again the basic rules being the subject of regulations emanating in the first place from Parliament.

The rent allowance could be limited in certain cases where it was felt that the rent was excessive in relation to the kind of accommodation occupied, or if it was felt that the applicant for Assistance was occupying accommodation at a rent level and of a standard out of proportion to his normal requirements. An interesting social consideration entered here.

It was recognized that it was reasonable for an elderly lady who had known better times to live in a private hotel on the south coast, but that most Assistance applicants should expect to occupy accommodation of a comparatively poor quality. Clearly then, on this point Executive Officers were required to make an assessment of people that was to some extent subjective. Such an assessment might be influenced by the values of the officer involved, but it might also be influenced by his assessment of the amount of pressure that would be likely to be put on him if he made a decision unfavourable to the applicant. The latter is an important point, to be discussed more fully later.

For the benefit of officers responsible for implementing these instructions at the local office further guidance was provided in the form of circulars from the Regional Office. Throughout most of the period the author worked for the NAB there was in operation a policy within his region which required that, in all cases where rents exceeded a given level, the rent allowance should be restricted to that level temporarily and that the 'case' (the papers relating to the application for Assistance) should be sent to Regional Office for decision. In this kind of case the procedure was for the Executive Officer to make a recommendation which the Manager would then endorse or comment upon before sending the papers to the Regional Office. This temporary refusal to give rent allowances in full, together with a tendency for the rent ceiling to be too low in some areas [. . .] came under fire in a *New Statesman* article.[8] Soon after the publication of that article the procedure was changed. Under the new policy, Executive Officers were instructed to give rent allowances in full unless they felt the rent was unreasonably high, in which case they were to restrict the allowance temporarily and submit the papers to Regional Office together with arguments for restricting the allowance. This was a significant change of policy, which the individual who was 'temporary Manager' of the office at that time presented as 'merely a change of procedure'.

Another form of restriction of rent allowance which was the subject of special instructions from the Regional Office related to immigrant households. It was suggested that in the absence of rent books or in households where 'communal living arrangements' existed, rent allowances should be restricted to very low levels. This instruction gave considerable scope for the exercise of the prejudices of some Executive Officers. The adoption of a harsh and stereotyped policy was moreover made easy by the fact that immigrants rarely made excessive demands and very rarely contested the allowances they were given. Whether or not 'communal living arrangements' existed prior to application for Assistance, they were certainly made necessary by such low allowances. This is one of several examples of the way in which Executive Officers tended to have the greatest scope for the use of discretion in dealing with those applicants for Assistance who were least well informed of their rights and least likely to appeal or complain.

Turning now to the scope of discretion in relation to the basic 'Scale rates', Executive Officers were given powers to reduce the basic allowances in certain cases. The best publicly known example of such restriction was the 'wage stop', the limitation of the allowance given to an unemployed man below what he could be expected to earn if he got a job. It is not proposed to discuss this as an example of discretion as, though clearly decisions had to be taken on expected earnings and so on, the rules for this procedure laid down in the 'A' code were fairly specific. Moreover, they derived originally from the National Assistance Act itself. A far more significant area of discretion was involved in dealing with unemployed men who had recently ceased work, or whose unemployment benefit had been stopped for six weeks by the Ministry of Labour on the grounds that they had left a job without due cause, had unreasonably refused a job, or had been sacked for 'industrial misconduct'.

These two types of case can be taken together because similar procedures were adopted for both. In the first case, the 'A' code instructed that it was reasonable to expect that men who had been in well-paid employment for some time could manage on unemployment benefit without any supplementation from the NAB for a period of up to a month after falling out of work. Unemployment benefit was, of course, an insurance benefit normally at a level substantially below the 'need' levels defined in the National Assistance regulations. In practice, the difference between the two scales tended to be roughly the amount of the rent allowance.

In the second case, the principle of expecting men to be able to subsist temporarily on an income at the level of unemployment benefit was developed further by the argument that men who had been refused unemployment benefit for one of the forms of misconduct listed should not be able to come to the Assistance Board for a similar or larger amount. Accordingly, the policy was to pay those men at a level about five shillings [a deduction of 10 per cent or less] below the normal unemployment benefit rate. But such a restriction was to be made, in the words of the code, 'bearing in mind an overriding responsibility to meet need'. The 'A' code included qualifications of this kind wherever a comparatively harsh policy was advocated.

On account of the fact that most of the applicants for Assistance to whom these latter instructions applied were newly unemployed, and that their allowances were subject to changes week by week, most of the payments involving reductions of the kind described above were made in the office. This was possible on account of the fact that the National Assistance Board office served a comparatively small and compact area.

Moreover, the Employment Exchange was very close by, and this department required unemployed men to call at least twice a week. Consequently, the procedure adopted with unemployed men in these categories tended to follow the basic instructions fairly rigidly, leaving the 'overriding responsibility to meet need' to be taken care of if one's action was challenged in any way. The consequence was a series of running battles with the more demanding applicants in which an initial minimum payment might be followed by a series of return calls at the office, of phone calls from social workers and others, or of demands for appeal forms. Inevitably this kind of continued pressure meant that the position of officers responsible for payments at the office was a task thoroughly disliked by the EOs. Inevitably, too, this crude approach to the 'overriding responsibility' tended to operate to the disadvantage of the meek.

So far we have concentrated on powers to make deductions from basic allowances. Now let us turn to the slightly less controversial power of Executive Officers to make additions to allowances to cater for special needs. Most of these additions went to elderly people and fell into three categories: laundry allowances, allowances to meet the extra expense involved in special invalid diets, and allowances to purchase extra coal in winter. All these three types of allowance were far from standardized throughout the office. The laundry allowance was given almost automatically if an elderly or sick person sent things to a laundry, but officers differed widely in their readiness to accept such claims from, at one extreme, the officer who would argue 'you really ought not to try to wash your own sheets, let me include an allowance for that purpose' to the officer who would be very sceptical about all claims not backed by a sheaf of old laundry bills. With long-term cases such inequities would tend to be levelled up over the years, as officers changed duties, since all cases were revisited at least once a year if not more frequently, and it was obviously not normally expedient to reduce allowances. Reputations for harshness or generosity were well known throughout the office, and Clerical Officers, who did much of the revisiting, would – if recommending the upward revision of some allowance – seek to avoid submitting their cases to known harsh officers for approval, a practice that involved evading the formal channels in many cases.

Special diet allowances were even more haphazard, both because officers' assessments of their costs varied considerably and because revisions in relation to changing costs or needs were very erratic. The amounts of fuel allowances, on the other hand, were standardized by managerial edict; the difficulty here was to achieve any consistency about who should have them. Officers were required to take into account the general health and mobility of the applicant, together with the state of his or her accommodation. Naturally, it was impossible for any very clear rules to be laid down on the evaluation of factors of this kind.

Executive Officers also had powers to give grants for special needs, primarily, that is, for clothes and household requisites. They were limited in the amount they could give at any one time, having to seek regional approval for grants in excess of a fixed figure, which was laid down centrally. This did not stop the giving of a number of smaller grants in fairly quick succession. The need for such grants came primarily from the applicants with children, partly because of the heavy wear and tear on clothing and partly because a high proportion of the pensioners had small amounts of capital sufficient for them to meet such 'exceptional needs', as they were termed, themselves. The family cases were primarily the families of the unemployed, of deserted wives and unmarried mothers. Consequently demands for special grants came from a sector of the population with which the officers of the Board were far less likely to sympathize than was the case with the special needs of the elderly. For this reason there was far less consistency within the office as a whole with regard to 'exceptional needs grants'. What is more, it was possible to discern with regard to these grants the same pattern of reluctant yielding to pressure, the same tendency for the demanding to get more than the meek, that could be observed in the treatment of the newly unemployed or of people with high rents.

In the description of the field of discretion of Executive Officers given above it has not been intended to give the impression that officers in any way departed from the spirit of their instructions. Rather it is suggested that they were given discretionary freedom in areas in which it was inevitable that individual attitudes would lead to wide variations in the treatment of the public. The only area described above in which there was, in the author's view, widespread abuse of discretionary power was in the treatment of immigrants' rents, where stereotyped assumptions of overcrowding and of untruthfulness determined behaviour towards persons who rarely knew how to present their own cases. And even here the encouragement for such abuse came from a highly ambiguous regional circular.

However, there was one way in which officers did depart very considerably from the instructions they were given on the use of discretion. This departure arose from the accessibility of the office to all able-bodied applicants for Assistance, and constituted what was described as 'mucking applicants around'. One example of this has already been quoted, the payment of the lowest possible amount to unemployed men, leaving them to protest then or later if they were disposed to do so. Another example was the avoidance of the ponderous and long-winded procedure for dealing with fraud by simply cutting off an allowance and filing away the 'case-papers'. If the person stayed away

one assumed the procedure was justified; if he, or she, came back for
more, then one would have to make a further payment and start the
laborious process of accumulating evidence of the suspected fraud. This
tactic was particularly used with unmarried mothers or deserted wives
where they were suspected of a continuing relationship with a man, the
aim being to make it more difficult for the woman to get money from
the NAB than from the man. The particular difficulty here was that in
order to prosecute one of these women, one had to prove not only that
she was living with a man but also that she was receiving money from
him. Failing this, one could only prosecute the man, another difficult
procedure and an unrewarding one if he was not the woman's husband,
as his only liability would then be his children, if any, and even then
only a limited one. In this type of case inevitably the woman often came
back for more Assistance, hence 'mucking around' consisted of giving
small payments, after a long wait in the office, the inadequacy of which
forced her continually to re-apply for Assistance. The official doctrine
on this kind of case was (a) not to make large payments when marital
reconciliation seemed imminent, and (b) in case of suspected fraud to
secure regular written statements from the person which might subsequently be produced as false statements in court. The point here is that
official doctrine was adjusted into a procedure whose rationale was that
applicants who were not genuine would give up trying to get Assistance
if it involved so much bother. Such an approach avoided the considerable amount of work involved in building up evidence against a
suspected fraudulent applicant and in preparing a case to be sent to the
legal experts at Headquarters for decision on the action to be taken.
Such cases tended to involve a great deal of frustration for Executive
Officers arising from their inability to provide the kind of evidence that
would satisfy the lawyers that court action was justifiable.

The control of discretion

The job of the National Assistance Board was defined in the National
Assistance Act 1948, and in the regulations passed by Parliament under
the terms of that Act. However, for the Executive Officer in a local
office of the Board this basic statutory framework had been enormously
developed into a large number of instructions found in the 'Codes'. The
basic manual for day-to-day work on applications for Assistance was the
'A' Code, a loose-leaf book of several hundred pages that was subject to
continuous amendment. But this was supplemented by other 'Codes', in
particular one in which procedures for dealing with fraud and overpay-
ments were laid down and one giving instructions on procedures for
attempting to receive payments from missing husbands and fathers.

Office procedures and personnel regulations were found in yet another code, the 'G' Code, a manual largely derived from the Treasury's Estacode. These codes were supplemented by circulars both from Headquarters and from the Regional Office. Finally, on matters of local significance the Manager also issued additional instructions from time to time.

Despite all this volume of instructions the areas of ambiguity, many of which have been described above, still existed. Amongst the specific instructions, officers were continually reminded of the need to take into account special circumstances and of their 'overriding responsibility to meet need'.

The new Executive Officer, that is the officer who came to the Board from outside the civil service or from another department, received approximately three months' training. Three weeks of the three months were taken up with a training course at Headquarters. Primarily this course was concerned with procedures, how to interview, how to complete a report, how to calculate allowances, and so on. It was thus merely an oral introduction to the 'Codes'. The rest of the training period involved primarily sitting-in with experienced officers, with the Manager taking some interest in the training process, according to his disposition and work load.[9] Training was therefore very largely instruction from one's peers, which meant of course that as far as the exercise of discretion was concerned one was subjected to a process in which the collective values of the Executive Officers, rather than the views of one's superiors, were impressed upon one. This point is emphasized not to suggest that there was any explicit conflict between the values of Executive Officers and their superiors, but rather because of its significance for the argument that will be developed later that, under pressure from outside, the Board tended to let a double standard exist. The comparatively repressive behaviour of Executive Officers was condoned, and in some ways encouraged, unless the Board was subject to pressure from outside when, at least from the Executive Officer's point of view, it appeared to disavow the actions of its 'front-line' employees.

The view that there was little pressure on the actions of Executive Officers from above, in the absence of complaints, is borne out when one considers the various forms of routine check upon their work. The Manager or Deputy Manager regularly checked the paperwork done by Executive Officers when dealing with new applicants for Assistance. Yet the procedure involved in authorizing payments normally entailed the writing of a report justifying discretionary action, so that in the absence of actual mistakes it was difficult for the Manager to find any grounds for objecting to his Executive Officer's actions. Moreover, a checking procedure of this kind was directed primarily at finding cases where too

much had been paid; it did not readily throw up cases where needs had
been neglected. After all, if they had been neglected they would not be
commented on in the EO's report. This was also true of the spot checks
made upon the work of the office by the Regional Office and by a team
of auditors from Headquarters.

Thus, once again, we are thrown back upon the fact that the only real
control over the actions of Executive Officers when they took a harsh
line was the protests of the individuals who were thus made to suffer.
These came in a variety of forms, the most common of which was the
direct complaint from the applicant, often delivered by means of a visit
to the office. Just as the Board's officers sought to wear down those they
suspected of fraud by making them call again and again at the office, so
aggrieved applicants would seek to wear down their 'adversaries' by a
similar process.

A more sophisticated weapon by which individuals sought to have
their allowances raised was the 'appeal'. This created a situation in
which the original decision had to be re-scrutinized in order that it might
be justified before an Appeal Tribunal. More appeals were withdrawn
than ever went to the Appeal Tribunal, largely because an appeal would
provoke the revision of a harsh or hasty decision. During much of the
time the author worked at the Area Office the local Appeal Tribunal
had as chairman a man who was very critical of the Board and who
regarded some of the common interpretations of the Act by the Board
as unreasonably harsh. Since the Manager disliked continually losing
appeals the tendency was to anticipate the tribunal decision whenever
an individual appealed.

Apart from appealing, applicants for Assistance often sought to
secure revision of their cases by getting someone to complain on their
behalf. The most effective method of doing this was to approach an
M.P. An M.P.'s enquiry produced the same kind of reaction as an
appeal. Moreover, in this case someone high in the Headquarters staff
of the Board had to be satisfied with the line taken in the treatment of
the applicant. Apart from M.P.s' enquiries, complaints also came in
from influential local citizens and from social workers. Once again, if
these complaints came in at managerial level then the Executive Officer
would be required fully to justify his action. In the same way a few
applicants, generally the more educated ones, sought to make repre-
sentations to senior officials of the Board at regional or Headquarters
level. This again would create a situation in which a decision had to be
justified to someone higher up the hierarchy.

All these methods of levelling a complaint provide evidence for the
contention, expressed earlier, that in the face of ambiguous rules those
applicants who strongly contested decisions tended to receive the most
favourable treatment. What is more, the more subtle the methods they

used in pursuing their own 'rights' the greater the chance they had of achieving something. Thus, the largely illiterate applicant who simply pestered the local office, and who might often adopt a very aggressive approach, was very much resented by most officers, who gave him as little as they could possibly get away with. On the other hand, the middle class applicant who appealed, or wrote to his M.P. or telephoned Headquarters, would probably receive an interview with the Manager at which he was able to argue his own case most cogently.

Hence the double standard pointed out above. To explain this more fully one must first reiterate the point that almost all the controversial instructions in the codes were double-edged; all the sections urging repressive action included reminders about the need to take such action with care, reminders about the 'overriding responsibility to meet need'. These escape clauses were used whenever trouble arose over a particular decision. A protest from an applicant tended to be treated as evidence of unmet 'need'. It was thus inevitable that in the event of a complaint the Manager was rarely able to defend the action of his Executive Officer. This created a situation in which in the ordinary run of work it was the job of managers and other more senior officials to encourage their staff to be economical, to encourage them to pay as little as possible, certainly as far as some types of case were concerned; yet when a complaint arose over an individual case a hard decision taken at the Executive Officer level was rarely upheld. This situation was very damaging to Executive Officer morale and a continual cause of complaint within the office. To understand fully the relationship between the decision-making process and the pressure upon it described above we need to explore the values prevalent within the office.

Values

In explaining the behaviour of public officials in a context in which they are given quite considerable discretionary powers it is important to take into account their values. It is particularly important to discuss values in dealing with discretionary actions of National Assistance Board officers, because in many ways the framers of the National Assistance Act failed to follow Simon's advice to politicians to deal with the main value problems at the policy-making stage.[10] The traditional attitude to the poor had been to regard them, in the absence of unambiguous evidence to the contrary, as undeserving individuals on whom public money should be spent most sparingly. The National Assistance Act seemed to turn its back on this doctrine, yet it failed to jettison the view entirely and it failed to provide financial resources sufficient to enable the Board to avoid having to distinguish between the claims made by applicants, particularly as regards their more unusual needs. Consequently the onus of distinguishing between the 'deserving' and the 'undeserving' poor tended to fall upon the officer dealing with the applicant in the field, just as it had fallen upon the relieving officer in the past. Whilst the politicians and administrators who framed the Act would not have wished to have espoused the notion of the 'undeserving poor', they felt unwilling to risk the public criticism that would have resulted from an approach to poverty that involved ignoring the potential waste on the 'work-shy' and the fraudulent applicant in order adequately to meet the needs of the majority of applicants. Extravagance in meeting the needs of the poor produces public criticism of the Government more readily than any other form of extravagance.

In order to remove all discretionary responsibility from the civil servant in the field the Government would have had substantially to increase expenditure on the forms of benefit given as of right, and to devise objective means of assessing the more ambiguous claims to help which came from, for example, the deserted wife. The insurance principle for statutory benefits would have had to be rejected, and all disqualification rules, such as those applied to unemployment benefit claimants who have left jobs voluntarily, would have had to be abandoned. Hence it was inevitable that the policy makers did in some measure delegate responsibility for making value decisions about the worthiness of certain applicants for relief, since the complexity of the issues involved defeated any attempt to resolve all the value issues at policy-making level. Thus, this study not only presents evidence for Simon's proposition that decision-making is not confined to the upper reaches of administrative organization, but also suggests that Simon's view that value decisions can be reserved to policy makers at the top may, in certain circumstances, be open to challenge. [. . .]

In turning to examine the values of NAB officers we must avoid laying too much emphasis on middle class norms of respectability and contempt for those 'unable to help themselves'. To do this would be to belittle NAB officers, many of whom made real efforts to understand the people amongst whom they worked. A more correct picture of the social attitudes prevailing in the office in which the author worked would be to make it clear that at one extreme there were those whose attitude to their clientele was one in which the safeguarding of public funds from the grasp of the poor was a primary consideration, whilst at the other extreme were some officers who readily recognized the inadequacy of the allowances they were empowered to grant and who were always on the lookout for their clients' needs. Perhaps the prevalent attitude was a combination of these two positions in which most officers sought to do as much as possible for the old and undeniably sick, but few had very much time for the long-term unemployed or for the women whose family life was of an unstable kind. In as much as these were the common attitudes it is unreasonable to represent the NAB officer as anything other than typical of the society from which he is drawn. Hence, when he was required to be a little tough he found such action quite justifiable in terms of his values and, naturally, he was offended whenever his superiors forced him to depart from such a line.

Such a feeling of offence was reinforced by the fact that the NAB Executive Officer prided himself on being a man (or woman) who could stand on his own feet and take decisions himself. To many civil servants a job in the NAB was something to be avoided at all costs. There was thus in the department a small number of Executive Officers who were severely disgruntled. However, many of the rest had opted for this kind of work or had found that it had certain attractions for them. These attractions particularly consisted in the freedom they had to organize their working day, half of which would very probably be spent outside the office, and in the range of discretion which they possessed, giving them far greater responsibilities than was typical for a civil servant of their grade. For the new officer, proving oneself in the eyes of one's colleagues largely consisted in showing that one could accept this burden of responsibility and that one could take decisions and stand by those decisions in the face of pressure upon one. Prestige attached to being able to handle the difficult customer in the office without giving in to him. Much gossip within the department was concerned with the handling of difficult people; the recounting of incidents served both as an emotional outlet and as a means of demonstrating ability to 'handle' people.

This emphasis on personal decision-making meant, above all, avoiding having to seek the advice of the Manager on any problem, a situation very similar to that found by Blau in his study of a law enforcement agency, where he suggested that to consult one's superior was regarded as to reveal oneself as incompetent.[11] In the light of this one can see why the response of the higher echelons of the NAB to complaints provoked so much resentment amongst the Executive Officers. It was not only a case of 'management' reversing sound decisions, but also unwarranted intervention from people one felt should be expected to protect one from criticism: intervention moreover from people who normally agreed with you – who even encouraged you in the kind of action for which they now seemed to be condemning you. One's superiors, it was felt, were too ready to give way to expediency rather than reason. [. . .]

The advantages of the National Assistance Board's approach derived from its flexibility. The Act enabled it to adjust its rules over time, in response to changing public needs and the public attitudes, without recourse to Parliament. Moreover, the Board itself maintained very flexible internal operating rules so that exceptional examples of need could be given consideration. Relative therefore to many other government departments, and particularly to the Ministry of Pensions and National Insurance, the National Assistance Board was comparatively unbureaucratic. The decentralization of decision-making into the hands of individual Executive Officer also contributed to this unbureaucratic approach with the use of the tiresome procedure of reference to superiors – so often identified as characteristic of bureaucratic organization – kept to a minimum. Given such flexibility, individual officers could be encouraged to adopt a human approach to the meeting of need, to take a pride in making a contribution to the discovery of neglected people and to the rehabilitation of the demoralized.

The disadvantages of the approach to poverty adopted by the Board were equally rooted in the flexibility of the system adopted. The ambiguity of the rules and the decentralization of decision-taking were inevitably productive of inconsistency. Such inconsistency was particularly apparent on any issue where there was a lack of consensus on the right thing to do. Such dissensus was inevitably rooted in controversy about social values, often taking place in a political context outside the Board. And, naturally enough, differences of opinion on such issues were found within the ranks of the Board's staff too. Over the years since the passing of the National Assistance Act there had been an increasing liberalization of many of the interpretations of the Act's instructions. Such liberalization was often unwelcome to those who had accepted the more repressive regime under which they had learned their job. They thus felt that much of the pressure to change came from superiors who were too ready to accept progressive ideas on the treatment of poverty forced upon them by pressure groups; and, of course, the tendency of the pressure groups to fight specific cases in order to bring general changes was particularly resented. Hence the tension that was particularly associated with the appeal and the complaint.

But it would be wrong to suggest that the internal tension consisted merely of more progressive superiors pressurizing less progressive subordinates. After all, since superior officers, and particularly those in the Higher Executive grades (who were the people with whom the Executive Officer came into close contact), tended to have been trained in the earlier years of the Board's history – or even to have been trained before 1948 in one of its predecessors – they too had learned the job under a more repressive regime. Hence, they also could be expected to be ambivalent towards change and subject to the kind of tension described above. It is not proposed here to try to analyse their motivations: our concern is with the situation of the Executive Officer.

Therefore let us merely say that the existence of difference of opinion amongst his superiors obviously contributed to the ambiguity of the pressures upon the Executive Officer. Thus even the Executive Officer who was sympathetic to progressive viewpoints felt the pressure of a system that was adjusting to changing ideas inconsistently and often reluctantly, both because of doubts among his superiors and among his colleagues.

It may thus be suggested that these tensions had an impact upon the orientation of the Executive Officer to the public, and that in some respects they produced rigidity in behaviour and therefore undermined some of the advantages gained from the absence of bureaucratic constraints. Leadership studies have suggested that inconsistency and apparent arbitrariness on the part of leaders is productive of rigid and over-cautious behaviour.[12]

Moreover, the inexperienced and idealistic Executive Officer was also likely to find, as Blau has suggested,[13] that he experienced tensions associated with 'reality shock' as he discovered that the poor often did not measure up to the idealistic notions he had entertained about them.

Finally, tendencies of this kind will, moreover, have been compounded by the enormous pressure of work which made it necessary for Executive Officers to spend little time dealing with the special and exceptional problems of their clients.

Thus the flexible approach to the public characteristic of the National Assistance Board produced an unbureaucratic approach to the public untypical of a government department, yet such an approach was not entirely successful on account of the tensions and conflicts that inevitably accompanied such a personalized and decentralized system of administration.

Notes

1. Audrey Harvey, *Casualties of the Welfare State*, Fabian Tract No. 321.
2. The latter point is central to Max Weber's analysis of bureaucracy (*The Theory of Social and Economic Organization*, trans. T. Parsons, Glencoe, Ill.: Free Press, 1947, pp. 329–40), while the former argument derives from many of Weber's critics (see particularly R. K. Merton, 'Bureaucratic structures and personality' in *Social Theory and Social Structure*, Glencoe, Ill.: Free Press, 1957, pp. 195–206). See also A. W. Gouldner, 'Red tape as a social problem', in R. K. Merton, *et al.* (eds.) *Reader in Bureaucracy*, Glencoe, Ill.: Free Press 1952, pp. 410–18).
3. P. M. Blau, *The Dynamics of Bureaucracy*, Chicago, University of Chicago Press, 1955.
4. R. G. Francis and R. C. Stone, *Service and Procedure in Bureaucracy*, Minneapolis: University of Minnesota Press, 1956.

5. A. W. Gouldner, *Patterns of Industrial Bureaucracy*, Glencoe, Ill.: Free Press, 1954.
6. M. Crozier, *The Bureaucratic Phenomenon*, London, Tavistock, 1964.
7. R. Bendix, 'Bureaucracy: the problem and its setting', *American Sociological Review*, Vol. 12, 1947, p. 507.
8. Audrey Harvey, 'Poor man's rent', *New Statesman*, Vol. 64, 13 July 1962, p. 42.
9. For an account of training procedures see K. R. Stowe, 'Staff training in the National Assistance Board: problems and policies', *Public Administration*, Vol. 39, Winter 1961, pp. 331–52.
10. H. A. Simon, *Administrative Behaviour*, 2nd edn., New York: Macmillan, 1957, Chapter III.
11. P. M. Blau, *op. cit.*, Chapter 7.
12. See, for example, H. C. Selvin, *The Effects of Leadership*, Glencoe Ill.: Free Press, 1960.
13. P. M. Blau, 'Orientation towards clients in a public welfare agency', *Administrative Science Quarterly*, Vol. 5, 1960, pp. 341–61.